CHILE & RAPA NUI
(EASTER ISLAND)

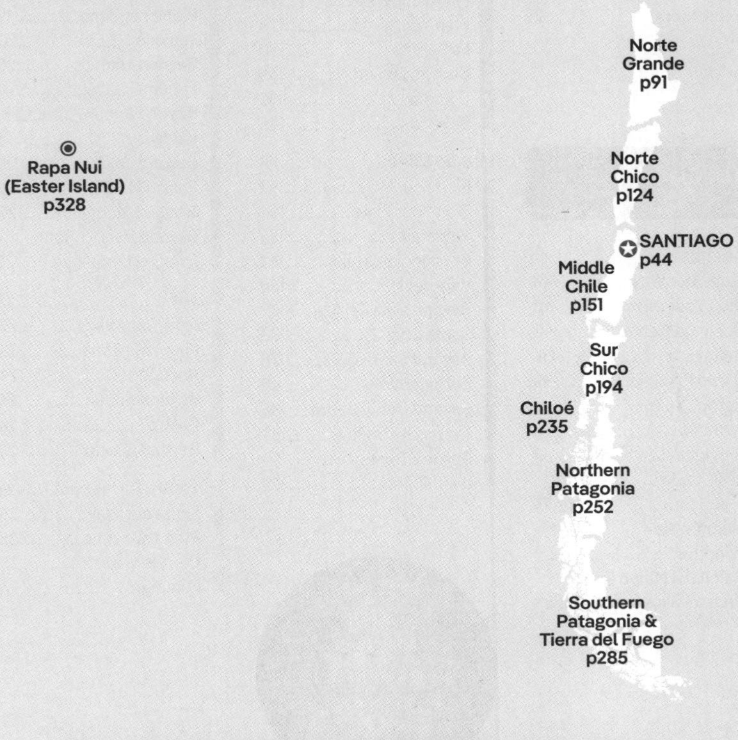

Norte
Grande
p91

◉
Rapa Nui
(Easter Island)
p328

Norte
Chico
p124

✪ SANTIAGO
p44

Middle
Chile
p151

Sur
Chico
p194

Chiloé
p235

Northern
Patagonia
p252

Southern
Patagonia &
Tierra del Fuego
p285

**Isabel Albiston, Ashley Harrell, Mark Johanson,
Shafik Meghji, Kevin Raub**

CONTENTS

Plan Your Trip

The Guide

Cerro Santa Lucía (p52)

**Traditional dancer (p334),
Rapa Nui**

TOP LEFT: PIERRE-YVES BABELON/SHUTTERSTOCK ©; BOTTOM LEFT: ANGELA MEIER/SHUTTERSTOCK ©; RIGHT: ANTONIO SALAVERRY/SHUTTERSTOCK ©

San Pedro de Atacama (p96)

TOP: MAURIZIO BERSANELLI/SHUTTERSTOCK ©

Inca trail through the Atacama Desert, San Pedro de Atacama (p96)

CHILE & RAPA NUI
THE JOURNEY BEGINS HERE

Chile is a country contemplating change. Although the progressive constitution was rejected in the referendum of 2022, the protests that preceded it represented a strong desire for reform. It's an interesting time to visit.

When I lived in Argentina, I often crossed the Andes to Chile, and I love the endless opportunities to connect with sublime landscapes. It's a place where it's easy to have an adventure, but there is space for reflection along the way. Nowhere is that more true than in the Atacama Desert. A snapshot can't convey the life and energy of the desert. It can be felt in the changing light, in the breezes and in the wildflowers that appear in the months following rain.

But my favorite spot is sitting in the shade of an *algarrobo* (carob tree) in the foothills of Cerro Mamalluca, overlooking Vicuña, watching the sun set behind the hills.

Isabel Albiston

@isabel_albiston

Isabel is a London-born writer who has lived in Argentina and traveled widely in South America.

My favourite experience is hiking along the pre-Incan trail from Putre to the Wilacabrani cave paintings (p122). It leads through a peaceful valley, full of butterflies and birds.

WHO GOES WHERE

Our writers and experts choose the places which, for them, define Chile & Rapa Nui.

A lover of road trips and self-proclaimed 'driving person,' Ashley was nonetheless slightly nervous about rolling solo on the very remote, extensively unpaved, livestock-dominated **Carretera Austral** (p258). The concerns subsided after she picked up a pair of hitchhikers and ended up spending five days in their company. That's just how it goes on the Carretera. Godspeed, Emil and Silvia.

Ashley Harrell

Ashley is a California-based freelance journalist who writes about travel and the outdoors. She's co-authored more than 50 Lonely Planet guidebooks across the Americas, Southeast Asia and Africa.

The prismatic port city of **Valparaíso** (p156) is kind of like that friend we all have whose life seems forever on the verge of complete chaos. You know the one: they're a little bit messy, unafraid to stick out in the crowd and up for whatever comes their way. They can drive you crazy sometimes, but you're so fascinated by their eccentricity and unpredictability that you'd do anything to absorb their energy just one more day.

Mark Johanson
@MarkOnTheMap

Mark writes about travel, food and sustainability in South America and beyond from his home in Santiago.

When it comes to isolation, adventure and dramatic landscapes, **Puerto Williams** (p318) is hard to beat. On the shores of the Beagle Channel, backed by the mighty Dientes de Navarino range, the world's southernmost city looks and feels like a small town. A captivating place, Puerto Williams can be challenging to reach – there are no road connections with the rest of Chile – but it's even harder to drag yourself away.

Shafik Meghji
@ShafikMeghji

Shafik is an award-winning journalist, travel writer and author of Crossed off the Map: Travels in Bolivia.

Though Pucón and Puerto Varas are kindred spirits in many ways, one difference is the proximity of its volcano. Volcán Villarrica is right there, barreling down on **Pucón** (p207) from just a few kilometers away. While undeniably fetching, it leaves you with a feeling that you're living life on the edge, a feeling made all the more ominous when the fiery red glow of its innards taint the clouds above.

Kevin Raub
@raubontheroad

Kevin is a Bologna-based travel journalist and craft beer connoisseur – and the co-author of over 110 Lonely Planet guidebooks on four continents.

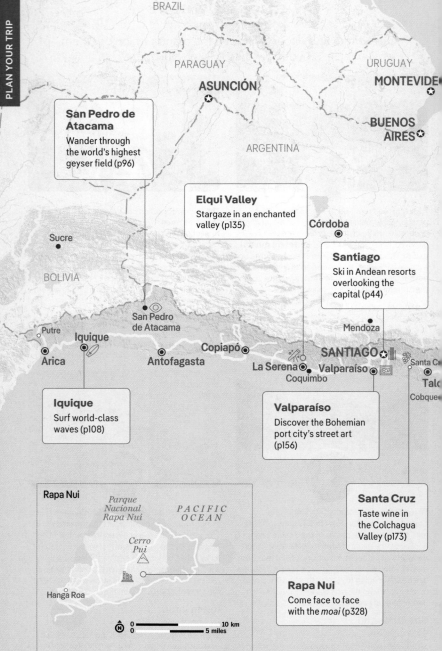

BRAZIL

PARAGUAY

URUGUAY

ASUNCIÓN

MONTEVIDE

ARGENTINA

BUENOS
AIRES

San Pedro de Atacama
Wander through the world's highest geyser field (p96)

Elqui Valley
Stargaze in an enchanted valley (p135)

Córdoba

Santiago
Ski in Andean resorts overlooking the capital (p44)

Sucre

BOLIVIA

San Pedro de Atacama

Mendoza

Putre

Iquique

Arica

Antofagasta

Copiapó

La Serena
Coquimbo

SANTIAGO

Valparaíso

Santa C

Talc

Cobque

Iquique
Surf world-class waves (p108)

Valparaíso
Discover the Bohemian port city's street art (p156)

Rapa Nui

Parque
Nacional
Rapa Nui

PACIFIC
OCEAN

Cerro
Pui

Hanga Roa

Santa Cruz
Taste wine in the Colchagua Valley (p173)

Rapa Nui
Come face to face with the *moai* (p328)

0   10 km
0   5 miles

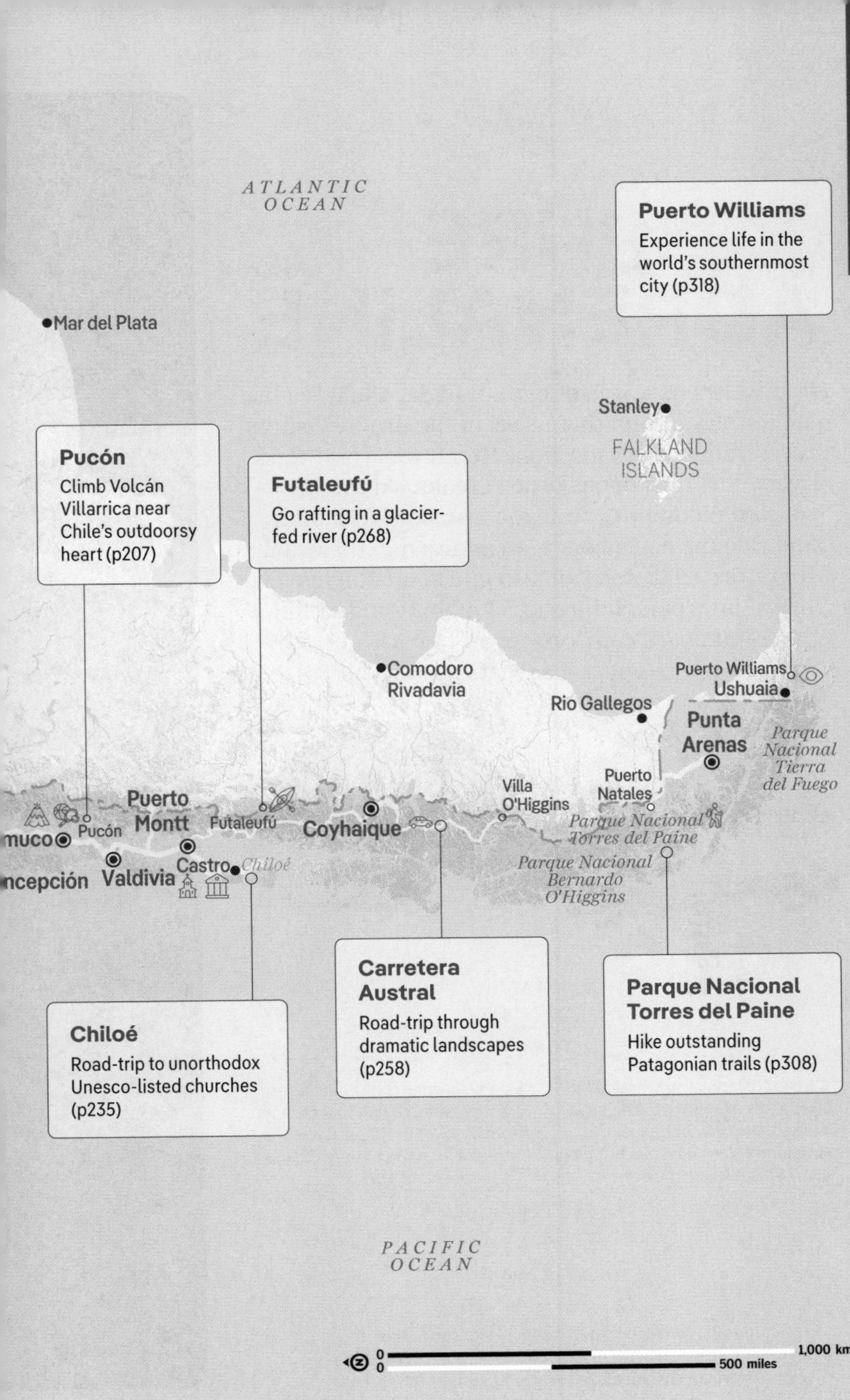

ATLANTIC OCEAN

● Mar del Plata

Puerto Williams
Experience life in the world's southernmost city (p318)

Stanley ●

FALKLAND ISLANDS

Pucón
Climb Volcán Villarrica near Chile's outdoorsy heart (p207)

Futaleufú
Go rafting in a glacier-fed river (p268)

● Comodoro Rivadavia

Puerto Williams
Río Gallegos   Ushuaia ●

Punta Arenas ◉   *Parque Nacional Tierra del Fuego*

Villa   Puerto
O'Higgins   Natales ●

△ 🦜   **Puerto**
🦜   **Montt**   Futaleufú ●   **Coyhaique** ◉   *Parque Nacional Torres del Paine*
muco ◉ Pucón ○
ncepción **Valdivia** 🏛️ Castro ● 🏛️ *Chiloé*   *Parque Nacional Bernardo O'Higgins*
◉   ◉

Chiloé
Road-trip to unorthodox Unesco-listed churches (p235)

Carretera Austral
Road-trip through dramatic landscapes (p258)

Parque Nacional Torres del Paine
Hike outstanding Patagonian trails (p308)

PACIFIC OCEAN

◎ 0 ————— 1,000 km
0 ————— 500 miles

PURE ADRENALINE

For travelers in search of natural highs, Chile is a big outdoor playground that packs in the thrills. Visitors travel from all over the globe to raft the world-class rivers, surf the famous beach breaks, ski the snow-dusted mountains, scale the fearsome volcanoes and ride the noble horses. In addition to the usual adventure sports, you can also find spine-tinglers like heli-skiing, paragliding, ice climbing, land sailing and sand-boarding. Don't forget to pack a healthy sense of adventure.

Gear

It's easy to rent kayaks, mountain bikes and surfboards, but if you're a serious mountaineer, kitesurfer or backcountry skier, consider bringing your own equipment.

Seasons

Ski season stretches from June to October, while rafting season lasts from October to March. Cycle the Carretera Austral between October and April.

The Big Event

In 2023, Santiago hosted the Pan American Games, the largest international multidisciplinary sports event in the Americas, which includes canoeing, surfing and cycling.

3
5
1
2
4

BEST ADRENALINE EXPERIENCES

Peer into the fiery belly of one of Chile's most active volcanoes, **Volcán Villarrica ①**, famous for its frequent explosions and lava effusions. (p211)

Raft or kayak the exhilarating Class IV and V whitewater runs on the stunning, glacier-fed **Río Futaleufú ②**. (p269)

Surf one of the most famous waves in the Americas, the perfect left break at **Punta de Lobos ③** in Pichilemu. (p179)

Jump into the saddle and trot around an *estancia* **④** (grazing ranch) like one of Chile's gauchos in Northern Patagonia. (p264)

Ski down an active volcano at Chile's prettiest winter resort, **Termas de Chillán ⑤**, and celebrate with a soak in hotsprings. (p190)

Parque Nacional Torres del Paine (p308)

UNFORGETTABLE LANDSCAPES

The Land of Fire encompasses some of the most eye-popping scenery on the planet, and the diversity of the landscape truly boggles the mind. Up and down Chile's 4300km stretch, you'll find parched dunes, fertile valleys, smoking volcanoes, ancient forests, creeping glaciers and breezy fjords. And that's just the tip of the iceberg (you'll see those here too!).

Protected Land

Chile has more than 100 national parks, monuments and reserves. Showstopping parks like Torres del Paine are inundated with visitors, but the majority remain underutilized.

Looking Up

The Chilean Andes repeatedly top 6000m. The highest peak is 6893m Ojos del Salado, the second-highest point in South America and the world's highest active volcano.

BEST LANDSCAPE EXPERIENCES

Behold the magnificent granite spires, blue lakes and cracking glaciers of **Parque Nacional Torres del Paine ❶**. (p308)

Take in America's southernmost outpost of **Puerto Williams ❷**. (p318)

Catch a sand dune sunset of surreal purples, pinks and yellows at **Valle de la Luna ❸**. (p98)

Drive through the charred volcanic desertscapes, forests and canyons of **Parque Nacional Conguillío ❹**. (p204)

Roll down the 1240km **Carretera Austral ❺**, perhaps the world's most scenic road trip. (p258)

WINE COUNTRY

Chile is one of the world's largest wine producers, with vineyards spanning hundreds of kilometers across multiple valleys. The climate varies from hot and dry to cool and wet, resulting in a delicious array of deep reds, crisp whites and floral rosés. In the tasting rooms, you'll have no trouble finding a suitable selection.

Past & Present

Missionaries and conquistadors brought wine to Chile in the mid-1500s, and Jesuit priests cultivated early vineyards of rustic pais grapes. Today, Chile has around 800 wineries.

Harvest Season

Chile's wine country harvests white grapes from February to mid-March. The red grape harvest begins in mid-March and continues through late April or early May.

Planning Ahead

Although it's possible to walk up to some wineries, you're better off booking tours at least a day in advance, particularly if they include a meal.

BEST WINE EXPERIENCES

Stay close to the capital and try powerful reds like cabernet sauvignon in **Maipo Valley ❶**. (p80)

Visit the most opulent wineries in Chile in its most famous region, **Colchagua Valley ❷**, where big cabernets and Carmeneres reign supreme. (p175)

Try cool-climate wines such as pinot noir and sauvignon blanc near Valparaíso in **Casablanca Valley ❸**. (p163)

Explore the Wild West of Chilean wine with old vines and funky natural wines in **Itata Valley ❹**. (p187)

Santa Cruz ❺ celebrates the grape harvest with stands from local wineries in the plaza, a crowned harvest queen, songs and folk dancing . (p173)

HIKES OF A LIFETIME

With a 4000km backbone of the rugged Andes and all the gorgeous terrain that comes with them, Chile is a hiker's paradise. But the country has more than just mountain scenery, with trails running the gamut through scarred desert and temperate rainforest, along icy lakes and raging rivers and up to volcano craters and calving glaciers. Patagonia is particularly dazzling in this department, but the Lakes District, the Atacama Desert and the area around Santiago also have great hikes.

Responsible Hiking

Pack out your trash, be cautious with campfires and don't feed wildlife. Pay the required fees before traversing private property. Leave livestock gates as you find them.

Best Time to Hike

Patagonia hiking is best in summer (December to February). Hike the Atacama Desert from June to January and Rapa Nui between March and December.

Routes of the Park

This extensive trail spans more than 2700km from Puerto Montt to Cape Horn (one-third of Chile), connecting 17 national parks and more than 60 towns.

BEST HIKING EXPERIENCES

Take on **Sendero Enladrillado ❶**, one of Middle Chile's best full-day hikes into the Andes. (p180)

Don the heavy pack and hike the world famous **W Trek** (p309) or **Paine Circuit ❷** (p310) in Parque Nacional Torres del Paine.

Dive into the **Dientes de Navarino Circuit ❸**, a five-day walk through wild high country fringed by razor-faced peaks. (p321)

Ascend **Cerro Castillo ❹** for a closer look at its basalt spires and sparkling laguna, or go all out on a four-day adventure. (p266)

Trek all the way across **Parque Nacional Patagonia ❺**, between the Valle de Chacabuco and Lago Jeinimeni sectors. (p278)

LEFT: FIIPHOTO/SHUTTERSTOCK ©. RIGHT: DUDAREV MIKHAIL/SHUTTERSTOCK ©. FAR RIGHT: JOSHUA RESNICK/SHUTTERSTOCK ©

Valparaíso (p156)

URBAN EXPLORATION

The streets of Chile's best cities are practically works of art, chock full of narrow winding staircases, vibrant street-art murals, expansive food markets and cheerful architecture. Standout urban centers include Santiago, Valparaíso, Castro and Concepción, and oftentimes the most rewarding way to explore these places is simply to wander.

The Capital

Santiago is a major metropolis that seven million people call home, and no other Chilean city comes close to rivaling its size, cultural cache or political influence.

Urbanization

Since the 1930s, the majority of Chileans have lived in urban areas. Today, around 90% of the country's population lives in cities, a figure that's still rising.

BEST URBAN EXPERIENCES

Ogle the colorful backsides of houses built in (on stilts) in **Castro ❶**. (p246)

Wander Santiago's **Barrio Italia ❷**, ducking into wine shops, boutiques and cafes. (p73)

Follow in the footsteps of poets, artists and philosophers and get lost amid the colorful jumble of hills in **Valparaíso ❸**. (p156)

Admire murals and sample live music in **Concepción ❹**, the cradle of Chilean rock. (p188)

Take a walking tour of **Santiago Centro ❺**, stopping at plazas, eateries, museums and cathedrals. (p50)

REMOTE GETAWAYS

Whether you fancy the Atacama Desert, the isolated parts of the Carretera Austral, the barren Tierra del Fuego or lesser-explored glaciers and fjords of the Patagonian ice fields, the options for dropping off the map are endless in Chile. Of course, it also has the pinnacle of all seclusion, Rapa Nui, the remotest Pacific isle.

④

③

②①

⑤

Tips for Remote Travel

Build in some extra days in case the weather doesn't cooperate, particularly in Patagonia. Bring plenty of snacks and water and pack the right clothing and gear.

Forget the Phone

Don't assume you'll have wi-fi or cell service. If you're using a smartphone, download map data in advance for the areas where you'll be traveling.

Check for Flights

Low-cost airlines such as Sky Airline and JetSmart operate regional flights to remote and underserved destinations in Chile.

BEST REMOTE EXPERIENCES

Stow away for a few days in Sur Chico's wonderful **Refugio Tinquilco ①**, surrounded by fabulous nature trails. (p212)

Venture to a patch of paradise at **Caleta Cóndor ②**, a protected stretch of hard-to-reach coastline. (p230)

Fly to the most remote commercial airport in the world on **Rapa Nui ③** to visit the towering *moai*. (p328)

Venture high into the altiplano to **Parque Nacional Volcán Isluga ④**, a spectacular Andean landscape. (p115)

Spend a few days exploring distant and seldom-visited glaciers by boat in **Parque Nacional Laguna San Rafael ⑤**. (p272)

XAVIER GALLEGO MORELL/SHUTTERSTOCK ©

Andean condor

EYE ON THE WILD

Chile is home to enormous plant diversity as well as a deep roster of creatures on land, in the skies and in the sea. Camelids bound through national parks, as does the occasional huemul, an endangered deer that's become a national symbol. Andean condors glide by high peaks, and the cold Humboldt Current brings abundant marine life.

Endemic Species

Chile's landscapes are bounded by ocean, desert and mountains, paving the way for endemic species. Archipiélago Juan Fernández has 101 plant species found nowhere else on Earth.

Plants

Chile's unique flora arguably rivals its fauna, with temperate rainforests, prehistoric-looking nalca (an edible rhubarb cousin), and more than 20 different cactuses and succulents.

BEST WILDLIFE EXPERIENCES

Track Humboldt and Magellanic penguins at **Monumento Natural Islotes de Puñihuil ❶**. (p244)

Don your binoculars at **Reserva Nacional Los Flamencos ❷** to see Chilean, Andean and James' flamingos. (p102)

Spend several days in **Parque Nacional Patagonia ❸** for guaranteed guanaco sightings. (p278)

Embark on whale-watching boat and kayak trips in **Marine Parque Francisco Coloane ❹**. (p297)

Watch Andean condors up close at the **Punta del Monte ❺** estancia. (p265)

Andean ceramics, Museo Arqueológico San Miguel de Azapa (p121)

HISTORY REVISITED

The land now called Chile contains one of the oldest inhabited sites in the Americas, and archaeologists are still working to unearth and understand this region's human history. Do some investigating of your own into the country's ancient ruins, ghost towns, colonial buildings and long-held customs that make Chile's past feel present.

Human Inhabitants

A footprint discovered in Monte Verde points to human habitation in Chile as early as 12,500 years ago, a millennium before the Clovis people crossed the Bering Land Bridge.

Living History

Seek out spots that bring Chile's history to life. Board a battleship in Iquique, ride like a gaucho and tour Chilote villages where people still use ancestral inventions.

BEST HISTORY EXPERIENCES

Behold the collection of mummies displayed at **Museo Arqueológico San Miguel de Azapa ❶**. (p121)

Get spooked in the eerie ghost towns of **Humberstone** and **Santa Laura ❷**. (p114)

Pop into Chiloé's Unesco-listed **wooden churches ❸**, which are a colorful mashup of European and indigenous design. (p247)

Take in the architecture, museums and cemetery of **Punta Arenas ❹**. (p290)

Learn about the Tangata Manu Birdman cult of Rapa Nui in the **Orongo Ceremonial Village ❺**. (p339)

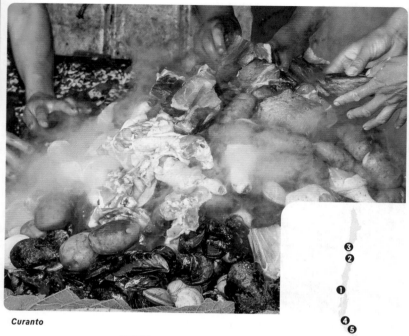

MAXMAXIMOVPHOTOGRAPHY/SHUTTERSTOCK ©

Curanto

FOOD & DRINK

Whether you enjoy grabbing a cocktail or a coffee at a buzzy cafe, sampling the goods at a traditional kitchen or splurging on a high-end restaurant meal, Chile has you covered. Everything grows in the country's Mediterranean climate, meaning plenty of local and seasonal produce, plus fresh meat from the ranches and fish straight off the boat.

Markets

Budget travelers are well served in food markets such as Santiago's La Vega Central, where vendors hawk their goods, and Mercado Central, where seafood lunches are tops.

Asados

Don't leave Chile without attending a traditional *asado* barbecue over a wood fire. Equal parts feast and social event, *asados* often take place on ranches.

BEST EATING EXPERIENCES

Devour a steaming heap of ***curanto*** ❶ (meat, potato and seafood stew), the pinnacle of Chiloé's culinary pedigree. (p242)

Dine at **Boragó** ❷, one of the 50 best restaurants on the planet. (p77)

Visit the **pisco distilleries** ❸ of the Elqui Valley. (p139)

Feast on ***cordero al palo*** ❹ (slow-cooked spit-roasted lamb), a regional speciality of Patagonia. (p305)

Order fresh **centolla** ❺ (king crab) with your pasta dish, risotto, crêpe, salad or sandwich in Tierra del Fuego. (p292)

ALUK/SHUTTERSTOCK ©

Musician, near San Pedro de Atacama (p96)

UNIQUE VILLAGES

Time seems to tick a little slower in Chile's villages. These remote outposts allow you to get off the tourist circuit and soak in the culture, observe traditions passed down through generations and get to know the country's rural locales. Their backdrops – deserts, mountains and ice fields – are nothing to sneeze at either.

Homestays

For a memorable and authentic experience in rural Chile, stay at *casas de familia* (homestays) owned and operated by locals. For a list of options, visit turismoruralchile.cl.

Logistics

Bring cash when you visit remote areas. Get small bills because it can be difficult to change money. Fill up on gas often if you're driving.

BEST VILLAGE EXPERIENCES

Visit the traditional artist village of **Pomaire ❶** for a pottery workshop. (p164)

Wander the boardwalks of **Caleta Tortel ❷**, an isolated lumber and fishing village. (p276)

Pause your adventures to saunter the dusty streets of **San Pedro de Atacama ❸**. (p96)

Boat down to the most southerly village on Earth, **Puerto Toro ❹** and hang out with its 12 residents. (p322)

Relax, ride a horse and enjoy some true Chilean hospitality in **Palena ❺**, a quiet mountain town. (p271)

19

REGIONS & CITIES

Find the places that tick all your boxes.

Santiago

BEATING HEART OF THE NATION

Chile's capital occupies a dramatic setting beneath the Andes, which can be viewed from the top of Cerro San Cristóbal. Learn about the country's fascinating history at the museums in the city center, and then enjoy the restaurants, galleries and shops of bohemian Bellavista, Lastarria and Barrio Italia.

p44

Rapa Nui
(Easter Island)
p328
◉

Rapa Nui

POLYNESIA'S LEGENDARY OPEN-AIR MUSEUM

What brings most people to Rapa Nui are the island's historical sites and ruins, especially the enigmatic *moai,* the mysterious megalithic statues whose very presence leaves the viewer guessing. Head to the remote island's biggest town, Hanga Roa, to experience Polynesian culture, including traditional dances.

p328

Chiloé

MISTY AND MYTHOLOGICAL MARITIME ISLAND

Isla Grande de Chiloé bewitches visitors with its Unesco-listed wooden churches and intriguing mythology. The provincial capital, Castro, has distinctive architecture to see, while the town of Ancud is the gateway to adventures in windswept hills, misty forests and remote national parks.

p235

Northern Patagonia

MOUNTAINS, RIVERS, GLACIERS AND FJORDS

Driving through mountain scenery and old-growth forest on the partially paved Carretera Austral is one of the world's great road trips. Don't miss the opportunity to see the fast-melting glaciers of Parque Nacional Laguna San Rafael. And adrenaline seekers can raft in the turquoise river of the Futaleufú valley.

p252

Norte Chico

BEACHES, STARGAZING AND VERDANT VALLEYS

La Serena is a charming city with a broad sandy beach. Further north are the gorgeous white sands of Bahía Inglesa and Parque Nacional Pan de Azúcar. Taste pisco at the distilleries of the Elqui Valley, which is also one of the world's top locations for stargazing.

p124

Norte Grande

DESERT, ALTIPLANO AND SURF

Head to San Pedro de Atacama to explore the rock formations and steaming geysers of the surrounding area. Surf by day and party by night in Iquique and Arica. Use Putre as a base to explore the high-altitude lakes of Parque Nacional Lauca.

p91

Norte
Grande
p91

**Norte
Chico
p124**

Middle Chile

SURF, SKI AND SAVOR WINE

The bohemian port city of Valparaíso is packed with street art, while neighboring Viña del Mar is a more polished coastal city with excellent museums. Taste wine in the Colchagua Valley, surf in Maitencillo, and hike or ski in the Andes.

p151

SANTIAGO
p44

**Middle Chile
p151**

Sur
Chico
p194

Sur Chico

OMINOUS VOLCANOES, PRISTINE WATERWAYS AND OUTDOOR ADVENTURES

Active volcanoes and glistening lakes bring lovers of adventure to this region, where Pucón is a base for climbing Volcán Villarrica. Experience the culture of the area's ethnic groups: La Araucanía is the heartland of the indigenous Mapuche, while Puerto Varas is a German-settled town by Lago Llanquihue.

p194

**Chiloé
p235**

**Northern
Patagonia
p252**

Southern Patagonia & Tierra del Fuego

END-OF-THE-WORLD ADVENTURES

This sparsely populated region has some of Chile's most dramatic scenery, much of it contained within Parque Nacional Torres del Paine, which can be traversed on a trek. In Tierra del Fuego, Puerto Williams is a base for exploring the Beagle Channel and hiking the Dientes de Navarino range.

**Southern
Patagonia &
Tierra del Fuego
p285**

p285

SL-PHOTOGRAPHY/SHUTTERSTOCK ©

Moai at Ahu Tongariki (p342), Rapa Nui

ITINERARIES

Cities, Wine & Rapa Nui

Allow: 12 days   **Distance:** 575km, plus a flight

This journey takes you from the Chilean capital of Santiago into the surrounding wine valleys, with stops for seafood and beach strolls along the central coast. Afterward, it's off to the colorful hills of Valparaíso before flying away to Rapa Nui for a Polynesian adventure. Encounter the enigmatic *moai* that confound archaeologists to this day.

❶ SANTIAGO ⏱ 2 DAYS

Start in **Santiago** (p44), exploring the capital's museums, plazas and parks. Stroll around Lastarria and Barrio Italia, visit bustling markets in Centro, and dine at top-class restaurants. In the evening, watch as the sunset bathes the Andes in an amber glow.

🚗 2 hours

🚗 **Detour:** Take public transportation to the nearby Maipo Valley wineries for a taste of Chilean wine. ⏱ 1 hour

❷ SANTA CRUZ ⏱ 1 DAY

Next, it's off to **Santa Cruz** (p173), the quaint town at the heart of the Colchagua Valley, Chile's preeminent wine region. Cabernet sauvignon and Carmenere are the main grape varietals here, but you'll find everything from malbec to chardonnay. In the mornings, check out the town's excellent museums.

🚗 2½ hours

❸ MATANZAS ⏱ 1 DAY

Long gray-sand beaches, pounding surf and magazine-worthy architecture welcome you to the lovely little seaside village of **Matanzas** (p165). It's your chance to relax by the sea, take long leisurely beach strolls and dine on fresh-caught fish dishes. Detour to neighboring villages, such as La Boca, for dramatic observation decks overlooking the Pacific Ocean.

🚗 3 hours

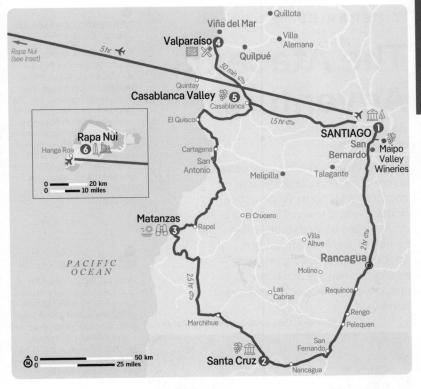

4 VALPARAÍSO ⏱ 1 DAY

Soak in the artistic charms of **Valparaíso** (p156), many visitors' favorite Chilean city. Sprawling across more than three dozen hills, the heart of the action lies on Cerros Alegre and Concepción, whose buildings are blanketed in murals. With some of the best hotels and restaurants, as well as romantic hilltop promenades, it promises an enchanting experience.

🚗 30 minutes

5 CASABLANCA VALLEY ⏱ 1 DAY

Missing wine country already? Head inland from Valparaíso to the **Casablanca Valley** (p163) to sample cool-climate wines like sauvignon blanc and pinot noir. On a tasting or tour of the stately wineries, you may find that bottles are notably fresher – and often lower in alcohol – than elsewhere in Chile.

🚗 1½ hours, ✈ 5 hours

6 RAPA NUI ⏱ 5 DAYS

Finish off your trip with a flight to the world's most remote commercial airport on **Rapa Nui** (p328), a Chilean territory in the middle of the South Pacific. This small island has an outsized reputation thanks to its enigmatic monolithic human figures known as *moai,* but it has other archaeological sites too, including the ceremonial village of Orongo, located atop a volcano.

ITINERARIES

The Atacama Adventure

Allow: 10 days
Distance: 900km

Explore the driest non-polar desert on earth on this epic adventure into Chile's far north. Begin at the popular resort town of San Pedro de Atacama before setting off in search of ancient petroglyphs, adobe villages, puffing geysers, soaring volcanoes and high-altitude lagoons speckled with pink flamingos.

Valle de la Luna (p98), San Pedro de Atacama

SKREIDZELEU/SHUTTERSTOCK ©

① SAN PEDRO DE ATACAMA
⏱ 3 DAYS

Ease into the harsh desert environment in **San Pedro de Atacama** (p96), an adobe resort town and the region's most tourist-friendly oasis. Use this town as a base for daytime trips to nearby salt flats, sand dunes and archaeological ruins, such as Aldea de Tulor, as well as sunset over the lunar-like landscapes of Valle de la Luna and nighttime stargazing at the public observatories.

🚗 1½ hours

② EL TATIO GEYSERS ⏱ 1 DAY

Once you're fully acclimatized to the altitude, it's time to head above 4000m to visit **El Tatio** (p102), the largest geyser field in the Southern Hemisphere and one of the highest-elevation geothermal areas in the world. On the way to this dramatic site, you'll pass traditional Andean villages, cactus-filled valleys and *bofedales* (swampy alluvial grasslands), home to wild vicuñas and domesticated llamas.

🚗 5½ hours

③ IQUIQUE ⏱ 2 DAYS

It's a *long* drive to the coastal city of **Iquique** (p108), but along the way, you'll pass a number of sites that make it worth your while, including the giant geoglyphs of Geoglifos de Pintados, the festival village of La Tirana, and the eerie ghost towns of Humberstone and Santa Laura. Dedicate the next day to Iquique itself, relaxing on its golden beaches.

🚗 3½ hours

④ ARICA ⏱ 1 DAY

Chile's northernmost city, **Arica** (p116), was built atop a cemetery used by the Chinchorro, an ancient fishing culture who were the first to artificially mummify their dead. Dozens of their mummies are on display in a small museum in town, as well as a larger museum in the nearby Azapa Valley. Arica is also home to War of the Pacific battlefields, surf breaks and stellar sea-facing restaurants.

🚗 2½ hours

⑤ PUTRE ⏱ 1 DAY

The tiny Aymara village of **Putre** (p122) is the last real outpost in Chile on the highway to La Paz. At an altitude of about 3370m, it's a great staging ground for trips into the high-Andean parks along the border with Bolivia. Spend a day acclimatizing before venturing further afield in search of hot springs, volcanoes and wildlife.

🚗 45 minutes

⑥ PARQUE NACIONAL LAUCA ⏱ 2 DAYS

Parque Nacional Lauca (p123) is quite literally one of Chile's most breathtaking national parks. Lorded over by giant volcanoes taller than 6000m, it's brimming with wildlife. Snowmelt creates azure-colored lagoons that are home to hundreds of pink flamingos.

🏞 **Detour:** On the second day, take an adventure-filled detour to Reserva Natural Las Vicuñas. ⏱ 1½ hours

ITINERARIES

The Lakes & Volcanoes Route

Allow: 10 days
Distance: 815km

Yes, this journey shows off tons of Chile's lakes and volcanoes, but equally attractive are the dense temperate rainforests, bucolic pastures and steamy geothermal baths. It's also the heartland of the country's largest indigenous group, the Mapuche, whose influence is felt in many towns along the way.

Lago Panguipulli, between Valdivia (p214) and Huilo-Huilo (p218)

CACIO MURILLO/SHUTTERSTOCK ©

① CASTRO ⏱ 2 DAYS

Castro (p246) is the main city on the Chiloé Archipelago and the best place to see its colorful *palafito* houses, which are set on stilts above the sea. Use it as a base to explore the island's Unesco-listed wooden churches (pictured below), temperate forests and fabulous restaurants, which showcase a cuisine based around local seafood and endemic potatoes.

🚗 3½ hours

② PUERTO VARAS ⏱ 2 DAYS

You'll feel the German influence left by early settlers the minute you arrive in the resort town of **Puerto Varas** (p224), though the landscape here is a world away. Set on the mirror-like Lago Llanquihue and blessed with front-row volcano views, it makes a comfortable base for trips into nearby parklands filled with raging waterfalls, emerald lagoons and dense forests of giant alerce trees.

🚗 2½ hours

③ VALDIVIA ⏱ 1 DAY

Divert back to the coast to call in at the buzzy university town of **Valdivia** (p214), known for its youthful energy, riverside attractions and, above all else, Spanish forts. It's also the epicenter of craft beer in Chile thanks to the influence of hometown icon Cervecería Kunstmann. Head just outside of town and you'll enter the temperate Valdivian rainforest.

🚗 2½ hours

LOCOMOTIVE74/SHUTTERSTOCK ©

4
HUILO-HUILO ⏱ 2 DAYS

Spend a few days inside a fairy-tale wonderland on the grounds of **Huilo-Huilo** (p218), a private biological reserve with whimsical wooden lodgings. Trails – many of which are family-friendly – lead to thundering waterfalls, riverside beaches and thermal baths. You'll also find a museum of indigenous artifacts, a bike park, a brewery and craft workshops. The Mocho-Choshuenco volcano looms over it all.

🚗 2 hours

5
PUCÓN ⏱ 2 DAYS

The posh resort town of **Pucón** (p207) is a hub of adventure sports, sitting alongside Lago Villarrica in the puffing glare of its namesake volcano. Several public and private parklands lie within easy day-tripping distance, including the Parque Nacional Villarrica and Parque Nacional Huerquehue. There are also a half-dozen hot springs – none more famous than Termas Geométricas (pictured below).

🚗 2½ hours

6
PARQUE NACIONAL CONGUILLÍO ⏱ 1 DAY

Nowhere can you appreciate the time-warping allure of Chile's ancient araucaria trees more profoundly than within **Parque Nacional Conguillío** (p204). Centered on a teal lake and lorded over by Volcán Llaima – one of the most active in Chile – this park is a landscape photographer's dream, with the umbrella-like trees atop verdant green hills everywhere you look. **27**

LARYSALITVIN/SHUTTERSTOCK ©

ITINERARIES

Patagonia Explorer

Allow: 14 days

Distance: 500km, plus one ferry

Take a trip on the wild side down the famed Carretera Austral (Southern Highway), the only artery through northern Chilean Patagonia, and then hop on a ferry for a ride south through foggy fjords to Puerto Natales, gateway to Torres del Paine, one of South America's most iconic national parks.

Mirador Las Torres (p312), Parque Nacional Torres del Paine

DAVID IONUT/SHUTTERSTOCK ©

❶ CERRO CASTILLO
⏱ 2 DAYS

Fly into the airport in Balmaceda and take the Carretera Austral south on the winding road to **Cerro Castillo** (p266; pictured below), a small town at the base of a castle-like massif. You've arrived in wild Patagonia. On day two, live the gaucho experience and go for a horseback riding trip, or hike the trails of the national park to vibrant Andean lagoons.

🚌 2 hours

❷ PUERTO RÍO TRANQUILO
⏱ 1 DAY

Continue south to **Puerto Río Tranquilo** (p261), the base for kayak and boat excursions to the famed Capillas de Mármol, better known as the 'Marble Caves.' Spend a half day at these sculpted geological formations and the rest of the day traveling into the nearby Valle Exploradores to get a peek at the Northern Patagonian Ice Field.

🚌 3 hours

❸ PARQUE NACIONAL PATAGONIA ⏱ 2 DAYS

Ground zero for efforts to reintroduce endangered animals into the Patagonian wilderness, **Parque Nacional Patagonia** (p278) is *the* place to go for wildlife watching. This park – set up by American philanthropists in 2018 – is among the finest in southern Chile, with great infrastructure and a nice network of hiking and biking trails to complement a museum, lodge and restaurant.

🚌 4 hours

DUDAREV MIKHAIL/SHUTTERSTOCK ©

④
CALETA TORTEL ⏱ 2 DAYS

Dreamy wooden boardwalks crisscross forested hills to reach the guesthouses, restaurants and homes of **Caleta Tortel** (p276), an isolated hamlet that feels ripped from a fairy tale. Stroll alongside the milky green bay or hike nearby trails to sweeping overlooks. Be sure to time your trip around the weekly ferries to Puerto Natales, which pass through stunningly remote fjords over about 40 hours.

⛴ *40 hours*

⑤
PUERTO NATALES ⏱ 2 DAYS

Southern Patagonia's iconic resort town, **Puerto Natales** (p300) is your staging ground for visits to nearby Torres del Paine. More than that, it's a quaint little village with a great waterfront promenade, large caves that once housed giant mylodons, cozy restaurants and a beloved gin distillery.

🚌 *1 hour*

⑥
TORRES DEL PAINE ⏱ 5 DAYS

Cap off your Patagonia adventure with a five-day hike along the famed W Trek through **Parque Nacional Torres del Paine** (p308). Along the way, you'll pass the three granite spires that give the park its name, as well as crackling glaciers (pictured above), golden pampas and lakes the color of a blue highlighter. With campgrounds, shelters and even some hotels, you can do the trek as luxe or budget as you'd like.

WHEN **TO GO**

With a diverse range of climates, long and skinny Chile has highlights to experience all year.

Apart from Chile's southernmost tip, which is best visited in summer, this varied country has opportunities for outdoor activities, wildlife watching and cultural experiences throughout the year. Spring is a beautiful time to visit Santiago, when the weather is balmy and the purple-blossomed jacaranda trees are in bloom, while fall is when the grapes are harvested at Chile's vineyards and pisco distilleries. In winter the far south can be inaccessible, but it's peak season at Chile's ski resorts near Santiago and at Termas de Chillán, the best time for big-wave surfing in Iquique and Arica, and a good time to visit the Atacama Desert (but bring warm clothes for the cold desert nights).

Avoid the Crowds

December through February is peak season, when Chileans take beach vacations and Patagonia is at its best (and most expensive). The shoulder seasons (September to November and March to May) are the best times to bag a bargain at coastal resorts and in the south.

⊗ I LIVE HERE

WINTER STARS

**Alfredo Burgos Rivera has lived in Vicuña all his life. He works at the Centro Astronómico Omega.
@omegaastronomico**

The Elqui Valley has clear skies all year-round, but for me, winter is the best time for astronomical observation. You can see Saturn, which is the most beautiful planet to observe and is not always visible in summer. The Milky Way appears clearer, and you can see the constellation Sagittarius. But when I was a child, I loved summer in Vicuña, especially the festivals.

THE ATACAMA DESERT

Covering 105,000 sq km of northern Chile, the Atacama Desert is the driest nonpolar desert on Earth. The average temperature is a relatively mild 18°C. The dry, cloudless conditions and absence of light pollution are perfect for stargazing.

LEFT: ABRIENDOMUNDO/SHUTTERSTOCK ©;
RIGHT: DREAMART123/SHUTTERSTOCK ©;

Stargazing (p99), Atacama Desert

Weather Through the Year

JANUARY	**FEBRUARY**	**MARCH**	**APRIL**	**MAY**	**JUNE**
Avg daytime max: **25°C**	Avg daytime max: **15°C**	Avg daytime max: **27°C**	Avg daytime max: **18°C**	Avg daytime max: **20°C**	Avg daytime max: **4°C**
Days of rainfall: **0** (Iquique)	Days of rainfall: **14** (Punta Arenas)	Days of rainfall: **1** (Santiago)	Days of rainfall: **1** (La Serena)	Days of rainfall: **0** (Iquique)	Days of rainfall: **11** (Punta Arenas)

VARIED CLIMATES

The climate of the central region is Mediterranean, with cool winters and hot summers, in which Chile's vineyards thrive. In Patagonia the climate is oceanic, with high rainfall, low temperatures and prevailing westerly winds.

Chile's Major Festivals

The **Teatro a Mil** performing arts festival dominates the cultural scene in Santiago (p44), with street and theater performances by international artists. **January**

First held in 1960, **Festival Internacional de la Canción de Viña del Mar** (p168) is one of South America's biggest and longest-running music festivals. It is broadcast live across the continent. **February**

Chilean independence is celebrated during **Fiestas Patrias** (p155) with barbecues, *terremotos* (wine shakes with pineapple ice cream and bitters) and merrymaking all over the country. The celebrations are particularly exuberant in Middle Chile. **September**

Chile's biggest **New Year's Eve** (p155) bash takes place in Valparaíso, where revelers fill open balconies and streets to dance, drink and watch fireworks on the bay. It's traditional to eat a spoonful of lentils as the clock strikes midnight. **December**

SUMMER AT THE BEACH

Camila Ahumada Tiska is from Caldera, where she has a bike rental shop and juice bar. @tiska.caldera

Summer is my favorite time of year in Caldera because I love the beach. But in January and February, the beaches are full of people, so I prefer March, when it's still hot but the crowds have gone. Whenever I have time, I go for a swim at Playa Loreta, a quiet family beach where the water is warm and there are few waves.

Bahía Inglesa (p146), Caldera

COLD OCEAN WATER

The Humboldt Current that flows along the Chilean coast keeps the Pacific Ocean cool year-round. The temperature of the water is usually between 15°C and 17°C off the coast of central Chile, around 21°C in Iquique and 9°C in the south.

Local Religious & Cultural Festivals

Festival Costumbrista celebrates the traditional customs of Chiloé (p235), with folk music, dancing and plenty of food. **February**

Tapati Rapa Nui (p332) is a huge cultural festival that takes place over two weeks, which involves a series of colorful dance, music and cultural contests on Rapa Nui. **February**

The streets of Arica vibrate with performances by brass bands and colorfully costumed Andean dancing troupes for the **Carnaval Andino con la Fuerza del Sol** (p94). The celebrations include three days of elaborate street parades. **February**

Chile's most spectacular religious festival is held in honor of the **Virgin of Carmen** (p115). For 10 days thousands of pilgrims, costumed dancers and bands fill the streets of La Tirana, a small inland village near Iquique. **July**

JULY	**AUGUST**	**SEPTEMBER**	**OCTOBER**	**NOVEMBER**	**DECEMBER**
Avg daytime max: **16°C**	Avg daytime max: **16°C**	Avg daytime max: **19°C**	Avg daytime max: **23°C**	Avg daytime max: **19°C**	Avg daytime max: **14°C**
Days of rainfall: **7** (Santiago)	Days of rainfall: **3** (La Serena)	Days of rainfall: **0** (Iquique)	Days of rainfall: **3** (Santiago)	Days of rainfall: **1** (La Serena)	Days of rainfall: **14** (Punta Arenas)

LEFT: TOLOBALAGUER.COM/SHUTTERSTOCK ©. RIGHT: CINEMATIC COLLECTION/ALAMY STOCK PHOTO ©

W Trek (p309), Parque Nacional Torres del Paine

GET PREPARED FOR CHILE

Useful things to load in your bag, your ears and your brain.

Clothes

Layers: Chilean summer days are hot, but when the sun goes down, the temperature drops in many parts of the country. In the north, mornings on the coast are surprisingly cool and often cloudy because of a coastal mist called *camanchaca*.

Thermals: Needed to keep warm at night in the Andes, Patagonia and for some winter nights in the Atacama Desert.

Hats: Necessary to keep the strong sun off your head, particularly in the desert areas of the north and in the Andes. Bring a wooly hat for the mountains and Patagonia.

Rain jacket: Bring a rain- and wind-proof jacket for Patagonia and the mountains.

Manners

It's polite to use the **formal usted verb form** when speaking to strangers and elders, and to address them as *señor* or *señora*.

Chileans tend to be quieter than their South American neighbors. Avoid talking too loudly in public places.

Hard bargaining is not common in Chile. Some light, friendly negotiation on price is usually fine, but demanding a discount could cause offense.

Comfortable walking shoes and hiking boots for trails: You'll be glad to have your feet encased in sturdy shoes when walking over rough terrain.

📖 READ

The House of the Spirits (Isabel Allende; 1982) A magic-realist tale following three generations in a country resembling Chile.

Twenty Love Poems and a Song of Despair (Pablo Neruda; 1924) By the writer who won the 1971 Nobel Prize in Literature.

By Night in Chile (Roberto Bolaño; 2000) Satirical reflection on a priest's life as an instructor to Pinochet.

My Tender Matador (Pedro Lemebel; 2001) A lonely older man is befriended by a revolutionary in this funny and moving novel.

Words

buenos días / buenas tardes is how to greet strangers; the phrases translate as 'good morning'/'good afternoon.'

hola is a less formal way to say 'hello'; use it with people you know.

por favor means please.

gracias means thank you.

de nada is the equivalent of 'you're welcome' and is used in reply to 'gracias.'

cómo estai is a Chilean variant of **cómo estás?**, an informal way of asking 'how are you?'

nos vemos is the equivalent of the phrase 'see you.' It usually sounds more like 'no vemo' because Chileans often don't pronounce the 's' at the end of words.

po is a filler word that Chileans frequently use for emphasis, but which doesn't

mean anything on its own. It's often added to the end of words: **sí** ('yes') becomes **sipo** and **no** becomes **nopo**.

harta is used a lot by Chileans to mean a large number or a lot of something.

¿cachai? is a Chilean phrase that roughly translates as 'got it?' or 'okay?'

al tiro means right now, a Chilean alternative for **ahora**.

weón is Chilean slang that should be used with care. It can be used as a strong insult, for example toward someone who cuts in front of you in line. However, it can also be used as a form of greeting between friends, but context is everything. Using it at the wrong moment could be offensive.

bacán means good.

filete means really good.

📺 WATCH

No (Pablo Larraín; 2012; pictured) Follows the publicist behind the 'no' campaign in the 1988 referendum on the Pinochet regime.

A Fantastic Woman (Sebastián Lelio; 2017) A transgender woman in Santiago faces prejudices and grieves after her boyfriend's death.

Machuca (Andrés Wood; 2004) During the final months of Allende's government, two boys from different socio-economic backgrounds become friends.

The Maid (Sebastián Silva; 2009) A maid who has worked 20 years for the same family attempts to hold on to her job.

Gloria (Sebastián Lelio; 2013) A middle-aged divorcée reenters the dating scene with mixed success.

🎧 LISTEN

Norma (Mon Laferte; 2018) She got her first break on a Chilean talent show and has become one of Chile's biggest stars.

Invisible (La Ley; 1995) After the death of founder Andrés Bobe in 1994, the Chilean rock band's fourth album brought them international success.

Quilapayún (Quilapayún; 1967) Though Quilapayún has gone through many iterations and musical genres, the first album included mostly Andean music.

Mamalluca (Los Jaivas; 1999) Inspired by the mountain that overlooks Vicuña in the Elqui Valley and recorded with a symphony orchestra.

LARISA BLINOVA/SHUTTERSTOCK ©

Pastel de jaiba

THE FOOD SCENE

Seafood, olive oil, wine and farm-fresh veggies are the key components of Chile's most iconic plates.

When was the last time you set foot in a Chilean restaurant? Never? For many visitors, a trip to the country is their first experience with Chilean cuisine, which can feel intimidating. Don't let it be. You've no doubt seen Chilean sea bass or wines like Carmenere on restaurant menus. Chilean salmon, fruits and berries are exported around the world, so you've likely eaten Chilean food before – you just didn't know it.

Unlike its neighbors on the far side of the Andes, Chilean cuisine is less about meat and more about fish, meaning you can expect amazingly fresh seafood anywhere you go. Add to the mix hearty stews, pillowy empanadas, gooey sweets and wildly affordable wines, and you begin to paint the picture.

Chile is an incredibly long country, spanning 4270km from end to end, which means the food in Arica in the far north is nothing like the food in Punta Arenas in the far south. Here's what to expect from Chilean cuisine from top to bottom.

Dining in the Desert

The vast majority of the Atacama's residents live in cities along the coast, where seafood dominates the local diet. *Ostiones* (scallops) and *locos* (a mollusk similar to abalone) are the biggest delicacies. The former is often served in its shell with a parmesan topping, while the latter comes atop salad with a dollop of mayonnaise.

Inland destinations like San Pedro de Atacama and Putre share much more in common

---

Best Chilean Dishes

CEVICHE
Raw fish mixed with onions, peppers, cilantro and lime juice.

POROTOS GRANADOS CON MAZAMORRA
Summer stew made from cranberry beans, maize kernels and squash.

PASTEL DE JAIBA
Crab meat cooked with cheese and cream in an earthenware bowl.

with neighboring Bolivia, with quinoa, llama meat and *charqui* (the original beef jerky) more prevalent here. Tea made from the coca leaf is also consumed to fight off altitude sickness, while cocktails and ice creams often feature the citrusy desert herb *rica-rica*.

Mediterranean Charms of Central Chile

Central Chile is one of the world's most productive agricultural regions, filled with vegetable gardens, fruit orchards and vineyards. That's why many people eat meals based on what's in season and available at the market, be it artichokes in the spring or squash in the fall.

No matter the dish, dinners almost always involve a glass or two of red wine, while brandy from the valleys just north of Santiago finds its way into the pisco sours served alongside pre-dinner ceviches.

Most Chileans shun spicy food, but the smoked chili pepper *merkén,* typical of Mapuche cuisine, is increasingly prevalent.

Meat & Potatoes in Patagonia

The dishes of southern Chile are much heartier – and meatier – than elsewhere in the country. Chiloé, in particular, has a large number of unique preparations based around its endemic potatoes, which are

turned into breads, stews and even desserts. *Curanto* – in which meat, fish and potatoes are cooked with heated rocks in an earthen hole – is one of South America's oldest continuously practiced culinary traditions.

Further south in Patagonia, lamb is the staple meat, often cooked over an open flame. You'll also find *centolla* (king crab) and many mushroom dishes, while desserts and pisco sours feature the omnipresent *calafate* berries.

FOOD & WINE FESTIVALS

Fiestas Costumbristas (p256) Small towns across southern Chile throw elaborate summer fairs in January and February, often with roast lamb and pig.

Cocinas del Pacífico (p128) This international food fair takes over tiny Bahía Inglesa each February as chefs experiment with the Atacama's coastal ingredients.

Fiesta de la Vendimia Colchagua (p154) Chile's preeminent wine region celebrates the harvest in late March or early April with grape-stomping, traditional foods and lots of vino.

Día Nacional del Pisco (p129) Towns across the Elqui Valley honor the national day of pisco on May 15 with flowing cocktails and bartender-led workshops.

Fiestas Patrias (p155 and p333) *Fondas* (food fairs) pop up across Chile in September for Independence Day celebrations, serving traditional street foods like empanadas.

Centolla

Pisco sour cocktails

PASTEL DE CHOCLO	CALDILLO DE CONGRIO	MACHAS A LA PARMESANA	CORDERO AL PALO	CHARQUICÁN
Similar to shepherd's pie but with corn mash instead of potatoes.	Fish soup made with veggies, cream and boiled conger eel.	Saltwater clams baked with a white wine and parmesan topping.	Lamb slow-roasted over an open flame, typically in Patagonia.	Pre-Columbian stew of potatoes, squash and dried *charqui* (jerky).

35

Local Specialities

Seafood Staples

Paila marina Tomato-based shellfish stew.

Choritos con arroz Mussels with rice.

Pulmay Shellfish, sausages, chicken and potatoes piled high in a bowl.

Tiradito Raw fish cut sashimi-style and served in a sweet or spicy sauce.

Chupe de centolla King crab casserole.

Snacks & Street Food

Empanadas Baked or fried turnovers.

Completos Hot dogs topped in mashed avocado.

Anticuchos Meat grilled on a stick.

Churrasco Italiano Sandwich of thin-sliced steak, tomatoes, mayo and avocado.

Choripán Grilled chorizo on a toasted bun.

Dare to Try

Piure An orange tunicate with a taste similar to sea urchin.

Cochayuyo Southern bull kelp that makes a great vegan ceviche.

Lengua de vaca Cow's tongue cooked in salted water until tender.

Calzones rotos

Prieta A dark black sausage filled with blood.

Lapas Slimy sea limpets often served in fried empanadas.

Sweet Treats

Calzones rotos Literally 'ripped underwear'; fried pastries with orange or lemon zest and powdered sugar.

Cuchuflí Tubular chocolate sweets filled with *manjar* (dulce de leche).

Mote con huesillos Sweet drink made from rehydrating dried peaches and adding husked wheat berries.

Kuchen de nuéz A dense pie made from walnuts.

Alfajores Cookie sandwiches covered in chocolate and filled with *manjar*.

MEALS OF A LIFETIME

Boragó (p77) Offering a culinary journey from Patagonia to the Atacama Desert in Santiago, it's listed among the 50 best restaurants in the world.

Tío Jacinto (p105) An unassuming seafood restaurant in Antofagasta with a big reputation among local foodies.

Te Moai Sunset (p337) Eat exquisite fresh-caught tuna or mahi-mahi in a ceviche or *tiradito* (raw fish cut sashimi-style) with views over Rapa Nui's famed *moai*.

Rucalaf (p248) This woodsy restaurant with a chalkboard menu rescues the unique plates and endemic ingredients of Chiloé.

CB Gastronomia Patagonia (p265) Regional dishes like lamb carpaccio and roasted morels shine at this experimental Coyhaique institution.

THE YEAR IN FOOD

SPRING

Fiestas Patrias celebrations in September are filled with *fondas,* where you can find empanadas, *anticuchos* (meat grilled on a stick) and *terremotos* (shakes made from sweet wine and pineapple ice cream).

SUMMER

Bean stews abound in the summer months, as do corn dishes such as *pastel de choclo* and *humitas* (like a Mexican tamale). In central Chile vendors sell the refreshing drink *mote con huesillos*.

FALL

Cooler air ushers in the season of *cazuelas,* stews made from a variety of meats and vegetables, and hearty *charquicán*. Harvest festivals at vineyards mean lots of wine drinking.

WINTER

On cold rainy days, Chileans prepare *sopaipillas,* small fried disks made from flour and pumpkin. If there are leftovers, they make *sopaipillas pasadas,* dousing them in a warm, thick molasses sauce.

Curanto al hoyo (meat, potato and seafood stew; p353)

SHARPTOYOU/SHUTTERSTOCK ©

W Trek (p309), Parque Nacional Torres del Paine

THE OUTDOORS

Home to a dazzling array of landscapes, Chile is an outdoor playground for lovers of nature and adventure sports enthusiasts.

Otherworldly deserts and shimmering ice fields, towering mountains and temperate rainforests, sandy beaches and crystalline lakes, rustling grasslands and far-flung islands: Chile's geography is remarkably diverse. Across the length and breadth of the country exist endless possibilities for outdoor adventures on foot or skis, by bike or horse, or in a raft or kayak, to name just a few of the options. As well as plenty to satisfy adrenaline junkies – including volcano climbing and canyoning – Chile offers many more relaxed experiences, such as stargazing and penguin-spotting.

Walking, Hiking & Mountaineering

Few countries compare with Chile when it comes to world-class trails. Most routes are in national parks and private reserves, and all levels of ability have excellent options, from easy half-day hikes along well-marked routes to testing backcountry expeditions into the wilderness lasting a week or more. Many can be done independently, but guides are widely available.

The most famous trails are in Patagonia, notably the W Trek and Paine Circuit in the sublime Parque Nacional Torres del Paine. Alternatively, you can strap on your crampons and go ice-hiking across the park's glaciers.

Further south, in Tierra del Fuego, the spectacular Dientes de Navarino Circuit offers a more rugged challenge. The Sur Chico region – notably the Huilo-Huilo Biological Reserve and Parque Nacional Villarrica – and the Chiloé Archipelago also have a wealth of memorable trails.

Adventure Sports

HORSEBACK RIDING
Ride with *baqueanos* (cowboys) across vast sheep ranches near **Puerto Natales** (p306) in Southern Patagonia.

PARAGLIDING
Soar above Cerro Dragón, a giant sand dune looming over the northern city of **Iquique** (p112).

SKIING & SNOWBOARDING
Check out one of Chile's renowned winter sports resorts, such as **Portillo** (p86) or **Valle Nevado** (p85).

FAMILY ADVENTURES

Spot penguins at **Monumento Natural Los Pingüinos** (p298) and **Reserva Nacional Pingüino de Humboldt** (p141).
Go stargazing in the light-pollution-free skies of the **Atacama Desert** (p99) or the **Elqui Valley** (p138).

Zipline, ride horses and whitewater raft at the private **Cascada de Las Ánimas** (p86) nature reserve.
Meet the mesmerizing *moai* and follow easy walking trails on **Rapa Nui** (p328).
Lose yourself in the magical landscapes of the **Huilo-**

Huilo Biological Reserve (p218) in Sur Chico.
Spend a day at the beach at a family-friendly resort near **La Serena** (p134) or **Bahía Inglesa** (p146), both in Norte Chico.
Sandboard down dunes near **San Pedro de Atacama** (p99) and **Iquique** (p112).

Northern Chile provides starkly different landscapes but similarly impressive hiking options. Highlights include Parque Nacional Pan de Azúcar in Norte Chico and Parque Nacional Lauca, and the area around San Pedro de Atacama in Norte Grande. There are even some good hiking options within striking distance of the capital, including in Parque Nacional Glaciares de Santiago.

Chile is also an excellent destination for mountaineering and ice climbing, with hundreds of peaks from which to choose.

Rafting & Kayaking

Chile's countless rivers, lakes, fjords and channels make it a hot spot for whitewater rafting and kayaking. The demanding but exhilarating Río Futaleufú in northern Patagonia is internationally renowned for its Class IV and V rapids, while rivers around Pucón in Sur Chico offer less technical runs.

Southern Patagonia has good options for rafting and kayaking, including in and around Parque Nacional Torres del Paine and on the Strait of Magellan, where you can spot whales. In Chiloé, you can paddle through the captivating sunken forests of Chepu at dawn. The Cajón del Maipo, a gorge southeast of Santiago, is another good spot for whitewater rafting.

Cycling & Mountain Biking

Chile abounds with leisurely cycles and epic rides. Bike rental and repair shops are common, particularly in the bigger towns and popular tourist destinations.

The San Pedro de Atacama and Sur Chico regions are both particularly popular with mountain bikers. If you have more time – and energy – try the challenging but spectacular ride along the 1240km-long Carretera Austral. A few intrepid cyclists have even set themselves the challenge of cycling the entire length of Chile, from the Atacama Desert to Tierra del Fuego.

An increasing number of tour operators – including in Puerto Natales – offer guided and self-guided e-bike rides.

BEST SPOTS

For the best outdoor spots and routes, see the map on p40.

©GUAXINIM/SHUTTERSTOCK ©

Bridge over Río Futaleufú (p269)

SCUBA DIVING
Explore dive sites off the coast of **Rapa Nui** (p337) and in the small towns around **Valparaíso** (p164).

SURFING
Find big breaks and long left-handers at **Pichilemu** (p179), Chile's surfing capital, or head north to **Iquique** (p112) and **Arica** (p119).

VOLCANO CLIMBING
Reach the 6893m summit of **Ojos del Salado** (p149), the world's highest active volcano, in Norte Chico.

CANYONING
Head into the countryside around **Puerto Varas** (p224) and **Pucón** (p210) for opportunities to rappel down waterfalls and navigate canyons.

ACTION AREAS

Where to find Chile's best outdoor activities.

Walking, Hiking & Mountaineering

① Parque Nacional Torres del Paine (p308)
② Dientes de Navarino Circuit (p321)
③ Huilo-Huilo Biological Reserve (p218)
④ Parque Nacional Villarrica (p211)
⑤ Chiloé (p251)
⑥ Parque Nacional Pan de Azúcar (p147)
⑦ Parque Nacional Lauca (p123)
⑧ Ojos del Salado (p149)

Rafting & Kayaking

① Río Futaleufú (p269)
② Pucón (p207)
③ Parque Nacional Torres del Paine (p313)
④ Strait of Magellan (p297)
⑤ Chiloé (p245)
⑥ Cajón del Maipo (p89)

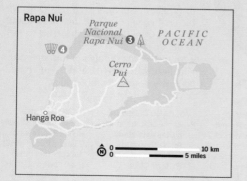

ATLANTIC OCEAN

●Mar del Plata

Stanley ●

FALKLAND ISLANDS

Cycling & Mountain Biking

1 San Pedro de Atacama (p99)
2 Sur Chico (p194)
3 Carretera Austral (p258)
4 Puerto Natales (p300)

●Comodoro Rivadavia

Puerto Williams
Ushuaia●

Rio Gallegos

Punta Arenas

Parque Nacional Tierra del Fuego

Parque Nacional Patagonia
Villa O'Higgins

Puerto Natales

Puerto Montt
Futaleufú
Coyhaique

Parque Nacional Torres del Paine

uco
Pucón
Castro *Chiloé*
cepción Valdivia

Surfing & Scuba Diving

1 Arica (p119)
2 Iquique (p112)
3 Pichilemu (p179)
4 Rapa Nui (p337)
5 Juan Fernández Archipelago (p360)
6 Cobquecura (p184)

National Parks

1 Parque Nacional Torres del Paine (p308)
2 Parque Nacional Patagonia (p278)
3 Parque Nacional Rapa Nui (p341)
4 Parque Nacional Lauca (p123)
5 Parque Nacional Pumalín (p262)
6 Parque Nacional Conguillío (p204)
7 Parque Nacional Nevado Tres Cruces (p148)
8 Parque Nacional Villarrica (p211)
9 Parque Nacional Queulat (p263)

0   1,000 km
0   500 miles

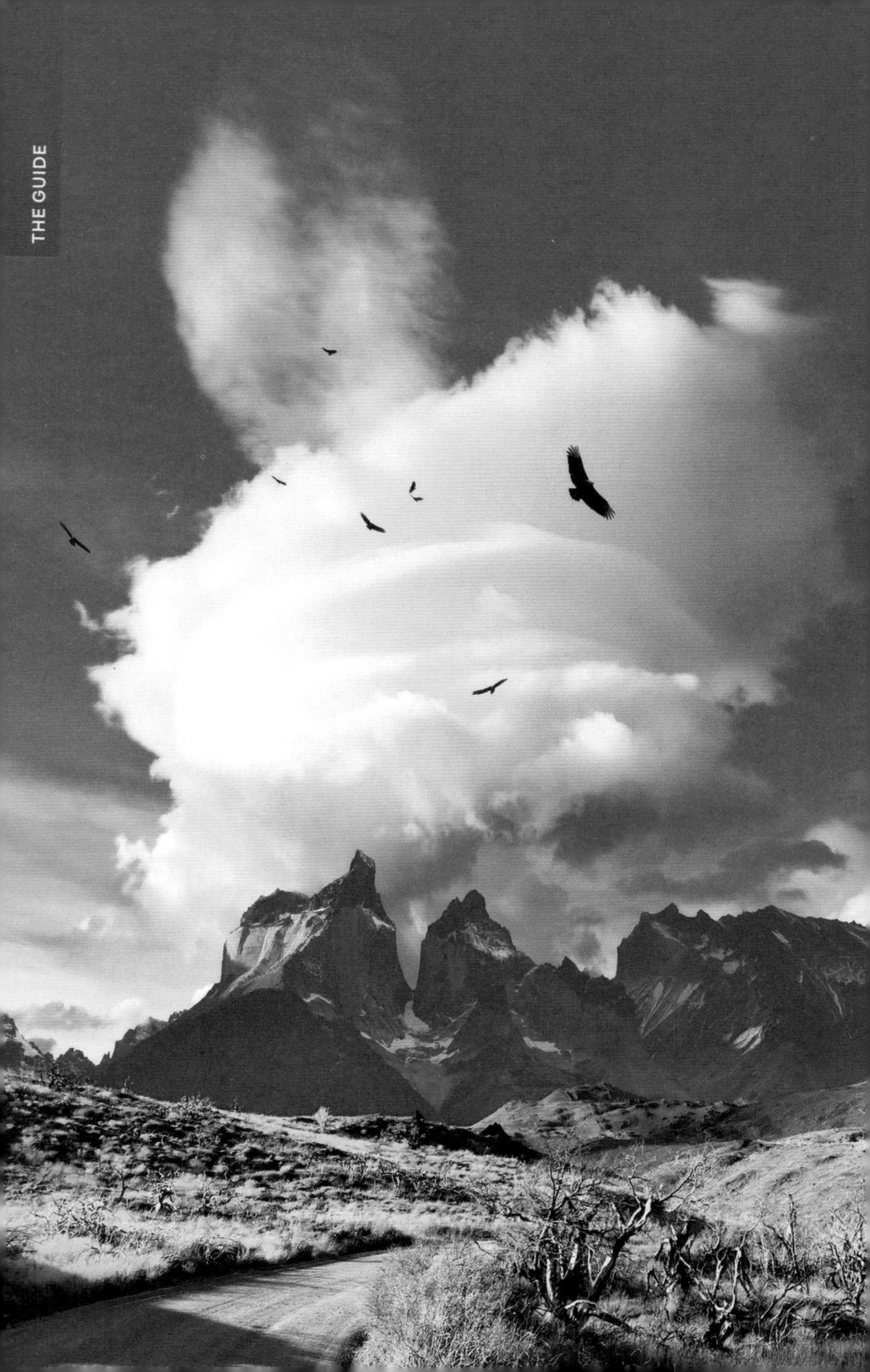

CHILE & RAPA NUI

THE GUIDE

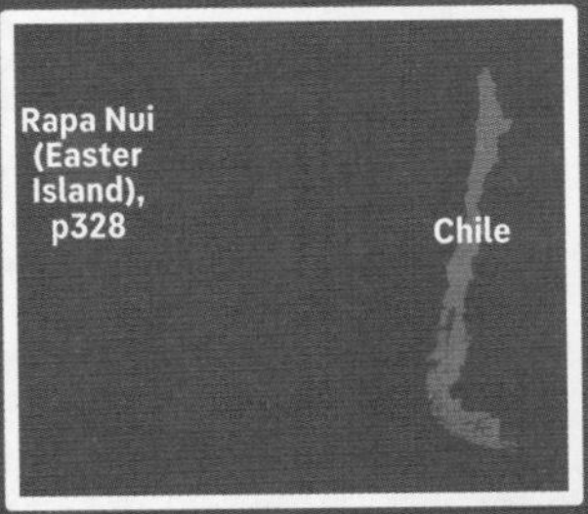

Rapa Nui (Easter Island), p328
Chile

Chapters in this section are organised by hubs and their surrounding areas. We see the hub as your base in the destination, where you'll find unique experiences, local insights, insider tips and expert recommendations. It's also your gateway to the surrounding area, where you'll see what and how much you can do from there.

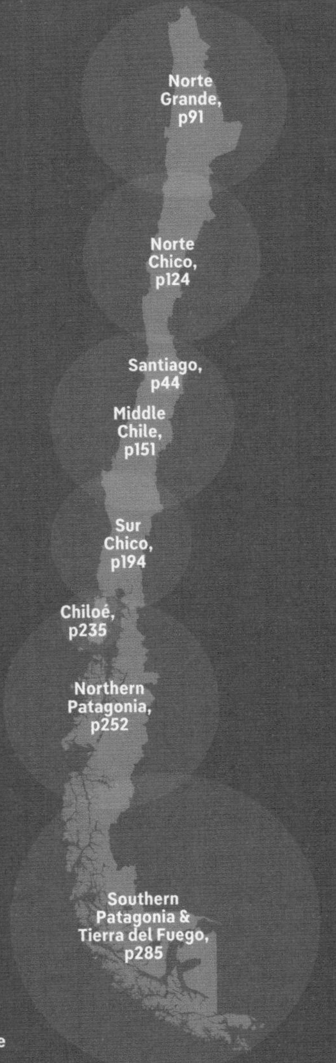

Norte Grande, p91
Norte Chico, p124
Santiago, p44
Middle Chile, p151
Sur Chico, p194
Chiloé, p235
Northern Patagonia, p252
Southern Patagonia & Tierra del Fuego, p285

Los Cuernos (p309), Parque Nacional Torres del Paine

SANTIAGO

BEATING HEART OF THE NATION

Nearly every trip to Chile begins in its sprawling capital, an overlooked city brimming with culture, character and boundless sunshine.

Few global capitals boast such a dramatic setting as Santiago, whose glittery skyscrapers and towering apartment blocks rise like beanstalks from a sun-drenched valley. To the west, you'll find the rolling hills of the Coastal Range, and to the east are the Andes, where you can ski, hike and raft amid the largest peaks outside the Himalayas. The metropolis below is a veritable urban jungle home to seven million people, including growing immigrant populations from Haiti, Peru, Colombia and Venezuela who have all left their mark.

Chileans from elsewhere love to say that *Santiago no es Chile* ('Santiago is not Chile'), yet almost half of the population – 40% of all Chileans – lives in the metropolitan region. No other Chilean city comes even close in size or influence. In fact, nothing happens in the country without people in the capital calling the shots. That's why, in many ways, Santiago *is* Chile. If you want to check the pulse of the nation, spend time in its beating heart.

Vast and sprawling in size, Santiago defies easy categorization. Perhaps it's best thought of as a collection of distinct neighborhoods, each with its own flavor. Centro is the city's historic core, home to stately government buildings and the best museums and cultural centers. More bohemian are neighborhoods like Lastarria, Bellavista and Barrio Italia, known respectively for dining, nightlife and shopping. The more affluent eastern neighborhoods, including Las Condes and Vitacura, are modern, shiny and high-rise, offering a vision of Chile's future. If the grit of urban life begins to wear on you, it's also easy enough to find yourself twirling a glass of Carmenere at one of the world-class wineries on the city's periphery.

Travelers have historically viewed the Chilean capital as a necessary evil before onward journeys to Patagonia, Rapa Nui or the Atacama Desert. But it really is worth more than a one-night stopover. Stick around for a few days, and you'll discover a fascinating city full of syncopated cultural currents, madhouse parties, frenetic markets, expansive museums, hilly parks and top-flight restaurants.

EDNO KAZUTO MORIGUCHI/SHUTTERSTOCK ©

THE MAIN AREAS

SANTIAGO CENTRO
The historic heart.
p50

BELLAVISTA
Parks and nightlife.
p56

BARRIO FRANKLIN
Food and markets.
p61

BARRIOS YUNGAY & BRASIL
Bastions of heritage.
p63

DIEGO GRANDI/SHUTTERSTOCK ©

Left: Winery, near Santiago (p80); above: *Teleféricos* (cable cars; p59)

0 — 1 km
0 — 0.5 miles

FROM THE AIRPORT

The cheapest way to get downtown from the airport is via public bus 555 or private buses Turbus and Centropuerto, which take you to Pajaritos, where you can transfer to the metro. For a shared or private taxi, stop by the counters just after customs.

Cementerio General

← *Aeropuerto Internacional Arturo Merino Benítez (15km)*

Parque Los Reyes

La Vega Central

Bellavista
p56

La Chascona

Mercado Central

Santiago Centro
p50

Museo de la Memoria y los Derechos Humanos

NAVE

Museo Chileno de Arte Precolombino

Bocanáriz

Cerro Santa Lucía

Teatro Municipal de Santiago

Centro Cultural Matucana 100

Barrios Yungay & Brasil
p63

Centro Cultural La Moneda

BICYCLE

Though surrounded by mountains, Santiago itself is actually pretty flat and excellent for biking with a growing network of *ciclovías* (bike lanes). For east-west travel, the *ciclovía* alongside Río Mapocho is particularly handy. A few competing bikeshare companies operate here; Bike Itaú is the most common.

PUBLIC TRANSPORT

The Santiago Metro is one of the best public transport systems in the Americas and the easiest way to get around town. Purchase a Tarjeta bip! card at any station and top it up with cash to use both the metro and public buses.

Parque O'Higgins

Barrio Franklin
p61

Persa Bíobío

*Parque
Metropolitano
(Cerro San Cristóbal)*

**Cajón del Maipo
& the Andean
Ski Resorts**
p83

**Las Condes
& Vitacura**
p75

*Pueblito Los
Domínicos (4km)*

*Parque de las
Esculturas*

*Estadio
Francés*

**Providencia
& Ñuñoa**
p68

TAXI

Taxis are readily available throughout
the city, though many travelers
prefer the ease and safety of using
rideshare apps like Uber and Cabify.
Short journeys are typically quite
affordable. These rideshare apps
are technically illegal at the airport,
though many use them clandestinely.

Find Your Way

Santiago is large and spread out, though the
neighborhoods most visitors frequent are just north
and south of the Río Mapocho. In general, in this
socioeconomically divided city, the further east you
travel away from the historic center (and toward the
Andes), the richer the communities become.

**Maipo Valley
Wineries**
p80

Plan Your Days

Santiago is less a unified city than it is an unwieldy collection of disparate neighborhoods that are best tackled barrio by barrio.

JOSE LUIS STEPHENS/SHUTTERSTOCK ©

Palacio de La Moneda (p54)

Day 1

Morning

● Stroll through Santiago Centro, starting at historic Plaza de Armas and ending at **Palacio de La Moneda** (p54), the presidential palace. For some culture along the way, include stops at **Museo Chileno de Arte Precolombino** (p53) or **Centro Cultural La Moneda** (CCLM; p52).

Afternoon

● Wander through the vibrant markets of **La Vega Central** (p53) and **Mercado Central** (p53). Head to **Barrio Lastarria** (p55) to check out its art museums. Break for happy hour at **Chipe Libre** (p55) for pisco sours or **Bocanáriz** (p81) for Chilean wine.

Evening

● Stick around in Lastarria for dinner. Check out what's playing at **GAM** (p55) or **Teatro Municipal de Santiago** (p52).

You'll Also Want to...

Travel beyond the city center, hit the ski slopes, hike in the Andes, visit some wineries and get off the beaten path.

HIKE IN THE ANDES

Escape into **Cajón del Maipo** (p83) to hike alongside arcing condors before retreating to a thermal bath.

TASTE WINE IN MAIPO VALLEY

Within an hour of the city are a dozen wineries like **Viña Santa Rita** (p82) offering tastings and tours.

SKI IN THE ANDES

In winter, head to **Portillo** (p86) or **Valle Nevado** (p85) from some of the best skiing in the Southern Hemisphere.

Day 2

Morning

● Take a scenic cable car ride to the top of **Cerro San Cristóbal** (p59) to get your bearings and understand the city's dramatic Andean setting.

Afternoon

● Catch the **funicular** (p59) back down and head to **Barrio Italia** (p73) for lunch and a leisurely walk, getting lost in its excellent shopping arcades.

Evening

● Try Chile's 'fourth meal,' *once* (p74), or simply go big on dinner plans in one of the superb cafes or restaurants of **Providencia** (p68). If you still have energy, head to the bars and clubs of **Bellavista** (p56) for a nightcap or a night on the town.

Day 3

Morning

● Start with a somber history lesson at **Museo de la Memoria y los Derechos Humanos** (p65), which offers necessary context on Chile's turbulent times. Stick around to explore other museums near **Parque Quinta Normal** (p67).

Afternoon

● Stroll into Barrio Yungay for lunch at **Peluquería Francesa** (p65), exploring the vibrant **murals** (p67) on its historic streets. Take the L1 metro across town to **Barrio El Golf** (p78) to see the vast contrast between Santiago old and new.

Evening

● Watch the sunset over the modern Santiago skyline at **Parque Bicentenario** (p77) before wining and dining in the ritzy streets of **Vitacura** (p79).

BUY CHILEAN CRAFTS

Travel to the craft market of **Pueblito Los Dominicos** (p77) to stock up on souvenirs to take home.

GET LOST IN BARRIO FRANKLIN

On weekends, head to this southerly market neighborhood to visit the hip **Factoría Franklin** (p62).

EXPLORE MORE PARKS

Walk up lovely little **Cerro Santa Lucía** (p52) in Santiago Centro for a serene escape and great views.

WATCH A SOCCER MATCH

On game day, there's nowhere else you'll want to be than **Estadio Nacional** (p69), Chile's largest stadium.

SANTIAGO CENTRO

THE HISTORIC HEART

Wedge-shaped Centro is the oldest and busiest part of Santiago. It's hemmed in by three fiendishly hard-to-cross borders: the Río Mapocho, the Autopista Central expressway and the Alameda, where the central railing puts your vaulting skills to the test. Architecturally, the Centro is exuberant rather than elegant because countless earthquakes have battered the city. Haphazardly maintained 19th-century buildings sit alongside the odd modern high-rise, while its crowded *paseos* (pedestrian streets) are lined with inexpensive clothing stores, fast-food joints and *cafés con piernas,* coffee shops staffed with scantily clad waitresses.

Government offices, the presidential palace and the banking district are also here, making it the center of civic life. Some excellent museums are scattered throughout, but it pays to head to other neighborhoods for lunch, dinner and accommodations, unless you opt to stay near the lovely little pocket of bohemia that is Lastarria or the stately cobblestoned alleyways of Barrio París-Londres.

TOP TIP

Back-to-back blows (a social uprising and a pandemic) took a heavy toll on Centro, with many businesses decamping for richer parts of town. They're coming back, but Centro remains worse for wear. If you're street smart – and leave valuables in your hotel – you should be just fine.

Barrio París-Londres

GUBIN YURY/SHUTTERSTOCK ©

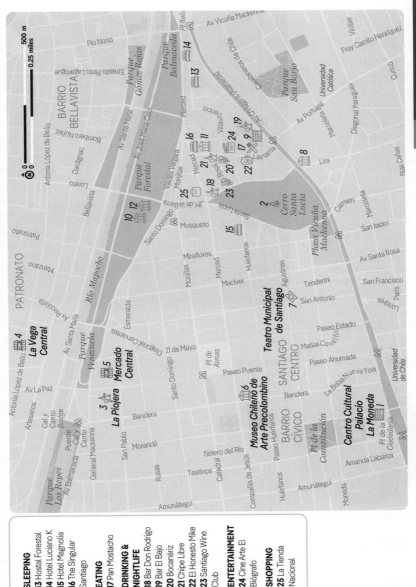

HIGHLIGHTS

1 Centro Cultural Palacio La Moneda
2 Cerro Santa Lucia
3 La Piojera
4 La Vega Central
5 Mercado Central
6 Museo Chileno de Arte Precolombino
7 Teatro Municipal de Santiago

SIGHTS

8 Centro de Extensión UC
9 Centro Gabriela Mistral
10 Museo de Arte Contemporáneo
11 Museo de Artes Visuales
12 Museo Nacional de Bellas Artes

SLEEPING

13 Hostal Forestal
14 Hotel Luciano K
15 Hotel Magnolia
16 The Singular Santiago

EATING

17 Pan Mostacho

DRINKING & NIGHTLIFE

18 Bar Don Rodrigo
19 Bar El Bajo
20 Bocanáriz
21 Chipe Libre
22 El Honesto Mike
23 Santiago Wine Club

ENTERTAINMENT

24 Cine Arte El Biógrafo

SHOPPING

25 La Tienda Nacional

Teatro Municipal de Santiago

A NIGHT AT THE THEATER

The exquisite neoclassical Teatro Municipal de Santiago is the most prestigious performing arts venue in the city. Home to the Ópera Nacional de Chile, it also hosts world-class ballet, classical music and visiting acts. It's one of the few institutions left in Latin America to not only have in-house chamber orchestra, ballet and opera companies, but also to make its own sets, props and costumes. To arrange a guided tour of Chile's oldest continually operating theater, contact visitasguiadas@municipal.cl or check the website to see what's playing.

Sleeping Beauty ballet, Teatro Municipal de Santiago

Cerro Santa Lucía

AN URBAN OASIS

Take a break from the chaos of Centro with an afternoon stroll through this lovingly manicured 63,300 sq m park, known to the indigenous Mapuche as Cerro Huelén. It was 19th-century mayor Benjamín Vicuña Mackenna who transformed this hill into one of the city's most memorable green spaces. A web of trails and steep stone stairs leads through terraces to the Torre Mirador at the top, and a scattering of chapels and other interesting buildings are in between, including a small 200-year-old 'castle,' Castillo Hidalgo. The main entrance lies by the cake-like Fuente Neptuno fountain.

Fuente Neptuno fountain

Centro Cultural La Moneda

ART, CRAFTS AND CINEMA

Underground art takes on a new meaning at Centro Cultural La Moneda (CCLM), one of Chile's leading cultural institutions, located directly beneath the presidential palace. The vault-like complex holds four small gallery spaces dedicated to cultural heritage, photography, design and children's programs, as well as two grand halls that host lavish traveling shows and locally produced exhibitions spanning art, architecture, and human and natural history. The national cinema, Cineteca Nacional de Chile, is also based here and hosts festivals regularly. The grand hall at the center of CCLM is used for concerts, book fairs and monumental sculptures. If that's not enough, the top floor has several gift stores, including the most spectacular craft shop from Fundación Artesanías de Chile.

Museo Chileno de Arte Precolombino

☐ Museo Chileno de Arte Precolombino

STRIKING ARTIFACTS FROM THE ANCIENT AMERICAS

Exquisite pottery from most major pre-Columbian cultures is the backbone of Santiago's finest museum. Star exhibits include dozens of intricately molded anthropomorphic vessels, hefty Maya stone steles, towering Mapuche totems and an intricate Andean textile display. More unusual are the wooden vomit spatulas used by Amazonian shamans before taking psychoactive powders. Unfortunately, the entire 2nd floor (or some 750 pieces) has been closed for some time because of a lack of funds exacerbated by the pandemic and social uprising. Check in advance to see what's on view.

🏪 La Vega Central & Mercado Central

EXPLORE SANTIAGO'S LARGEST MARKETS

La Vega Central is Santiago's sprawling vegetable market and has become so unwieldy that the government built a more tourist-friendly version, Tirso de Molina, just in front. Decide your comfort level, pick your market and look out for local fruits such as *tuna* (prickly pear) and *cherimoya* (similar to soursop), as well as vegetables like *papas chilotas* (colorful potatoes endemic to Chiloé). Across Río Mapocho at the beautiful wrought-iron Mercado Central, the gleaming piles of fresh fish and crustaceans atop mounds of sparkling ice thrill foodies and photographers. Look for staples from the Pacific coast, including *congrio* (conger eel), *locos* (Chilean abalone), *piure* (an orange tunicate) and *erizos* (sea urchins). Though tempting, the touristy restaurants here aren't very good.

Mercado Central

🍸 La Piojera

HOME OF THE TERREMOTO

No dive bar in Chile is more iconic than La Piojera, where the walls are the colors of ketchup and mustard, the tables are permanently sticky and the air is often filled with the guitar strums of wandering musicians. Sure, you could dine on *chorrillana* (fries piled high with meat and fried egg), but the real reason to come is for a *terremoto*. Typically reserved for Fiestas Patrias celebrations, the drink is kind of like a wine shake with pineapple ice cream, pipeño (a sweet white vino) and fernet (a bitter). As its name implies (*terremoto* means 'earthquake'), the drink might leave you shaking.

WALKING TOUR OF SANTIAGO'S HISTORIC CORE

This scenic walk starts at the core of Santiago Centro, **1 Plaza de Armas**, the symbolic heart of the city since 1541. These days, it holds a fountain celebrating *libertador* (liberator) Simón Bolívar and dozens of Chilean wine palms. Towering above the northwestern corner is the neoclassical **2 Catedral Metropolitana**, built between 1748 and 1800. At the northern edge of the plaza is the stately history museum **3 Museo Historico Nacional**, while the porticos on the eastern edge hold a string of nice restaurants, including **4 Comedor Central**. Take Compañia de Jesús west from the plaza past **5 Museo Chileno de Arte Precolombino** to the **6 Palacio de los Tribunales de Justicia de Santiago**, a neoclassical building housing Chile's Supreme Court. Continue west to San Martín and then walk one block south to visit **7 Palacio Pereira**, a gorgeous

mansion renovated to house Chile's constitutional convention between 2021 and 2022. It has an excellent cafe, as well as rotating art exhibitions. Continue south one block more and then head east to **8 Plaza de la Constitución**, a flag-filled park in front of the presidential palace, **9 Palacio de La Moneda**. Designed by Italian architect Joaquín Toesca in the late 18th century, it was originally the official mint. The north facade was badly damaged by air-force missile attacks during the 1973 military coup when President Salvador Allende, who refused to leave, was overthrown. A **10 monument** honoring the fallen socialist leader now stands in the plaza. Drop beneath La Moneda to check out the art at **11 CCLM** before finishing up with a meal nearby at **12 Salvador Cocina y Café**, a classically inspired Chilean lunch spot with an upmarket twist.

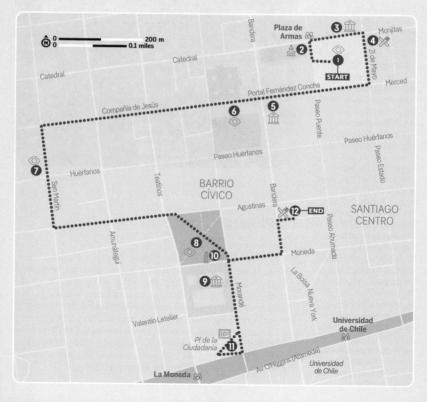

Centro Gabriela Mistral

MORE IN SANTIAGO CENTRO

Centro's Art & Culture Scene

STROLLING BOHEMIAN LASTARRIA

More than anywhere else, it's Barrio Lastarria that wins the hearts of most Santiago visitors. Sandwiched between Parque Forestal, Cerro Santa Lucía and Plaza Italia, Lastarria is the city center at its finest. The star attraction is Centro Gabriela Mistral (**GAM**), a striking cultural and performing arts venue with concerts, theater, dance and other shows most days of the week. Drop by to check out the rotating art exhibits on the bottom floor, the iconic architecture (which vaults and cantilevers on the inside and looks like a giant rusty cheese grater from the street), the little plazas, murals, cafes and more.

Nearby, José Victorino Lastarria is Santiago's most charming street, lined with cafes and restaurants and packed with buskers (including some running delightful pinhole theaters, known as *lambe lambe*). **Cine Arte El Biógrafo** is Santiago's preeminent art-house cinema, and sleek little Museo de Artes Visuales (**MAVI**) has four open-plan galleries of contemporary art. Nearby are some great stores, including La Tienda Nacional for books, music and gifts, and **Santiago Wine Club** for unconventional wines.

At the far end of the barrio from GAM is the Museo Nacional de Bellas Artes and the attached Museo de Arte Contemporáneo (**MAC**), both of which are housed in a stately neoclassical palace built as part of Chile's centenary celebrations in 1910. The former is a fine arts museum with a solid permanent collection of Chilean art, while the latter stages temporary shows of photography, design, sculpture, installation, web art and other modern forms. Both are free to visit.

BEST PLACES TO STAY IN CENTRO

Hotel Magnolia
This artfully designed hotel masterfully intertwines old and new in a restored 1920s building. $$$

Hostal Forestal
You won't find a nicer bed at this price point in Lastarria. There's a communal kitchen, dorms and private rooms. $

Hotel Luciano K
This stylish boutique with a great roof terrace lies in an historic building with art deco designs. $$

The Singular Santiago
The coolest luxury hotel in Santiago; it's worth a trip to the rooftop bar even if not staying. $$$

 WHERE TO DRINK IN LASTARRIA

Bar El Bajo
Artists and performers flock here after shows at GAM to down cocktails in an equally theatrical setting.

Chipe Libre
Even though it's always packed, Chipe Libre remains Santiago's only pisco bar. You decide: Chilean or Peruvian?

Bar Don Rodrigo
Lastarria's bohemia is on full display at this red-lit piano bar with cheap drinks and timeless appeal.

BELLAVISTA

PARKS AND NIGHTLIFE

Tourists often associate Bellavista with Pablo Neruda's house and the Virgin Mary statue, which looms over the city from the hilltop park on Cerro San Cristóbal. For locals, Bellavista equals *carrete* (nightlife). Partying until the wee hours makes this neighborhood's colorful lanes and cobbled squares deliciously sleepy by day. The leafy residential streets east of Mallinkrodt are perfect for aimless wandering, while the graffitied blocks west of it are a photographer's paradise.

In the heart of it all is Patio Bellavista, a giant dining and shopping zone that, while worth a wander, is a rather expensive tourist trap. The best bars and restaurants are in the streets beyond, including Pío Nono (known for its cheap and casual drinking dens), Bombero Núñez (the gay district) and Constitución (which is best for dining). You'll also find several small theaters, great hotels and underground clubs sprinkled amid the neighborhood's low-rise buildings.

TOP TIP

Don't be surprised if you show up at a club at 11pm and find it closed. Many places don't even open their doors until midnight, and they won't get packed until an hour or two later. Plenty of sit-down bars open around 7pm.

Patio Bellavista

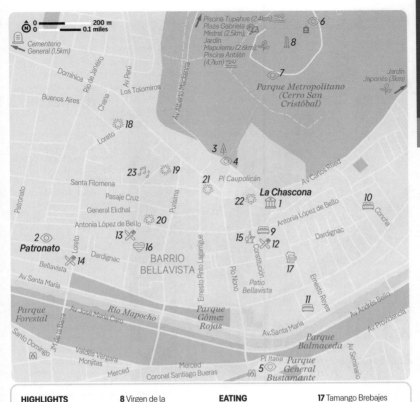

HIGHLIGHTS
1 La Chascona
2 Patronato

SIGHTS
3 Cerro San Cristóbal
4 Funicular
5 Plaza de la Dignidad
6 Teleférico
7 Terraza Bellavista

8 Virgen de la Inmaculada Concepción

SLEEPING
9 Castillo Rojo
10 Eco-Hostal Tambo Verde
11 Hotel Boutique Santiago Suite

EATING
12 Bar El Retiro
13 Dae Jang Kum
14 Sarita Colonia

DRINKING & NIGHTLIFE
15 AlmodoBar
16 Infierno Divas

17 Tamango Brebajes House of Beer

ENTERTAINMENT
18 Club Vita
19 El Clan
20 Illuminati
21 KLAMA
22 La Feria
23 Thelonious

Cementerio General

CITY OF TOMBS

Cementerio General

More than just a graveyard, Santiago's Cementerio General is a veritable city of tombs, many adorned with works by famous local sculptors. The names above the crypts read like a who's who of Chilean history: its most tumultuous moments are attested to by Salvador Allende's tomb and the Memorial del Detenido Desaparecido y del Ejecutado Político, a memorial to the 'disappeared' of Pinochet's dictatorship. The cemetery lies about 2km northwest of Bellavista in the Recoleta neighborhood. Alternatively, take the metro to Cementerios station.

La Chascona

Patronato

CHEAP SHOPS AND
INTERNATIONAL DINING

This barrio within a barrio, roughly bordered by Recoleta, Loreto, Bellavista and Dominica streets, is home to many of Santiago's 20th-century immigrant communities, particularly Koreans, Chinese and Palestinians. In fact, the largest Palestinian community outside of the Middle East lives in Chile. The colorful, slightly run-down blocks are lined with antique buildings and illuminated by neon signs, and a soundtrack of cumbia always seems to keep the beat in the background. Poke around the bare-bones supermarkets, feast on Korean food and wander through the clothing market to watch shoppers haggling over dresses and Chinese slippers.

La Chascona

PABLO NERUDA'S COLORFUL HOME

When poet Pablo Neruda needed a secret hideaway to spend time with his mistress Matilde Urrutia, he built La Chascona (loosely translated as 'Messy Hair'), the name inspired by her unruly curls. Neruda, of course, was a great lover of the sea, so the dining room is modeled on a ship's cabin and the living room on a lighthouse. Audio tours (available in English, French, German, Portuguese and Spanish) take you through the history of the building and the collection of colored glass, shells, furniture and artwork by famous friends. Sadly much more was lost when the house was ransacked during the dictatorship. The Fundación Neruda, which maintains Neruda's three houses, has its headquarters here and runs a lovely gift shop.

Street art in Patronato

View from Cerro San Cristóbal

MORE IN BELLAVISTA

Parks, Playgrounds & Viewpoints

EXPLORING PARQUE METROPOLITANO

You'll find the best views of Santiago from the peaks and viewpoints of Parque Metropolitano, better known locally as **Cerro San Cristóbal**. At 737 hectares, the park is Santiago's largest green space, but it's still decidedly urban: a funicular carries you from Bellavista to the top on one side, while a *teleférico* (cable car) swoops you away on the other toward Providencia.

A snowy white 14m-high statue of the Virgen de la Inmaculada Concepción towers atop the *cumbre* (summit) at the Bellavista end and is visible from everywhere downtown. The benches at its feet are the outdoor church where Pope John Paul II said Mass in 1984. Just below is Terraza Bellavista, with a few snack stands and extraordinary city views. *Mote con huesillo* (a drink made from dried peaches and husked wheat berries) is the classic park treat. To get here, take a steep switchbacked dirt trail or the funicular from Plaza Caupolicán. Alternatively, you can enter the park from Providencia at the northern end of Pedro de Valdivia and board the *teleférico*.

ZONA CERO: PLAZA DE LA DIGNIDAD

Santiago's central roundabout – known alternatively as Plaza Italia or Plaza Baquedano – has long been a destination where citizens gather to celebrate the nation's highs (like *fútbol* victories) and vent frustrations over its lows. Following the social unrest that began in October 2019, it became ground zero for a massive protest movement (known as the *Estallido Social*) with crowds gathered here almost daily until the start of the pandemic in March 2020. More than one million Chileans congregated here on October 25, 2019, to protest rising living costs, unemployment, privatization and inequality. Many now refer to the landmark as Plaza de la Dignidad in response to the movement's core mission: a fight for more dignity.

 WHERE TO EAT IN BELLAVISTA

Bar El Retiro
This playful, atmospheric resto-bar with a giant patio is the ultimate crowd-pleaser with affordable tapas. **$**

Dae Jang Kum
In-the-know locals go wild for the sublime seafood at this authentic no-frills Korean restaurant. **$$**

Sarita Colonia
Kitsch to the max, this queer hangout does stellar Peruvian-fusion cuisine and killer pisco sours. **$$$**

**BEST PLACES
FOR CRAFT BEER**

**Tamango Brebajes
House of Beer**
Try the Corta
Corriente hazy IPA at
this lively resto-bar
from Santiago's best
craft beer producer.

El Honesto Mike
Santiago's original
beer bar is still
going strong with
an unrivaled tap
list, American-style
burgers and three
locations.

Oculto Beergarden
This hidden hipster
beer garden has
20 taps of Chilean
drafts and excellent
pairings, such as
tacos and sushi.

**Cervecería
Intrinsical**
The original neon-lit
craft brewery in
Barrio Brasil grew
so popular there's
now an outpost in
Providencia too.

Other attractions on the hillside include **Jardín Mapulemu**, a botanical garden; the child-oriented **Plaza Gabriela Mistral**, featuring attractive wooden playground equipment and an interactive water fountain; and two huge public swimming pools with sweeping city views, Piscina Tupahue and Piscina Antilén. The small but perfectly landscaped **Jardín Japonés** (Japanese Garden) is just above the Pedro de Valdivia entrance.

Piscolas & Parties Until Dawn

NIGHTLIFE IN BELLAVISTA

Each evening when the sun drops behind the Coastal Range, Bellavista kicks into action. Nowhere else in Santiago lives for the night quite like this hard-partying barrio, which has clubs for all tastes and desires. Those who prefer something mellow and intellectual head to live music venues like **Thelonious**, an intimate early-evening bar for jazz aficionados with well-priced wines and shared plates. Other live music venues in the area typically double as clubs with DJ sets later in the evening, including El Clan and **KLAMA**. The former is more experimental in its musical offerings, while the latter leans heavy on emerging rock acts.

For underground electronic dance music (EDM), there's nowhere better than La Feria, Santiago's most famous nightclub, which boasts visiting DJs from Berlin to Brooklyn. Though compact, it regularly packs a capacity crowd of 300 and is one of the only clubs in the world to operate with 100% clean energy.

LGBTIQ+ visitors will find in Bellavista the most welcoming spots in all of Chile. Nights typically kick off at early-opening bars like kitschy **AlmodoBar**, whose wild decor goes for sensory overload. From there, drag fans can bar hop down Bombero Núñez looking for the most happening show. **Infierno Divas** tends to pack the biggest crowds with both comedy and music acts on its hypnotic stage. Nearby **Illuminati** is a sure-bet club for pop music, as well as memorable dance floor photos, which you can stage against its glow-in-the-dark walls. For something more underground and electronic, **Club Vita** ticks all the right boxes. No matter where you end up, you may as well join the crowd and order some strong *piscolas* (pisco and Coca-Cola).

 WHERE TO STAY IN BELLAVISTA

Castillo Rojo
Bellavista's most atmospheric digs, located in a firehouse-red mansion with a serene patio and vintage decor. **$$$**

Eco-Hostal Tambo Verde
Just removed enough from the bars to be a quiet, clean oasis for budgeteers. Great breakfasts. **$**

**Hotel Boutique
Santiago Suite**
Boutique hotel quality at a budget price makes this an affordable option. **$**

BARRIO FRANKLIN

FOOD AND MARKETS

The chaotic working-class neighborhood of Barrio Franklin rarely features on travelers' itineraries, but its sprawling weekend street markets are truly a sight to behold. Santiaguinos flock here to purchase everything from antique furniture to records, toys, video games, clothing and a wild assortment of eccentric curios – all at great value. In recent years, the neighborhood has drawn the attention of emerging chefs, brewers, distillers, artists and makers of all kinds, who have infused it with a newfound cool. Gentrified it most certainly is not, but suddenly it has surprisingly refined restaurants, superb art galleries and hipster-filled distillery-bars. Weekend fairs bring in lovers of everything from wine to fashion.

Trying to navigate the labyrinthine markets and clogged streets is basically impossible, so expect to get lost. Watch your pockets here; thefts are not uncommon. For a safe and enjoyable visit, stick to the key spots mentioned in this section.

TOP TIP

The markets and shops of Barrio Franklin are for the most part operational only on the weekends. Many of the restaurants are hopping only for lunch on Saturdays and Sundays. Time your visit between about 10am and 4pm, after which many things begin to shut down. The area is best avoided at night.

Art Galleries

SEE THE LATEST AND GREATEST

Want to discover the next big thing in Chilean art? The galleries of Barrio Franklin are some of the best in town to learn about emerging talent. Spaces include **AFA Galería**, a small industrial spot in Factoría Franklin with rotating exhibitions and an excellent gift shop. Even larger and more ambitious are **Factoría Santa Rosa** and **Galería 314**, which lie within Persa Santa Rosa (part of Persa Biobío). The latter two are particularly adept at sniffing out young artists before they hit it big abroad.

TOP: LARYSALUTVIN/SHUTTERSTOCK ©; BOTTOM: KARI KITTELL/ALAMY STOCK PHOTO ©

Antiques for sale

Persa Biobío

MARKET MADNESS

Persa Biobío

Art, antiques, furniture, knickknacks and fascinating old junk fill the cluttered stalls of this famous flea market, which sprawls across several blocks north and south of Bío Bío. Sifting through the jumble each weekend to find vintage rocks glasses, antique brandy snifters, cowboy spurs and 1970s magazines is truly an eye-opening experience. Increasingly, the market has also drawn top chefs who've opened experimental restaurants like Willimapu, serving fusion Mapuche cuisine, and DeMo, one of the best brunches in town. The latter is located within Persa Victor Manuel, the flea market's artsiest and hippest corner.

Factoría Franklin

HIPSTER HEAVEN

This former industrial complex has been transformed into one of Santiago's coolest destinations for lovers of food, strong drinks and edgy art. Each weekend, its doors fling open, and creators showcase their wares, including craft brewers, coffee roasters, vermouth makers, cheese wizards and bean-to-bar chocolatiers. Gin flows like water, with no fewer than three distilleries competing to bottle up the best local botanicals. Wash those G&Ts down with kimchi and ramen at Mirai Food Lab or a tangy sandwich at Barra de Pickles, a pickle bar from the vinegar mavens at By María. Check Instagram (@factoria_franklin) to see what's happening because events take place every weekend, including art fairs, design expos and themed wine tastings.

BARRIOS YUNGAY & BRASIL

BASTIONS OF HERITAGE

Toss aside the map, but don't forget your camera – wandering through the slightly gritty barrios west of the city center is like stepping back in time. Characterized by vibrant street murals, old-fashioned homes, long abandoned trolley tracks, low-key markets and hole-in-the-wall eateries, these historic barrios offer a charming counterpoint to the high-rise glitz of Santiago's eastern business sectors.

Once some of the wealthiest quarters in the 1800s, they fell into disrepair by the 1940s. In the decades that followed – when city planners saw skyscrapers as progress manifested – they remained an ode to a forgotten era. Rediscovered in the post-dictatorship decades, they're blossoming anew thanks to heritage-minded old-timers, young Chilean artists and immigrants from Peru, Haiti and Venezuela. Barrio Yungay, in particular, has flourished since Chile's youngest-ever president, Gabriel Boric, chose to move here at the start of his term in 2022.

TOP TIP

These barrios have higher crime rates than most areas frequented by tourists. Visitors typically have no issues, particularly during daylight hours, though it's smart to be aware of your surroundings. Plaza Brasil is best avoided after dark. The arrival of Chile's president to Barrio Yungay in 2022 has brought a stronger police presence.

Barrio Yungay

ROBERTHARDING/ALAMY STOCK PHOTO ©

BARRIOS YUNGAY & BRASIL

N 0 — 500 m
0 — 0.25 miles

Rosas

Museo de la Memoria y los Derechos Humanos
5

BARRIO YUNGAY

Plaza Yungay

Santo Domingo

Santo Domingo

M Maturana

Catedral

Ricardo Cumming

El Huaso Enrique 3

NAVE 6

Peluquería Francesa 7

Compañía de Jesús

Pl Brasil

12

4

Espacio Gárgola

Cueto

García Reyes

Huérfanos

BARRIO BRASIL

Agustinas

Moneda

11 9

Av Portales

Av Portales

Bulnes

13

Moneda

15

10

Las Palmeras

Chacabuco

Herrera

Mapú

Esperanza

Libertad

Moneda

Erasmo Escala

14

8

2 **Centro Cultural Matucana 100**

Universidad de Santiago

Erasmo Escala

Maestranza Restaurante (4km);
Pulpería Santa Elvira (4km);
Museo Cielo Abierto (8km)

Matucana

Romero

República

Pasaje República

Carrera

Blondie 1

Av O'Higgins (Alameda)

Av España

Av República

Cifuentes

Echaurren

Amaia Restaurante (10km)

Estación Central

Av Exposición

San Borja

Salvador Sanfuentes

Sazié

Grajales

Grajales

Latorre

Gorbea

HIGHLIGHTS
1 Blondie
2 Centro Cultural Matucana 100
3 El Huaso Enrique
4 Espacio Gárgola
5 Museo de la Memoria y los Derechos Humanos

6 NAVE
7 Peluquería Francesa

SIGHTS
8 Museo Artequin
9 Museo de Arte Contemporáneo Quinta Normal

10 Museo Ferroviario de Santiago
11 Museo Nacional de Historia Natural
12 Parque Quinta Normal

EATING
13 Creme Caramel Pastelería
14 Squella Restaurant

DRINKING & NIGHTLIFE
15 Cervecería Intrinsical

Centro Cultural Matucana 100

Centro Cultural Matucana 100

EDGY ART

Matucana 100 is one of Santiago's most experimental cultural centers with youthful, left-leaning programs and a packed calendar of cultural events. The ever-growing complex – located in a huge redbrick building that formerly served as government warehouses, plus a hangar-like addition – includes a small cinema, a large theater and several gallery spaces of differing sizes. Visit by day to see the art and stick around in the evening for a fringe theater production or a screening of an art-house movie. Forward-thinking to the max, it's the kind of space that would not be out of place in any major liberal hub.

Peluquería Francesa

BARBERSHOP TURNED RESTAURANT

This long-running restaurant – which also goes by the name Boulevard Lavaud – is an iconic Barrio Yungay institution with exposed brick walls, mismatched antique furniture and curios galore. The menu blends French and Chilean traditions (think duck a l'orange and almond-dusted cow tongue), and weekends often bring live music. As the name implies, it's also a working barbershop with stylists busy quaffing hair in the attached room. The placemats – with maps of Barrio Yungay's sites – serve as a great guide to the surrounding neighborhood.

Museo de la Memoria y los Derechos Humanos

Museo de la Memoria y los Derechos Humanos

A TOUGH BUT ESSENTIAL EXPERIENCE

A powerful piece of self-reflection, this striking 'museum of memory' explores the terrifying human rights violations and large-scale 'disappearances' that took place under Chile's military rule, when some 40,000 victims were subjected to torture and execution. It's an unmissable stop to learn not only about this dark period in Chilean history, but also how its repercussions vibrate across society to this day. One of the few Chilean museums with English translations, exhibits take you on a journey from the 1973 coup (often called 'the other 9/11' because of the date) up to the return to democracy in 1990 and the search for justice thereafter. Protest art and artifacts, victim testimonials, and photos of the disappeared make it a visceral experience.

Peluquería Francesa

65

NAVE

INTIMATE
PERFORMANCE SPACE

When NAVE opened to the public in 2015, it was a grand symbol of Barrio Yungay's emergence as an artistic hub of western Santiago. This experimental cultural center built within the walls of a 20th-century mansion invites artists in residence to showcase their works across dance, performance, music and theater. Quality varies wildly depending on who's in town, and the experimental nature of the pieces might not be for all tastes (many are still works in progress). With just 146 seats, however, intimacy is guaranteed.

Cueca dancers

Blondie

A CULT CLASSIC FOR NIGHTLIFE

The disco that never dies, Blondie is a bona fide Santiago institution. Opened within the old Cine Alessandri in 1993, it's been going strong for three decades, but it's never left behind its '90s-era love for new wave, post-punk and Brit-pop. Add to the mix some pop divas and modern indie tastemakers and you have the Blondie of today: a multi-floor dance club that draws the most diverse crowd in town. You can be young or old, queer or straight, punk or pop – Blondie welcomes everyone with open arms and encourages you to be your wildest self.

Blondie

Cueca Music

CHILE'S NATIONAL DANCE

Outside of Fiestas Patrias celebrations in September, it can be hard for visitors to see Chile's national dance, *cueca*, which imitates the courtship rituals of a rooster and hen. Old-school institutions in Barrio Yungay are among the few places left that proudly keep this tradition alive throughout the year. On weekend nights, the bar El Huaso Enrique overflows with patrons watching as proud dancers take to the stage, handkerchief in hand, ready to stomp the floor and twirl around their partner. Nearby Espacio Gárgola often has *cueca* on Saturday evenings. El Huaso Enrique isn't really known for its food, but Espacio Gárgola prepares excellent traditional dishes and cocktails served up in a quirky two-floor space that couldn't be more Chilean.

Museums of Parque Quinta Normal

ART, TRAINS AND NATURAL HISTORY

Parque Quinta Normal is the cultural nucleolus of Santiago's more working-class western barrios. This 40-hectare park, though unkempt on its edges, has a lovely core with an emerald green lagoon filled with swans and pedal boats. It has half-dozen museums, but only a few are worth your time. Start at the stately **Museo Nacional de Historia Natural**, whose 1st floor offers a great introduction to the flora, fauna and geography of Chile from the Atacama to Patagonia, plus Antarctica and the Pacific islands. A highlight is the giant skeleton of a sei whale. Kids love the immersive dioramas, as well as watching the scientists at work behind glass walls. Unfortunately, the museum has only sporadic English-language info, and the 2nd floor has been closed since the 2010 earthquake.

Rail fans will enjoy the antique trains at nearby **Museo Ferroviario de Santiago**. Education and entertainment come together at Museo Artequin, a museum with copies of famous artworks hung at kiddy height in a striking cast iron and glass structure. For older art lovers, **Museo de Arte Contemporáneo (MAC) Quinta Normal** offers an edgier and more experimental curatorial line than the main MAC museum in Bellas Artes.

Old Streets, New Murals

STROLL THROUGH ART AND HISTORY

Barrio Yungay has a pride of heritage in protecting both buildings and culture that you won't find anywhere else in Santiago. That's because residents mobilized in 2006 to form the city's first community-led heritage organization. The result is a low-rise district with a strong sense of identity and commitment to honoring the past. The checker-tiled **Pasaje Adriana Cousiño** and cobblestone **Pasaje Lucrecia Valdés** are among the most scenic spots to get a sense of the area's glory days.

One of the best reasons to visit this part of town is to wander Yungay's sleepy streets, gazing at the astounding murals covering the historic homes. **Artistas Yungay** (artistasyungay.cl) frequently hosts open houses and events showcasing the works of local artists, but you can come any time of the year and spot lavish murals from the likes of Sofrenia, STFI, PabloEtrom, Pikoenelojo Stencil and others. The streets between Parque Portales and Santo Domingo are generally your best bet.

For more Santiago street art, head south to the **Museo Cielo Abierto**, which is like an open-air graffiti museum.

OFF-THE-BEATEN-PATH CHILEAN RESTAURANTS

Amaia Restaurante
Chile's most famous Mapuche chef prepares hearty southern dishes at this colorful Maipú restaurant, whose plates honor endemic berries, herbs and potatoes. $$

Pulpería Santa Elvira
One of Santiago's finest restaurants. It's in an old Chilean home in Barrio Matta, pairing antiques and grandma-style hominess with ultra-modern cooking across multiple courses. $$$

Maestranza Restaurante
The perennial waitlist attests to the greatness of this classic lunch stall in Barrio Franklin, whose hand-written menu features dishes rarely served outside the Chilean home. $

 WHERE TO EAT IN BARRIOS YUNGAY & BRASIL

Creme Caramel Pastelería
It's so unassuming you'd have no idea how flavor-packed the treats are at this vegan-friendly bakery. $

Squella Restaurant
The oysters, the wines, the rooftop, the on-point service: Squella may be Santiago's greatest seafood restaurant. $$

Cervecería Intrinsical
The west side's most happening craft brewery with Chilean-style pub grub. $

PROVIDENCIA & ÑUÑOA

SHOPS AND CAFES

Providencia and Ñuñoa are leafy middle-class neighborhoods sandwiched between Santiago's historic center to the west and the glassy skyscrapers of the business districts to the east. While short on major attractions, they nevertheless make a peaceful base in the heart of the city for anyone interested in shopping, dining and people-watching. Cafe culture thrives here more than anywhere else, while the food scene is the best in the city.

Providencia, in particular, is packed with great hotels, boutique stores, third-wave coffee shops, innovative restaurants and hopping bars, mostly along the streets just north and south of its namesake avenue. Ñuñoa is more residential and among the fastest-growing sectors of the city thanks to two metro lines opened between 2017 and 2019 that've finally connected it to the public transport grid. Barrio Italia, which is split between the two municipalities, is the hippest place in the city and well worth a leisurely stroll.

TOP TIP

Providencia and Ñuñoa are crisscrossed by some of Santiago's most serene *ciclovías* (bike lanes), particularly along Río Mapocho, Tobalaba, Av Pocuro, Av Ricardo Lyon and Montenegro. Many streets shut down entirely on Sunday mornings (until 2pm) for CicloRecreoVía, a mass cycling event. Look for cheap bikeshare rentals like Bike Itaú.

Providencia

JOSE LUIS STEPHENS/SHUTTERSTOCK ©

Estadio Nacional de Chile

FOR THE SOCCER FANS

On the whole, Chileans are a pretty calm bunch – until they step foot in a *fútbol* (soccer) stadium. The most dramatic matches are against local rivals like Argentina, when 'Chi-Chi-Chi-Lay-Lay-Lay' reverberates through the Estadio Nacional. This 48,665-seat stadium also hosts the city's largest concerts (mostly global superstars on tour). Despite all the fun experienced here today, Estadio Nacional actually has a dark history as a detention center for more than 40,000 people following the 1973 coup that ushered in Chile's military junta.

Parque de las Esculturas

Chilean soccer fans

Parque de las Esculturas

A SERENE SCULPTURE PARK

Not only does this park offer a great view of the city's modern skyline to the east, but it also has a ton of rare araucaria trees, which tend to attract the vivacious green monk parakeets. Scattered in between are dozens of sculptures from local and international artists, and many pieces have QR codes you can scan for additional insights. An octagonal gallery in the center hosts rotating art exhibits. The park, a popular picnic spot, is often filled with smooching teens and twenty-somethings who have yet to move out of their parents' homes (and need a place to make out!).

Drugstore

HOME OF LOCAL BRANDS

Discerning Chileans eschew the city's megamalls for this vibrant (and confusingly named) shopping complex, which is geared around young designers, artists and authors. Men, in particular, will find some of the best and most affordable Chilean fashion at shops like Snog, Bastardo and Mo Store. Beloved local shoe brand Bestias also has an outpost. Several bookshops sell gorgeous coffee table books, though you'll find few English-language titles. Most stores lie underground, while the top floor holds cafes such as La Resistencia. On the weekends, local farmers sell organic produce at a market out back. The streets surrounding Drugstore to the east and west have some of Providencia's best bars and restaurants.

PROVIDENCIA & ÑUÑOA

0   500 m
0   0.25 miles

HIGHLIGHTS
1 Bao Bar
2 Bar Porfirio
3 Drugstore
4 Parque de las Esculturas
5 Pepperland

SIGHTS
6 D2l Art Projects

SLEEPING
7 Carmènère eco Hotel
8 Hostal Vitalia
9 Hotel Boutique Le Reve

EATING
10 Café de la Candelaria
11 CORA Bistró
12 Fiol Dulcería
13 InPasta
14 La Popular Infante
15 Lomit's
16 Óbolo
17 Piso Uno
18 Sapiens
19 Silvestre Bistró
20 Violeta Restaurant

DRINKING & NIGHTLIFE
21 Bar Rapa Nui
22 Bravo 95l
23 Café Black Mamba
24 Chueca
25 Graciélo Bar
26 La Cava del Barrio
27 La Pastora Coffee House

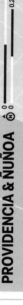
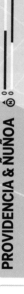

PI P de Valdivia

Parque Inés de Suárez

Av Antonio Varas

Santa Isabel

◎ Estadio Nacional (1.4km);
La Vinocracia (1.8km);
Plaza Ñuñoa (1.8km) ◎

Bao Bar

1
5

Pepperland

Av Antonio Varas

Pocuro

Elena Blanco

Av Manuel Montt

Av Manuel Montt

Av Francisco Bilbao

Santa Isabel

José Manuel Infante

José Manuel Infante

Av José Infante

Rancagua

14

Av José Infante

21

Julio Prado

Santa Isabel

Lautaro

Caupolicán

Av Salvador

Av José Infante

Av Salvador

Marín

Tegualda

Girardi

31 32

20
10

19

16

Av Salvador

Quebec

Av Francisco Bilbao

29

18

Av Italia

26

8

Av Condell

M Concha

30

Emilio Vaisse

24

13

12

Av Condell

Santa Victoria

Marín

Av Seminario

Parque General Bustamante

Mujica

Rancagua

7

Cyclist, Providencia

Plaza Ñuñoa

Av Manuel Montt

DRINKING AND DINING

Sometimes called Barrio Manuel Montt, this long avenue linking Providencia with Ñuñoa has grown into one of the city's principal zones for drinking and dining. Because of the presence of several private universities in the area, it tends to draw a younger crowd, and places skew more casual and affordable than elsewhere on the east side of Santiago. The avenue is densely packed with drinking and dining spots just south of Nueva Providencia, but some of the best resto-bars – including Bar Porfirio, Bao Bar and Pepperland – lie further south near Eliodoro Yañez.

Plaza Ñuñoa

'ÑUÑORK CITY'

Ñuñoa has a reputation among Santiaguinos as a neighborhood full of middle-class hippies who love their vegan cafes, plant shops, cannabis brownies and endless evening *carretes* (parties). Nowhere is that more apparent than at Plaza Ñuñoa, the leafy heart of the barrio, which is surrounded by low-key and pretension-free restaurants, bars and nightclubs, many of which have live music on the weekends. This pretty plaza has also been the site of some of the city's largest (and almost always peaceful) protests, particularly during the social uprising of 2019–20.

TOP: IGNACIO BUSTAMANTE/SHUTTERSTOCK © BOTTOM: JOSE LUIS STEPHENS/SHUTTERSTOCK ©

Gran Torre Santiago

Gran Torre Santiago

SHOPPING CENTER WITH A VIEW

This 62-story skyscraper is the tallest building in South America and the fourth-tallest in the southern hemisphere. Famously empty – save for a handful of floors – it's often seen by locals as an emblem of the greed and hubris of Chile's billionaire class. That said, visitors do enjoy riding to the top for 360-degree views of the entire city (smog permitting) at an observation deck known as Sky Costanera. The building complex also houses Costanera Center, the largest shopping mall in South America, which is your best bet for any camping, backpacking or snow sports items you might need for trips into the Andes. The mall similarly contains one of the city's best supermarkets (Jumbo), movie theaters (Cineplanet) and department stores (Falabella).

GERARDO ERNESTO CAMACHO/SHUTTERSTOCK ©

Barrio Italia

I LIVE HERE: CULTURE

Felipe Bascuñán, deputy director of CCLM, shares his recommendations for the best places for culture in the neighborhood.

D21 Art Projects
This small gallery showcases contemporary Chilean visual artists. It's hidden on the 2nd floor of an old apartment building (buzz D21) next to an old-school '70s-style *caracol* (snail-shaped shopping center).

Centro de Extensión UC
Inside a 100-year-old convent you'll find two art galleries – Galería Macchina and Espacio Vilches – which show young artists, as well as stages for concerts, movies and plays.

Ojoporojo Tienda
This concept store focuses on art books, as well as zines, funky t-shirts and printmaking, all done in-house. Check Instagram (@ojoporojo.cl) for frequent workshops.

MORE IN PROVIDENCIA & ÑUÑOA

Santiago's Hippest Hood

STROLLING AROUND BARRIO ITALIA

Barrio Italia is not a neighborhood you visit with an agenda. Rather, it's the most exciting place in Santiago for a wander, particularly on Sunday afternoons when the rest of the city shutters. Split between Providencia and Ñuñoa, it's one of those rare places that's managed to gentrify while keeping its low-rise identity and blue-collar roots.

The name comes from the Italians who moved here at the start of the 20th century to work at the Girardi hat factory. Though the factory is long closed, fashion still plays a key role at labyrinthine shopping arcades like Estacion Italia, whose boutiques sell made-in-Chile shoes, sunglasses and clothing. Other arcades, often built into creaky old homes, sell records, books, crafts and curios; check out **Tienda Larry** for funky home goods. Many have hip cafes and coffee shops tucked into the interior patio, such as the vegan food bastion **Sapiens**. In between all the modern shops on Av Condell and Av Italia are plenty of old-school antique stores with workers out front in coveralls busy painting and polishing.

 WHERE TO STAY IN PROVIDENCIA & ÑUÑOA

Carménère eco Hotel
Sustainability meets sophistication at this stylish wine-themed hotel on a quiet Barrio Italia side street. **$$$**

Hostal Vitalia
You can't beat the location of this small, homey hostel at the heart of Barrio Italia. **$**

Hotel Boutique Le Reve
This high-end boutique is a leafy oasis covered in ivy and blessed with a French-inspired courtyard. **$$$**

**BEST RESTAU-
RANTS IN PROVI-
DENCIA & ÑUÑOA**

CORA Bistró
The imaginative
flavors, painterly
plating and off-piste
sommelier-led wine
offerings make for a
fabulous fine-dining
experience in a
casual setting with
reasonable prices. $$

Piso Uno
Learn why Chileans
are hooked on Nikkei
cuisine (Peruvian-
Japanese fusion) at
this loungy and lively
resto-bar. $$$

Lomit's
For cheap eats,
professional service
and old-school vibes,
you can't beat this
traditional sandwich
bar. $

Rishtedar
Like your Indian
food paired with
pisco sours? This
atmospheric spot
does the nation's best
curries and tandoori
chicken. $$

Barrio Italia is also home to the city's best wine shops, including **La Cava del Barrio**, which works only with small-scale and boutique producers, and **Vinoteca Italia**, which has frequent tastings. Those with a sweet tooth should head to **Fiol Dulceria** for wildly inventive confections or the bean-to-bar chocolate factory **Óbolo**. Veggie hotspot **Violeta Restaurant**, pasta perfectionists **InPasta** and funky farm-to-table **Silvestre Bistró** are the neighborhood's hottest restaurants. The gin drinks at **Ruca Bar** and hip LGBTIQ+ crowd at **Chueca** keep the area packed well after dark.

Discover Chile's 'Fourth Meal'

FORGET TEA TIME; IT'S LA ONCE

British teatime (elevenses) arrived in Chile via English-owned saltpeter mines and spread like wildfire, morphing into a unique late afternoon 'fourth meal' known as *once* ('eleven,' in Spanish). Typically, it involves a sweet and salty mix of breads, pastries, cheese, eggs and mashed avocado consumed with tea or coffee. While there is an entire chain dedicated to this meal – **Tavelli** – you're better off going to some of the independent cafes and bakeries that Providencia is famous for.

Chile is, by far, the largest bread consumer in Latin America. The roll-like *marraqueta* and biscuit-like *hallulla* are most common, but you'll find an astounding variety at less traditional bakeries such as **Pan Mostacho** and **La Popular Infante** (which has legendary sourdough). For a more sweets-focused *once*, try the edible pastry art at **Roberto Muñoz Patisserie**. If you want a cafe that will do all the work for you by preparing its own *once* menu, **Café de la Candelaria**, in an interior patio in Barrio Italia, is a no-brainer.

Those who prefer to visit cafes for their morning fix instead will be pleasantly surprised to learn that Santiago has shed its addiction to Nescafé. Fantastic coffee shops include **Café Black Mamba**, **La Pastora Coffee House** and the oh-so-trendy **Casino Latriana**, which also runs a series of clandestine dinner parties.

 WHERE TO DRINK IN PROVIDENCIA & ÑUÑOA

Gracielo Bar
Craft cocktails and tapas draw
crowds to both the rooftop
and stylish interior of this old
mansion.

Bravo 951
This hipster hangout has
frequent fiestas, fairs and DJs.
Otherwise, it's all cocktails and
comfort food.

Bar Rapa Nui
A must for lovers of dive bars,
local traditions and jolting
piscolas (pisco and Coca-
Cola).

LAS CONDES & VITACURA

SKYSCRAPER CENTRAL

Glittering skyscrapers, security-heavy apartment blocks and shiny new megamalls: Las Condes is determined to be the international face of modern Chile. Sprawling off toward the Andes, it finds its groove best in Barrio El Golf, a leafy neighborhood home to posh restaurants, gorgeous mansions and luxe hotels that's sometimes referred to by its ironic nickname: 'Sanhattan.' The streets just north and south of Parque Araucano are similarly high-rise and hopping but more business-minded and dominated by international chains.

To the north, the even ritzier neighborhood of Vitacura contains Santiago's most exclusive shopping streets, posh art galleries, high-end bars and famous restaurants. The most vibrant quarter is east of the spectacular Parque Bicentenario on the crisscrossing avenues of Nueva Costanera, Vitacura and Alonso de Córdova. As you'd expect, these upper-class neighborhoods see a steady stream of business travelers. While they lack some of the soul found elsewhere, they deliver on fashion, shopping and good eats.

TOP TIP

These two neighborhoods can feel like an entirely different version of Santiago. In fact, many of their residents never travel west of Av Tobalaba to the city's less affluent sectors. You, however, may want to: prices here tend to be on par with (or exceed) those in major European or North American cities.

Las Condes

JOSE LUIS STEPHENS/SHUTTERSTOCK ©

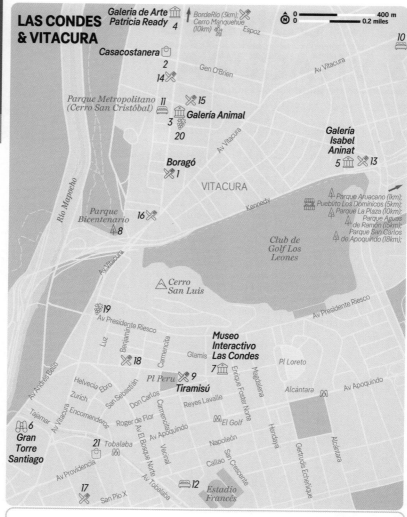

LAS CONDES & VITACURA

HIGHLIGHTS
1 Boragó
2 Casacostanera
3 Galería Animal
4 Galeria de Arte Patricia Ready
5 Galería Isabel Aninat
6 Gran Torre Santiago

7 Museo Interactivo Las Condes
8 Parque Bicentenario
9 Tiramisú

SLEEPING
10 Hotel Bidaosa
11 NOI Vitacura
12 Select by Time

EATING
13 CV Galería
14 La Calma by Fredes
15 La Mesa
16 La Punta
17 Rishtedar
18 Tip y Tap

DRINKING & NIGHTLIFE
19 Les Dix Vins
20 Vinolia

SHOPPING
21 Ojoporojo Tienda

Pueblito Los Domínicos

CRAFT GOODS

Beyond the lovely Artesanías de Chile stores (including the one here), you won't find anywhere better in Santiago to purchase quality craft goods that were actually made in Chile. This mock village at the end of the L1 metro line in Las Condes houses dozens of small stores, art galleries and traditional lunch cafes. As you stroll around, look for lapis lazuli jewelry, genuine Andean textiles, hand-carved wooden bowls, tightly woven baskets and ceramics with indigenous motifs. You're likely to walk away with a memorable souvenir.

Chilean textiles

Boragó

CHILE'S FINEST RESTAURANT

The concept of Chilean fine dining really only began with the arrival of chef Rodolfo Guzmán's groundbreaking eatery Boragó, which has been listed among the World's 50 Best Restaurants for a decade. Guzmán takes visitors on a multicourse culinary journey through little-known endemic ingredients found in the valleys, fjords and hills between Patagonia and the Atacama Desert. More affordable than most meals of this caliber, it truly is an experience you won't soon forget, particularly when combined with the unconventional Chilean wine pairings. Located in a minimalist building facing Cerro Manquehue, the restaurant includes a mind-blowing food lab where Guzmán dreams up his creations.

Boragó

Parque Bicentenario

SNOOZE UNDER THE SKYLINE

This serene urban oasis was created, as the name suggests, in celebration of the Chilean bicentennial. In addition to more than 4000 trees, the park has manicured footpaths, public sculptures, bird-filled lagoons, playgrounds and food vendors, including the fine-dining restaurant Mestizo, which is great for a sundowner looking back over the gleaming 'Sanhattan' skyline. The park also hosts open-air movie screenings and frequent fairs for everything from fashion to wine and designer goods. For a great pedaling excursion, grab a public bike from Bike Itaú and head to the *ciclovía* (bike lane) alongside the Río Mapocho just outside the western edge of the park. From there, you can bike northeast along the river for 6km, enjoying spectacular views of Cerro Manquehue and the distant Andes.

Parque Araucano

A PARK WITH A MALL

Parque Araucano

Surrounded by glassy skyscrapers, Parque Araucano is a true green refuge and one of the city's prettiest parks with a lovely rose garden, fantastic playgrounds, dancing water fountains, a skate zone, sports fields and a small educational theme park called KidZania. Many people, particularly South Americans from neighboring countries, head to this 22-hectare park en route to the American-style mall of the same name, which lies on its northern edge and is home to high-end global brands, colossal department stores and tons of open-air dining.

Vitacura Art Galleries

FOR DISCERNING CONNOISSEURS

An important nexus for the exhibition of contemporary Chilean art – and a choice spot to observe fashionistas in their natural habitat – is the gallery circuit around Av Alonso de Córdova. Those seriously considering a purchase should head to **Galería Animal**, which has a sophisticated collection of contemporary art in a stunning multilevel space. For the works of more emerging artists – plus a bookshop and cafe – head to **Galería de Arte Patricia Ready**. In the artsy **CV Galeria**, the well-respected Galería Isabel Aninat has exhibited the works of major Chilean and international artists since 1983, including Joan Miró and Antoni Gaudí.

Isidora Goyenechea

Isidora Goyenechea & Nueva Costanera

HIGH-END AVENUES

These two wide *avenidas* are the heart and soul of their respective neighborhoods. In Barrio El Golf (Las Condes), Isidora Goyenechea has shed its addiction to international chain restaurants and transformed into a more dynamic dining destination, particularly around Plaza Peru where Italian restaurant Tiramisú draws huge lines. Interspersed between the dining options are a few clothing and homeware stores, as well as the kid-friendly technology museum Museo Interactivo Las Condes. In Vitacura, Nueva Costanera is Santiago's most exclusive shopping street with several designer boutiques (Karyn Coo, Lia Fernández, SISA) and a high-end open-air mall (Casacostanera). Dining, too, is excellent, with many of the city's most renowned restaurants (La Calma, Dondoh, Osaka, Aquí Está Coco) paying a premium to be here.

Cerro Provincia

MORE IN LAS CONDES & VITACURA

Take a Hike

RISING INTO THE CORDILLERA

Hiking enthusiasts gearing up for treks in Patagonia should consider some of the excellent routes into the precordillera that are accessible by public transportation or taxi on the easternmost edge of Las Condes. Asociación Parque Cordillera runs several private parks here, all of which must be entered by 1pm at the latest, depending on the hike. Check the website (asociacionparquecordillera.cl) for maps, rules and regulations.

The 17km round-trip hike to the **Salto de Apoquindo** waterfall in **Parque Aguas de Ramón** is one of the most scenic and shaded options enjoyed by experienced trekkers, though the shorter 6.5km **Sendero Los Peumos** is equally picturesque. Those looking to scale some pre-Andean slopes should head instead to the neighboring parks **Parque La Plaza** and **Parque San Carlos de Apoquindo**, where you can summit **Morro Las Papas** (1357m, 7km) or continue to the more challenging **Alto Las Vizcachas** (1871m, 10km). Both offer sweeping views back over Santiago. Parque San Carlos de Apoquindo also has some less-traveled (and more formidable) trails to summits like **Alto del Naranjo** (1890m, 13km) and **Cerro Provincia** (2750m, 22km).

Closer to town in Vitacura (and not part of the Asociación Parque Cordillera), you'll find **Cerro Manquehue**, the highest peak within Santiago. The short but strenuous 5km round-trip climb to its 1639m summit is one of the most popular hikes in the city. If possible, plan your trip for just after it rains to get the best (that is, smog-free) views.

WHERE TO EAT IN LAS CONDES & VITACURA

La Mesa
Sustainable sourcing is at the heart of all its meals. $$$

La Calma by Fredes
Puts the entire Pacific coast on a plate in a local seafood extravaganza. $$$

La Punta
Might just make the best empanadas in Santiago. $

Tip y Tap
Eastern Santiago chain with affordable down-home cooking. $

BordeRio
Find many of Vitacura's most popular eateries in this riverside dining complex. $$$

CV Galería
See and be seen at this art-minded dining destination. $$$

 WHERE TO STAY IN LAS CONDES & VITACURA

Select by Time
Excellent value spot with classy decor, a rooftop pool and a quiet plaza-facing location. $$

Hotel Bidasoa
Oh-so-trendy Bidasoa has an alluring tropical-chic vibe and buzzy vegan-friendly restaurant to boot. $$$

NOI Vitacura
The prime location on Nueva Costanera, in-house spa and rooftop lounge are all highlights. $$$

MAIPO VALLEY WINERIES

VINES AND WINES

When you've had your fill of Santiago's museums and plazas, head south of the city center to check out the gorgeous family vineyards and mass-production wine operators of the Maipo Valley. Big-bodied reds are what this place is all about. Varietals such as merlot, Carmenere and syrah are all present, but it's cabernet sauvignon that's the real star. In fact, Maipo Valley cab sauvs are some of the most exported Chilean wines, featured in stores and restaurants around the world. Pastoral Pirque is at the heart of the valley and is its most picturesque sector with several wineries, restaurants and hotels. You don't actually have to leave Santiago at all to taste some amazing Maipo Valley wines. Not only are there wineries within city limits, but there's also a growing number of excellent *vinobars* where you can sample an array of intriguing bottles.

TOP TIP

Many of the Maipo Valley wineries require advance reservation to visit and only offer guided tours, not tastings (Viña Santa Rita and Concha y Toro are exceptions). You'll find more multilingual guides here than in other Chilean wine valleys, and creative tours include sunset dinners and bike rides through the vines.

Viña Cousiño Macul

HISTORY AND LEGENDS

Viña Cousiño Macul is one of the only vineyards still carving a green patch within Santiago's urban sprawl (though most of the vines are now 40km away in Buin) thanks to its historic winery building, which dates from 1872. In addition to the traditional tours, which are packed with Chilean wine history and include three tastings, you can also book a cycling tour through the vines that includes four tastings. Public bus 418 drops you right out front.

Wine, Viña Cousiño Macul

Concha y Toro

GLOBALLY FAMOUS WINES

Concha y Toro is Latin America's largest wine producer and one of the 10 biggest wine brands on Earth. Thanks to its global name recognition, it's also the most-visited winery in Chile and has excellent infrastructure for receiving guests and welcoming them in several languages. You can sign up for a variety of different tours of the lavish grounds or simply show up to the on-site wine bar, Bodega 1883, and sample wines by the glass or flight. Though not nearly as surprising or personal as other wineries, it's nevertheless one of the few reachable by public transportation from Santiago.

Concha y Toro

Santiago Wine Bars

THE BOOM OF VINOBARS

You don't have to leave Santiago to try some of the best wines from nearby vineyards. **Bocanáriz** in Lastarria is the grande dame of wine bars, credited with inspiring the boom in the early aughts. The newer **Les Dix Vins**, in Barrio El Golf, pairs rare Chilean bottles with their French cousins. It also hosts nightly events such as live jazz, cheese tastings and oyster evenings. Low-key **La Vinocracia**, near Plaza Nuñoa, boasts one of the largest wine lists in South America. Every Monday, it opens dozens of premium bottles and pours them for just CH\$1000 per glass. In Vitacura, **Vinolia** is like a cinema for wine lovers with multisensory tastings in a theater-like setting.

Chile Wine Trails

TOURING WINE COUNTRY

This Aussie-run company offers bespoke tours of Chilean wine country departing from and returning to Santiago. All tours are for small, personal groups and are hosted by bilingual guides. Day trips to the Maipo Valley might include stops at several vineyards for tastings, as well as a visit to the artists' village of Pomaire for a pottery workshop or a picnic lunch among the vines. Chile Wine Trails also runs day trips to the nearby Casablanca, Aconcagua and San Antonio valleys, and multiday trips to Colchagua Valley.

Tour through Viña Santa Rita

TOP: FREE WIND 2014/SHUTTERSTOCK ©. BOTTOM: KAROL KOZLOWSKI PREMIUM RM/ALAMY STOCK PHOTO ©

Wine tasting, Viña Santa Rita

Alyan Family Wines

SUNSET SESSIONS

Alyan lies in a dreamy landscape at the foot of the Andes and is one of greater Santiago's most tourist-friendly vineyards. Unlike most wineries, which run tours during the day, it focuses instead on the evenings. For up to four hours, you'll drink chardonnays and cabernets and snack on charcuterie boards as you travel to various points across the manicured grounds. The culmination is a meal at sunset on the top floor of the winery, with views toward the Coastal Range. While groups for the sunset experience can be large, there's no denying the value for money.

Viña Santa Rita

RESTAURANTS, ACCOMMODATIONS AND OPULENCE

If you only visit one winery in the Maipo Valley, make it Viña Santa Rita, which has enough activities to keep you around for hours. Not only are there a variety of different tours (on bike, in a horse-drawn carriage, with a picnic), but there's also a lavish museum of pre-Columbian art that rivals the Museo Chileno de Arte Precolombino in Santiago. Dining options span all budgets, with an on-site cafe offering affordable lunches and a restaurant producing more elaborate wine-paired meals. Santa Rita's character-rich hotel, Casa Real, located at the heart of a rambling 40-hectare botanical garden, makes an alluring base for overnighting in the countryside just beyond Santiago city limits. The website (santarita.com) has instructions on how to visit by public transport.

CAJÓN DEL MAIPO & THE ANDEAN SKI RESORTS

HIKING AND NATURE

The mountains above Santiago see a buzz of activity during the austral ski season (June to September). Most ski resorts – including Valle Nevado, Farellones, El Colorado and La Parva – lie above the tree line in the Tres Valles, making it easy to plan a trip to several different places across the span of a few days. Other ski resorts are just north near Los Andes (Portillo) or south in the Cajón del Maipo (Lagunillas). All are accessible from Santiago, though sleeping high in the Andes can be a charming, if expensive, experience.

Some resorts operate summer activities – typically hiking and downhill mountain biking – but it's Cajón del Maipo that really shines this time of year as Santiaguinos escape the heat for cooler climes. Spring is the most beautiful time to visit, when winter snows melt and leave the landscape remarkably green. By contrast, the hills turn brown and thirsty by fall.

TOP TIP

Public buses travel to San José de Maipo year-round and continue to Baños Morales (at the end of the Cajón del Maipo) daily in summer and weekends only in winter. To get to the ski resorts of Tres Valles, several companies in Las Condes offer shuttle buses in season.

Valle Nevado (p85)

FOTO ARENA LTDA/ALAMY STOCK PHOTO ©

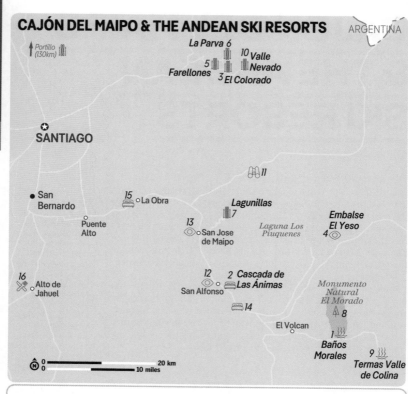

CAJÓN DEL MAIPO & THE ANDEAN SKI RESORTS

ARGENTINA

HIGHLIGHTS
1 Baños Morales
2 Cascada de Las Ánimas
3 El Colorado
4 Embalse El Yeso
5 Farellones
6 La Parva

7 Lagunillas
8 Monumento Natural El Morado
9 Termas Valle de Colina
10 Valle Nevado

SIGHTS
11 Mirador de Cóndores
12 San Alfonso

13 San José de Maipo

ACTIVITIES, COURSES & TOURS
see 13 Rutavertical Rafting

SLEEPING
14 Cabañas y Camping Parque Almendro

see 12 Hotel Altiplanico Cajón del Maipo
15 Lodge El Morado

EATING
see 12 Casa Chocolate
see 12 Cervecería y Pizzería Jauría
16 Mitifuu

El Colorado & Farellones

FAMILY FUN IN THE SNOW

El Colorado

The runs at kid-friendly Farellones tend to attract beginner skiers and boarders who are newbies to snow sports and hoping to spend the day in school. Families also come here to go tubing, sledding or zip-lining. Those with existing skills will have a much better time at sister property El Colorado. Together, they have 19 lifts, 101 runs and a maximum height of 3333m above sea level. Most runs are geared toward intermediate skiers, though experts will find some options too. The terrain park at El Colorado is touted as the largest in Chile.

84

Gondola, Valle Nevado

La Parva

GORTEX AND GLAMOUR

It may be the smallest of the Tres Valles ski resorts, but La Parva is also the most exclusive, oriented toward posh Chilean families rather than the powder-and-party pack. Private cottages and condos make up the ski base of Villa La Parva, where 15 lifts take you to its 48 runs, the highest of which starts at 3574m above sea level. There's a terrain park, plus plenty of off-piste skiing. Snow permitting, the intrepid can ski onward to Valle Nevado or El Colorado.

Valle Nevado

WORLD-FAMOUS SLOPES

Modeled on European setups, foreigner-friendly Valle Nevado boasts almost 900 hectares of skiable terrain, the largest in South America. It's also the best maintained of Santiago's resorts and has the most challenging runs (beginner slopes make it good for kids too). Thirteen chairlifts or surface lifts – and a kick-ass six-person gondola – take you to high-altitude start points up to 3670m for 39 groomed runs. Adrenaline levels run high here: there's a snow park, good off-piste action and heli-skiing (in the summer, it also runs a bike park). Ski-in Hotel Valle Nevado is the best-appointed option in the area with a heated outdoor pool, spa and fire-lit lounge. It's the only South American resort on the global passes IKON and Mountain Collective.

La Parva

Laguna del Inca

Portillo

HISTORIC AND EPIC

Set around the spectacular alpine lake of Laguna del Inca, Portillo is one of Chile's most renowned resorts. The US, Austrian and Italian national teams have used it as a base for their summer training, and the 200 km/h speed barrier was first broken here. Some of its terrain is suitable for novices, but it's hard-core powder junkies who really thrive. Altitudes range from 2590m to 3310m on its 35 slopes, which span 500 hectares of skiable terrain. Portillo is a bit far from Santiago on the mountain pass to Mendoza (and within eyesight of the largest peak in the Americas, Aconcagua). You could theoretically visit for the day, but its distance makes it more of an outright destination, with lodgings for all budgets.

Cascada de Las Ánimas

PRIVATE MOUNTAIN RESERVE

Organized activities are the only way to visit this private nature reserve, which takes its name from a waterfall reached by the shortest walk on offer. Guided half-day hikes head into the hills, and you can go rafting and horseback riding (it's a working ranch). The lodgings are among the most character-rich in the area. The premium suites at Cascada Lodge boast a rustic-chic design, stone features, mosaic tilework and king-size beds. There are also lofted domes, log cabins, serene riverside bungalows and a shaded campsite. A spa, pool and restaurant mean you'll never want to leave.

TOP: FRIEDRICHSMEIER / GETTY IMAGES ©. BOTTOM: LEON WERDINGER/ALAMY STOCK PHOTO ©

Cascada de Las Ánimas

Lagunillas

COZY LITTLE RESORT

Being the only ski resort in Cajón del Maipo has its pros and cons. The pros: A cozy atmosphere, way cheaper rates for both ski tickets and lodging, and much less traffic if you're descending to Santiago after a long day on the slopes. The cons: Its lower altitude (2100m) means less snow and shorter seasons. It also has just three lifts and 13 runs, though the real joy is off-piste skiing across 200 hectares of terrain.

Monumento Natural El Morado

TREK TO A GLACIER

Hike into this small park from the entrance at Baños Morales to view Glaciar San Francisco, one of the closest glaciers to Santiago. It takes about two hours (6km) to reach the banks of the sparkling Laguna El Morado, which has fabulous views of both the glacier and the nearly 5000m summit of Cerro El Morado. The landscape is arguably best seen in winter, when you can do this hike with snowshoes. For safety reasons, entrance to the park is only before 12:30pm.

Hiker, Monumento Natural El Morado

Embalse El Yeso

A CLOUD-HUGGING RESERVOIR

Embalse El Yeso is one of the most common day trips offered from Santiago. Formed by the damming of the Río Yeso (part of the Maipo River Basin), this mirror-like blue-green reservoir is an important source of drinking water for the city below. Popular for fishing and windsurfing, most visitors come to take photographs of the high Andes from a lofty vantage point of more than 2500m. It's possible to continue from here to the remote Termas del Plomo, a wild geothermal pool at nearly 3000m. For that, you'll need a 4x4 vehicle, some pre-planning and a real sense of adventure.

Embalse El Yeso

Baños Morales & Termas Valle de Colina

REMOTE AND WELCOMING HOT SPRINGS

Baños Morales is the tiny hub at the end of the paved road into Cajón del Maipo with some hostels, campgrounds and lunch restaurants, as well as plenty of loitering *huasos* (cowboys) who will happily lead you on horseback-riding trips into the backcountry.

The main attraction in town is Centro Termal Baños Morales, which has two thermally heated pools of orange-brown water. Far superior is Termas Valle de Colina, a collection of gem-like thermal baths 13km further down an unpaved road toward Argentina (a 4x4

is recommended, though it's usually manageable with a high-clearance vehicle). These turquoise pools offer wowing views over rugged Andean peaks and will have you feeling a world away from Santiago. Toilets and showers mean you can change on-site.

WHY I LOVE CAJÓN DEL MAIPO & THE ANDEAN SKI RESORTS

Mark Johanson,
Writer

The view of the Andes from Santiago on a clear day is absolutely magical, particularly at sunset as the mountains don an amber hue. Few cities in the world can boast such massive peaks right in their backyard. That's what's always attracted me to this city. You can be strolling beneath glass skyscrapers one minute and then hiking to a glacier, skiing down a summit, rafting Class IV rapids or bathing in a remote thermal pool just 90 minutes later. The mountains are always present in Santiago. They help you orient yourself when you're lost and can reorient your mind when you're having a bad day.

ABRIENDOMUNDO/SHUTTERSTOCK ©

Hikers, Cajón del Maipo

MORE IN CAJÓN DEL MAIPO & THE ANDEAN SKI RESORTS

Soar with the Condors

HIKING HIGH ABOVE SANTIAGO

Parque Nacional Glaciares de Santiago, in the Andes high above the capital, was created in 2022 to protect 18,000 hectares of glaciers (vital to the city's water supply) and key habitat for native fauna, such as black-chested buzzard eagles, colocolo wildcats, pumas and Andean condors. The announcement was the culmination of a grassroots movement called **Queremos Parque** (queremosparque.cl), which gathered more signatures than any other environmental campaign in Chilean history.

Unfortunately, the park protects lands only above 3600m – far from any existing roads and far from democratizing these mountains for the citizens of Santiago below (the goal of Queremos Parque, which wants to break down long-standing barriers to mountain access created by local energy interests). Visitors can nevertheless explore the lands Queremos Parque hopes will one day be included in the park by driving into the Cajón del Maipo and diverting toward **El Alfalfal**. Here, you'll find greater Santiago's most spectacular half-day

 WHERE TO EAT IN CAJÓN DEL MAIPO

Cervecería y Pizzería Jauría
The valley's hipster hangout with house-brewed beers and excellent pizzas to match. **$$**

Casa Chocolate
House-made chocolates, hot chocolates, gelatos, sweets and coffees sold in an enchanting fairy-tale-like setting. **$**

Mitifuu
Excellent service, an English-language menu and hearty meat dishes make this woodsy restaurant a real charmer. **$$$**

hike, **Mirador de Cóndores**, a 9km out-and-back trail that takes you up to a clifftop where condors soar at eye level. Just past El Alfalfal, the **Olivares** and **Colorado river valleys** are absolutely stunning alpine landscapes, but should be explored with a guide. You can hike to the tiered thermal pools of **Baños Azules**, high-altitude wetlands (known as *bofedales*) or the ethereal wind-carved ice blades called *penitentes*.

White Water

RAFTING THE RÍO MAIPO

The Río Maipo rages in whitewater rapids with few calm areas as it carves its way through the Cajón del Maipo between the towns of **San Alfonso** and **San José de Maipo**. In fact, rafters here are sometimes tossed into the water. Still, it's far less hazardous than when the first kayakers descended in the 1980s and found themselves facing automatic weapons as they passed the grounds of General Pinochet's estate in **El Melocotón** (the narrow bedrock chute here, one of the river's more entertaining rapids, is now known as **El Pinocho**, the ex-dictator's nickname).

The 9km section between El Melocotón and San José de Maipo is the most common for rafting trips, with the highest waters in spring as the snow melts. In lower waters (February to October) when it's safer, you can also raft the section beginning in San Alfonso. Water temperatures hover around 9°C year-round.

Most operators are based in San José de Maipo, including **Rutavertical Rafting**, which runs popular one-hour trips led by enthusiastic multilingual guides. You'll descend Class III or IV rapids, taking in some lovely gorges before ending up back in town. Allow about 2½ hours in total for the briefing, outfitting and drive upriver to the starting point. Helmets, wetsuits and lifejackets are provided, and there are lockers to store your belongings.

TIME TO TREK

If you don't have the time to travel into Cajón del Maipo, **Asociación Parque Cordillera** (p79) runs several private parks in Las Condes where you can take public transportation to the trailhead and set off to summit pre-Andean peaks.

WORLD CAPITAL OF MOUNTAIN TOURISM?

Santiago is in the midst of an ambitious 10-year program funded by CORFO (a government agency for economic growth) to transform itself into a 'world capital of mountain tourism' by 2030. The public-private partnership known as Andes Santiago (andesstgo.cl) is leading the charge. It's been busy training mountain guides to international standards, enhancing the local tourism offering and developing public use plans for city-adjacent parklands. It also has plans to build a 150km hut-to-hut hike through the Central Andes linking the Tres Valles ski resorts with Cajón del Maipo. The hope is that people will begin to see Santiago as a kind of Kathmandu of the Andes.

 WHERE TO STAY IN CAJÓN DEL MAIPO

| **Lodge El Morado** The swankiest option near El Morado and the hot springs with a spa and wide-open views. **$$$** | **Hotel Altiplanico Cajon del Maipo** One of the few proper hotels here, it has the feel of a hip mountain resort. **$$$** | **Cabañas y Camping Parque Almendro** This large complex has riverside campsites, plus cabins, a pool and seasonal cafe. **$** |

Above: Vicuñas, Norte Grande; right: Valle de la Luna (p98)

NORTE GRANDE

DESERT, ALTIPLANO AND SURF

From the wonderland of San Pedro de Atacama to the surfing breaks of the coast, Chile's northern tip offers high-octane adventures.

At Chile's northernmost tip, the region of Arica and Parinacota is where the Atacama Desert begins, sandwiched between the Andes and the crashing waves of the Pacific Ocean. Despite the extreme desert aridity, the region has sustained humans for many thousands of years. Some of the area's earliest inhabitants were the Chinchorro, who left behind an extraordinary collection of mummies.

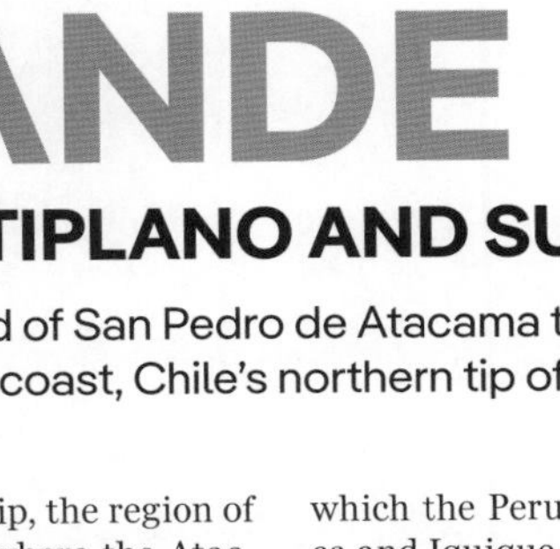

Despite its distance from Santiago, Norte Grande has always played a strong role in Chile's political and economic arenas, mostly because of the mineral wealth buried beneath its surface. The desert sands are a source of nitrate that was once vital to the region's economy. Its monetary value was one of the prompts for the War of the Pacific (1879–83), after which the Peruvian coastal cities of Arica and Iquique became Chilean territory. These days, both cities are known as surfing hot spots.

The altiplano (high plain) of the country's northeast is an Andean heartland. Dispersed Aymara communities come together for traditional festivals featuring brass bands, dancing and colorful costumes. Amid the snow-capped volcanoes of the surrounding landscape, vicuñas and alpacas graze at *bofedales*, high-altitude marshland areas with unique flora and fauna.

Norte Grande's star attraction is the adobe village of San Pedro de Atacama, a day trip from the world's highest geyser field and astounding desert formations.

THE MAIN AREAS

SAN PEDRO DE ATACAMA	**ANTOFAGASTA**	**IQUIQUE**	**ARICA**
Desert adventures.	Norte Grande's largest city.	Surfing and nightlife.	Beaches, waves and history.
p96	p104	p108	p116

Find Your Way

Norte Grande covers a large area of northern Chile, including vast expanses of arid desert. The coastal cities and the precordillera town of San Pedro de Atacama are cultural centers and make good bases for exploration.

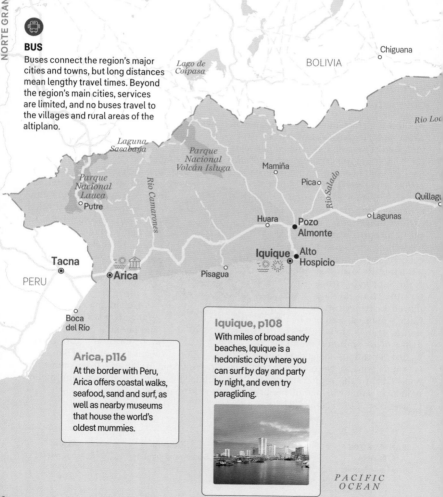

BUS

Buses connect the region's major cities and towns, but long distances mean lengthy travel times. Beyond the region's main cities, services are limited, and no buses travel to the villages and rural areas of the altiplano.

Chiguana

BOLIVIA

Lago de Coipasa

Río Loa

Laguna Sacabaya

Parque Nacional Volcán Isluga

Mamiña

Pica

Río Salado

Quillagu

Parque Nacional Lauca

Putre

Río Camarones

Huara

Lagunas

Pozo Almonte

Iquique · Alto Hospicio

Tacna

Arica

Pisagua

PERU

Boca del Río

Iquique, p108

With miles of broad sandy beaches, Iquique is a hedonistic city where you can surf by day and party by night, and even try paragliding.

Arica, p116

At the border with Peru, Arica offers coastal walks, seafood, sand and surf, as well as nearby museums that house the world's oldest mummies.

PACIFIC OCEAN

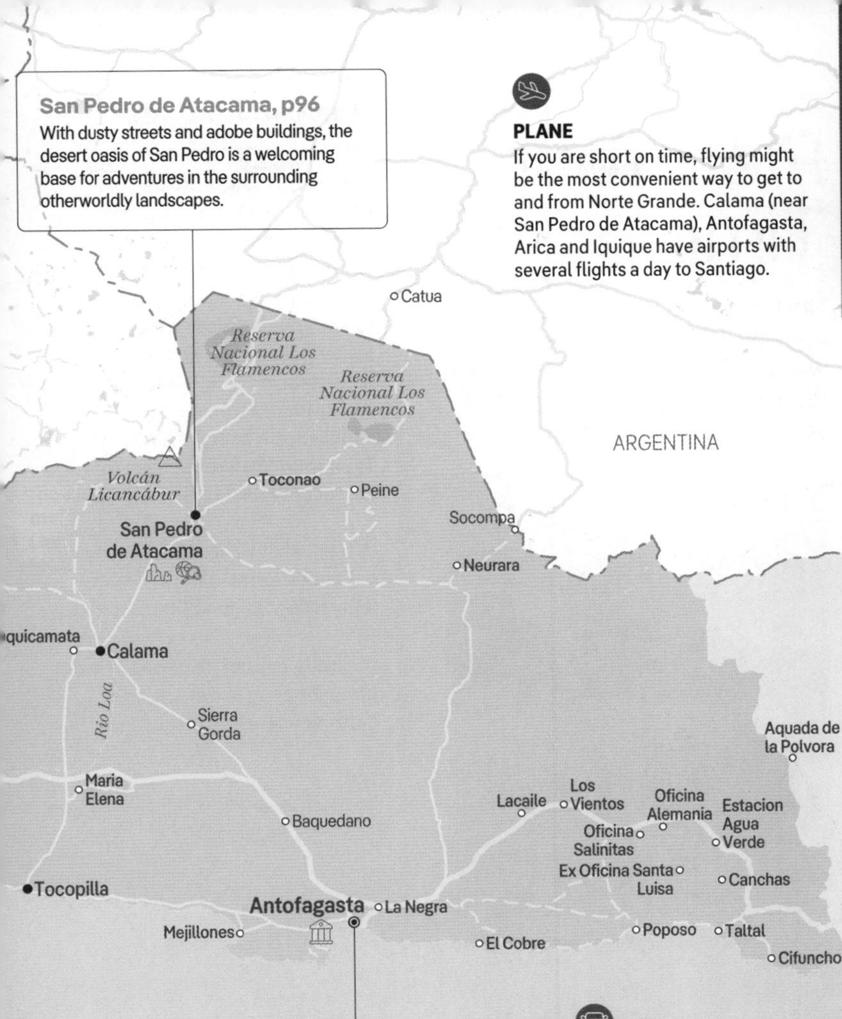

San Pedro de Atacama, p96
With dusty streets and adobe buildings, the desert oasis of San Pedro is a welcoming base for adventures in the surrounding otherworldly landscapes.

PLANE
If you are short on time, flying might be the most convenient way to get to and from Norte Grande. Calama (near San Pedro de Atacama), Antofagasta, Arica and Iquique have airports with several flights a day to Santiago.

Catua

Reserva Nacional Los Flamencos

Reserva Nacional Los Flamencos

ARGENTINA

Volcán Licancábur

Toconao

Peine

San Pedro de Atacama

Socompa

Neurara

Chuquicamata

Calama

Río Loa

Sierra Gorda

Aquada de la Polvora

María Elena

Baquedano

Lacaile

Los Vientos

Oficina Alemania

Estacion Agua Verde

Oficina Salinitas

Ex Oficina Santa Luisa

Canchas

Tocopilla

Antofagasta

La Negra

Mejillones

El Cobre

Poposo

Taltal

Cifuncho

Antofagasta, p104
The museums and historic buildings of this major urban center make an interesting stop. Pick up supplies in the city's shopping malls.

CAR
Unless you take tours, renting a car is the best way to discover the areas beyond the region's major urban hubs. Driving is the only way to get to certain remote sites in the Atacama Desert.

0 — 200 km
0 — 100 miles

Plan Your Time

Norte Grande covers a large area, and many of the most worthwhile sights are miles apart. Plan ahead to make the most of your time on the road.

Valle de la Luna (p98)

Pressed for Time

● Focus on **San Pedro de Atacama** (p96), where you can explore as much as you have time to squeeze in. Start with adventures near town to adjust to the altitude. Spend a day exploring the **Valle de Catarpe** (p99) by bike, hiking at the **Pukará de Quitor** (p98) or visiting the intriguing remains of the **Aldea de Tulor** (p100) before catching the sunset at **Valle de la Luna** (p98).

● Next, float in the salty waters of **Laguna Cejar** (p102) and spot flamingos at **Laguna Chaxa** (p102).

● Finally, rise before dawn to visit the spluttering and steaming **El Tatio Geysers** (p102).

Seasonal Highlights

The desert nights are cold in winter, which is also the best season for big wave surfing. In late summer, the oasis of San Pedro de Atacama is at its greenest.

JANUARY
Summer brings vacationers to the **beaches** of Arica (p119) and Iquique (p112). Book accommodations in advance.

FEBRUARY
Thousands of spectators gather to see the brass bands and dancing troops of Arica's **Carnaval Andino con la Fuerza del Sol**.

MARCH
In February or March, **Carnaval** is celebrated in San Pedro de Atacama with costumed dancers and parades.

A Week in the North

● Extend your time in **San Pedro** (p96) to fit in a trip to see the colors of the **Valle del Arcoiris** (p103) and the gallery of rock art at **Petroglifos de Yerbas Buenas** (p103) before moving on to **Iquique** (p108). Spend the morning **surfing** (p112) and the afternoon exploring the **historic center** (p110). Drink a sunset cocktail at the **Península de Cavancha** (p111).

● Head to **Arica** (p116) and cycle along the coast to the **Cuevas de Anzota** (p119) in the morning. Spend the afternoon discovering the mummies of **Museo de Sitio Colón 10** (p117) and the **Azapa Valley** (p121).

If You Have More TIme

● After exploring **San Pedro** (p96), spend a couple of days in **Iquique** (p108), allowing time to relax on the **beach** (p112) and to visit the eerie ghost towns of **Humberstone** and **Santa Laura** (p114).

● Move on to **Arica** (p116), where you can extend your stay to include time to surf.

● Next, take a trip to the precordillera town of **Putre** (p122), which you can use as a base for hikes to see cave art, to soak in hot springs, and to take day trips to the stunning altiplano lakes of **Parque Nacional Lauca** (p123) and the **Surire salt flats** (p123).

MAY
Held annually in Iquique, **Héroes de Mayo Pro** is one of Chile's biggest surf events and attracts the world's best surfers.

JUNE
Timed to commemorate the Battle of Arica of June 7, 1880, **Semana Ariqueña** (Arica Week) features parades, concerts and fireworks.

JULY
Pilgrims flock to La Tirana for 10 days of religious parades and dancing in celebration of the **Virgin of Carmen** (p115).

AUGUST
On August 10, miners gather in Tarapacá to celebrate their patron saint **San Lorenzo** with bands and parades.

95

SAN PEDRO DE ATACAMA

San Pedro de Atacama

✪ Santiago

On the approach to town, the precordillera oasis of San Pedro first appears as a splash of green amid the sands and coffee-colored landscapes of the Atacama Desert. Most travelers feel instantly at ease as they wander the dusty streets of this good-vibes village.

Adrenaline junkies will find endless opportunities for adventure, from sand-boarding to hot-air balloon rides. On the outskirts of San Pedro, several valleys with otherworldly rock formations can be reached by bike. Soothe aching muscles with a massage or stretching out in a yoga class in town. At night, agencies offer stargazing tours away from the lights of the town.

Visible from the village is the conical peak of Volcán Licancabur (5916m), a sacred mountain for the indigenous Lickan Antay community. People still practice irrigated farming in the *ayllus* (small indigenous communities). Many farm on terraces that are more than 1000 years old.

TOP TIP

Mountain biking is a convenient way to get around San Pedro and explore the surrounding area, including excursions to Valle de la Muerte, Valle de la Luna and Aldea de Tulor. Several agencies along Caracoles rent bikes and supply maps. Wear sunblock and bring plenty of water.

Volcán Licancabur

FERNANDO TATAY/SHUTTERSTOCK ©

FLAVORS OF THE ATACAMA DESERT

Rica-rica
This fragrant herb is endemic to the region. It is sometimes sprinkled on top of pisco sours.

Pingo-pingo
A desert plant that's used to make tea to treat colds. It's also a natural aphrodisiac.

Picante de conejo
A slow-cooked rabbit dish that is typical of the region.

Patasca Atacameña
This traditional maize-based stew is prepared to celebrate religious festivals.

Ayrampo
The red seeds of this cactus flower can be used to flavor ice cream. Try it at Heladería Babalú on Caracoles.

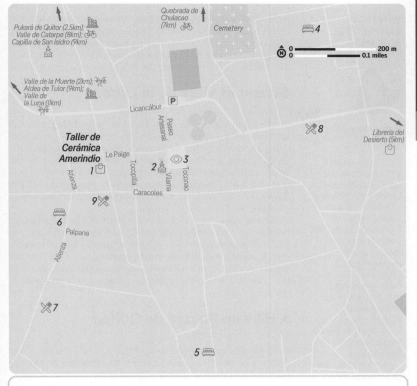

HIGHLIGHTS	SIGHTS	SLEEPING	EATING
1 Taller de Cerámica Amerindio	**2** Iglesia San Pedro	**4** Backpackers San Pedro	**7** Baltinache
	3 Plaza de Armas	**5** Hostal Quinta Adela	**8** Franchuteria
		6 Hotel Poblado Kimal	**9** La Casona

Exploring San Pedro

A STROLL AROUND TOWN

San Pedro is easy to explore on foot. Most of the town's tour agencies, restaurants and other tourist services are located along pedestrianized **Caracoles** and the streets leading off it. One block north of Caracoles is pretty **Plaza de Armas**, where you can stop for a snack at one of several cafes and restaurants with outdoor tables overlooking the greenery.

Take a look at **Iglesia San Pedro**, west of the plaza. The building dates from the 17th century, though the current adobe walls were built in 1745 and the bell tower was added in 1890. Don't miss the church's *cardón* (cactus wood) roof.

On Calle Calama is the **Taller de Cerámica Amerindio**, the workshop of ceramicist Fernando Alfaro, who molds

MORE INDIGENOUS ART

Several of the indigenous symbols used in Fernando Alfaro's work can be seen in the incredible gallery of rock art known as the **Petroglifos de Yerbas Buenas** (p103). Ceramics found at **Aldea de Tulor** (p100) are displayed in the on-site museum.

pieces from local clay using traditional techniques. His work reflects the indigenous style of the Atacama region, and some pieces feature symbols that can be observed in nearby rock art. Alfaro has lived a fascinating life; one of his pieces, *El Abrazo*, is inspired by a hug he once shared with Nelson Mandela. The shelves of his workshop are full of his ceramics for sale.

Sunset at Valle de la Luna

MOON-LIKE LANDSCAPES

Find a perch high on the sand dunes of **Valle de la Luna** and get ready for the show as the sun dips below the horizon. Suddenly, the distant ring of volcanoes, the crinkled peaks of the Cordillera de la Sal, and the surreal lunar landscapes of the valley are infused with intense purples, pinks and golds. Several short, well-marked walking trails to viewpoints take in the valley's unusual lunar-like geological formations, which are the result of years of erosion.

Located 15km west of San Pedro, Valle de la Luna can be reached by car or mountain bike (make sure you have lights and a reflective vest if you plan to return by bike after sunset). It is also San Pedro's most popular tour. Trips usually depart around 4pm and include a sunset cocktail. To avoid the crowds, visit in the morning, though you'll miss out on the sunset colors.

A Hike up Pukará de Quitor

ANCIENT HILL FORTRESS

On a hillside on the left bank of the Río San Pedro, a 3km walk, cycle or drive north of town, the **Pukará de Quitor** encompasses the 12th-century ruins of some 200 structures. The site was at one time a permanent settlement and was later used by the indigenous Lickan Antay people as a defensive fort against Spanish colonizers. In part because of the protected position of the fortress, it took the Spanish 20 years to overcome the Pukará de Quitor and defeat its defenders, whom they subsequently killed.

The ruins, which hug the hillside, can be viewed from a walking trail. The path passes several viewpoints on the way to the hilltop, which overlooks the Valle de la Muerte and the distant volcanoes. The walk takes around 1½ hours. Bring water, sunscreen and a hat.

From the entrance to the complex, a separate trail leads to a plaza with a magnificent *algarrobo* (carob) tree. Nearby, look for the carvings of several large faces in the rock.

 WHERE TO STAY IN SAN PEDRO DE ATACAMA

Backpackers San Pedro
This hostel has shared dorms, guest kitchens, and a patio with hammocks and a firepit. **$**

Hostal Quinta Adela
Views over orchards and hammocks create a relaxed atmosphere at this friendly guesthouse. **$$**

Hotel Poblado Kimal
Right off Caracoles, Kimal has two pools and spacious adobe bungalows set in lush gardens. **$$$**

Sunset, Valle de la Luna

Valle de Catarpe by Bike

ROCKY GORGES, SAND AND VIEWS

Located 4km north of San Pedro, just beyond Pukará de Quitor, **Valle de Catarpe** has mountain-biking trails that wind through narrow gorges between sun-scorched rocks, over sand dunes and past peaks with hiking trails that offer far-reaching views. From the entrance, where you must sign in and out, the full 14km loop takes around three hours by bike. Bring plenty of water.

The trail runs parallel to the river before branching off to the **Quebrada de Chulacao**, a ravine where a narrow, sandy trail passes between looming rock formations and overhangs that glow in the light of the sun. Be prepared to get off and lift your bike up steps in the rocks at several points in the trail.

After emerging into a more open area, the trail passes a signposted path to a viewpoint. Climb the hill for views of Volcán Licancabur. Once back on your bike, you can choose to retrace your path back through the Quebrada de Chilacao or to continue along the trail, which soon becomes more challenging, with deeper sand and steeper inclines. It leads to **Capilla de San Isidro**, a tiny hilltop church.

BEST ACTIVITIES IN SAN PEDRO DE ATACAMA

Sand-boarding
Slide down 150m-high dunes on a board during this adrenaline-pumping activity.

Horseback riding
Explore the desert dunes and canyons on horseback. Trips range from two hours to several days.

Climbing
Nearby peaks to scale include the volcanoes Sairecabur (5971m) and Láscar (5592m).

Hot-air balloon ride
Fly over the desert during a dawn hot-air balloon ride and catch the sunrise over the volcanoes.

Stargazing
Astronomy tours take place in light-free spots outside town, with explanations and telescope-assisted observations.

 WHERE TO EAT IN SAN PEDRO DE ATACAMA

Franchuteria
This French bakery serves authentic pastries, croissants, sandwiches and baguettes in a delightful garden. $

La Casona
A typical Chilean restaurant with ample indoor and outdoor seating, firepits and live music. $$$

Baltinache
Atacameño restaurant offering a three-course menu featuring local ingredients such as rabbit and rica-rica. $$$

LEGENDS OF THE ATACAMA DESERT

According to local lore, everything that can be seen in the area around San Pedro, from the volcanoes and the flamingos to the stars of the cosmos, has a story to tell. One of the most popular is the story of the volcano Licancabur and his love for the mountain Quimal, who was banished to the other side of the valley. Once a year, in June, the shadow of Licancabur reaches Quimal, and the lovers are reunited.

Librería del Desierto near San Pedro sells beautifully illustrated books recounting tales of the Atacama Desert and the stars, including editions with text in Spanish, English and Ckunsa, the local indigenous language.

From here, follow the dusty road along the river bank back to the entrance. You might spot a farmer taking his llamas, goats and sheep out to graze along the way.

Otherworldly Landscapes of Valle de la Muerte

SAND DUNES AND JAGGED ROCKS

An easy 3km bike ride or long walk west of San Pedro is the striking **Valle de la Muerte** (Death Valley), also known as Valle de Marte (Mars Valley) for its desolate red-hued landscape. Explore the towering sand banks and an inhospitable landscape of incisor-like rocks on the 4km walk that loops through the valley, passing a viewpoint that looks out to the distant cordillera.

The dunes are a popular spot for **sand-boarding**, and excursions are offered by several agencies in San Pedro.

Archaeological Wonder

INDIGENOUS CULTURE AND HISTORIC RUINS

The excavated adobe structures at **Aldea de Tulor** form one of the region's most significant archaeological sites. The area was settled 2500 years ago in what was then a lush valley, but it was abandoned in 300 CE when the oasis dried up. The site is 11km southwest of San Pedro and can be reached by car or mountain bike.

The local Lickan Antay community (the indigenous population, also known as Atacameños) manage the site and provide guided tours of the ruins. A reconstruction of a typical dwelling shows how people lived in interconnected circular adobe houses in the valley. Nearby are the partially excavated structures of the original *aldea* (village), surrounded by a perimeter wall.

Explanations are infused with the guide's personal connection to the landscape and the significance of the site, where the ancestors of the Lickan Antay once lived. The valley is a beautiful setting in which to learn more about the group's traditional beliefs, local legends associated with the surrounding volcanoes, and the importance of nature in Lickan Antay culture.

A small museum has a display of ceramics found at the site, along with a gallery on the local flora and fauna.

GETTING AROUND

San Pedro is easily navigated on foot or by bike. Nearby sites can be reached by mountain bike, by car or on a tour. Buses for Calama (1½ hours) depart throughout the day from San Pedro bus terminal, 1km south of Plaza de Armas.

Beyond San Pedro de Atacama

San Pedro is surrounded by some of northern Chile's most spectacular scenery, and opportunities for adventure abound.

Beyond the dusty streets of San Pedro lie steaming geyser fields, flamingo-strewn mountain lakes and volcanic peaks within day-tripping distance. Most people visit the main sights on tours, but it's also possible to explore in your own vehicle or on multiday trekking or horseback riding trips. The mining town of Calama is the location of the nearest airport to San Pedro.

Several of the area's most visited sites are within the 740-sq-km Reserva Nacional Los Flamencos, co-managed by Conaf (the National Forest Corporation) and the local Lickan Antay indigenous community. In 2023, Conaf reported that closing the Salar de Tara sector to tourists in 2018 had allowed native wildlife to return to the area.

El Tatio Geysers
Valle del Arcoiris
Petroglifos de Yerbas Buenas
Termas de Puritama
San Pedro de Atacama
Atacama Large Millimeter/submillimeter Array
Reserva Nacional Los Flamencos

TOP TIP

Allow time to acclimatize to the altitude in San Pedro (2400m) before visiting the Tatio Geysers (4300m) or the altiplano lakes (4000m).

Andean flamingo, Reserva Nacional Los Flamencos (p102)

DIEGO GRANDI/SHUTTERSTOCK ©

WILDLIFE AROUND SAN PEDRO DE ATACAMA

Flamingo
Andean flamingos have black-tipped wing feathers, while Chilean flamingos do not. The James' flamingo, the smallest of the three, can be identified by its red legs and yellow and black beak.

Vicuña
Spot these delicate camelids at high altitudes, particularly around the altiplano lakes.

Ñandú
South America's largest birds; also known as rheas or suris.

Flamingo Spotting

VOLCANOES, SALT FLATS AND LAKES

The 740-sq-km **Reserva Nacional Los Flamencos** contains some of northern Chile's most spectacular scenery: vast salt flats, russet-colored ridges and topaz lakes set against a backdrop of soaring mountain peaks.

Just 22km south of San Pedro, **Laguna Cejar** is a lake with water so salty that you effortlessly float on the surface. It's a spectacular setting in which to kick back and admire the surrounding mountains and volcanoes. The complex has changing rooms and showers and is open to individuals in the mornings and tour groups in the afternoons (closed Tuesdays). A boardwalk leads to the neighboring lake, **Laguna Piedra**, where it is sometimes possible to see flamingos (swimming is not permitted).

A further 40km south, **Laguna Chaxa** sits within the jagged crusts of the **Salar de Atacama**. This important flamingo-breeding site is a good place to spot Chilean, Andean and James' flamingos, as well as plovers, coots and ducks. An interpretive trail provides views of the birds.

Continue up into the mountains, passing the traditional village of **Socaire**, to reach viewpoints for the altiplano lakes of **Laguna Miñiques** and **Miscanti**. The shimmering blue surface of the lakes looks all the more stunning against a backdrop of chiseled snow-covered peaks. Further still is **Laguna Tuyajto**, at 4000m. The lake is known for the *piedras rojas* (red rocks) that line the shore. A walking trail leads to the water's edge.

Gurgling Geysers

WORLD'S HIGHEST GEYSER FIELD

Visiting the world-famous **El Tatio Geysers** at daybreak is a visceral experience that envelops the senses: the sight of swirling columns of steam against the backdrop of looming volcanoes and the rising sun; the distinctive egg-like smell of sulfide gases; the sound of bubbling, spurting and hissing; and the feel of the freezing dawn as the body attempts to keep warm. This field of some 80 gurgling geysers is a window into the past, revealing a glimpse of what the world might have been like as the first life forms emerged. Be careful not to stray off the paths because there is a danger of falling through the thin crust into the scalding water.

The geysers are 80km north of San Pedro. Most people visit on a tour from San Pedro, which leave at around 5am to catch dawn at the geyser field. It's also possible to come by

 WHERE TO EAT IN CALAMA

Om Cafe
Colorful cafe with a good-value daily lunch menu, which includes vegetarian options. **$**

Osumi Sushi
Japanese restaurant offering a wide selection of sushi rolls along with hot dishes. **$$**

Pasión Peruana
With several branches in town, this restaurant serves generous portions of typical Peruvian dishes. **$$**

MARANADE/SHUTTERSTOCK ©

Valle del Arcoiris

car, but there is no public transport. The fields are open until late morning, but they are most atmospheric at daybreak.

Rainbow-Colored Rocks

ROCK ART AND MULTICOLORED LANDSCAPES

About 70km north of San Pedro lies the **Valle del Arcoiris** (Rainbow Valley), so called because of the remarkable hues of the multicolored rocks. The distinct shades are easiest to see in the morning sun and on cloudy days. It's a peaceful spot, where you might spot a guanaco or two watching from a nearby ledge. The valley is in the Río Grande Basin. Get here on a tour or by car. The turnoff is on the road between San Pedro and Calama.

South of the Valle del Arcoiris, in the Quebrada de Yerbas Buenas, is an impressive gallery of rock art. The **Petroglifos de Yerbas Buenas** were created over hundreds of years, when the rocks were a meeting place for people from across the cordillera to trade knowledge and produce. Look for petroglyphs (engravings) depicting serpents, flamingos, foxes and the life cycle of llamas. The human figures with outstretched arms probably represent shamans. Other petroglyphs appear to relate to Andean astronomy: the seasonal position of the shapes of camelids in the dark spaces of the night sky indicated when it was time to reap and sow crops.

ATACAMA OBSERVATORIES

Thanks to its clear skies and absence of light pollution, the Atacama Desert is home to a number of important observatories.

Atacama Large Millimeter/submillimeter Array (ALMA), 40km southeast of San Pedro, is the world's largest ground-based astronomy project. It comprises 66 giant antennas, interstellar 'ears' that simulate a telescope to detect faint objects in space. Tours are offered on weekends.

The European Southern Observatory (ESO) has four 8.2m Very Large Telescopes at its futuristic **Paranal Observatory**, 130km south of Antofagasta. Daytime tours of the facilities take place on Saturdays. The ESO's forthcoming Extremely Large Telescope (ELT), on nearby **Cerro Armazones**, is expected to revolutionize ground-based space observation when it begins operating in 2027.

GETTING AROUND

Tour agencies in San Pedro offer guided excursions to the sights that surround the town. It is also possible to visit them by car, and car rental is available in Calama. Buses connect San Pedro with Calama, which has onward bus connections to Antofagasta, Iquique, Arica and elsewhere. Calama's airport has several daily flights to Santiago.

ANTOFAGASTA

Antofagasta is a sprawling port city and the major urban center of northern Chile. Beyond the high-rise concrete and hustle of city life, Antofagasta has some interesting museums and elegant architecture to discover. Nearby, a giant granite hand in the desert to the south and a natural rock arch in the ocean to the north make fun excursions from the city. The port handles most of the minerals from Atacama, especially the copper from Chuquicamata, and it's still a major import-export node for Bolivia, which lost the region during the War of the Pacific.

Antofagasta's immigrant population has increased in recent years, and most are nationals of Colombia and Bolivia. Many non-Chileans in Antofagasta have struggled to find work and often find themselves living in precarious situations. Statistics from 2022 indicated that more than 900 people were living on the streets of the city, which has a population of around 390,000.

TOP TIP

Antofagasta's main sights can be seen in a day, so you don't need to schedule too much time here. The city center and Barrio Histórico can be explored on foot during the day. Avoid walking around the city center after dark. It's safer to take a taxi or Uber.

SLEEPING
1 Hotel Paola

EATING
2 Tío Jacinto

ENTERTAINMENT
3 Café del Sol

SHOPPING
4 Mercado Central
5 Terminal Pesquero

ELENA CHIKANOVA/SHUTTERSTOCK ©

Mano del Desierto

THE DESERT HAND

Located 70km south of Antofagasta, by the Ruta 5 Panamericana, the **Mano del Desierto** is a soaring granite hand reaching out from the desert sand. Mario Irarrázabal, the sculptor who created the 11m-high work, has said that it is up to the the observer to decide what the hand means.

The sculpture makes for striking photographs. It appears particularly otherworldly when photographed at night against the backdrop of the star-filled sky.

Northern Chile's Mining History

MUSEUM AND MINING OFFICE REMAINS

A worthwhile museum is located at the site of the remains of the former Bolivian Huanchaca Company building. Though the complex appears to be the ruins of an ancient settlement, the **Ruinas de Huanchaca** actually date from the late 19th century. The company was one of the richest silver-mining operations of the late 1800s. More than 1000 people once worked at the site, which was used as a foundry and refinery for raw materials mined at Pulacayo in Potosí, Bolivia. The ruins have national monument status, and you can take photos but can't enter them. Climb up the steps to the left of the museum door for the best views.

Inside the museum, start at the mining gallery, which focuses on life in the pampas mining towns during the nitrate-mining boom and includes displays on the children who worked there. Scan QR codes to read English translations of the museum panels.

On the patios between the galleries, look for the evocative mining murals by Luis Núñez San Martín, who also created

NITRATE MINING GHOST TOWNS

Near Iquique, the abandoned former mining towns of **Humberstone** and **Santa Laura** (p114) are now preserved as museums. These ghost towns serve as relics of the region's nitrate mining days.

WHERE TO STAY & EAT IN ANTOFAGASTA

Hotel Paola
A smart city center hotel with a roof terrace and well-equipped rooms. **$$$**

Tío Jacinto
This small family-run seafood restaurant is one of the region's best; excellent wine list too. **$$$**

Café del Sol
A *peña* (folk-music venue) with live Andean music and a menu of hearty Chilean mains. **$$**

The grand buildings of Antofagasta's Barrio Histórico serve as a reminder of the wealth generated by the 19th-century nitrate boom. Start at **1 Plaza Colón**, a beautiful 19th-century square with fountains, palm trees and bougainvillea. The centerpiece is the Torre Reloj, a gift from the British community who had mining interests in the region, built in 1911. On the corner of Antonio José de Sucre and José de San Martín, the exterior walls of the **2 Teatro Municipal** are the canvas for a mural by Luis Núñez San Martín that pays homage to the region's mining history. Across the square, the landmark building that was once the city's central post office is now the magnificent **3 Biblioteca Regional de Antofagasta**, a public library. Look inside the palace-like building, which was completed in 1930. Walk two blocks east along Jorge Washington to **4 Centro**

Cultural Estación de Antofagasta, a gallery space that hosts interesting exhibitions. On Bolívar, take a look at the bottle-green **5 Estación Ferrocarril** (1887), the restored terminus of the defunct Antofagasta–La Paz railway. It's closed to the public, but you can see several old engines and British-style telephone boxes through the western railings. Turn left onto Adrónico Abaroa to see a large-scale **6 mural** by San Martín depicting a pampas mining town, as well as a series of colorful mosaic reliefs. Back on Bolívar, the former Aduana (customs house) now houses the **7 Museo Regional**, with displays on natural history and local culture. Don't miss the models of indigenous rafts. Pass the wooden balustrades of the **8 former maritime administration building**, dating to 1910, and continue to the restored **9 Muelle Salitrero** (Nitrate Pier).

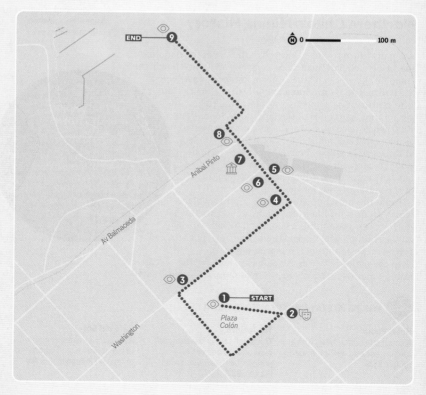

works in Antofagasta's Barrio Histórico. The clever design means that the ruins are visible above the murals.

A further gallery displays back-lit, blown-up space photographs taken at the European Southern Observatory (ESO) La Silla, 170km north of La Serena in Norte Chico.

In front of the museum entrance, don't miss *Out of Sync,* an installation of 10,000 ceramic daffodils by celebrated sculptor Fernando Casasempere.

Natural Rock Arch in the Ocean

COASTAL VIEWPOINT

The enormous offshore arch at **Monumento Natural La Portada** can be viewed from the cliffs 20km north of Antofagasta. Topped by marine sediments and supported by a sturdy volcanic base, the stack was eroded into a natural arch by the waves of the Pacific Ocean. It is the centerpiece of a protected zone managed by Conaf, which is a habitat for Humboldt penguins, sea lions, seals, terns and peregrine falcons.

Walk the 70m-long path along the clifftops and take in the views of la Portada and the beaches 50m below. Snapping photos, gazing out to sea and admiring the squawking seabirds are the main activities here. A steep set of stairs down to the shoreline was closed after being deemed unsafe. Check the Conaf website (conaf.cl) to see whether the coastal path has reopened. Get here on a northbound bus from Antofagasta (it's a 2km walk from the highway) or by car.

Lunch at an Antofagasta Market

FRESH JUICES AND SEAFOOD

Housed in a beautiful former railway station at Plaza Sotomayor, the **Mercado Central** indoor market is packed with butchers' stalls and fruit and produce vendors, as well as informal restaurants serving typical Chilean lunchtime dishes, such as soups and empanadas, and fresh juices.

By the seafront, you might spot sea lions and pelicans outside the busy fish market at the **Terminal Pesquero.** Inside are a dozen or so stalls serving hearty seafood soups, ceviche and fried fish.

MUSIC OF NORTE GRANDE

In many ways, the music of northern Chile is similar to the sounds of the altiplano regions of Bolivia and Peru. Typical instruments include *bombos* (drum), *sikus* (panpipe), *quenas* (flute) and *charangos* (a stringed instrument). Brass marching bands are another important tradition in the region. Hear them at celebrations and events including the Virgin of Carmen festival (p115) in La Tirana.

Beyond the traditional music of the mountain villages, it is possible to hear the influence of Andean rhythms in the work of contemporary artists from Norte Grande, such as Paulina Camus and Natalia Norte. You can hear Andean folk and local bands at **Café del Sol** in Antofagasta.

GETTING AROUND

Buses run throughout the city. To get to the Ruinas de Huanchaca, take bus 103 from Plaza Colón to Calle Sangra. Buses also operate to destinations throughout northern Chile and to Santiago from the terminal 4km north of town. They go between the terminal and the city center, or you can take a taxi or Uber. Aeropuerto Cerro Moreno, 25km north of the city, has flights to Santiago and other destinations.

IQUIQUE

Iquique ●

✪ Santiago

On a golden crescent of coastline, Iquique is a haven for vacationing Chileans, who stroll its beachfront boardwalks, surf its waves and paraglide off the sandy cliffs that loom above it. This city is a hive of activity by day and night, from early morning open-air aerobics classes by Playa La Gaviota to afternoon beach volleyball sessions and sunset cocktails at the Península de Cavancha. The urban sand dune at Cerro Dragón is a popular spot for sand-boarding.

A number of museums reflect the importance of the 19th-century mining boom and the War of the Pacific in shaping Iquique. The renovated wood-framed buildings on the street of Baquedano date from a time when Iquique was an export hub for nitrate from the mines of Humberstone and Santa Laura. After the nitrate bust, Iquique was reborn as a fishing port. Sample the seafood at one of the city's excellent restaurants.

TOP TIP

Iquique is a pleasant city to navigate on foot or by bicycle. The Mall Zofri shopping complex is near some sketchy neighborhoods, so it's safer to get there by taxi or Uber. At night, avoid walking in quiet areas where few people are in the streets.

Paragliding, Iquique

LUCAS NISHIMOTO/SHUTTERSTOCK ©

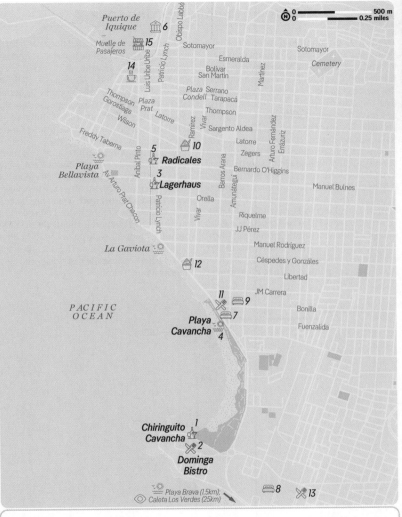

PACIFIC OCEAN

Puerto de Iquique

Muelle de Pasajeros

Playa Bellavista

La Gaviota

Playa Cavancha

Chiringuito Cavancha

Dominga Bistro

Playa Brava (1.5km);
Caleta Los Verdes (25km)

Cemetery

0 500 m
0 0.25 miles

HIGHLIGHTS
1 Chiringuito Cavancha
2 Dominga Bistro
3 Lagerhaus
4 Playa Cavancha
5 Radicales

SIGHTS
6 Museo Corbeta Esmeralda

SLEEPING
7 Backpacker's Hostel Iquique
8 NH Iquique
9 Sunfish Hotel

EATING
10 Fábrica de Chumbeques M.Koo
11 La Mulata
12 Marrasquino
13 Santorini

DRINKING & NIGHTLIFE
14 Ciocciata

SHOPPING
15 Caleta Riquelme

The 1km walk along Baquedano to Plaza Prat takes in the best of Iquique's historic buildings. Start at **1 Monumento Boya Esmeralda**, a copy of the buoy that marks the location of the *Esmeralda* wreck, and pass the statue of *Esmeralda* captain Arturo Prat at **2 Plaza 21 de Mayo** to reach the broad boulevard of Baquedano. The restored buildings here were constructed from Oregon pine between 1820 and 1920, during the nitrate mining days. To the north, a customs house built in 1871 now contains the **3 Museo Naval**, which displays artifacts salvaged from the *Esmeralda*. Continue along Baquedano to Bernardo O'Higgins. Here you'll see **4 Palacio Astoreca**, a 1904 mansion built for a nitrate tycoon that's now a cultural center hosting contemporary art exhibitions in the elaborate interior. Back on Baquedano, pop into **5 Pájaro en Mano** to browse the locally designed posters, t-shirts and mugs. Motifs include historic characters from the pampas nitrate mines and images associated with the festival of La Tirana (p115). Nearby, stop to explore the galleries of the **6 Museo Regional**, housed in the city's former courthouse that dates from 1892. Alongside permanent exhibits on regional history, the museum hosts some interesting temporary exhibitions. Continue for two blocks to reach **7 Plaza Prat**, with its 1877 **8 Torre Reloj** (clock tower). On the southern edge of the square is the neoclassical **9 Teatro Municipal**, which has hosted operas and plays since 1890. The showiest building on Plaza Prat is the **10 Casino Español**, a Moorish-style palace built in 1904 that is now a restaurant. Head inside for a look at the dazzling tile work, coffered ceilings and fanciful murals.

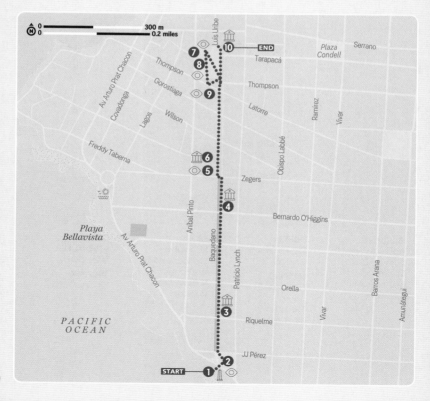

Museo Corbeta Esmeralda

Onboard the Museo Corbeta Esmeralda

REPLICA WARSHIP MUSEUM

Occupying a prime position in Iquique's port, the **Museo Corbeta Esmeralda** is housed in a replica of its sunken namesake warship and tells the story of the ship's role in the War of the Pacific (1879–83), in which Chile defeated a Peruvian–Bolivian alliance and increased its territory in the north. The wreck of the original ship remains nearby at the bottom of the ocean, and a buoy marks its location. Arturo Prat captained the ship, and his name graces plazas and avenues across the country.

Book ahead (museoesmeralda.cl) for a guided tour of the ship in Spanish or an audio guide in English. The museum (closed Monday) reflects a patriotic telling of the War of the Pacific and depicts life on board in the recreated staff quarters; the replica *Esmeralda* was constructed using the original drawings. Don't miss the doctor's cabin complete with medicines and surgical instruments.

Nearby, the restaurants above the fish market at **Caleta Riquelme** make a good place for lunch.

A Night Out in Iquique

BEACHSIDE RESTAURANTS AND BARS

South of Playa Cavancha, the **Península de Cavancha** is the location of some prime real estate in the form of flash apartment blocks, as well as a number of restaurants and bars where crowds of young people gather for '*la previa*' (early evening

BEST PLACES TO EAT IN IQUIQUE

La Mulata
Ocean views and fantastic Peruvian-Japanese dishes make La Mulata a top choice. $$$

Santorini
Head here for exceptional Greek food served on a bougainvillea-draped patio. $$

Ciocciata
City center cafe serving coffee, sandwiches and cakes. $$

Marrasquino
Seafront cake and ice cream shop with a huge selection of flavors. $

Fábrica de Chumbeques M.Koo
The best place in town to try *chumbeques*: cookies filled with mango, lemon, guava, passionfruit or *manjar* (dulce de leche). $

 WHERE TO STAY IN IQUIQUE

Backpacker's Hostel Iquique
Right by Playa Cavancha, this sociable hostel has a kitchen, bar and cafe. $

NH Iquique
This branch of the NH hotel chain is one of Iquique's nicest hotels; has ocean views. $$$

Sunfish Hotel
High-rise hotel near Playa Cavancha with spacious rooms and a rooftop pool. $$$

drinks). At the southern end of Cavancha Beach, **Chiringuito Cavancha** is a fashionable place where the outdoor tables overlook the ocean waves; book ahead. Running down the center of the peninsula, **Filomena Valenzuela** is a boulevard lined with buzzy bars and restaurants, from high-end sushi places to pizza joints and sports bars. **Dominga Bistro** is a good choice for seafood and cocktails. It has indoor and outdoor seating and a luxe contemporary decor.

After dinner and drinks on the peninsula, head to the bars on the pedestrian drag of **Baquedano**. Try the two floors and warren of rooms at **Radicales**. Nearby **Lagerhaus** is the place to go for craft beer.

Iquique Beach Life

SUN, SEA AND SURF

Iquique's most popular beach is **Playa Cavancha**, a beautiful expanse of sand backed by palm trees and grass. The ocean water here is some of the warmest in Chile. Not only is it safe to swim, but it's also suitable for surfing, body-boarding, kayaking and stand-up paddleboarding. Cavancha is usually quiet in the mornings, but it gets busy on summer afternoons. Surfers and body-boarders have less competition for early morning breaks at the north end of the beach. Several operators rent surfboards and offer lessons.

Because mornings in Iquique are generally cool, it can be a lovely time to go for a cycle, run or walk along the coast. Head south along the walking or cycling paths at Playa Cavancha to reach **Playa Brava**, a broad sandy beach. The water here is not suitable for swimming. In the evenings, the luminous pinks and oranges of the sunsets are not to be missed.

In May, the world's top surfers arrive in Iquique for the **Héroes de Mayo Pro** surfing competition. The event attracts some 200 surfers, who compete to win thousands of dollars in prize money and improve their rankings in the World Surf League. The competition involves surfing the Ola El Colegio wave to the north of Playa Cavancha.

Caleta Los Verdes, a small cove 25km south of Iquique, is known for its excellent fish restaurants. The **Copa Verano Iquique** body-boarding competition takes place at Caleta Los Verdes every January.

SURFING NORTE GRANDE

To surf more of northern Chile's best waves, head to **Playa Las Machas** (p119) in Arica, where the water is warm and the waves are suitable for surfers of all levels.

GETTING AROUND

Colectivos (shared taxis) are a convenient way to get around the city. Long-distance buses to Arica, Calama, Antofagasta and Santiago leave from the Terminal Rodoviario, 4km north of Playa Cavancha. Aeropuerto Diego Aracena is 40km south of Iquique, with flights to Santiago and Arica.

Beyond Iquique

The desert beyond Iquique bears the marks of history. It also hosts one of Chile's most important religious festivals.

Parque Nacional
Volcán Isluga
Colchane
Pisagua
Humberstone
and Santa Laura
Giant of the
Atacama
Villablanca
Iquique
La Tirana
Cerros
Pintados

Traveling inland from Iquique, ghost towns punctuate the desert, eerie relics of once flourishing nitrate-mining communities that are now museums. Nearby, mysterious geoglyphs left on the barren landscape speak of a more distant past, when the area was a trade route between the mountains and the coast.

From the Panamericana, the road from Huara to Colchane climbs through the foothills to the mountains and volcanoes of the altiplano, where Parque Nacional Volcán Isluga offers isolated natural beauty. Cultural traditions are kept alive in the communities of the nearby Aymara villages, where people keep alpacas and llamas and weave textiles from their wool. The pisco sours and high-rise real estate of Iquique seem a world away.

TOP TIP

During the Virgin of Carmen festival, buses from La Tirana to Iquique and Pica run throughout the day. Book accommodations in advance.

Cerros Pintados (p115)

HOLGER LEUE/GETTY IMAGES ©

CHILE'S DARK PAST

Located 120km north of Iquique, Pisagua was one of Chile's most important ports during the 19th-century nitrate-mining boom. But these days, Pisagua is better known as the site of a camp for political prisoners during Pinochet's military dictatorship (1973–89) and for the subsequent discovery of an unmarked mass grave in the local cemetery.

The cemetery is on a hillside 3km north of town. A memorial plaque marks the site of the pit beneath the rock face where the grave containing the bodies of 21 political prisoners was uncovered. The presence of bullet wounds indicated that they had been shot to death.

JEREMY RICHARDS/SHUTTERSTOCK ©

Santa Laura

Mining Ghost Towns

NITRATE MINES TURNED MUSEUMS

Once home to a thriving community of nitrate mine workers and their families, the abandoned towns of **Humberstone** and **Santa Laura** are now preserved as museums. The buildings in these eerie ghost towns have protected status in tribute to the people whose hard work fueled the nitrate boom. Established in 1872 as La Pampa, the town of Humberstone once buzzed with life, but after the development of synthetic nitrates, the site closed in 1960.

Visiting the abandoned towns is a disconcerting experience. Humberstone and Santa Laura's industrial structures and desert backdrop make them interesting subjects for photography. Some buildings are restored, but others are crumbling, so take care when exploring. At the entrance to Humberstone, the houses contain small museums displaying themed collections of items found on the site: whole walls covered with strange ensembles of children's toys, cooking implements and work tools.

A 2km walk or drive west of Humberstone is the smaller town of Santa Laura, which is part of the same museum but has fewer exhibits than Humberstone. The museums can be visited on a half-day trip from Iquique (45 minutes by bus or car).

 WHERE TO STAY & EAT BEYOND IQUIQUE

Hostal Inka Thaki
Just about the only option in town, this Colchane guesthouse has a restaurant and hot showers. **$**

Hostal La Roca
Run by a friendly couple, this Pisagua guesthouse has charming rooms and ocean views. **$**

Restaurante Qori Inti
In Pica, this Andean restaurant serves typical dishes such as rabbit, llama and quinoa soup. **$$**

Celebrating La Tirana's Virgin of Carmen

COSTUMES, BRASS BANDS AND DANCING

The **Virgin of Carmen** festival is one of Chile's most spectacular religious events, and as many as 250,000 costumed dancers, musicians and festival-goers fill the streets of the otherwise sleepy town of **La Tirana**. The town's origins are connected to the legend of the Inca princess known as La Tirana, who resisted the Spanish invaders and was killed after falling in love with a Spanish man. The village was established at the site of her grave.

On July 15, excitement mounts, and at midnight, fireworks mark the beginning of the festival. July 16 begins with a dawn mass, after which the virgin is paraded through the village, followed by a grand procession with dancing and brass bands.

During the festival, shuttle buses run between La Tirana and Iquique throughout the day and night, taking revelers back to their accommodations.

Adventures in the Altiplano

ANDEAN LANDSCAPES AND CULTURE

High in the altiplano, some 250km beyond Iquique, is **Parque Nacional Volcán Isluga**, where snow-topped conical volcanoes and marshy *bofedales* are home to guanacos, vicuñas and ñandú. The high-altitude flora of the zone includes cacti that grow as tall as 4m. Within the boundaries of the park is Volcán Isluga, where a 6km walking trail leads to the summit (allow eight hours). Near the volcano is the uninhabited village of Isluga. During religious festivals, the scattered residents of the surrounding area gather at the 17th-century adobe church. The village of **Colchane** on the Bolivian border is one of the few places in the area with accommodations.

South of Colchane, the traditional Aymara village of **Villablanca** enjoys a privileged location, surrounded by sacred mountains and volcanoes. The village of simple adobe houses and a charming church is not geared toward tourism, but visitors receive a warm welcome. Ask about buying traditional handwoven alpaca-wool textiles and handmade guitars. Take a walk at **Laguna Villablanca**, a beautiful spot visited by flamingos and local farmers, who bring their llamas and alpacas to graze on its shores.

MYSTERIOUS DESERT GEOGLYPHS

Measuring some 100m in length, the **Giant of the Atacama** is one of the world's biggest geoglyphs (large motifs created in the landscape by adding stones, removing earth or a mixture of both). The Tarapacá Giant, as it is also known, is estimated to date from around 900 CE and could represent a shaman. It can be seen on the isolated slope of Cerro Unita, 14km east of Huara on the road to Colchane.

Further south, some 420 geoglyphs can be viewed at **Cerros Pintados**, where the designs include human and animal figures. It is believed these geoglyphs relate to the routes of ancient llama caravans and might have indicated the location of water sources.

GETTING AROUND

To reach Humberstone and Santa Laura, take the bus from Iquique toward Pozo Almonte with the bus company Santa Angela. It's a short walk to the museums from the highway. Daily buses link Iquique and La Tirana, and transport runs throughout the day during the festival. Buses from Iquique to Oruro (Bolivia) stop in Colchane, but you'll need your own vehicle to reach Parque Nacional Volcán Isluga and other nearby villages.

ARICA

Arica ●

✪ Santiago

With a pleasant climate, miles of sandy beaches and a laid-back surf culture, Arica is a charming city to kick back in for a while. Beyond the city's upbeat atmosphere, Chile's historically tense relationship with neighboring Peru looms large at sites commemorating the 19th-century War of the Pacific, during which Arica became a Chilean city. The hilltop site of an important battle is marked with a huge Chilean flag that might almost be visible in Peru.

Arica's past conflicts are a blip on the timeline compared with the history of the Chinchorro culture that lived in the area some 7000 years ago and left behind intriguing burial sites. Along the coast, a walking trail passes through caves once used by the Chinchorro culture as a base for hunting and fishing. At that unspoiled spot, it's easy to imagine life many thousands of years ago.

TOP TIP

Time your visit to take in one of Arica's colorful festivals. The Carnaval Andino Con la Fuerza del Sol takes place in February, and Semana Ariqueña happens in June.

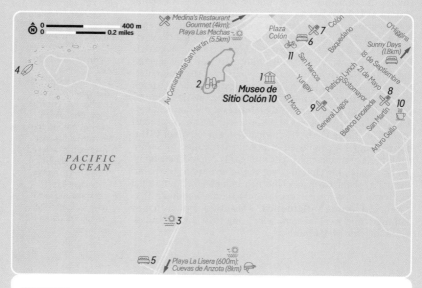

HIGHLIGHTS
1 Museo de Sitio Colón 10

SIGHTS
2 El Morro
3 Playa El Laucho

ACTIVITIES, COURSES & TOURS
4 Isla del Alacrán

SLEEPING
5 Hotel Arica
6 Hotel Casa Beltrán

EATING
7 Cafe del Mar
8 Los Aleros de 21
9 Salteñas y Empanadas Caupolicán

DRINKING & NIGHTLIFE
10 Salon de Te 890

TRANSPORT
11 Turismo Chogña

Cuevas de Anzota (p119)

Excavated Chinchorro Burial Ground

ANCIENT HUMAN REMAINS

Near Arica's city center, the **Museo de Sitio Colón 10** displays the remains of 48 ancient people in their original positions. In the late 19th century, a house was built here. Look for a preserved section of the building's original walls near the museum ticket desk. In 2004, when architects began excavating the site to prepare the ground for a new hotel, they came across a number of bones in the ground. These remains were later determined to be those of the Chinchorro people.

The Chinchorros lived in the coastal areas of what is now northern Chile and southern Peru between 8000 and 2000 BCE, during which time their burial procedures evolved. The burial ground at Sitio Colón 10 is believed to date from the later period, between 4200 and 3800 BCE, when bodies were no longer mummified but were instead covered with plant fibers and seabird feathers. The bodies remained preserved underground because of the dry climate and the high salt content of the earth.

On the 1st floor of the small museum, you can view the remains as they were found. Walk over the glass panels covering the bodies to look closely at details such as grass skirts and

BEST PLACES TO EAT IN ARICA

Salteñas y Empanadas Caupolicán
The best place in town for Chilean empanadas and Bolivian *salteñas* (filled savory pastries). $

Salón de Té 890
Cheerful tearoom offering sandwiches and cakes; don't miss the signature *siete sabores* (seven flavors) cake. $

Cafe del Mar
Long menu of burgers, sandwiches, snacks and desserts. $$

Medina's Restaurant Gourmet
Near Playa Las Machas, this restaurant is worth the trip for its superb Peruvian food. $$$

Los Aleros de 21
Neighborhood restaurant serving excellent Chilean grilled meat and seafood dishes. $$$

 WHERE TO STAY IN ARICA

Sunny Days
An easygoing guesthouse near Playa de Chinchorro, 2km northeast of Arica city center. $

Hotel Casa Beltrán
City center boutique hotel, where the spacious rooms come equipped with all the mod-cons. $$

Hotel Arica
Large, ocean-front resort near Playa Laucho, with cabins overlooking the water and a beachfront pool. $$$

This walk takes in Arica's most important historical sites. Start at the **1 Estación de Ferrocarril Arica–La Paz**, the former terminal of the railway that linked Bolivia with the coast. Walk across the square to the **2 Ex Aduana**, the city's former customs house that's now a cultural center. Designed by Gustave Eiffel, the building was prefabricated in Paris and assembled on-site in 1874. Pop inside to see the original floor tiles and wrought-iron spiral staircase. The galleries house temporary exhibitions by local artists. Walk across **3 Plaza Colón**, passing palm trees and fountains, to **4 Catedral San Marcos**. Eiffel designed this Gothic-style church, prefabricated in France in 1870 and shipped to Arica, before his famous Parisian tower. The construction is made of stamped

and molded cast iron, coated with paint. Take a look at the ironwork of the cathedral's interior. Walk up 7 de Julio and turn right onto Colón. At the corner of Yungay, stop to see the elegant wooden verandas of **5 Casa Bolognesi**. The building was once the headquarters of Peruvian commander Bolognesi, who was killed in 1880 during the War of the Pacific. It is now the Peruvian consulate. Walk uphill for one block to reach **6 Museo de Sitio Colón 10**. Allow at least an hour at the museum to view the fascinating remains of a Chinchorro burial site. On the hillside behind the museum, steps lead up to the **7 Mirador de la Virgen** shrine for views over the city and ocean. If you have the energy, tackle the steep path to the left of the Mirador up to **8 El Morro**, a hilltop military memorial.

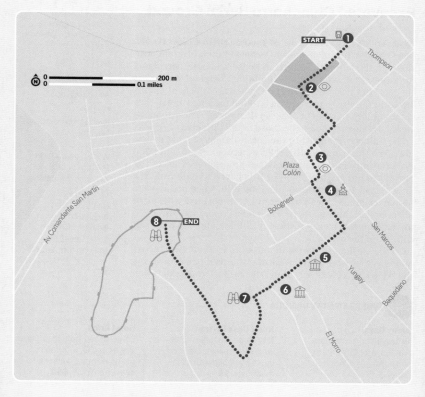

feathers. Numbered panels on the walls identify the remains underfoot, including a child with painted red hair and wigs made from human hair. An infant wears a black mask made from clay.

Upstairs, a gallery displays replicas of anthropomorphic figures found at nearby Chinchorro burial sites. Replicas of fishing hooks and nets made from plant fibers show the Chinchorros' lifestyle as expert fishers and divers.

Historic Hillside

MILITARY MEMORIAL AND VIEWS

Arica's most prominent landmark is **El Morro**, an imposing coffee-colored shoulder of rock that looms 110m above the city. On it flies a huge Chilean flag. The hilltop can be accessed via a steep path from the top of Colón or by road. It offers impressive views of the city, port and Pacific Ocean.

The headland was the site of a crucial battle in 1880 during the War of the Pacific, when the Chilean army took El Morro from Peruvian forces in less than an hour. Atop the hill, the battle is remembered at a military museum and at the Tomb of an Unknown Soldier. A walking trail loops around the hillside, passing the various military statues and memorials.

Coastal Route to Cuevas de Anzota

BEACHES, CAVES AND WILDLIFE

The coastal road south of Arica passes the city's best beaches on the way to the Cuevas de Anzota. The 10km route makes a scenic cycle, and **Turismo Chogña** rents bikes.

From Plaza Colón, take the cycle path south along Av Comandante San Martín. The first beach you'll reach is **Playa El Laucho**, where the water is suitable for swimming. Further south, **Playa La Lisera** is a prettier beach with changing rooms and showers.

The coastal road ends at the jagged cliffs and rocky shorelines of **Cuevas de Anzota** (closed Monday), where a 2.2km interpretive trail leads under rocky overhangs and into caves (allow 40 minutes). Thousands of years ago, the caves were used as shelter and as a burial site by the Chinchorro culture. Admission to the trail is free, but you must sign a waiver and wear a protective helmet. Watch for sea lions and otters.

MORE CHINCHORRO MUMMIES

Don't miss the remarkable collection of mummies displayed at the **Museo Arqueológico San Miguel de Azapa** (p121), 12km east of Arica. The mummies at Azapa were found at various locations in the surrounding area.

ARICA'S BEST WAVES

North of Arica's city center, **Playa Las Machas** is a surfers' haunt with waves suitable for all levels. Several places offer lessons and rent boards. July sees the biggest breaks, attracting pro surfers from around the world.

As well as Playa Las Machas, expert surfers also hit the towering waves of **El Gringo** (also known as the Chilean Pipeline) and **El Buey** at Isla del Alacrán, an expert point break west of Club de Yates.

GETTING AROUND

Local buses connect Arica city center with Playa Las Machas and the bus station, which has connections to Iquique, Calama, Antofagasta and Santiago. Aeropuerto Internacional Chacalluta is 18km north of Arica, with daily flights to Santiago.

Beyond Arica

Arica is the gateway to the Azapa Valley, the villages of the precordillera and the dizzying heights of the altiplano.

Putre

Arica　Valle de
Lluta　Parque Nacional
Lauca

Museo Arqueológico
San Miguel de Azapa　Termas de
Polloquere

Monumento Natural
Salar de Surire

The area surrounding Arica has a similarly upbeat atmosphere to the city, and it feels less desolate than some of the desert areas further south. The Azapa Valley is an important research center for the area's fascinating Chinchorro mummies, and there's a local sense of pride in the importance of these relics of an ancient culture.

Nearby, Ruta 11 rises into the hills of the precordillera, where Aymara villages are brightened with colorful flowers, butterflies and hummingbirds. Putre makes a welcoming base for adventures high onto the altiplano, where the dazzling waters of Lago Chungurá lap the shores at over 4000m. This biodiverse area is replete with wildlife from vicuñas to flamingos.

TOP TIP

At 3530m, Putre is an ideal acclimatization stop on the way to Parque Nacional Lauca on the altiplano.

Hummingbird, Azapa Valley

JOSE ARCOS AGUILAR/SHUTTERSTOCK ©

Chinchorro mummies

THE WORLD'S OLDEST MUMMIES

The Chinchorro mummies are the oldest known artificially preserved bodies in the world, predating their Egyptian counterparts by more than 2000 years. Several hundred mummies have been found, created by the Chinchorro people, who fished and hunted along the coast of what is now southern Peru and northern Chile from around 8000 BCE.

The mummification process involved removing the internal organs; drying out the corpse; repacking the body with sticks, reeds, clay and animal fur; reassembling the corpse; attaching a wig of human hair and a clay mask; and painting the corpse with black manganese. In later years, red ocher was used.

Chinchorro Mummies of the Azapa Valley

9000 YEARS OF HISTORY

The **Museo Arqueológico San Miguel de Azapa** is home to some of the world's oldest mummies. Set amid lush gardens, the museum has several sections. Start in the gallery that covers the region's history from 7000 BCE to the Spanish invasion. The well thought-out displays focus on the cultures from the various time periods, with original ceramics, agricultural tools and textiles. One room is dedicated to the production of olive oil in the Azapa Valley, complete with a huge 18th-century olive press.

Across the gardens, a second gallery houses an exhibition dedicated to the Chinchorro mummies, with display cases featuring tools, clothing and adornments used in the burial process. The mummies themselves are in the final display cases.

It is easy to get to the museum from Arica by bus or shared taxi (30 minutes). Allow one to two hours to view the exhibitions.

 WHERE TO STAY IN PUTRE

Terrace Lodge
This guesthouse has neat, heated rooms with mountain views; the gardens are visited by hummingbirds. **$$**

Hostal Vientos del Altiplano
A well-run guesthouse offering simple, heated rooms with balconies overlooking the gardens. **$$**

Pachamama Hostel
Rooms share bathrooms at this traveler-friendly hostel, which has a kitchen and central patio. **$**

I LIVE HERE: TRAVEL TIPS FROM PUTRE

Odlanier Veliz, who works at the Putre tourist office, shares the top tips and trips from the village.

Acclimatize
It's essential to spend time in the precordillera to acclimatize before visiting the altiplano. Take a road trip to the villages of Saxamar, Tignamar and Belén, where you should try the local goat's cheese.

Hot Springs
Head to nearby Termas de Jurasi and Termas de las Cuevas.

Suriplaza
North of Putre, Suriplaza is known as the hills of colors because of the browns, reds, greens and golds of the landscape.

When to go
The best time to visit is from March to May, when the landscape is at its greenest following the rain.

Volcán Parinacota

Hiking Near Putre

ANCIENT TRAIL AND ROCK ART

The precordillera village of **Putre**, 150km east of Arica (three hours by bus or car), makes a good base for venturing further onto the altiplano. You can take in the mountain scenery surrounding the Aymara village on a half-day hike.

Walk west from the square and follow the road past the school and down to the river. Cross the river and continue along the road, with the river to your left, until you reach a flat area with a number of farm buildings. Continue across the field and take the furthest north of two paths (it is easy to get lost here). When you see a building on your right, look for a steep path down to the river, cross over and climb up to reach a narrow path hugging the hillside.

You are now on the **Sendero de Wilacabrani**, a pre-Inca trail that was part of the route from the altiplano to the coast. Continue along the narrow stony path, passing a waterfall. When you see a house, look for a trail to your right leading to some **cave paintings** of llamas and other images.

 WHERE TO EAT IN PUTRE ───────────

Casona del Rey
Putre's best restaurant offers a range of dishes made with local produce, including excellent pizzas. **$$**

Suma Q'antati
Good-value local restaurant serving a typical Andean lunch menu of soup, a main dish and fruit. **$**

Rosamel
At the plaza, Rosamel has a long menu of Andean dishes, including several vegetarian options. **$$**

Exploring Lauca National Park

HIGH-ALTITUDE LAKES AND VOLCANOES.

The breathtaking altiplano landscapes of **Parque Nacional Lauca** lie 50km east of Putre (one hour by car) along the Ruta 11. Though it's possible to visit on a day trip from Arica, it's a good idea to spend at least one night in Putre to acclimatize. The elevation of the park's main sight, Lago Chungará, is 4517m.

Several viewpoints take in the perfect, snow-capped cone of **Volcán Parinacota**. Walk along the trail at the shores of the glistening **Lago Chungará** (around 20 minutes), where picnic tables make an idyllic spot for lunch. The park's vast array of wildlife includes vicuña, viscacha and condors.

It's worth taking a short detour to the village of **Parinacota** for a stroll and to see the typical Andean church. The restaurant **Uta Kala Don Leo** serves meals, but call ahead to make a reservation (+56 98 895 3373).

See Flamingos at the Salt Flats

STEAMING ALTIPLANO LAKE

The salt flats at **Monumento Natural Salar de Surire** are a remote wilderness with thermal springs for bathing and wildlife watching, which can be visited on a tour or by car as a day trip from Putre. The unpaved road south to the Salar passes several *bofedales*, waterlogged areas of lush spongy ground where vicuñas, guanacos and ñandú come to graze. Stop to look at the 19th-century stone and adobe church in the tiny, isolated village of **Guallatiri**.

Continue to **Termas de Polloquere**, a spectacular lake where you can take a dip in the thermal waters, but bear in mind that you won't be able to rinse off afterward. The site is not staffed, so you have to judge the temperature of the water yourself. Take care because some areas are hotter than others. Once you're submerged in the water, soak in the awesome views of the salt flats and volcanoes. It's common to spot three species of flamingo, which come to the isolated salt flats to nest.

Bring food and water with you, leave early and allow around eight hours. Find out about current road conditions before setting off (roads may be impassable after rain); the tourist office in Putre can help.

SOUTH TO ISLUGA

From Monumento Natural Salar de Surire, the road continues south to the village of Colchane, near **Parque Nacional Volcán Isluga** (p115). Check road conditions before attempting this adventurous and isolated route.

VALLE DE LLUTA GEOGLYPHS

The barren slopes of Lluta Valley are the canvas for a number of geoglyphs, known as the **Gigantes de Lluta**. Figures to look for include a frog, an eagle, llamas and humans. See them near the roadside of Ruta 11, just after the turnoff from the Panamericana. The geoglyphs are a reminder of the importance of the valley as a route for pre-Inca trade caravans between Tiwanaku in modern-day Bolivia and the Pacific coast. Further geoglyphs are visible on the hillsides of the Azapa Valley. Look for them on the way to the museum at San Miguel de Azapa (p121).

GETTING AROUND

Colectivos (shared taxis) to San Miguel pass the entrance to Museo Arqueológico San Miguel de Azapa. They leave from the corner of Chacabuco and Patricio Lynch in Arica. One bus a day runs between Arica and Putre. To get to Parque Nacional Lauca and beyond, you'll need your own vehicle or take a tour.

NORTE CHICO

BEACHES, STARGAZING AND VERDANT VALLEYS

A sliver of land packed with wildlife-rich nature reserves, charming cities and mystical valleys, Chile's 'Little North' is small but diverse.

Between the Andes and the ocean, the Atacama Desert extends north from La Serena. To the east of the city, the Elqui River is fringed by a strip of green. In this mystical valley, grapes are distilled into pisco, and astronomical observatories aim their telescopes towards the cloudless night sky. The landscapes here inspired the work of poet Gabriela Mistral.

A string of pretty beaches line the coast, from the resorts near La Serena to the unspoiled strips of sand in Bahía Inglesa and Pan de Azúcar. Thanks to the Humboldt Current, the Pacific Ocean here is a plentiful source of fish. Nature reserves in the region work to protect the area's marine life, including Humboldt penguins. The cold ocean current is also the reason for the *camanchaca*, a sea mist that gathers over coastal areas in the mornings.

Deep below the desert lie the minerals on which the local economy depends. However, the narrowly averted tragedy of the trapped miners at Mina San José serves as a reminder of the dangers of the industry, while plans for a controversial mega mine have been met with resistance from environmental groups.

Though the desert might appear desolate, beneath the surface it is teeming with life. Dormant wildflower seeds await the rain. In the years of sufficient rainfall, the desert is transformed with a blanket of colorful wildflowers.

THE MAIN AREAS

LA SERENA
Historic buildings and sandy beaches.
p130

CALDERA
Coastal resort and mining port.
p142

Left: Faro (p132), La Serena; above: Bahía Inglesa (p146)

Find Your Way

Norte Chico encompasses rugged unspoiled coastline, popular beach resorts, swathes of empty desert, verdant valleys and remote Andean mountains. La Serena and Caldera are cultural hubs and strategic bases from which to explore the region.

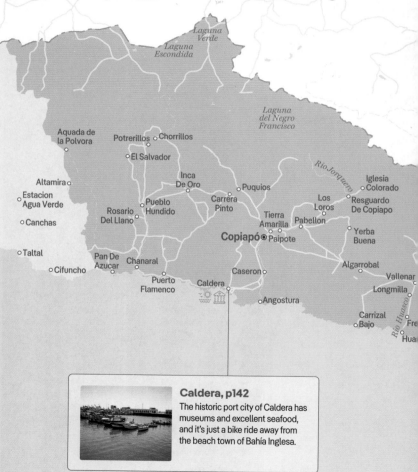

Laguna Verde

Laguna Escondida

Laguna del Negro Francisco

Aquada de la Polvora

Potrerillos   Chorrillos

El Salvador

Inca De Oro

Altamira

Estacion Agua Verde

Canchas

Rosario Del Llano

Pueblo Hundido

Carrera Pinto

Puquios

Río Jorquero

Iglesia Colorado

Los Loros

Resguardo De Copiapo

Tierra Amarilla

Pabellon

Copiapó   Paipote

Yerba Buena

Taltal

Pan De Azucar

Chanaral

Cifuncho

Puerto Flamenco

Caldera

Caseron

Angostura

Algarrobal

Vallenar

Longmilla

Carrizal Bajo

Río Huasco

Fre

Hua

Caldera, p142

The historic port city of Caldera has museums and excellent seafood, and it's just a bike ride away from the beach town of Bahía Inglesa.

0   100 km
0   50 miles

ARGENTINA

BUS

Buses connect cities and towns along the coast and in the Elqui Valley, and they are generally a cheap and efficient way to get around. However, several places, including the region's national parks and nature reserves, are not served by public transport.

CAR

Renting a car offers the opportunity to reach Norte Chico's less accessible areas. The region's main highways are in good condition; however, it is easy to get lost in remote mountainous areas, where there is also the risk of ice and snow on the roads.

TOUR

Joining a tour is often the most cost- and time-efficient way to visit some of Norte Chico's national parks and nature reserves. Going with an expert guide also offers an element of safety when visiting tricky-to-navigate areas.

Rio los Patos

Chollay
El Transito
San Felix
Guanta
Cabrito
La Campana
Vizcachitas
Domeyko
El Tamba
Incoguosi
Quebrada Honda
La Serena
Higuerita
Choros Bajos
Rio Turbio
Rio Elqui
Quebraditas
El Chanar
Rapel
Samo Alto
Andacollo
Algarrobo
El Penon
Tongoy
Cerillos
Puetro Aldea
Rio Grande
Caren
Guatulame
Monte Patria
Ovalle
Punitaqui
Rio Cogoti
Combarabala
Pama
Salamanca
Illapel
Canela Baja
Quillaicillo
Maitencillo
Cuncumen
Pintacura
Chigualoco
Huentelauquen
Guanguali
Quilimari
Los Vilos
Rio Choapa
Rio Limari

La Serena, p130

Chile's second-oldest city is home to an elegant main square, historic buildings, a bustling covered market and a broad sandy beach.

PACIFIC OCEAN

Plan Your Time

Norte Chico is a region you won't want to rush through. Allow time to linger in the valley towns and beach resorts that pull you in.

Coquimbo (p136)

Pressed for Time

● Head straight to **La Serena** (p130) to explore the **city center** (p131), shop for **local produce** (p133), stroll the beach at sunset and feast on seafood.

● Breathe in the ocean breeze on a **cycling tour** (p132) along the coast to **Coquimbo** (p136), where the historic buildings of Barrio Inglés are surrounded by fabulous murals.

● Travel east into the lush Elqui Valley. Use the town of Vicuña as your base and visit the valley's **pisco distilleries** (p139) by day and take a **stargazing tour** (p138) at a nearby observatory at night. Take in the area's natural beauty on a **bike ride** or **hike** (p137).

MARK PITT IMAGES/SHUTTERSTOCK ©

Seasonal Highlights

The summer months of January and February bring hot weather, and beach resorts fill with vacationers. December through March is the best time to spot whales.

JANUARY
Verano en La Serena features a program of cultural events including traditional folkloric dance, ballet and theater performances.

FEBRUARY
The **Cocinas del Pacífico** international food festival is held in Bahía Inglesa, with talks, cooking demonstrations and plenty of tastings.

MARCH
A good month to visit the **pisco distilleries** of the Elqui Valley, where grapes are harvested between February and May.

Five Days to Travel Around

● After two days in La Serena and the Elqui Valley, take a day trip to **Reserva Nacional Pingüino de Humboldt** (p141), where you can see penguins, sea lions and possibly whales.

● Next, head north to **Caldera** (p142). Spend a morning exploring the city's **museums** (p143) and then take a bike ride along the coast, stopping for lunch at **Bahía Inglesa** (p146) before checking out the fossils at Parque Paleontológico Los Dedos.

● Take a day trip to **Parque Nacional Pan de Azúcar** (p147), where you can hike to viewpoints and relax on pristine beaches.

A Week Long Stay

● Start at the beaches south of **La Serena** (p130), where you can surf at **Playa Totoralillo** (p134) and eat seafood in **Tongoy** (p137).

● After exploring La Serena and the Elqui Valley, head north to **Caldera** (p142) and use the city as a base for trips to nearby beaches. Take a day to explore the coast south of Caldera as far as **Playa La Virgen** (p146) and another day to head north via the **Orbicular Granite nature sanctuary** (p147) to **Parque Nacional Pan de Azúcar** (p147).

● Spend the last two days in the mountains at the remote and isolated **Parque Nacional Nevado Tres Cruces** (p148).

MAY

On May 15, towns in the Elqui and Limarí valleys celebrate the **Día Nacional del Pisco** with parties and cocktails.

JULY

In Caldera, the **Fiesta de la Recreación** commemorates the inauguration of Chile's first railroad with a series of cultural events.

OCTOBER

La Serena hosts **FECILS**, a five-day international film festival with screenings taking place around the city.

DECEMBER

From December 23–27, the town of **Andacollo** near La Serena hosts a religious festival, including traditional folkloric dances.

LA SERENA

La Serena ✪ Santiago

Chile's second-oldest city is a regional capital and a popular beach resort. Not only is La Serena a relaxed and pleasant city to explore, with several beautiful sandy beaches nearby, but it also benefits from a bounty of local produce from the Elqui and Limarí valleys and fresh seafood caught by fishing boats from the neighboring port city of Coquimbo.

Spanish colonizers selected La Serena's location at a strategic point between Santiago and Peru in an area long inhabited by the indigenous Diaguitas. Much of the city center architecture appears to be in a Spanish colonial style, but while some buildings do date to that period, most were built in the late 1940s as part of President Gabriel González Videla's 'Plan Serena.' President from 1946 to 1952, González Videla was a La Serena native and a controversial figure. The house he once owned on Plaza de Armas is now a museum.

TOP TIP

The tourist office at Plaza de Armas is an excellent source of information about La Serena and the surrounding region. Accommodations book up fast in January and February, during which time many hotels require a minimum two-night stay.

La Serena

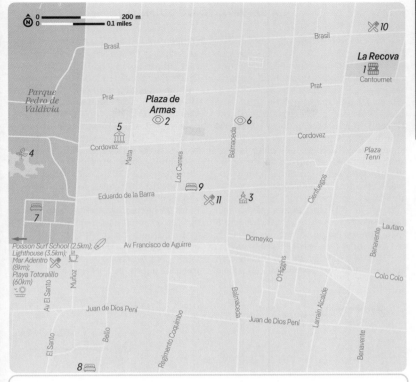

HIGHLIGHTS
1 La Recova
2 Plaza de Armas

SIGHTS
3 Iglesia San Francisco

4 Jardín Japonés
5 Museo Histórico Casa Gabriel González Videla
6 Patio Colonial

SLEEPING
7 Hostal El Arbol
8 Hostal El Punto
9 Terra Diaguita

EATING
10 Donde El Guatón
11 La Terrazza

Plazas, Gardens & Historic Buildings

EXPLORING LA SERENA'S HISTORIC CENTER

La Serena's tree-shaded streets and pretty stone buildings make the compact historic center a pleasure to explore on foot. Allow a couple of hours for a leisurely stroll with plenty of stops.

Start at the lush **Plaza de Armas** and join the locals as they lounge on benches, lulled by the sounds of the square's fountain. On the southwestern corner of the plaza is **Museo Casa Gabriel González Videla**, a museum named after and largely dedicated to Chile's president from 1946 to 1952. Located in a 19th-century house once owned by González Videla, the museum houses some interesting curios, including elaborately decorated *mates* (drinking gourds).

SOUVENIR SHOPPING

Two blocks east of Patio Colonial, **La Recova** (p133) is a vibrant covered market that is a good place to shop for local produce, artisan crafts and jewelry.

This scenic cycle follows the Av del Mar coastal road that links bougie La Serena with its gritty port-city neighbor Coquimbo. Allow at least three hours to cycle there and back with stops.

From **1 La Serena**, use the bike lane on Av Francisco de Aguirre to reach the **2 Faro**, the lighthouse at the northern end of Av del Mar. Admire the expanse of golden sand and the coastline before cycling south along the bike lane with the ocean on your right. As you reach Coquimbo, the bike lane ends just before Mall Vivo. Continue along Av Costanera. On your right, you'll see the **3 Terminal Pesquero**, a fish market where the catch of the day is served up at low-key restaurants. Stop for lunch and look out at fishing boats bobbing in the bay. Turn left onto Francisco Bilbao, continue uphill for three blocks and then turn

right onto José Santiago Aldunate. Continue straight to reach the restored 19th-century buildings of Barrio Inglés (the English Quarter). Several of the houses have plaques outlining their history. Look out for **4 Casa Wilson** (1880), **5 Casa Bauza** (1889) and **6 Casa Vicens** (1846). Nearby is the **7 Genesis Mural**, which depicts the history of Coquimbo. Take a look inside the **8 Centro Cultural Palace**, which hosts exhibitions and cultural events. Don't miss the tiled courtyard space. Continue straight on Regimiento Coquimbo, passing the port, and then turn right onto Cam. Al Fuerte to reach **9 Fuerte Coquimbo**, a 19th-century fortification built on the rocks at the northeastern tip of the peninsula, with views over the bay. From the lookout towers, you might spot pelicans and other seabirds as you gaze out to the crashing waves.

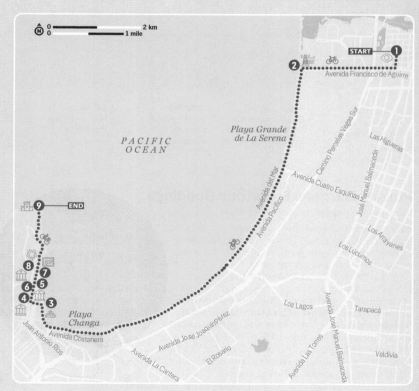

Bike track along La Serena's beach (p134)

West of Plaza de Armas, the tranquil **Jardín Japonés** has landscaped Japanese rock gardens, pagodas, arched bridges, turtle-filled ponds and a heart-shaped island to explore. Don't miss the collection of bonsai trees in the plant nursery.

Walk east along pretty Eduardo La Barra and stop to look at the 16th-century **Iglesia San Francisco**. It is the only church to have survived a fire caused by English pirate Bartholomew Sharp, who torched La Serena in 1680. Admire the details of the decorative facade and elegant bell tower. Inside, the simple stone walls and wooden ceilings give the church a stark beauty.

One block north of the church, on Av Balmaceda, **Patio Colonial** is a pedestrianized alleyway lined with colorful potted plants and shops selling books, jewelry and chocolates. Several cafes with outdoor tables make a great place to stop for a drink or a snack.

Shop at an Artisan Market

GEMSTONES, LEATHER GOODS AND PAPAYA

Three blocks east of Plaza de Armas, **La Recova** is a covered market with stalls selling artisan crafts and local produce. You'll find the favorite local fruit papaya preserved in

 WHERE TO STAY IN LA SERENA

Terra Diaguita
Leafy patios and creatively decorated spaces set this hotel apart. Bikes are available to rent. **$$**

Hostal El Arbol
This friendly downtown hostel has private rooms, shared dorms, a kitchen and a cozy living room. **$**

Hostal El Punto
Centrally located and colorfully decorated hostel with helpful staff, sun terraces and an on-site cafe. **$**

BEST RESTAURANTS IN LA SERENA

Lighthouse
Beachside cafe offering sandwiches, burgers, excellent cakes and the best coffee in town. $$

La Terrazza
With indoor and outdoor tables, this buzzy restaurant is a great spot for pizza, pasta or drinks. $$

Donde El Guaton
Traditional restaurant serving grilled meats and other classic Chilean dishes in a charming covered patio. $$

Mar Adentro
On the coastal road between La Serena and Coquimbo, this restaurant and bar specializes in fish and seafood. $$$

OSCARGUTZO/SHUTTERSTOCK ©

Surfing, La Serena

many different forms, from strips of dried fruit to papaya marshmallows, jams, juices and cakes. As well as the typical stalls selling Andean wool clothing and blankets, look out for high-quality handcrafted leather goods sold by the local artisans who made them. La Recova is also a good place to shop for *combarbalita*, a multicolored volcanic stone found only in nearby Combarbalá, and lapis lazuli from the Limarí Valley. Vendors are friendly and happy to chat about their wares.

Hit the Beach

SUN, SEA AND SAND

The miles of broad sandy beaches lining the coast between La Serena and Coquimbo are one of the area's biggest draws. Beaches are manned by lifeguards during the summer, but be careful of strong currents. It's also possible to surf, windsurf and sail. The best spots for water sports are south of the city of Coquimbo, including the beautiful **Playa Totoralillo**. In La Serena, **Poisson Surf School** offers lessons and rents out boards.

COASTAL BEACH RESORTS

South of La Serena are a number of popular sandy beaches, including several in the resort town of **Tongoy** (p137). In summer (January and February), they are often packed with holidaymakers.

Look carefully at the sand dunes and you might notice the purple wildflowers malvilla and suspiro del mar. Birds to watch out for include oystercatchers, snowy plovers and curlews.

Parallel to the beach is a broad promenade, cycling lane and coastal road lined with bars and restaurants. It is a particularly beautiful spot at sunset.

GETTING AROUND

The bus terminal is 1km south of Plaza de Armas. Parking is tricky in the city center. If you are driving, ask at your accommodations where to park. The city center is easy to explore on foot. Cycling is a good way to reach the beach and venture further along the coast. Rent bikes from Hostal Luna del Mar. Use official radio taxis (agree the price before setting off) or Uber to travel between the city center and the beach at night.

Beyond La Serena

La Serena is the gateway to a wealth of adventures in the captivating Elqui Valley and coastal beach resorts.

Reserva Nacional
● Pingüino de Humboldt

La Serena ● Observatorio
Coquimbo ● Cerro Mamalluca
● Vicuña
Tongoy ● ● Guanaqueros
Parque Nacional
Bosque Fray Jorge
● ● Valle del Encanto

The area surrounding La Serena offers so much to explore, from wildlife-watching boat trips and cloud forest walks to coastal beach resorts. East of La Serena, the fertile grounds of the Elqui Valley produce grapes that are turned into pisco at several distilleries, and the town of Vicuña makes an excellent base for exploring the valley. Thanks to the area's cloudless skies, the hills around Vicuña offer spectacular views of the night sky and are the location of some of the world's leading astronomy centers, as well as observatories that offer guided stargazing experiences.

Further into the valley, Pisco Elqui is a laid-back village with opportunities for mountain-biking and horseback-riding excursions in the surrounding mountains.

TOP TIP

Although it's possible to visit the Elqui Valley on a day trip, it's worth spending the night in Vicuña or Pisco Elqui.

Pisco Elqui (p139)

GUAXINIM/SHUTTERSTOCK ©

ROCK ART

Throughout northern Chile, you'll find examples of intriguing rock art left by the people who inhabited the area over a period of some 4000 years. An extensive gallery of rock art can be found in **Valle del Encanto**, 120km south of La Serena and 20km west of Ovalle. The art has been attributed to the Molle, Ánimas and Diaguitas cultures.

Elements of this rock art include pictographs (pictures on rocks painted with vegetable and mineral pigments), petroglyphs (rock engravings of various sizes, making use of different techniques) and *piedras tacitas* (rocks with round, coffee-cup-sized holes that were probably used as mortars to grind ceremonial plants and food).

MARK PITT IMAGES/SHUTTERSTOCK ©

Cruz del Tercer Milenio

Take in the View

ASCENDING COQUIMBO'S LANDMARK CROSS

Visible from the beaches of La Serena, **Cruz del Tercer Milenio** is an 83m-high concrete cross in the hills of Coquimbo that offers outstanding views. On the 1st floor is a religious museum, and to access the viewing platforms, you'll need to buy a museum ticket. Take an elevator up to the viewpoint at 70m, from which the entire bay is visible.

Coquimbo is a 30-minute bus trip from La Serena. The cross is near some unsafe neighborhoods, so take a taxi from Coquimbo's bus terminal or Mall Vivo.

A Night Out in Coquimbo

PORT-SIDE REVELRY

On the weekends, revelers spill out onto the streets from the bars and clubs of Coquimbo's Barrio Inglés. Grab a taxi to Calle José Santiago Aldunate (a 30-minute drive from La Serena) and take your pick of places between Las Heras and Plaza Vicuña Mackenna. Try **Mi Bar Coquimbo** for cocktails and live music, including jazz nights. The area can be sketchy after dark, so don't wander off the main drag.

 WHERE TO STAY IN ELQUI VALLEY

Campo de Cielo
Overnight in a Bedouin tent beneath starry skies at this magical camp in the hills near Vicuña. **$**

Alfa Aldea
Located amid vineyards on the outskirts of Vicuña, this guesthouse has simple rooms and mountain views. **$$**

Luna de Cuarzo
Self-catering cabins on a mountain property near Cochiguaz, with pools and a hot tub. **$$**

Seafood in Tongoy

SCALLOPS BY THE BEACH

The lively, upmarket beach resort of **Tongoy** makes an easy day trip by bus or car from La Serena. The scenic coastal drive takes about an hour, allowing plenty of time to stroll the beaches, stop for a seafood lunch and take a dip in the sea.

At the **Terminal Pesquero fish market**, vendors serve fresh seafood, including scallops, clams, oysters, crab, sole and turbot. Locals insist Tongoy scallops (*ostiones*) are the best in Chile. Seafood restaurants line Av Costanera, which runs parallel to the broad sands of **Playa Grande**. **La Bahía Restaurante** is a good choice for lunch. On the northern side of the peninsula, **Playa Socos** is a sheltered spot for a dip.

The bus from La Serena to Tongoy stops in Guanaqueros, so get off to see the town's famous long white-sand beach. You might even squeeze in another plate of seafood. The buzzy beachside restaurant **El Pequeño** serves some of the best in town.

A Walk in the Clouds

MIRACULOUS POCKET OF TEMPERATE FOREST

Scientists travel from around the world to study the unique vegetation of **Parque Nacional Bosque Fray Jorge**, a patch of green between the desert and the ocean that's a Unesco World Biosphere Reserve. Of the four ecosystems within the park, the most remarkable is the remnant of temperate forest that subsists amid cactus-riddled semi-desert thanks to its precise elevation and the moisture of the *camanchaca* (p148), a thick mist that rolls in from the Pacific ocean. This dense, vegetation-rich forest is of the same type as the Valdivian temperate forests found some 1000km further south. One of the best times to visit is in the morning, when condensation from the *camanchaca* leaves the plants dripping wet. At around noon, the white cushion of clouds that hovers over the sea gradually drifts over the forest's base.

Inside the park, an accessible 1km-long interpretative trail leads through a semiarid ecosystem and then winds through the moss-covered trees of the cloud forest and along a ridge above the ocean. The park is home to skunks, foxes and up to 120 different bird species. Look out for small hawks perched on cacti and search the skies to catch eagles hunting for prey. But wildlife is not the park's biggest draw; rather it's the fact that such a forest exists in an area of semi-desert, a natural relic of the past.

BEST BEACHES NEAR LA SERENA

Playa el Faro
The nearest beach to La Serena makes a romantic spot for a sunset walk.

Punta de Teatinos
A wildlife-rich wetlands area 10km north of La Serena that's great for bird watching.

Playa Totoralillo
A beautiful white-sand beach 15km south of Coquimbo; suitable for swimming, snorkeling and fishing.

Playa de Guanaqueros
Clear waters and a long stretch of sand make this a popular beach with families.

Playa Socos
Sheltered sandy beach in Tongoy that's perfect for swimming, kayaking or stand-up paddleboarding.

COQUIMBO'S BARRIO INGLÉS BY DAY

The restored 19th-century buildings of the English Quarter can be reached by bike from **La Serena** (p132). Check out the schedule of events at Centro Cultural Palace, which include theater performances and live music.

WHERE TO EAT IN ELQUI VALLEY

Heladería La Bilbaina
Family-run artisanal ice cream shop in Vicuña offering flavors like fig and *copao* (cactus). $

Chivato Negro
Vicuña bar and restaurant serving pizzas, sandwiches and salads, with a garden and cozy fires. $$

Cervecería Guayacán
Sample local Guayacán craft beer and feast on pizzas and burgers; branches in Vicuña and Pisco Elqui. $$

ASTRONOMICAL OBSERVATORIES

Because of its cloud-free skies and lack of light pollution, northern Chile is considered the best place in the world to observe the stars. Many of the world's astronomical centers are located here. It may be possible to arrange a daytime tour of the facilities at the **Cerro Tololo Inter-American Observatory** near Vicuña and view the two 8.1m telescopes of **Gemini South** and neighboring **SOAR telescope** at Cerro Pachón.

Due to begin operation in 2024, the **Vera Rubin Observatory**'s Legacy Survey of Space and Time (LSST) will deliver a 500-petabyte set of images hoped to reveal more about the structure and evolution of the universe.

There is no public transport to the park, which is a two-hour drive south of La Serena. The final section of road is steep, rough and dusty, and it can become impassable after rain. Pay the park admission fees in advance on the Conaf website (conaf.cl).

Stargazing in the Elqui Valley

STARS, PLANETS AND DISTANT GALAXIES

When the sun dips behind the hills of the Elqui Valley, the star-filled night sky over Vicuña is a truly awesome sight. Observatories close to town offer astronomical explanations and the chance to see Saturn's rings, Jupiter's moons and distant galaxies through telescopes. It's possible to visit on a tour or by car (one hour) from La Serena, but most people prefer to stay overnight in Vicuña. Visibility is best on or around a new moon when skies are darkest.

The most popular stargazing tour is at the purpose-built **Observatorio Cerro Mamalluca**, but large group sizes mean there can be some waiting in line for a chance to glimpse galaxies, star clusters and nebulae through the telescopes. The observatory's office at Plaza Gabriela Mistral in Vicuña sells tickets for the bilingual nightly tours and the shuttle bus service from Vicuña to the observatory.

Nearby, at the foot of Cerro Mamalluca, **Centro Astronómico Omega** offers personalized tours incorporating elements of traditional Andean astronomy, astrology and observations through three different telescopes. What you see depends on the season. In summer, you might observe the Orion and Tarantula nebulae; globular clusters including 47 Tucanae; the Jewel Box star cluster; the Andromeda and Sculptor galaxies; and the planets Jupiter, Saturn, Mars, Venus and Mercury. In winter, expect to see the Omega, Lagoon and Dumbbell nebulae; the Ghost of Jupiter; the Omega Centauri globular cluster; the Sombrero galaxy; and Mars. Viewings of the moon depend on the lunar phase.

On the outskirts of Vicuña, **Alfa Aldea** offers tours that start with a talk on astronomy, including a 3D film set to an evocative soundtrack by Chilean musician Joakín Bello. Once your sense of wonder has been duly sparked, the tour emerges into the star-filled sky for observations through a telescope.

Positioned far away from any light pollution in the hills 17km south of Vicuña, **Observatorio del Pangue** offers nightly small-group observations using several powerful telescopes. Tours are offered in English, Spanish and French, and transport is provided from Vicuña.

 WHERE TO EAT IN ELQUI VALLEY

Delicias del Sol
Dishes are cooked using an innovative method that harnesses sun rays at this solar restaurant in Villaseca. **$$**

El Bosque
Lunch is served in an idyllic outdoor woodland setting on the banks of a river in Horcón. **$$**

Alóe Restorán
Exquisite Chilean dishes, an excellent wine list and expertly mixed cocktails are offered at this Vicuña restaurant. **$$$**

JESS KRAFT/SHUTTERSTOCK ©

Elqui Valley at night

The Elqui Valley Pisco Trail

DISTILLERIES, VINEYARDS AND BREWERIES

The climate of the lush Elqui Valley is well suited to growing the varieties of grapes used to produce pisco. These pisco distilleries are located along the 40km route from Vicuña (one hour's drive east of La Serena) to just south of Pisco Elqui. Most are within walking distance of the Vicuña to Pisco Elqui bus route. Beyond Pisco Elqui, you'll need to rent a bike to reach Doña Josefa and Fundo los Nichos. It's possible to visit them all in one day if you go easy on the tastings.

Within walking distance of Vicuña's Plaza Gabriela Mistral, **Planta Pisco Capel** is an artisan distillery with a small pisco museum. Cocktail-mixing classes are available, along with regular tours and tastings.

East of Vicuña is **Pisquera Aba**, where tours include all aspects of production and end in the tasting room for samples of the boutique distillery's range of products, including some innovative fruit blends. Around Christmas, you'll be offered Cola de Mono, a traditional holiday beverage made with pisco, coffee, milk and spices. In the nearby village of Diaguitas is **Cevecería Guayacán**, a highly rated craft brewery that derives most of its electricity from solar panels. It's worth stopping by for a brewery tour, tasting or lunch under the canopy in the beer garden. North of Montegrande, **Cavas del Valle** is a boutique winery that offers tours and tastings, after which you'll probably want to buy a bottle of syrah or two.

I LIVE HERE: EXPLORING BEYOND VICUÑA

Max Elicer, owner of Campo de Cielo (@campo_de_cielo_mamalluca), shares his top things to do.

Ride the railway
Cycle along the former railway line from Vicuña to Diaguitas, a village with listed adobe houses and access to the Río Elqui. Cool off in the water and eat a picnic in the shade of the willow trees.

Temple talks
The Eco Truly Hare Krishna temple opens its doors on Sundays for vegetarian food, talks and meditation.

On the trail
Hike the trail at Laguna el Cepo in Cochiguaz. You can also do the route on horseback.

Surfing
The reservoir at Pulcaro Dam is one of the best places in the world for kitesurfing and windsurfing because of the consistent wind.

 WHERE TO STAY & EAT IN GUANAQUEROS & TONGOY

Akítespero
Peaceful, self-catering apartments in Guanaqueros with terraces and sea views. **$**

La Bahía
Grab a table by the ocean for plates of scallops and sole at this restaurant in Tongoy. **$$**

El Pequeño
This Guanaqueros restaurant serves platters of crab, shrimp, scallops, seafood empanadas and freshly caught fish. **$$**

Destileria Pisco Mistral

CLOSE ENCOUNTERS IN COCHIGUAZ

The secluded area east of Montegrande along Río Cochiguaz is claimed by locals to be blessed with a powerful energy. It's easy to believe there is something special in the shimmer of quartz in the ground, the crystal-clear waters of the river, the looming presence of the mountains and the rustle of the wind in the trees. Not surprisingly, the area is popular with mystics and healers, and Cochiguaz even has a Buddhist stupa, replete with Tibetan prayer flags fluttering in the breeze. Perhaps it's not only earthlings who are drawn to the energies of Cochiguaz: several UFO sightings have been reported in the area.

In Pisco Elqui, **Destileria Pisco Mistral** is one of the region's best known and highly regarded pisco producers. Tours of the museum and distillery, which include a run-through of the distilling process, must be booked in advance (piscomistral.cl). Afterward, allow time to wander around the laid-back town and admire the pretty church before continuing south.

The family-run artisan distillery **Doña Josefa** is worth a stop for a quick tour and tasting before heading onto nearby **Fundo los Nichos**. Established in 1868, this distillery still produces pisco using traditional methods, and the tours are perhaps the most interesting of those in the Elqui Valley. They include a good explanation of the grape-harvesting and distillery process and a look around the haunted cellars, with stories of secret societies, drunk presidents and ghosts along the way. By the time the tour is over, you might need the shots of pisco included in the tasting to steady your nerves.

In the Footsteps of Gabriela Mistral

DISCOVERING THE POET'S INSPIRATION

The life and work of Nobel Prize–winning poet Gabriela Mistral (1889–1957) is celebrated at a number of sites in her natal home of Vicuña and the village of Montegrande, where she lived as a child. Buses link La Serena with Vicuña (one hour) and Montegrande (a further 40 minutes). Allow around two hours to see the sights.

In Vicuña, **Museo Gabriela Mistral** (closed Mondays) includes a reconstruction of the poet's first home. In the main gallery space, blown-up extracts of Mistral's writing adorn the walls (in Spanish only), many of them referencing the local

 WHERE TO EAT NEAR RESERVA NACIONAL PINGÜINO DE HUMBOLDT

Los Troncos
This restaurant in Los Choros village offers simple, good-value dishes, including fresh fish and empanadas. $

Costa Bahia
A good place to stop for local seafood with ocean views in Punta de Choros. $$

El Pingüino
The restaurant at Marea Alta campsite has a menu that includes vegetarian options and homemade desserts. $$

landscape. Don't miss Mistral's desk and several hand-written letters. Outside, the 'poet's garden' is a beautifully landscaped space with views of the mountains and a fragrant lavender walk accompanied by a tablet of Mistral's poem *Lavender*. It is an appealing place to linger with a volume of Mistral's work, available at the on-site bookshop.

Mistral spent most of her childhood in Montegrande. Lucila Godoy Alcayaga, as she was known before she adopted the pen name Gabriela Mistral, attended the primary school where her older sister taught. As a small child, Mistral lived with her sister and mother in the dormitory attached to the school. The building is now the small **Museo Casa-Escuela Gabriela Mistral** dedicated to the writer, who as a teenager herself began working as a teacher. Also in Montegrande is Mistral's **mausoleum**. The path to her tombstone is lined with quotes and biographical details, and it's a fitting tribute to the poet's extraordinary life.

March of the Humboldt Penguin

WILDLIFE-WATCHING BOAT TRIPS

A day trip to the **Reserva Nacional Pingüino de Humboldt** is one of Norte Chico's best excursions. Boat trips around two of the reserve's three islands leave from Punta de Choros (1½ hours by car from La Serena). The easiest way to visit is on a tour with a La Serena-based agency, such as **Eco Turismo La Serena**. It's also possible to make your own way to Punta de Choros and arrange a boat trip from there.

At **Isla de Choros**, boats pass by for wildlife viewings but are not permitted to land. You'll see groups of Humboldt penguins; massive rookeries of gulls, cormorants and boobies; and basking sea lions. It is usually possible to make a one-hour landing at nearby **Isla Damas**. Bring cash for the Conaf park fees. Interpretive trails highlight the island's unique flora and offer vistas of the turquoise waters and white-sand beaches.

The third and largest island in the reserve is **Isla Chañaral**, which can be reached on a boat trip from Caleta Chañaral de Aceituno, 25km north of Punta de Choros. From December through March, there is a good chance of spotting whales in this stretch of water.

The drive from La Serena to Punta de Choros takes in some spectacular coastal views and desert landscapes. Keep your eyes peeled for guanacos near Quebrada Honda. Twenty kilometers east of Punta de Choros, the village of **Los Choros** is a good place to stop for lunch. Try locally grown olives and take a look at **Iglesia de San José**, built in 1600.

WILDLIFE-WATCHING IN THE HUMBOLDT ARCHIPELAGO

Humboldt penguin
The stars of the show can be seen waddling around Isla Choros.

Pelican
These large birds are easy to spot.

Red-legged cormorant
Often found in pairs on Isla Choros.

Sea lion
Look out for them basking on rocks.

Bottlenose dolphin
Pods often splash alongside boats.

Marine otters
These small mammals like to hide in rocks and crevices.

Humpback whale
If you're lucky you might spot these whales between December and March.

GETTING AROUND

Frequent buses connect La Serena with Vicuña, Montegrande and Pisco Elqui. Buses also run along the coast from La Serena to Coquimbo and Tongoy. The best way to reach Parque Nacional Bosque Fray Jorge and Reserva Nacional Pingüino de Humboldt is by car or by joining a tour from La Serena.

CALDERA

Caldera

☆ Santiago

Though nomadic groups had lived along this stretch of coast for thousands of years, Caldera's origins as a port city are strongly connected to the 19th-century mining boom. In 1849, the bay was identified by Massachusetts-born William Wheelwright as the site of a railway to transport minerals for export from the mines of Copiapó, transforming Caldera into an important mining port. Though the railway is now obsolete, the port continues to be used for copper exports. Caldera also has a thriving fishing industry.

Caldera is an easygoing place, with a sunny climate and neat rows of well-kept single-story houses with cacti growing in the front yards. During the summer months, the atmosphere changes as Chileans arrive for beach vacations and bars blare out music late into the night. Though Caldera has a beach, the white sands and clear sea of neighboring Bahía Inglesa are more beautiful.

TOP TIP

Many visitors prefer the beaches, restaurants and bars of neighboring Bahía Inglesa to those in Caldera. However, if you are on a tight budget, it might be cheaper to stay in Caldera and spend your days on the beach in Bahía Inglesa.

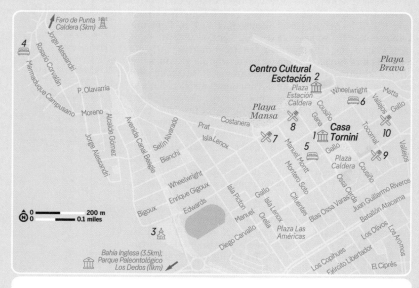

HIGHLIGHTS	SIGHTS	SLEEPING	EATING
1 Casa Tornini	**3** Gruta del Padre Negro	**4** Hostal El Faro	**7** Big Bang Caldera
2 Centro Cultural Esctación		**5** Hotel Costa Fósil	**see 1** Caffe Museo
		6 Hotel Quinta Estación	**10** El Cafe de Wheelwright
			8 Kavana Restobar
			9 Vecino Otto

BERNAT MATEU SALAT/SHUTTERSTOCK ©

Faro de Punta Caldera

Historic Caldera

ARCHITECTURE AND TRAINS

Book a tour of **Casa Tornini**, a red neoclassical mansion
built in 1875 as the home of American railway administrator
Thomas Smith and later acquired by Italian Bernardo Tornini Capelli. Tours of rooms with period furniture are led by
Capelli's great-grandson, who himself grew up in the house,
and offer a personal telling of local history.

Nearby is **Centro Cultural Esctación**. Built in 1850, the
beamed building was the terminus for South America's first
railroad, a great source of pride in Caldera. Today it houses
a paleontology museum, where you can see locally found fossils, and an exhibition space.

To the Lighthouse

BIRD-WATCHING AT CALDERA'S FARO

At the tip of Punta de Caldera, 5km northwest of Caldera's
main square, the red and white clapperboard **Faro de Punta
Caldera** sits perched on the rocks, surrounded by seabirds.
It's possible to cycle here, but be prepared for some steep
hills. Along the eastern side of the peninsula, the road to the
lighthouse offers good views of the colorful Caldera seafront

BEST RESTAURANTS IN CALDERA

Caffe Museo
Adjoining Casa
Tornini, this cafe
serves espresso
coffee, sandwiches
and cakes. $

Big Bang Caldera
Buzzy restaurant
where the quality of
the food and cocktails
is matched by stylish
decor. $$$

**El Cafe de
Wheelwright**
Located in a historic
building, this cafe,
restaurant and bar has
a counter loaded with
cakes. $$

Vecino Otto
Neighborhood
restaurant serving
generous portions
of grilled meats and
casseroles. $

Kavana Restobar
Friendly pub with
beers on tap and
a menu of fajitas,
burgers and bar
snacks. $$

 WHERE TO STAY IN CALDERA

Hostal El Faro
Located 2km west of town, this
cheery guesthouse offers sea
views and a small pool. $

Hotel Costa Fósil
Centrally located hotel with
friendly staff, breezy patios
and comfortable rooms. $$

Hotel Quinta Estación
Good breakfasts, spotless
rooms and a central location
make this hotel a top choice.
$$

22

THE GUIDE

NORTE CHICO

143

and port. On the final approach to the Faro, there is a sense
of isolation as an empty stretch of coast comes into view.

Built in 1868 from Oregon pine, the lighthouse is unusual because the building itself was designed to rotate (it is no
longer operational). It's a spot where you might want to linger amid the crashing waves and squawking seabirds. Look
out for pelicans, cormorants, boobies and gulls.

Cycling Along the Coast

BEACHES, DESERT AND DINOSAURS

Cycling is a fun way to explore the coast from Caldera to Bahía
Inglesa and beyond. Allow at least three hours to cycle to the
Parque Paleontológico and back, with stops.

The cycle path starts west of town, at the roundabout on
Carvallo. Before setting off toward Bahía Inglesa, look inside
Gruta del Padre Negro, an unusual church on Av Canal Beagle. The grotto-like stone building was constructed in 1940,
and the internal murals were added in 1978.

The coastal views along the 6km stretch of cycle path are
unspectacular, but after turning off the main road to reach
the beach (follow signs), the white sands and turquoise waters
of Bahía Inglesa come into view. There are plenty of restaurants where you can stop for lunch.

Continue along Av El Morro and pick up the cycle path along
Playa Las Machas. When the cycle path ends at the southern part of the beach, return to the main coastal road and cycle south for 7km, with the ocean on your right and the vast
empty sand dunes of the Atacama Desert to your left. Soon
you'll reach **Parque Paleontológico Los Dedos**, an open-
air fossil museum.

Park your bike at the entrance and take the 500m interpretative trail across the dunes. Along the way, you can
see the fossils of extinct mammals discovered at the
site, including gavialis, an extinct crocodile; mega-
lodon (or carcharodon), 15m-long mega sharks; ac-
rophoca, an ancestor of the seal; and the Caldera
penguin, which lived in the area some nine million
years ago. The site is named Los Dedos (the fingers) because the mounds of sand look like fingers.

GETTING AROUND

Caldera is easy to navigate on foot. Shared
taxis operate between Caldera and Bahía
Inglesa. You can also reach Bahía Inglesa
by bike on the cycle path. Tiska Bicicletas in
Caldera rents bikes. Buses run throughout the
day to Copiapó (one hour), which is a major

transport hub with bus connections north
and south. Long-distance buses from Caldera
are less frequent. Aeropuerto Desierto de
Atacama, 25km south of Caldera, has several
flights a day to Santiago.

Beyond Caldera

Parque Nacional
Pan de Azúcar

Parque Nacional
Nevado Tres Cruces

Bahía
Inglesa ● **Caldera**

Playa
La Virgen

Parque Nacional
Llanos de Challe

From pristine coast to vast expanses of desert
to Chile's highest peak, Caldera is surrounded by
diverse landscapes.

Caldera is 75km east of the regional capital, Copiapó, a pleasant city with some historic buildings. It was the 18th-century gold boom that led to the 1851 inauguration of South America's first railroad linking Copiapó with the port of Caldera. Today it is copper mining that brings jobs to the area. Located nearby is Mina San José, the former mine where 33 trapped workers were miraculously rescued in 2010.

Beyond the region's mining connections, there is great natural beauty to be discovered in the white sands of the coast and the majestic Andean mountains in the east. In certain years, the barren desert between them bursts into bloom, and the sand is carpeted with wildflowers.

TOP TIP

If you plan to visit the mountains, come prepared for daytime heat on the coast and cold Andean nights.

Corona de fraile (monk's crown; p148)

ABRIENDOMUNDO/SHUTTERSTOCK ©

145

THE PIRATES OF BAHÍA INGLESA

Bahía Inglesa (English Bay) takes its name from the British pirates who were seen in the area in the 17th century. Local legend has it that there is hidden treasure somewhere in the bay. In 1687, the pirate Edward Davis left his boat anchored offshore and spent almost a week in Bahía Inglesa. The length of his stay raised suspicions that he was looking for items he had buried nearby, without success.

Fox, Parque Nacional Pan de Azúcar

The Pristine Beaches of Bahía Inglesa

WHITE SAND AND TURQUOISE SEA

The rocky outcrops, crystal waters and white sands of **Bahía Inglesa** make it an idyllic vacationing spot. The best way to enjoy the chilled vibe of this charming resort is to lounge on the beach, take dips in the sea, and sip cocktails and eat seafood in the bay's fashionable bars and restaurants.

Huts at the beach rent out stand-up paddleboards and kayaks, and there are spots for diving and snorkeling around the bay. At **Playa Las Machas**, there are swings and dinosaur-themed children's play equipment, as well as ping-pong tables, volleyball courts, boardwalks and cycling trails.

THE COAST BY BIKE

A 6km cycle trail links Caldera with Bahía Inglesa. **Parque Paleontológico Los Dedos** (p144) is a further 7km south along the coastal road, in the direction of Playa La Virgen.

Coastal Road to Playa La Virgen

A SLICE OF PARADISE

From Bahía Inglesa, follow the coastal road 46km south to reach **Playa La Virgen**, a pristine white-sand beach resort which is considered one of Chile's most beautiful bays. En route, **Playa Chorrillos** is a good place to stop for a walk along a trail over the rocks and down to the beach. Further along the

WHERE TO STAY IN BAHÍA INGLESA

Nautel
Contemporary guesthouse by the beach with appealing patio spaces for lounging and an outdoor kitchen. **$$**

Coral de Bahía
In a prime location overlooking the beach, this chic hotel books up fast in summer. **$$$**

Hotel Rocas de Bahía
This hotel offers spacious rooms decorated with geometric designs, ocean-view balconies and a small pool. **$$$**

coast, the road passes the quiet beach at **Bahía Cisne**, the striking sandstone cliffs of **Salto del Gato** and the wetlands of the **Humedalas Salinas** at the mouth of the Copiapó River.

The drive from Caldera takes around one hour. If you have a car, it's an easy day trip. There are also cabins and a campsite at the beach for overnight stays. Tour agencies offer trips that highlight sights along the way.

Remembering the Miners' Rescue

MISSION TO SAVE THE 33

For 121 years, workers at **Mina San José**, 40km east of Caldera, went about their business of digging for copper deep in the Atacama Desert. But on the afternoon of August 5, 2010, disaster struck, and a cave-in trapped 33 miners 700m underground. The subsequent rescue mission was televised around the world, as the Chilean government, which took control of the rescue, oversaw the involvement of international drilling teams and experts from NASA. Finally, more than two months after the accident on October 13, 2010, an estimated audience of one billion viewers watched as the men were finally hoisted to freedom through a narrow shaft.

Following the accident, the mine ceased operation, but it reopened to visitors in 2015. A trip to the site (30 minutes by car from Caldera) is a moving experience. At the entrance are 33 flags (one for each of the miners, including one Bolivian). It was here that the miners' families and supporters set up camp and kept a round-the-clock vigil until the miners were rescued. Overlooking the mine is a small museum, with photographs, videos and a timeline of the rescue. Jorge Galleguillos, one of the 33 trapped miners, is usually at the museum to introduce visitors to the site and point out where the rescue mission took place.

In Copiapó (a 45-minute drive south of Mina San José), the specially built rescue capsule, in which the miners were raised up one by one, is displayed in the courtyard of the **Museo Regional de Atacama**. In the museum's mining gallery, look for the note that let the world know the miners were alive. It reads '*Estamos bien en el refugio los 33*' (We are fine in the shelter, the 33 of us).

Exploring Parque Nacional Pan de Azúcar

HIKING, BEACHES AND WILDLIFE-WATCHING

The white-sand beaches, hiking trails and fabulous flora, fauna and marine life of **Parque Nacional Pan de Azúcar** make it

I LIVE HERE: EXCURSIONS FROM CALDERA

Yerko Invernizzi of Thaqhiri Tour Atacama (@thaqhiri_tour_atacama) shares his tips on adventures from Caldera.

Orbicular Granite This nature sanctuary, 12km north of Caldera, is a stretch of beach with extremely rare formations of tonalite, created near the Earth's core and brought to the surface by tectonic movement.

Zoológico de Piedras 'Stone Zoo' is 3km further north. Over the years, wind and rain have eroded the sandstone to form what appear to be animal figures, depending on your imagination.

Termas de Juncal My favorite excursion is to these hot springs in the mountains where it's possible to bathe. Just getting there is an adventure, driving through rivers and passing waterfalls and sand dunes along the way.

 WHERE TO EAT IN BAHÍA INGLESA

Ostiones Vivos Right on the beach, this seafood shack serves plates of delectably fresh scallops (*ostiones*). $

Punto de Referencía A block from the waterfront, this cozy restaurant specializes in seafood, sushi and sashimi. $$

Coral Restaurant This restaurant at Coral de Bahía is perfect for ceviche and a glass of wine. $$$

MORNING SEA FOG

The *camanchaca* is a mist that drifts over coastal areas of northern Chile from the Pacific Ocean. When the cool ocean air – a result of the Humboldt current – meets the warm desert air, it rises and gets trapped against the hills, causing it to condense into a thick fog. It is this phenomenon that maintains the aridity of the Atacama Desert. An innovative solution to water scarcity in the region involves the collection of the *camanchaca*'s minute droplets using special mesh nets. You can see them on the hillsides north of Chañaral on the way to Pan de Azucar. At the Atrapaniebla craft brewery, water collected using fog catchers is used to make beer.

an appealing place to get back to nature. The park has several hiking trails. The starting point for the popular 2.5km **Mirador Grande** route is a 4km drive (or walk) from the Caleta, the area of the park with seafood restaurants and a pier. The views from the Mirador Grande are spectacular. Look out for guanacos and foxes along the way. If you don't have a vehicle and are happy to hike for longer, you can follow the quieter 11km **Mirador Chico** trail through cactus-strewn landscapes to a slightly lower viewpoint, where the views are no less rewarding.

The 5km **Aguada los Sapos** is a good coastal route for observing the desert flora, and the 4km **Las Lomitas** trail covers an inland area of rolling hills.

A short distance offshore, **Isla Pan de Azucar** is home to Humboldt penguins, sea lions and marine otters. Boat trips offer the chance to view the island's marine life up close. Launches leave from the pier when there are enough passengers to make the trip worthwhile.

It's possible to visit on a day trip from Caldera (1½ hours by car), but campsites and cabins are available for overnight stays. Register for park admission online in advance on the Conaf website (conaf.cl).

The Desert in Bloom

WILDFLOWERS IN THE SAND

In some years, an astonishing transformation takes place in Norte Chico's barren desert. If there has been heavy rainfall, the parched land erupts into a multicolored carpet of wildflowers, a phenomenon known as the *desierto florido* (the flowering desert). It usually occurs between July and September in wetter years. Look for *garra de león* (lion's claw), *suspiro de campo* (sigh of the field; a delicate white or purple flower), *pata de guanaco* (guanaco's hoof; a bright purple flower) and the yellow *corona de fraile* (monk's crown).

The flowers of the blooming desert can be seen in various places, though it's difficult to predict ahead of time whether the phenomenon will occur in any given year. One of the best spots is **Parque Nacional Llanos de Challe**, an isolated national park two hours drive south of Caldera, reachable only by car or tour.

Remote Mountain Lakes

VOLCANOES, FLAMINGOS AND SALT FLATS

High in the Andes, **Parque Nacional Nevado Tres Cruces** is hard to reach, but those who make the effort rave about its rugged beauty and solitude. The park is divided into two sec-

WHERE TO STAY & EAT IN COPIAPÓ

Cumbres de Atacama
A spotless hotel with spacious rooms, located within walking distance of the main plaza. **$$**

Aji Rocoto
This excellent Peruvian restaurant with a cheery patio is almost reason enough to visit Copiapó. **$$**

Legado
High-end restaurant serving grilled steaks, seafood risottos and creatively plated desserts. **$$$**

Salar de Pedernales

THE WORLD'S HIGHEST VOLCANO

Chile's highest peak is **Ojos del Salado**, close to Parque Nacional Nevado Tres Cruces at the border with Argentina. At 6893m, it is the second-highest peak in South America, after Aconcagua in Argentina, and the highest volcano in the world. It is possible to climb Ojos del Salado between November and March. The climb is not technically difficult, apart from the tricky final ascent, but the altitude makes it challenging. It is important to allow plenty of time to acclimatize before attempting to reach the summit. Agencies in Copiapó and Santiago run expeditions, which usually begin near Laguna Santa Rosa at 3600m.

tors: the larger Sector Laguna Santa Rosa, which includes the lake and the Salar de Maricunga salt flat, and the smaller Sector Laguna del Negro Francisco, where the lake attracts thousands of birds in the summer. Look out for Andean flamingos, Chilean flamingos and even a few James' flamingos. You'll also see vicuñas and guanacos roaming the nearby slopes.

Sector Santa Rosa is 150km east of Copiapó (230km east of Caldera), and Sector del Negro Francisco is a further 80km. Sector Santa Rosa has a campsite and cabins. It's easy to get lost on the rough, unmarked mountain roads, so consider taking a tour from Caldera or Copiapó. Multiday trips might include a visit to the beautiful **Salar de Pedernales**, a salt flat north of the park that's often visited by Andean flamingos.

GETTING AROUND

Most excursions from Caldera are tricky without a car. For short trips along the coast, consider renting a bicycle. If you don't have your own vehicle, you can reach Parque Nacional Pan de Azucar by taking a bus to Chañaral and a taxi from there to the park.

Arrange for the taxi driver to come back and pick you up. Alternatively, tour agencies in Caldera offer trips to Pan de Azucar, Parque Nacional Nevado Tres Cruces, Mina San José and Playa La Virgen.

Above: Colchagua Valley (p175); right: Surfing, Punta de Lobos (p179)

MIDDLE CHILE

SURF, SKI AND SAVOR WINE

From the disparate sister cities of Viña and Valparaíso to ritzy coastal enclaves, sun-kissed vinelands and high Andean resorts, Middle Chile pleases all tastes.

If you love wine, fine dining, never-ending springs, street art, clubbing, skiing, hiking, mountain biking, surfing or just lazing for days on wild coastlines, you're in luck. Middle Chile has a spot for all of these things and more.

Comparisons to the Mediterranean are obvious in both the climate and look of the region, with sun-kissed farmlands, rolling hills and rocky coastlines dotted with sandy beaches. It's also Chile's most important wine-producing area, and the vineyards and cozy bed and breakfasts of the Colchagua, Casablanca, Maule and Itata valleys will tickle your palate and enliven your senses.

Board riders find killer breaks up and down the coast, with surf culture exploding in towns like Maitencillo, Pichilemu, Matanzas and Cobquecura. Hikers and skiers love the lost lagoons and steep pistes found eastward in the Andes, while cultural explorers won't want to miss the hard-rocking musical exploits of Concepción and the murals and jumbled alleyways of Valparaíso.

The latter – alongside Santa Cruz in the Colchagua Valley – is plainly on the global travel circuit. Yet remarkably, given how close Middle Chile is to Santiago, much of it actually sees far fewer international visitors than you'll find in Patagonia or the Atacama.

Whether you're headed to the sea, summits or sunny central valleys, opportunities for getting lost in the bucolic Chilean countryside are everywhere.

THE MAIN AREAS

VALPARAÍSO	**VIÑA DEL MAR**	**SANTA CRUZ**	**COBQUECURA**	**TERMAS DE CHILLÁN**
Art-fueled bohemia. **p156**	Ritzy city by the sea. **p166**	Wines, vines and restaurants. **p173**	Surf, sand and sea lions. **p181**	Skiing down and hiking up volcanoes. **p189**

Find Your Way

Middle Chile is a vast region at the heart of the nation. Home to 75% of Chile's population, this area has excellent infrastructure for travel by car and public transport.

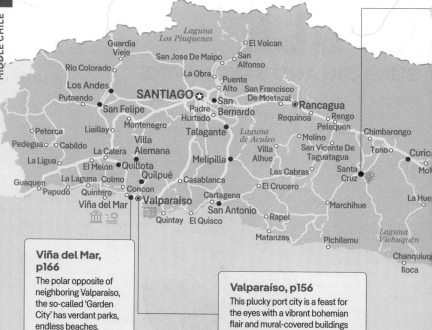

Viña del Mar, p166

The polar opposite of neighboring Valparaíso, the so-called 'Garden City' has verdant parks, endless beaches, manicured streets and excellent museums.

Valparaíso, p156

This plucky port city is a feast for the eyes with a vibrant bohemian flair and mural-covered buildings tumbling down its 42 hills.

CAR

A car is unnecessary in Viña del Mar and Valparaíso, but to reach the national parks in the Andes or to tour rural vineyards on your own, there really is no substitute. Bring cash for frequent tolls on Ruta 5 and other highways.

BUS

Bus travel in Middle Chile tends to involve hubs and spokes, particularly when heading south, where you may have to transfer in cities on Ruta 5 to reach your final destination. Coastal towns just north and south of Valparaíso are well connected by public transport.

TRAIN

One of the only trains still operating in Chile travels south from Santiago to Chillán, stopping in cities such as San Fernando, Curicó and Talca. Transfer to buses to reach destinations in the Andes or on the coast.

Santa Cruz, p173

Epicenter of Chile's fine wine industry, this attractive city with stylish hotels and restaurants is the launchpad for tastings or tours in Colchagua Valley.

Termas de Chillán, p189

Skiers flock here each winter to carve turns before bathing in thermal pools, while summers are all about hiking and biking below puffing volcanoes.

Laguna Llancanelo

alargue

Laguna del Maule

Chos Malal

ARGENTINA

Laguna de la Laja

San Clemente

Linares

San Blas   San Gregorio   Cato

lca   San Javier

Parral

Coihueco

Los Rastrojos   Antuco

San Carlos

Pinto   Yungay   Huepil

Río Ñuble   Termas de Chillán

Verquico   Chillán   Pemuco   Canteras

Campanario   Humano   Los Ángeles   Mulchen

San Nicolas   Bulnes

Cauquenes   Santa Juana

Cambrero   Puente Perales   El Parron   Ercilla   Victoria

nstitucion   Cancha Alegre   Quirihue

El Milagro   Tomeco   Yumbel   Nacimiento

Illoquilque

Loanco   Coelemu   Florida   Rere   San Rosendo   Santa Lucia   Angol

Cobquecura   Rafael   Roa   Laja

Dichato   Coihue   San Jeronimo

Boca De Itata   Tome   Chiguayante

Concepción   Poico Chico   Don Alfonso   Pillimpilli   Colonia Alemana

Talcahuano   Coronel   San Jose De Colico   Cayucupil   Los Notros   *Laguna Puyehue*

Canete   Pehuen   Quidico

Aguapie   Frutillar

Lebu

Río Biobío

Cobquecura, p181

This charming coastal hamlet draws lovers of big waves, leisurely beach strolls, paddles through bird-filled estuaries and golden sunsets over the Pacific.

PACIFIC OCEAN

0 ——— 100 km
0 ——— 50 miles

TOP: MICHELEPAUTASSO/SHUTTERSTOCK ©, BOTTOM: RALF LIEBHOLD/SHUTTERSTOCK ©

Plan Your Time

Pick your passion: Where to spend your time depends on whether you prefer vibrant city life, bucolic winelands, mountain trails or long, lazy dinners by the beach.

SKREIDZELEU/SHUTTERSTOCK ©

Valparaíso (p156)

Three Days to Travel Around

● Head straight to the coast, choosing either bohemian **Valparaíso** (p156) or put-together **Viña del Mar** (p166) as your base. No matter where you sleep, you can easily explore both cities. Spend the first day wandering the streets of Valparaíso, exploring the prismatic murals of **Cerro Alegre** and **Cerro Concepción** (p157) before touring **La Sebastiana** (p160), the whimsical home of poet Pablo Neruda. Afterward, hit up the museums, parks and wide beaches of Viña.

● On your third day, take a day trip along the coast, either south to quiet coves like **Quintay** (p164) or north to beaches such as **Maitencillo** (p171) and **Zapallar** (p171).

Seasonal Highlights

High season is summer on the coast and winter at Andean towns with ski resorts. The shoulder seasons are most ideal for hiking and wine tasting.

JANUARY
Tiny Olmué is immersed in folk music during **Festival del Huaso de Olmué** against the backdrop of Parque Nacional La Campana.

FEBRUARY
The lavish **Festival de Viña del Mar** draws top musicians from across Latin America to Viña's Quinta Vergara.

APRIL
Late March and early April are harvest season in the wine valleys, and celebrations include the **Fiesta de la Vendimia Colchagua**.

DIEGO SUGONIAEV/SHUTTERSTOCK ©, NICOLAS LISPERGUIER/SHUTTERSTOCK ©, JOSE LUIS STEPHENS/SHUTTERSTOCK ©

Middle Chile in a Week

● Add on time for wine tasting in the white-heavy **Casablanca Valley** (p163) or red-heavy **Colchagua Valley** (p175), using **Santa Cruz** (p173) as a base for the latter. Don't miss standout wineries like Viña MontGras and Viña Vik.

● Tasting complete, pick between the surf towns of **Pichilemu** (p179), a classic backpacker hub, or quieter and ritzier **Matanzas** (p165). Both have top-class dining and lodging.

● On your last day, swap the coast for the Andes, heading to a park like **Altos de Lircay** (p180), whose forested hills hold one of the region's best day hikes, Sendero Enladrillado.

If You Have More Time

● Continue south to explore the Andean playground of **Termas de Chillán** (p189). In winter, hit the slopes at **Nevados de Chillán** (p190). In summer, mountain bike down those same slopes or hike up to **Laguna del Huemul** (p191). Nearby **Laguna del Laja** (p193) has a cartoonishly conical volcano, plus more hiking and skiing.

● Down by the coast, finish up your trip to Middle Chile at **Cobquecura** (p181), a calm surf town with giant caves, ample wildlife watching and high-quality dining and lodging options. Travel from here to the **Itata Valley** (p187) for more wine-tasting or **Concepción** (p188) for another dose of culture.

JUNE

Fishing hamlets across the region celebrate the **Fiesta de San Pedro** with grand processions and decorated boats.

JULY

Ski season kicks into full gear at resorts like Nevados de Chillán as snowfall blankets the Andes.

SEPTEMBER

The **Fiestas Patrias** celebrations in Valparaíso are a wild affair with dancing, drag queens and bands galore.

DECEMBER

Nowhere in Chile goes as all out for **New Year's Eve** as Viña and Valparaíso, with fireworks exploding over the Pacific.

155

VALPARAÍSO

Syncopated, dilapidated, colorful and poetic, Valparaíso is a wonderful mess. Pablo Neruda, who drew much inspiration from this hard-working port town, said it best: 'Valparaíso, how absurd you are...you haven't combed your hair, you've never had time to get dressed, life has always surprised you.' Yet the Nobel Prize–winning poet wasn't the only artist to fall for Valparaíso's quixotic charms.

Painters, photographers and would-be philosophers have long been drawn to Chile's most unusual city. Along with the ever-shifting port population of sailors, dockworkers and sex workers, they've endowed gritty and gloriously spontaneous Valpo (as locals call it) with an edgy air of 'anything goes.' Add to this the spectacular faded beauty of its chaotic *cerros* (hills), some of the best street art in Latin America, a maze of steep, sinuous alleys and *escaleras* (stairways) piled high with crumbling mansions, and it's clear why some visitors spend more time here than in Santiago.

TOP TIP

Valparaíso has a reputation for being less safe than other Chilean cities. While the touristed hills (Alegre, Concepción, Carcel, Bellavista and Florida) see less petty crime, you should nevertheless be aware of your surroundings, particularly at night, and refrain from flashing any valuables. Savvy travelers will be just fine.

Valparaíso

JOHN W BANAGAN/GETTY IMAGES ©

BEST ART GALLERIES IN VALPARAÍSO

Bahía Utópica
This esteemed gallery sells the works of renowned local artists, including singer Mon Laferte and a large collection from Valpo's famed chronicler Loro Coirón.

Galería Artemark Online
A relative newcomer, it stages fresh exhibitions every month or so and has made a name for itself with its refined tastes.

Galería Espacio Rojo
Near Palacio Baburizza, this gallery has an eclectic collection of higher-end local art – some from big names – mixed in with kitschy souvenirs.

Art on Cerros Alegre & Concepción

EXPERIENCE AN OPEN-AIR MUSEUM

The mural-covered facades of **Cerro Alegre** and **Cerro Concepción** are an ever-changing canvas and undeniably Valparaíso's most seductive draw. Begin a prismatic walking tour at the top of **Ascensor El Peral**, where you'll find the rambling art nouveau **Palacio Baburizza**, which houses the city's fine arts museum. Continue across Paseo Yugoslavo and down Alvaro Besa until you reach **Paseo Gálvez**, a twisting alley blanketed in a kaleidoscope of competing colors and ideas. It's not uncommon to find muralists at work.

Several spectacular promenades split up the walk as you look out over the city from **Paseo Gervasoni** (where you can find a tourist information center) and **Paseo Atkinson**. Head down Beethoven from the latter to the aptly named **Escalera Piano** ('Piano Stairs') and then work your way over to Templeman, climbing uphill to the famous **We Are Not Hippies, We Are Happies** mural by Art+Believe. Nearby, on the gallery-lined Lautaro Rosas, is the **Museo Universitario del Grabado**, dedicated to Chilean printmaking. You'll find works by big names like Mario Toral, Roberto Matta and Beatriz Leyton.

Though works come and go, look out for local muralists such as Inti Castro, Anis and Un Kolor Distinto. For added context, sign up for an outing with **Valpo Street Art Tours**.

Strolling Plaza Sotomayor & El Plan

DISCOVER VALPARAÍSO'S FORMER GLORY

The flat strip of land between the ocean and hills is known as **El Plan**, and it contains nearly all of the city's public and commercial buildings. This area is a bit rough around the edges, but the crumbling grandeur of its historic edifices hints at how rich this port was until the Panama Canal stripped Valparaíso of its importance. Many of the graffiti-covered bank buildings are stunning when you pop inside to withdraw cash.

El Plan is divided into two sectors: **Barrio Puerto** and **El Almendral**. Focus your time on the former, beginning at **Plaza Sotomayor**, which is dominated by the periwinkle Renaissance Revival–style **Edificio Armada de Chile**. Directly in front of this navy-owned building is the **Monumento a Los Héroes de Iquique**, a grand monument dedicated to fallen sailors from the War of the Pacific. The plaza is typically packed with craft vendors, especially when a cruise ship is in town. Be careful of thru-traffic (including cars and buses) when walking.

Head from Plaza Sotomayor toward the ocean to reach **Muelle Prat**, a small harborside promenade where hawkers compete

WHERE HAVE ALL THE FUNICULARS GONE?

Riding up and down the *ascensores* (funiculars) and gazing across the jumbled hills of Valparaíso is one of the city's greatest joys. But of the 30 *ascensores* that once operated, only 16 remain. Of those, just five were working at the time of research (Polanco, San Agustín, El Peral, Reina Victoria and Barón). Ten others have been closed for more than a decade since the government purchased them in 2012. Some of the promised renovations haven't materialized. Others are years behind schedule, leaving both residents furious and tourists without easy access to some of the city's most important sites.

 WHERE TO EAT IN VALPARAÍSO

María María
This bakery's perennial waitlist speaks to the greatness of its sweets, coffees and brunches. **$**

La Caperucita y el Lobo
Valpo's reigning high-end dining experience, with beautifully plated dishes, solid service and inventive flavors. **$$$**

Circular
This seafood restaurant is so panoramic it feels like it's floating above the city. **$$**

HIGHLIGHTS
1 Escalera Piano
2 Parque Cultural de Valparaíso
3 Paseo Atkinson
4 Paseo Gálvez
5 Paseo Gervasoni
6 We Are Not Hippies, We Are Happies

SIGHTS
7 Ascensor El Peral
8 Ascensor Espíritu Santo
9 Bahía Utópica
10 Catedral de Valparaíso
11 Cerro Bellavista
12 Edificio Armada de Chile
13 Galería Artemark Online
14 Galería Espacio Rojo
15 Mercado Puerto
16 Monumento a Los Héroes de Iquique
17 Muelle Prat
18 Museo a Cielo Abierto
19 Museo Universitario del Grabado
20 Palacio Baburizza
21 Plaza Sotomayor
22 Plaza Victoria

SLEEPING
23 Fauna Hotel
24 Maki Hostel

EATING
25 Circular
26 La Caperucita y el Lobo
27 María María

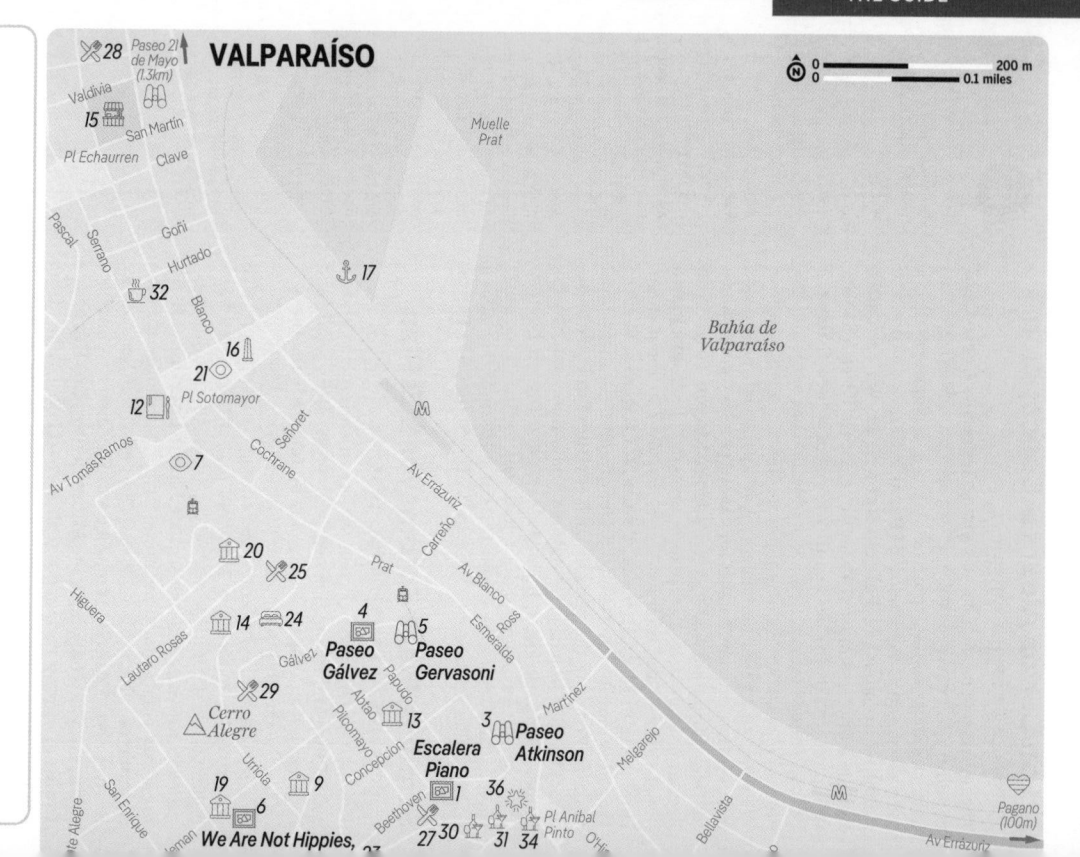

VALPARAÍSO

Yungay

 10

Av Pedro Montt

Independéncia

San Pedro (85km)

Pl Simón Bolívar

◎ 22

Chacabuco

La Espańita (650m)

Lira

Av Colón

Carrera

Lastra

E Ramírez

Condell

Huito

Aldunate

8

Edwards

San Pedro

✗ 26

Winebox (120m)

Av Baquedano

Verso Restaurante (50m); La Sebastiana (200m)

Mena

⚂ Cerro La Florida

Rudolph

Bernardo Ramos

18

△ Cerro Bellavista

Av Ramos

Ricardo Ferari

11

Calvo

Av Yerbas Buenas

Pirámide

Mackenna

Subida Ecuador

Pl Yungay

Cementerio Católico

Cementerio de Disidentes

△ Cerro Cárcel

Parque Cultural de Valparaíso ◎ 2

Cumming

Av Equador

☾ 35

△ Cerro San Juan de Dios

Newman

Pl Bismark

Elías

Atahualpa

28 Porto di Vino
29 Ropa Tendida Bar y Cocina

DRINKING & NIGHTLIFE
30 Bar del Tío
31 Bar Ritual
32 Callejón Café
33 Casa Cervecera Altamira
34 Cinzano

ENTERTAINMENT
35 La Quinta de los Nuñez
36 Máscara

Ascensore (funicular; p157)

Plaza Sotomayor (p157)

DIEGO GRANDI/SHUTTERSTOCK ©

CULTURE ON 'PRISON HILL'

Cerro Cárcel's **Parque Cultural Valparaíso** is one of the city's most ingenious creations: a striking cultural center built from the bones of a *cárcel* (prison) where dissidents were tortured during the dictatorship. Formerly a place of exclusion, it's now all about inclusion in the art, theater, music and dance found in both the main building and the center for innovation on the far side of a buzzing park. Also on this hill is **La Quinta de los Nuñez**, a clandestine folk venue that opens on Sundays for an unforgettable afternoon filled with cueca, tango and bolero music. It is a quintessential Valpo experience – and you'll likely be the only foreign visitor in the crowd.

to sell cheap **boat trips** past cranes, containers and sundry naval vessels out to spot frolicking sea lions. Walk north from the plaza and you'll enter the historic heart of gritty Barrio Puerto, which has gotten a slight facelift with some great third-wave coffee shops, such as **Callejón Café**, and wine-led restaurants like **Porto di Vino**. At the revived **Mercado Puerto**, you'll find veggies sold alongside handmade souvenirs and even garage wines. From Plaza Aduana, you can make the long walk up **Cerro Artillería** past its closed *ascensor* (funicular) to **Paseo 21 de Mayo** for sweeping views over everything you've just explored.

Descending Cerros Bellavista & Florida

PABLO NERUDA'S VALPO

Cerro Florida became one of Valparaíso's most iconic hills the day Nobel Prize–winning poet Pablo Neruda moved into the house known as **La Sebastiana** in 1961. Today, you can wander around the five floors, taking in the heart-stopping views over the harbor while ogling the late writer's vast collection of global curios, including a carousel horse from Spain, a

 WHERE TO STAY IN VALPARAÍSO

Fauna Hotel
An architectural stunner with calming wood-paneled rooms and a fabulous restaurant for sundowners. **$$$**

Winebox
This wildly inventive container hotel on Cerro Florida is also Chile's first urban winery. **$$**

Maki Hostel
This solidly run hostel has spacious dorms and even nicer private rooms at an unbeatable price. **$**

cow-shaped punch bowl from Italy and an embalmed scarlet ibis from Venezuela. As the accompanying audio guide notes, Neruda built his house as a toy so he could play with it from morning to night. Visiting this enchanting property offers a fascinating peek into his playful mind.

Around the corner from La Sebastiana is **Verso Restaurante**, whose artfully plated dishes and intriguing flavor combinations make an excellent follow-up. Of the many lunch options around, this restaurant is the best. Continue downhill and you'll drop into **Cerro Bellavista**, full of vibrant murals and mosaics. Unfortunately, the works from famous Chilean artists that line the **Museo a Cielo Abierto** ('Open Air Museum,' formerly the neighborhood's top attraction) have fallen into disrepair. The surrounding area is nevertheless hopping with some great restaurants and cafes. **Ascensor Espíritu Santo** takes you from here to just behind **Plaza Victoria**, a palm-shaded square lined with historic buildings, including Valparaíso's stoic **cathedral**.

Valparaíso After Dark

A NIGHT ON THE TOWN

Generations of Chileans have flocked to Valparaíso for one purpose: to dance the night away at one of its legendarily wild nightclubs, where the city's anything-goes attitude is on full display. Don't even dream of arriving before midnight or you'll be the only one on the dance floor. Instead, start the night off in one of the city's stellar bars. **Casa Cervecera Altamira** has an excellent spread of hazy IPAs and dry stouts alongside filling pub grub. For something stronger, **Bar del Tío** has the most imaginative (and ridiculously good-value) craft cocktails served in a sexy setting with mood-setting tunes. If you can't get in (it's absolutely packed on weekends), head across the street to **Bar Ritual**, a funky classic known for its cheap and potent pisco sours.

Where you go next depends on what kind of a night you want. For something classic, head to the city's oldest nightspot, **Cinzano**, which draws in salty sailors for traditional Chilean folk music. Nearby, **Máscara** blasts disco, new wave, divas and Britpop (a Chilean obsession) across two dance floors filled with an edgy crowd in their 20s and 30s. Though Máscara is very gay-friendly, many in the LGBTIQ+ community eventually make their way to **Pagano** for no-holds-barred fun, including wild drag shows. Other nightlife spots come and go, but these three never die.

I LIVE HERE: WHERE TO EAT LIKE A LOCAL

Marcelo del Pino, a local bartender, DJ and hospitality consultant, shares his favorite under-the-radar spots.

La Españita
This classic *fuente de soda* (neighborhood diner) is a great spot to try a *completo*, the Chilean version of a hot dog, or have a cold beer surrounded by retired sailors. $

San Pedro
Doña Rosana crafts wonders with what her husband Don Carlos harvests and fishes every day from the Pacific Ocean. Try their *loco* (a mollusk similar to abalone) and cheese deep-fried empanada. $

Ropa Tendida Bar y Cocina
This lovely terrace restaurant has a great cocktail menu and perfectly chosen selection of draft beers, all framed by a wonderful view of the city. $$

GETTING AROUND

You'll regret bringing a car to Valparaíso, whose labyrinthine streets sprawl across improbably steep hills. Roads are ostensibly two ways but can often fit only one car. It's better to travel around by bus or taxi. Most parts of the city are walkable, using the funiculars to avoid some (though certainly not all) hill climbs.

Beyond Valparaíso

Caleta Quintay •
• Valparaíso
Tunquen •
• Casablanca Valley
Casa de Isla Negra •
• Las Cruces

Matanzas •

Attractive resort towns, empty beaches and
opulent wineries give visitors plenty of reasons
to travel beyond Valparaíso.

As enchanting as Valparaíso can be, several days reveling in
its gritty glory will likely have you pining for the nearby countryside. Just 30 minutes southeast of city limits lie Chile's best
cool-climate vineyards, which produce crisp sauvignon blancs
and silky pinot noirs that are exported around the world. The
coastline due south of town, meanwhile, is remarkably untouched. It leads, over the course of an hour or so, to a series of attractive fishing coves, middle-class resort towns and
more working-class cities that inspired some of the nation's
most famous poets. Head a bit further south and you'll find
the hipster hangout of Matanzas, where the architecture is
as alluring as the waves curling across the gray-sand beach.

TOP TIP

The vineyards and
coastal resort towns near
Valparaíso get packed
on weekends. To save
money on lodging, travel
mid-week.

Vineyard, Casablanca Valley

FILIPELOPES/SHUTTERSTOCK ©

Wine barrels, Casablanca Valley

HOW TO VISIT CASABLANCA WINERIES

The wineries of Casablanca are gorgeous, well organized and take tourism seriously with on-site restaurants, creative experiences and multilingual guides. That said, visiting them isn't nearly as easy as it should be. Despite Casablanca's proximity to both Valparaíso and Santiago, casual drop-ins are often frowned upon. Most places request that you book in advance for a tour, tasting or lunch. The fees for these activities can be disproportionately high compared with the prices of the bottles, which tend to offer great value for money. It's rare to simply show up unannounced and expect that you will be able to sample wines, though some places do sell by the glass. The key is advance planning.

Cool-Climate Wines

WINE TASTING IN CASABLANCA VALLEY

A cool climate and temperatures that vary greatly from day to night have made Casablanca Chile's premier valley for white wines. Chardonnay and sauvignon blanc grow particularly well, though silky-smooth pinot noirs and surprisingly fresh syrahs keep red-lovers happy too. Because it's split in half by the highway to Santiago, 40km southeast of Valparaíso, the valley can feel like a sprawling place. Find your bearings at the **Ruta del Vino de Casablanca** info center on the main plaza, where you can pick up a map and learn about which places are open to visitors. Keep in mind, however, that not all wineries are members of the organization that runs this place.

West of town, **Casas del Bosque** is one of the area's most tourism-oriented wineries with a romantic hacienda-style tasting area. The wines are outstanding, though tours can feel a tad corporate and rushed. That's not the case at **Bodegas RE**, a nearby winery that specializes in wild blends such as syragnan (syrah and carignan) or chardonnoir (chardonnay and pinot noir). **Villard Fine Wines** is another boutique family-owned winery. It's set amid the rolling vines of the picturesque Tapihue area and, like Bodegas RE, offers

 WHERE TO STAY IN CASABLANCA VALLEY

Indomo Casablanca
These domes and tiny cabins on the grounds of Matetic Vineyards are geared toward families. **$$**

Hotel Casablanca BCW
A hacienda-style hotel with cozy firepits, a sauna and two pools with Carmenere-grape-colored waters. **$$$**

Residencial del Valle
This clean, family-run spot is one of the few budget options in Casablanca. **$**

A POTTER'S PARADISE

Halfway between the Coast of the Poets and Santiago lies **Pomaire**, a lively country town known for its skilled potters and classic Chilean cuisine. Several clay records have been set here, including the world's largest piggy bank, though you'll mostly find pots, tableware and souvenirs.

Giant football-sized empanadas are among the plates typical of the town, as are traditional barbecued meats. Most visitors are *huasos* (cowboys) from the nearby countryside, as evidenced by their dusty boots and flat-rimmed *chupalla* hats. While it's packed with day-trippers on weekends, the town can be deserted on weekdays.

Tunquen beach

more affordable tastings than other wineries. When you tire of vino – or need to appease the beer-lover in your group – head to **Cervecería CODA**. This hipster craft brewery is in an industrial complex north of town and specializes in IPAs.

The Coast of Poets

DRIVING SOUTH TO THE BEACHES

On a two-hour road trip south from Valparaíso, wild rambling countryside leads to stunning beaches and bustling coastal towns that inspired Chile's greatest poets. **Caleta Quintay**, a colorful little fishing cove tucked amid craggy cliffs, is the first stop. It's a lovely lunch spot and a hub for scuba diving, but most come to visit **Museo Ex Ballenera**, a museum that reveals how Quintay was one of the Pacific's largest whaling hubs between 1943 and 1967, when it processed approximately 13,700 cetaceans.

South of Quintay is a stretch of pine-covered coastline, thanks to the forestry industry. At its heart is **Tunquen**, a youthful jumble of second homes and remote restaurants like **Casa Tunquén**, which pairs sweeping views over a wild beach with creative seafood dishes. The area attracts those who want to

 WHERE TO STAY IN MATANZAS

OMZ - Olas de Matanzas
OMZ caters to all budgets with everything from Tetris-like cabins to a seafront lodge and woodsy campsites. **$$**

Hotel Surazo
The waves are just steps away from your window at this high-design beachfront hotel. **$$$**

Hostal Mar de Boca
This blufftop hostel in La Boca is a value-hunter's dream with sea views and guided tours. **$**

get away from it all. Nearby **Algarrobo** is just the opposite: a proudly middle-class resort town whose main beach is lorded over by the San Alfonso del Mar apartment complex, which boasts what was, until 2015, the world's largest pool. A better bet for visitors is nearby **Playa El Canelillo**, a jewel of a beach tucked into a protected forest.

Head south to travel along the **Coast of Poets**. The famous poet Pablo Neruda is buried at **Casa de Isla Negra**, the wildest of his three homes and a huge tourist attraction. No less beloved by Chileans are Nicanor Parra, who lived just south in **Las Cruces**, and Vicente Huidobro, whose museum is in historic (if gritty) **Cartagena** next door. If you make it to the end and don't want to turn around, stew in the poetic spirit of **Patio Ferreiro**, an art-filled B&B with passionate hosts.

Seaside Cool in Matanzas

SURF, SAND AND STYLE

Flip through the pages of architecture magazines and you'll often find images of the stunning cabins that line the Chilean coast near **Matanzas**, about 160km south of Valparaíso. Local firms like WMR Arquitectos have crafted a unique aesthetic for the region, dotting its sea cliffs with secondary homes notable for their boxy shapes, modular designs, pinewood frames and expansive glass facades. Fortunately for travelers, many of these homes are available to rent on sites like Airbnb. Mea nwhile, the same architects are behind restaurants and hotels in Matanzas and neighboring beach towns like **Puertecillo** and **Boca de Pupuya**, making the area a treat for lovers of modern design.

Windsurfers in particular flock to Matanzas for some of the most consistent conditions along the Chilean coast. Meanwhile, surfers head to the south end of Puertecillo where there's a sandy-bottomed left-point break. Everyone else comes to this coastline to stroll its long gray-sand beaches and explore its tiny hamlets, which are framed by pea-green hills. **La Boca**, north of Matanzas, is especially appealing. Here, the Río Rapel winds out into the Pacific, forming a scenic estuary ideal for kayaking and paddleboarding. Don't miss **Mirador La Boca**, a panoramic observation deck with a winding wooden walkway that leads to one of the area's most picturesque – yet least crowded – beaches.

WHERE TO EAT & DRINK AROUND MATANZAS

Surazo
You can't beat this hotel restaurant for a meal or sundowner right on the beach. Grilled seafood is the star, but it also has excellent (and more affordable) pizzas. $$$

Caleta de Pescadores
Seafood empanadas and cheap ceviches used to be the only thing you'd find here. Now stalls sell craft ice cream, espresso and fruit smoothies. $

Márola
Reservations are a must at this stunning seafront restaurant in neighboring Pupuya with hearty fish and meat dishes. $$$

GETTING AROUND

It's possible to get to towns like Matanzas, Casablanca and Algarrobo by bus, but many of the attractions lie further afield. If you want to tour the vineyards of Casablanca or casually explore the coastline, you'll want a car. Alternatively, you can base yourself in each hub and take guided tours or cycling trips.

VIÑA DEL MAR

Viña del Mar ✪ Santiago

Orderly Viña del Mar is a sharp contrast to the charming jumble of neighboring Valparaíso. Manicured boulevards lined with palm trees, stately palaces, a sprawling public beach and beautiful expansive parklands have earned it the nickname of *Ciudad Jardín* (Garden City). Its official name, which means 'Vineyard by the Sea,' stems from vines once planted here when the area was nothing more than a rural hacienda.

Viña tends to be more popular with South Americans and weekending well-to-do Santiaguinos than travelers from elsewhere, who opt instead for a day trip from Valparaíso. But it strikes all the right chords for certain types of visitors who prefer long lazy beach walks and the comforts that come from staying in a more affluent city. Whereas its neighbor colors its streets with graffiti, Viña does so with flowers. It's the Miami to Valpo's Berlin: cleaner, greener, flatter and more predictable.

TOP TIP

Viña del Mar is flat and compact, making it easy to tackle on foot. In general, the nicer shops and restaurants lie north of the estuary. Valparaíso is just 15 minutes away by bus, taxi or light rail, making it easy to explore both cities.

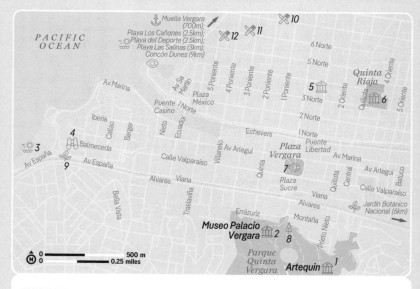

HIGHLIGHTS
1 Artequin
2 Museo Palacio Vergara

SIGHTS
3 Caleta Abarca
4 Mirador Jorge Alessandri
5 Museo de Arqueología e Historia Francisco Fonck
6 Palacio Rioja
7 Plaza Vergara
8 Quinta Vergara
9 Reloj de Flores

EATING
10 Bakery Lynch
11 Donde Willy
12 Ilo Mapu

Playa Los Cañones

Pick Your Favorite Beach

STROLLING VIÑA'S STELLAR COASTLINE

Viña del Mar is buzzing, but its greatest asset is the sandy coastline. To truly appreciate it, take a long and leisurely stroll. Get a taxi to drop you off at the city's northernmost beach, **Playa Las Salinas**, a protected bay and the safest place around for a swim. After a dip, begin the 3km walk south back to the heart of town. The first beach you'll come across is **Playa del Deporte**, which, true to its name (*deporte* means 'sport') has tons of public exercise equipment. Beach volleyball courts and a nice seafront amphitheater look back toward the towers of Valparaíso in the distance.

The beach changes names to **Playa Los Cañones** as you pass the naval academy (which has some cannonry on display). A flowery network of seafront paths leads you to the northern edge of Viña, where the skyline suddenly rises from one to 20-plus floors. You've now crossed into **Playa El Sol**, the busiest stretch, with several seafront vendors both formal and informal (many of the latter sell cheap fruit-flavored mojitos). North of the **Muelle Vergara** pier is a souvenir market. To the south is where the beach and its coastal path end. The path is just as nice on a bike or for a morning or evening run.

Museum-Hopping Around Viña

ARCHAEOLOGY, ART AND ARISTOCRACY

The beach might be Viña's main draw, but this city by the sea is also home to some of Middle Chile's better museums. Two of them are located in the Quinta Vergara park. **Museo Palacio**

STROLL ATOP CERRO CASTILLO

Cerro Castillo is a fantastic barrio for an afternoon stroll because it's elevated above the city and sea. On a leisurely walk, you'll find lovingly restored mansions, great city lookouts, a small 'castle' and **Palacio Presidencial de Cerro Castillo**, the summer palace of the president of Chile. The viewpoint at **Mirador Jorge Alessandri** is particularly dreamy, and you can drop down from there to **Reloj de Flores** (Flower Clock) and **Caleta Abarca** beach. The easiest way to reach the top is to take the street called Bajada Britannia (near Castillo Wulff) or Vista Hermosa (off Calle Valparaíso).

WHERE TO EAT IN VIÑA DEL MAR

Donde Willy
This famous family restaurant with down-home charm does excellent Chilean seafood dishes and wine pairings. **$$**

Bakery Lynch
This bakery-cafe with a woodsy aesthetic boasts affordable sweets and sandwiches; try the *mechada Italiana*. **$**

Ilo Mapu
Taste indigenous flavors of the southern forests at this gorgeous restaurant with Mapuche fusion cuisine. **$$$**

VIÑA'S STAR-MAKING FESTIVAL

Viña holds a special place in the hearts and minds of many Latin Americans who've grown up watching the annual **Festival Internacional de la Canción de Viña del Mar**, which takes place at the Anfiteatro de la Quinta Vergara on the third weekend of February. Some 15,000 spectators flock here – and 150 million more tune in to live broadcasts beamed across the region – as Latin American pop, rock and folk stars join top-tier global musicians for an all-out extravaganza. This massive event has launched the careers of everyone from Shakira to former festival host Sofia Vergara.

Vergara is a pretty-in-pink Venetian Gothic–style palace that houses a wonderful mix of 20th-century paintings and more modern works from regional artists. Beautifully restored, it reopened in 2021 with hypnotic floor tiles, dramatic chandeliers and first-rate exhibitions. Nearby **Artequin** is an educational museum for children that aims to bring them closer to art through interactive experiences.

Heading north past **Plaza Vergara**, the city's central square, is the **Museo de Arqueología e Historia Francisco Fonck**, a small museum of history and archaeology. You'll know you've arrived when you see a *moai* (monolithic statue) from Rapa Nui out front. Inside is a large collection of artifacts from Rapa Nui alongside arts and crafts from Chile's other indigenous cultures, including silver Mapuche jewelry and patterned Diaguitas ceramics. The 2nd floor is full of taxidermied Chilean fauna; the puma and condor are particularly spectacular.

The final museum worth visiting is **Palacio Rioja**, dedicated to the decorative arts of the 20th-century Chilean aristocracy. Housed in a grand French-inspired building, it also has a lovely cafe and occasional classical music concerts.

Garden City

PARKS, FLOWERS AND GREENERY

Learn why Chileans refer to Viña as *Ciudad Jardín* (Garden City) on a tour of its parks, gardens and green spaces. Begin at the foot of Cerro Castillo at the **Reloj de Flores**, a large and fully functioning clock made of meticulously manicured flowers. This quirky botanical landmark – crafted for the 1962 World Cup – is controlled by GPS and chimes every 15 minutes, drawing big crowds.

The **Quinta Vergara** park once belonged to one of the city's most illustrious families, the Alvares-Vergaras. This urban oasis is packed with a rainbow of flowers, curving palms and large patches of grass used by picnicking couples. With benches aplenty, it's a serene spot to relax in the shade of a fanning araucaria tree. The biggest park of them all is **Jardín Botánico Nacional**, Chile's national botanical garden, which lies 8km southeast of town. Its 400 hectares of parkland contain more than 3000 plant species, including the nearly extinct toromiro tree from Rapa Nui and a collection of rare endemic plants from Chile's Juan Fernández archipelago. Explore 26 different botanical collections along the scenic walking trails.

GETTING AROUND

Viña is relatively flat and easy to walk around. Public buses are plentiful and useful for getting from one side of town to the other. You can also ride them to neighboring Valparaíso, or alternatively, take the light rail Tren Limache-Puerto. Taxis (and some international taxi apps) also operate here.

Beyond Viña del Mar

Zapallar
Cachagua
Maitencillo

Concón

Parque Nacional
La Campana

Olmué

Viña del Mar

Quaint Chilean villages, ritzy coastal resorts and palm-filled hills ripe for hiking make greater Viña a traveler's treat.

The coast north of Viña del Mar is home to some of the swankiest enclaves in all of Chile. Wealthy Santiaguinos spend their summers here slurping scallops from their shells and downing bottles of dry rosé as the sun sets over the Pacific. Each weekend, urbanites depart the city en masse to frolic down the wide beaches of Maitencillo and Cachagua or the leafy cove of Zapallar. Follow suit if you're keen to hobnob with Chile's power players (and pay high prices to do so).

If you're a more athletic traveler, head slightly inland to Parque Nacional La Campana, which has soaring hills and the largest remaining forest of Chilean wine palms.

TOP TIP

Phone apps translate *ostiones* (a common dish along the coast) to oysters, but in Chile, *ostiones* are actually scallops.

Maitencillo (p171)

JOSE LUIS STEPHENS/SHUTTERSTOCK ©

COUNTRYSIDE CHARM IN OLMUÉ

With its backdrop of rolling green hills, plazas filled with wood-carved cowboys, and streets lined in palms and jacarandas, **Olmué** might just be the cutest town in central Chile. A popular resort destination for domestic tourists – though rarely visited by foreigners – it has a strong pride of character that's on full display each January when it hosts the **Festival del Huaso de Olmué**, a folk-music festival held in the grand Anfiteatro El Patagual. To visit (likely en route to La Campana) is to step back in time to the Chilean countryside of yore.

Chilean wine palm, Cerro La Campana

A Paradise of Palms

HIKING PARQUE NACIONAL LA CAMPANA

Many of the largest mountains in Chile's Coastal Range lie within the striking **Parque Nacional La Campana**, about 50km east of Viña by road. Peaks include **Cerro La Campana** (1890m), which Charles Darwin climbed in 1834. The 7km **Sendero Andinista** trail to its summit has become so popular that you need to book one of just 50 spots in advance (asp-ticket.cl). The other reason to visit La Campana is the park's 60,000 jubaea, or Chilean wine palms, which have the thickest trunks of any palm species.

Hikers hoping to walk amid the largest remaining forests of jubaea should head to the northerly **Ocoa** sector. To hike up La Campana, go instead to the southerly **Granizo** sector. A third ranger station lies at the entrance to the nearby **Cajón Grande** sector, which has some flatter hikes, as well as one path, the **Sendero El Portezuelo de Ocoa**, which takes you to an overlook of a palm-covered valley (6km one way).

There are no roads inside the park, nor are there working campgrounds (they've closed because of Chile's incessant drought). Unfortunately, you can no longer hike from one side

 WHERE TO STAY NEAR PARQUE NACIONAL LA CAMPANA

Domos Ocoa
A group of four will find these two-room domes near the Ocoa entrance a fantastic deal. **$**

Biosfera Lodge
Marvelous ovular domes – plus a pool, restaurant and yoga shala (studio) – spill down a hill by Cajón Grande. **$$$**

El Copihue
This resort-like hotel on the plaza in Olmué is filled with country charm and character. **$$**

of the park to the other, meaning you should choose your access point wisely. Ocoa is more remote with only basic tourist infrastructure. Cajón Grande and Granizo, however, lie on the edge of **Olmué**, a popular resort town with dozens of hotels, cabins and campgrounds, as well as public transportation.

Road-Tripping to Cachagua
DUNES, BEACHES AND PENGUINS

Heading an hour north from Viña does not mean escaping city life – at least not until you pass through the high-rises of neighboring **Reñaca** and **Concón**, the latter of which is known for its stellar seafood restaurants. Breathe your first big gulp of fresh air at **Ritoque**, a tiny jumble of bungalows, resto-bars and cabins (we love those at **La Ritoqueña**) that looks south over 15km of beach backed by empty rolling dunes. The wild surroundings beg to be explored on foot, bike or horseback.

Head north to **Maitencillo**, the resort of Chile's new rich. Its string of lovely beaches house hip restaurants, youthful stores and buzzing surf shops. It's also a great place to overnight along this stretch of coast at places like **Posada Portal del Sol** (a serene sea-facing guesthouse on a hilltop) or **Cabañas Hermansen** (crowd-pleasing cabins steps from the beach). Further north, you'll pass several high-end condo complexes before descending into sleepy **Cachagua**, whose dirt roads are lined with million-dollar mansions. At the northern edge of its beautiful wave-lapped bay is **Isla Cachagua**, an offshore island home to 3% of the world's remaining Humboldt penguins. You can't set foot on the island, but you can hire a boat taxi from the *caleta* (cove) in neighboring Zapallar to get closer. Inland from Cachagua is **Outlife Parque Aguas Claras**, a private park that protects some of the last undisturbed coastal forests on this coast, which exist in the arid climate thanks to the coastal fog.

Stroll the Zapallar Coast
A CHIC SEASIDE RESORT

About 70km north of Viña, **Zapallar** is the wealthiest seafront community in Chile and *the* place to hobnob with the rich and famous, who retire here on weekends and summer holidays. Its quiet downtown is little more than a jumble of hill-hugging homes mixed in with cafes, sweets shops, clothing boutiques and the odd gallery or two. The real action is at **Playa Zapallar**, the prettiest crescent of sand north of Viña, which is edged by dense green forests. Nowhere else around are the waters this calm for swimming.

BEST SEAFOOD RESTAURANTS IN CONCÓN & MAITENCILLO

Aquí Jaime
Down oysters, scallops and clams overlooking Concón's harbor. $$$

Empanadas El Hoyo
Seafront crab and cheese empanadas make this an unmissable cheap eat – if you can brave the crowds. $

5unset Lounge
Downtempo beats, wooden tables in the sand, haute Nikkei (Peruvian-Japanese fusion) dishes and, of course, epic sunsets draw devout diners. Try the sashimi-like *tiradito*. $$$

La Perla Del Pacífico
Tradition is the key to success at this long-running (and oft-copied) Concón staple, which knows its seafood like few others. $$

 WHERE TO STAY IN ZAPALLAR

Hotel Casa Zapallar
A high-design boutique hotel with plush beds, a handsome lounge and small plunge pool. $$

Casa Wilson
You can't beat the location of this historic B&B by the sea, which has a time-warping allure. $$$

Hostería Zapallar
This old-school inn with a shared kitchen is the closest thing to a budget option in Zapallar. $$

BEST WATER SPORTS ON THE CENTRAL COAST

Kayak Zapallar
The calm waters of Zapallar make it the most ideal spot for sea kayaking and paddleboarding. Check in advance here, and below, for English-speaking guides.

Escuela de Surf Maitencillo
This popular surf school in Maitencillo rents boards, runs classes and has a surfer-packed coffee spot on the beach.

Austral Divers
Quintay lures divers to its sunken whaling boats, which are now enveloped in underwater life. Austral Divers is the top operator and has its own dive hostel to boot.

Playa Zapallar (p171)

Walk north of the beach to find a stunning 2km-long **coastal path** past mansions with wildly landscaped gardens tumbling down to the sea. Walk south, and you'll see the **Caleta de Zapallar**, a small fishermen's wharf that doubles as a hub for kayaking and scuba diving. Zapallar's most famous seafood restaurant, **Chiringuito**, is next door and has oceanfront tables where you can watch as pelicans dive-bomb the sea. To the west is **Cerro La Cruz**, a small nature sanctuary with hiking trails. Divert south and you'll continue along the stone-hewn coastal path for several more kilometers of blissful strolling on trails carved around soaring boulders and wave-lapped coves. Those who can afford to stay along this dreamy coastline won't want to be based anywhere else.

GETTING AROUND

Buses regularly ply the coast from Viña's Terminal de Buses up to Zapallar and beyond, stopping at most resort towns along the way. To reach Olmué, you can buy a train-bus combination ticket with EFE (efe.cl) and take the light rail Tren Limache to Limache before connecting to a bus to Olmué or the Cajón Grande national park entrance.

SANTA CRUZ

Santa Cruz ●✪ Santiago

It was 1994 when a purple grape thought extinct for more than 100 years in its native Bordeaux was rediscovered in Chile mixed in with the merlot vines. Carmenere would go on over the next decades to become the nation's signature grape, representing it on wine shelves around the world. Nowhere does Carmenere better than the sun-scorched Colchagua Valley, a Mediterranean-like landscape of rolling hills blanketed in patchwork vines.

At the valley's heart is the sleepy city of Santa Cruz, which has a picturesque central plaza, several fine restaurants, surprising museums and a growing number of truly excellent hotels. The hacienda look (white adobe walls, red-tiled roofs and high ceilings with exposed wooden beams) is the defining aesthetic both here and in the nearby countryside, where you'll find the real *encanto* (charm) of the region. Taste some vino, visit with eccentric vintners and experience the lyrical pull of wine country.

TOP TIP

Though many wineries featured in this guidebook offer tastings for walk-up visitors, it's highly recommended to book 24 hours in advance for any tours, especially if they include a meal. Not all wineries are open daily. Many close on Sundays or early in the week.

Viña Santa Cruz (p176)

BEST MAULE VALLEY WINERIES

Viña Gillmore
Sample some experimental wines at this friendly winery, which offers tours and tastings and has an on-site barrel-themed lodge, Tabonkö. Ask about the origins of VIGNO, Maule's unique appellation.

Viña Balduzzi
Located right off the Pan-American Highway, this tourist-friendly vineyard does reservation-free tours and tastings.

Viña J Bouchon
Bouchon is making some of the most exciting wines in Chile. Book in advance to tour the stunning Mingre Estate, which also boasts a romantic high-end hotel, Casa Bouchon.

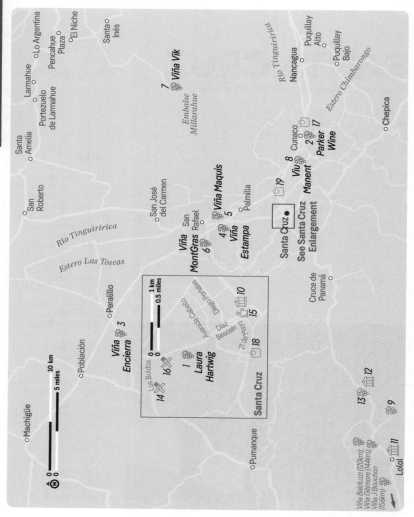

Map labels:

- Machigüe
- Lo Argentina
- Larmahue
- El Niche
- Santa Inés
- Pencahue Plaza
- Portezuelo de Larmahue
- Santa Amelia
- 7 Viña Vik
- Puquillay Alto
- Puquillay Bajo
- Río Tinguiririca
- Nancagua
- Chepica
- Estero Chambarongo
- San Roberto
- San José del Carmen
- Viña Maquis
- San Rafael
- Palmilla
- 8 Viu Manent
- Cunaco
- 2 Parker Wine
- 17
- 19
- Viña MontGras
- 4 Viña Estampa
- 5
- 6
- Santa Cruz
- See Santa Cruz Enlargement
- Cruce de Panamá
- Embalse Millarahue
- Río Tinguiririca
- Estero Las Toscas
- Peralillo
- Viña Encierra 3
- Población
- Pumanque
- Santa Cruz (enlargement)
- Los Boldos
- 14
- 16
- 1 Laura Hartwig
- Avenida Cabello
- Diego Portales
- Díaz Besoaín
- 21 de Mayo
- 10
- 15
- 18
- 13
- 12
- 9
- 11
- Lolol
- Viña Balduzzi (120km); Viña Gillmore (144km); Viña J Bouchon (155km)

Scale: 10 km / 5 miles; 1 km / 0.5 miles

Wine barrel, Viña Vik

The Power Players of Chilean Wine

TOUR CHILE'S RENOWNED WINERIES

The big wine estates of Colchagua Valley are multimillion-dollar operations whose showpiece *bodegas* (winery buildings) are lavish affairs. Case in point is Casa Silva, an opulent vineyard with an excellent restaurant overlooking a polo field where you can dine after taking a tour or tasting in the wine shop. And then there's **Viña Vik**, a sculptural opus built by renowned Chilean architect Smiljan Radic. It's a tad far from Santa Cruz (technically in neighboring Cachapoal Valley) – and grows its own organic vegetables – so you'll want to book a tour here with lunch at the art-filled **Pavilion Restaurant**.

At **Viu Manent**, a rare Chilean malbec specialist, you can choose from the budget-friendly cafe or sumptuous terrace restaurant **Rayuela** after embarking on any number of tastings or tours, many of which involve carriage rides. Sustainability-minded **Viña Maquis**, which has a cool brutalist winery building, has a gorgeous location at the intersection of two rivers. Tours, including one by bike, linger in this serene riverine landscape, while tastings showcase extraordinarily elegant wines, many of which are based around an unlikely grape (for Chile): cabernet franc.

If you make it to only one Colchagua Valley power player, go for **Viña MontGras**, the friendliest kid on the block with zero pretensions despite its stunning hacienda-style building and excellent bottles. Cab sauv and syrah are the specialties, and you can taste them in flights, after tours or by the glass. It's also one of the only spots offering a make-your-own wine experience, as well as three months of interactive harvest-focused tours between February and April.

Wines With Personality

TOURING COLCHAGUA'S BOUTIQUE VINEYARDS

Colchagua might be Chile's preeminent wine region, but that doesn't mean that it's only the domain of massive global exporters. At least a dozen smaller wineries offer a boutique – often more personalized – experience. At **Viña Encierra**, on the road to Marchigüe, you can sample exceptional Carmenere and red blends in the tiny tasting room or book ahead for a private lunch amid the vines. Petit verdot specialist **Laura Hartwig** – right on the edge of Santa Cruz – is exceptionally easy to visit. Pay a small fee for a glass (which you keep) and then fill it with all the wines you want to sample. You can also order a cheese board as you lounge in the shaded patio.

COLCHAGUA TASTING TIPS

Wine tasting in Colchagua Valley – and Chile, in general – can be frustrating for visitors who have been to other wine-producing countries and are accustomed to showing up unannounced to vineyards to sample their products. Wineries here often prefer that you reserve in advance for elaborate one- to two-hour tours, particularly in the Apalta area where the egos are high and prices inflated. In general, the wineries we recommend are more open to casual visitors – those who may do the occasional tour, but don't need to do three in one day. After all, sometimes you just want to try some wine – in a tasting or by the glass.

 WHERE TO EAT IN SANTA CRUZ

Time Coffee
Espresso coffees, sweets and cheap but hearty sandwiches are served in a lush garden off the plaza. $

Vino Bello
Scratch-made pastas are the specialty at this vineyard-facing Italian restaurant aligned for golden sunsets. $$$

Casa Colchagua
This excellent patio restaurant serves top-class Chilean fish and meat dishes alongside local wines. $$

The more modern **Viña Estampa** is a blend specialist, though it has a number of experimental single varietal options too. Stop by during the day for tours, walk-up tastings or lunch at the cafe. The real treat is coming in the late afternoon for a flight with snacks as the sun sets over the Coastal Range. Estampa is one of the only wineries open in the evenings (Thursday to Saturday). The most intimate experience of all is a tour of **Parker Wine**, a Californian-owned winery opened to the public in 2022 with 100-year-old vines making citrusy sémillon and textured cabernet sauvignon alongside funky ciders. Tours are by reservation only.

FOR WINE LOVERS

Want to get even further off the wine map? The **Itata Valley** (p187) is like the Wild West of Chilean vino and a fascinating place for lovers of natural and low-intervention wines.

Surprising Santa Cruz Museums

THE CULTURAL SIDE OF COLCHAGUA

Few visitors come to the Colchagua Valley imagining that they might find top-class museums, but thanks to the Fundación Cardoen, this valley is actually home to the finest repositories of pre-Columbian art, archaeology and historic artifacts beyond Santiago. The unmissable **Museo Colchagua** showcases the largest private natural-history collection in the country, including pre-Columbian mummies, ceramics, textiles and jewelry. A large exhibit details the 2010 Copiapó mining accident, when 33 miners were rescued from the bowels of the Earth after 69 days.

Two more of the foundation's museums are at **Viña Santa Cruz**, a lavish Disney-like winery about 25km west of downtown. At **Museo del Automóvil**, you'll find one of the DeLoreans used in *Back to the Future* alongside a host of other classic cars that enthusiasts will swoon over. The adjacent **Museo del Vino** is easily the largest wine museum in South America. Its collection takes you from the earliest days of wine production in the Caucuses up to wine's arrival in Chile and beyond. Highlights include an aroma room and tons of historic winemaking equipment. Unfortunately, signage is in Spanish only.

Perhaps as interesting as these museums is the wild story of their founder, Carlos Cardoen, who allegedly sold armaments to Iraq during Saddam Hussein's regime. On Interpol's wanted list for three decades – and unable to leave the country – he's become an instrumental figure in bringing tourism to his hometown.

BEST WINE TOURS

Ruta del Vino Colchagua
This association of Colchagua Valley wineries has an information office on the plaza to book tours (which don't include transport). See the options online (rutadelvino.cl).

Casa Suiza
Bike tours to small-scale wine producers (available in four languages) are the focus of this well-run operation, based out of the namesake hostel. You can also rent mountain or gravel bikes to go on your own.

Upscape
This well-regarded company runs high-end tours to Colchagua Valley combining food and wine experiences.

 WHERE TO SHOP IN SANTA CRUZ

Wine Outlet
Overstock wines at bargain basement prices, particularly if you buy a box of six.

Tienda Ecobazar
This artist-run co-op has a fabulous collection of crafts, cosmetics, ceramics, textiles and other artisan goods.

La Vinogarage
Sells quirky bottles from small-scale vintners you won't find anywhere else.

Laura Hartwig winery (p175)

Slow Down in Historic Lolol

SMALL-TOWN CHARM

Tiny Lolol leaves a big impression on visitors thanks to its steadfast dedication to maintaining its historic Spanish-colonial character. While there isn't a whole lot to do in town other than stroll its cobbled streets, you can visit the **Museo de la Artesanía** (another Fundación Cardoen museum). Chile has a proud history of folk art that's often overlooked by visitors, and this lovely museum takes you on a tour through regional craft traditions from the vibrant textiles of the Atacama to the wood carvings of Rapa Nui and basket weavings of Chiloé. Middle Chile is particularly well represented, including the folksy ceramics of Quinchamalí. Unfortunately, information panels are in Spanish only.

If you're inspired by the works, stop by **La Casa del Artesano** to buy anything from Chilean textiles to wood carvings, baskets or local honey to take home. Head to **Hacienda Araucano** just beyond the town limits for a vineyard tour and lunch (with prior reservation) at this sprawling organic estate from famed French winemaker François Lurton. The wines are notably fresher than elsewhere in Colchagua thanks to the influence of the Pacific.

WHY I LOVE SANTA CRUZ

Mark Johanson, writer

Ask me why I live in Chile and some version of that answer involves wine. Big family lunches here include endless rounds of vino as we wrap up desserts and segue into *sobremesa* (the tradition of chit-chatting at the table long after a meal finishes). Wine is such a big part of the nation's identity that when the Image of Chile Foundation set out to discover Chile's most emblematic symbol abroad, the result was not the snowcapped Andes or the *moai* of Rapa Nui (Easter Island); it was wine. But most of the best bottles never travel beyond these borders. That's why, for newcomers, taking a trip to Colchagua can be a revelatory experience.

GETTING AROUND

Santa Cruz has a growing network of bike lanes, but they don't extend beyond town where almost all of the wineries are. Roads can be dusty with zero shade, so most people either rent a car, book a tour with transport or get around by taxis or ridesharing apps.

Beyond Santa Cruz

Parque Nacional
Las Palmas
de Cocalán

Pichilemu

Cáhuil

Santa Cruz

Reserva Nacional
Río de Los Cipreses

Parque Nacional
Radal Siete
Tazas

Reserva Nacional
Altos de Lircay

Wild waves pound against gray-sand beaches while condors fly over snowcapped peaks in the surroundings of Santa Cruz.

One of the great joys of Chile is that when you find yourself in a central point like Santa Cruz, you're never more than 90 minutes away from the Pacific or the Andes. Heading west, you'll enter a serene coastline of wind-whipped beaches with hip resort towns and the wildest surf breaks in South America. Pichilemu, the biggest surf hub, offers some of the best-value beach lodgings within reach of the Colchagua Valley, as well as an array of stellar restaurants.

To the east, excellent high-Andean parks and reserves beckon active travelers. Often overlooked by foreigners who race to the Lake District or Patagonia, places like Altos de Lircay deserve a closer inspection.

TOP TIP

Most national parks and reserves in the Central Andes require advance registration (aspticket.cl) and are closed on Mondays. Plan accordingly.

Pichilemu

LMSPENCER/SHUTTERSTOCK ©

CHRISTIAN CREIXELL/ALAMY STOCK PHOTO ©

Surfer, Pichilemu

Surf, Sand & Smoothies

RIDING WAVES IN PICHILEMU

Wave gods and goddesses flock to **Pichilemu** year-round to brave the icy waters of Chile's unofficial surf capital, about 90km west of Santa Cruz. **La Puntilla** is the closest surfing spot to town and has a long and slow point break. **Punta de Lobos**, 6km to the south, is the real draw. It's a solid, heavy left break and as consistent as they come. The highly recommended English-language operation **Océanos Chile** can set you up with lessons, rentals and accommodations in its Surf House. Mere beach-going mortals should head to Pichilemu between December and March to sprawl across its long gray-sand beaches.

Downtown Pichilemu won't win any beauty pageants, but the outskirts are decidedly trendy with a unique pine-box aesthetic. The road to Punta de Lobos in particular is lined with quality restaurants, cafes and well-priced lodgings. Between rides, surfers fuel up on smoothies and vegan grain bowls at **Cúrcuma** or eye-opening coffees and matcha lattes at **Taller 2470**. They gather anew for sunset at **Los Piures**, a hipster social club with craft beers and inventive seafood tapas. Pichilemu's good-time vibes can quickly become addictive.

CÁHUIL SALT ROUTE

Cáhuil, 12km south of Pichilemu, is famous across Chile for its sea salts, which grace dishes in the nation's finest restaurants. Remarkably cheap, these chunky granules make a great gift for home cooks. When arriving – likely by car – you'll find vendors selling salt at a market near the entrance to town. It's better to follow the scenic route, **La Ruta de la Sal**, past the market, restaurants and craft shops into Cáhuil's picturesque estuary, which is home to 46 bird species, including swans and herons. Buy direct from the salters at places like **Barrancas**, a scenic farm that's open to visitors wanting to learn more about the process.

 WHERE TO STAY IN PICHILEMU

SudEste Hostel
Rare oceanfront hostel with a pool, dorms and absurdly cheap private rooms with unobstructed sea views. $

Surf Lodge Punta de Lobos
This woodsy complex has an attractive design and ample leisure zones, including pools and a spa. $$

Hostal Moreno
Cleanliness, friendliness, centrality and a leafy patio make this a solid budget option. $

NEARBY NATIONAL PARKS

When Santiaguinos want to escape the arid Central Valley for greener pastures, they come to **Reserva Nacional Río de Los Cipreses**. Two excellent campgrounds, family-friendly hiking trails and a dramatic evening migration of the *tricahue*, an olive-green burrowing parrot, make it deservedly popular.

To the south, **Parque Nacional Radal Siete Tazas** has two 50m waterfalls that tumble into emerald green swimming holes. But the highlight in these forested mountains is the *siete tazas*, a breathtaking series of seven pools carved out of black basalt by the Río Claro.

Meanwhile, some 35,000 jubaea (Chilean wine palms) form a perky forest at the little-visited **Parque Nacional Las Palmas de Cocalán** in the Coastal Range.

OBSCUR/SHUTTERSTOCK ©

Reserva Nacional Altos de Lircay

Climb into the Andes

HIKING ALTOS DE LIRCAY

The range of challenging hikes at the well-organized and easily accessible **Reserva Nacional Altos de Lircay** (180km southeast of Santa Cruz) will leave you – quite literally – short of breath. The park's star trail is **Sendero Enladrillado**, which is arguably the best day hike in the whole of Middle Chile, taking you to the top of a 2300m basalt plateau.

The trail starts with a two-hour stretch east along the **Sendero de Chile**, and then a signposted right-hand fork climbs steeply through dense forest for about an hour before leveling off. You eventually emerge onto the dead-flat platform of Enladrillado, which some people think is a UFO landing ground. To the west, you can see the flat-topped crater of **Volcán Descabezado** ('Headless Volcano') and next to it the sharp peak of **Cerro Azul**. The 10km one-way trek takes about four hours up and three down.

Consult park maps for how to link this trail with the **Sendero Laguna del Alto**, which leads to a mountain-ringed lagoon at 2000m. **Trekking Chile**, based out of the superb **Lodge Casa Chueca** in nearby Talca, sells topo maps and can arrange guides for day hikes or longer excursions like **Circuito los Cóndores**, a six-day high-Andean circuit. Other lodging options include **Camping Antahuara**, a shaded Conaf campground 800m beyond the Adminstración.

When you finish exploring the park, don't forget about the turquoise **Lago Colbún** down below. Encased in the Andean foothills, it's a serene spot for kayaking with several lodgings on its shores, including **Ecorefugio Spa**, a playful container hotel.

GETTING AROUND

Santa Cruz is not as well connected by public transportation as larger cities. Visiting nearby destinations often involves at least one transfer (typically in San Fernando). A car is the only practical way to travel high into the Andes without a lot of advance planning to catch the infrequent local buses from regional capitals along Ruta 5. In general, roads to the parks are in good condition.

COBQUECURA

Cobquecura ● ✈Santiago

Cobquecura is a quaint little seaside enclave with a pictur-esque core that nearly crumbled to bits in a 2010 earthquake. Its long, wide beaches with wild breaks and black sands at-tract surfers from around the world, but you don't need to be a wave-rider to enjoy its quiet charms. Always seemingly on the cusp of being discovered, 'Cobque' (as locals call it) nev-er feels overrun in the way that surf towns closer to Santia-go do. In fact, it's not uncommon to share the roads with ox-drawn wagons – such is the slow pace of life here.

To the north, the beach of Buchupureo has a string of excep-tional lodging options, while you'll find excellent seafront din-ing both here and on the next cove north, Pullay. Just south of town, Playa Rinconada is both the fishermen's hub and the calmest beach around for a swim.

TOP TIP

More than a single place, Cobquecura is really a string of separate beach towns running from Taucú in the south up to Buchupureo and Pullay in the north. Cobquecura itself has the most infrastructure, though Buchupureo has more of a resort feel and is where many travelers end up.

Pullay (p185)

PAUL KENNEDY/ALAMY STOCK PHOTO ©

WHERE TO EAT IN COBQUECURA

El Chiringuito de Pullay
This cash-only spot with yummy *pastel de jaiba* (crab casserole) is surfer central. $$

Salón Verde
Local sourcing, fresh seasonal produce and Itata Valley wines are the names of the game at this Pullay eatery. $$

Ruka Antu
A notch above other hotel restaurants with creative seafood dishes, including Peruvian-style risottos, as well as sweeping ocean views. $$$

Caleta Rinconada de Taucú
Devour supremely cheap ceviche made with just-caught seafood at this fish market. $

COBQUECURA

N

0 — 1 mile
0 — 2 km

HIGHLIGHTS
1 La Boca
2 La Lobería
3 Playa Rinconada
4 Pullay

SIGHTS
5 Parque Las Nalkas

ACTIVITIES, COURSES & TOURS
6 El Chiringuito de Pullay
7 Escuela Nanosurf Cobquecura
8 Iglesia de Piedra

SLEEPING
9 Complejo Turístico Ayekan
10 Hotel Boutique Kurayafu
11 View Buchupureo

EATING
12 Ruka Antu
13 Salón Verde

DRINKING
see 9 Café La Mano
14 Cervecería Kofke

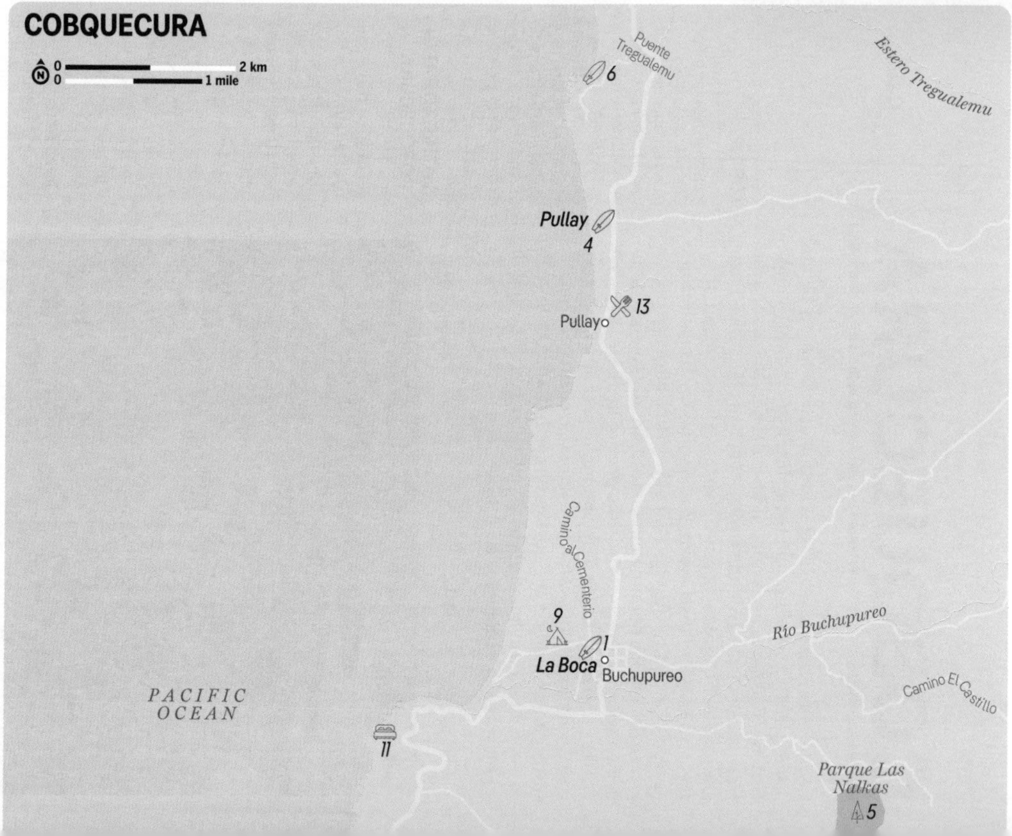

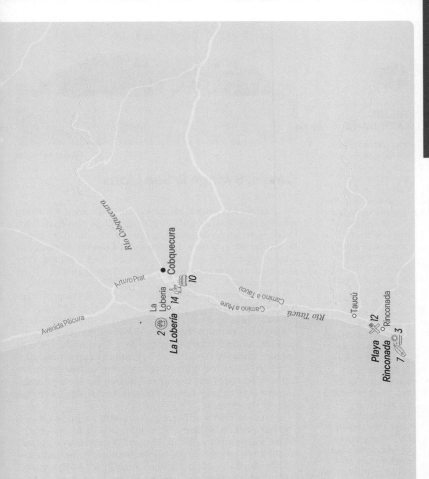

Río Cobquecura

Cobquecura

Arturo Prat

10

Avenida Pilicura

La
Lobería

14

La Lobería

2

Camino a Mure

Camino a Tauco

Río Taucú

Taucú

Playa
Rinconada

Rinconada

12

7   3

Sea lions (p184), Cobquecura

BIOSPHOTO/ALAMY STOCK PHOTO ©

FOR SURFERS

Punta de Lobos in **Pichilemu** (p179)
is – arguably – Chile's most famous
wave and a pilgrimage point for
surfers. If riding waves is your
raison d'être, then build a
trip around these two
destinations.

BIOSPHOTO/ALAMY STOCK PHOTO ©

Iglesia de Piedra

THE 2010 EARTHQUAKE

It was the middle of the night on February 27, 2010, when the ground beneath Cobquecura first began to wobble. The intense shaking lasted a full three minutes as an earthquake measuring 8.8 on the Richter scale struck just offshore. The sixth-strongest earthquake on record, it caused more than $5 billion in damage. Some 525 people lost their lives (mostly in the subsequent tsunami and landslides), and about 9% of the population in affected zones lost their homes. Cobquecura was particularly hard hit. The ground rose up 3m in some areas, sending many of its old adobe homes crumbling to the ground. Remarkably, on a visit today, you would hardly know anything happened here at all.

Caves, Swings & Sea Lions

STROLLING BY THE SEA

Cobquecura has several attractions that are great for a long wander, including its main 8km beach. Walk west from town to the water and a deep baying sound resonates from a rock formation 50m offshore. Known as **La Lobería**, it's home to a large colony of sunbathing sea lions. Each January, they give birth to new pups in a process visitors can smell from kilometers away.

Follow the coast road 4km north to reach the exquisite **Iglesia de Piedra** ('Stone Church'), a massive monolith containing huge caves that open to the ocean. The light inside them is majestic – perhaps that's why Cobquecura's pre-Hispanic inhabitants held ritual gatherings here. The Iglesia now contains an image of the Virgin Mary and is wrapped up in local legends. One has it that pregnant women shouldn't enter lest they be swept out to sea, and in fact, being swept away because of fast-rising tides is not uncommon. Heed warning signs at the entrance.

Continuing north to Buchupureo and then inland, you'll find **Parque Las Nalkas**, a 22-hectare private forest reserve. Whimsical nature trails lead to waterfalls, lookout points and giant hilltop swings begging for Instagram photos. Ruby-red boardwalks link a stunning collection of gravity-defying treehouses, which offer a compelling reason to stick around for a night or two.

Surf's Up

RIDING THE ICY WAVES

Surfers were the first to put Cobquecura on the travel map in the early 2000s, and they continue to be the area's most devout fans. But you don't need to be an expert to get in on the action. Beginners tend to find the best break south of town

 WHERE TO STAY IN COBQUECURA

Complejo Turístico Ayekan
Pitch a tent near the sea in a pretty clearing at the bottom of a eucalyptus-lined drive. **$**

Hotel Boutique Kurayafu
With local art, textiles and a lovely terrace, this boutique oozes character. **$$**

View Buchupureo
As the name implies, these window-encased cabins tumbling down a hill have unrivaled ocean views. **$$**

at **Playa Rinconada**, the busiest surf beach in summer with a small surf shop, surfer-focused campgrounds and several lunch stalls with cheap seafood empanadas. North of town is **Pullay**, a sandy left point that's fun for all levels with fast and strong waves that rush to the shore at predictable intervals. **La Boca** in Buchupureo is the standout break for pros with long lefts and excellent barrel time. Unfortunately, the beach right in Cobquecura is generally pounded by waves too choppy for riding.

Most waves in the area are left-breaking and best suited for intermediate or experienced riders. A thick wetsuit is a must any time of the year, with water temperatures hovering between 14°C and 17°C. **Escuela Nanosurf Cobquecura** is the most experienced surf school for those new to the sport, but for English-language instruction, you're better off heading to the smaller surf school at **El Chiringuito de Pullay**. Both places rent equipment at affordable rates, while the latter is arguably the biggest surfer hangout in the region. Another spot for a post-surf pint is **Cerveceria Kofke**, which has a funky aesthetic and great burgers, while morning riders head to **Café La Mano** for a caffeine fix.

Paddling & Bird-Watching

EXPLORING THE WILD COASTLINE

There are plenty of ways to get active during a stay along the gray-sand coastline of Cobquecura that don't involve hopping atop a surfboard. Those who prefer to stand up on a paddleboard will find several placid estuaries on which to roam – particularly in Taucú and Buchupureo, where rivers descending from the Andes stall before flowing out to the sea. **Stand Up Paddle Buchupureo** offers SUP classes and runs both daytime and nighttime paddle tours. If you enjoy sitting as you row, María Elvira at **Kayak Vilu Cobquecura** provides single and tandem kayaks to explore the shallow estuaries of Taucú, which are often filled with coots, swans, ducks and herons.

Ancestral Ecoturismo is a local tour agency that offers trips focused on both nature and patrimony. Guides take you to local wetlands, along bird-watching trails or to learn about the human history of the area. Note that, in most cases, English-language proficiency is low in Cobquecura's adventure tourism industry, but with enough patience, the understanding of a few key words and some good hand-gesturing, you can often get by just fine. Contact agencies a few days in advance to arrange an outing with an English-speaking guide.

IDENTIFYING SEAFOOD AT THE CALETA

Cobquecura's **Caleta Rinconada de Taucú** is a great place to become acquainted with the common seafood found along Chile's Central Coast. Crab (*jaiba*) is abundant here. It's typically mixed with parmesan, cream and breadcrumbs and baked in a clay dish to make *pastel de jaiba*. Also present are Chilean blue mussels (*choritos*), which are steamed with white wine, rice and garlic to make *arroz con choritos*. Southern bull kelp (*cochayuyo*) is a versatile seaweed used for salads and vegan ceviche. Meanwhile, jackknife clams (*navajuelas*) and the fleshy orange tunicate *piure* are sold in tubs here. The latter is eaten raw and has a taste akin to sea urchin.

GETTING AROUND

Buses coming into town from Chillán and Concepción often continue from Cobquecura on to Buchupureo and Pullay, making it possible (though not ideal) to get around by bus. That said, because this string of beaches sprawls for about 20km, those without their own transportation are best off picking one area and sticking to it. Hotels can generally arrange transfers and transport.

Beyond Cobquecura

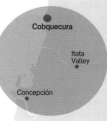

Cobquecura

Itata Valley

Concepción

Within a 125km radius of Cobquecura, you can find yourself in unconventional wineries or Chile's most underrated city.

Heading inland from Cobquecura, the ungrafted, bush-trained vines of the Itata Valley sprawl across rolling green hills otherwise blanketed in forests of pine and eucalyptus. The southern frontier of Chilean wine country has a completely different look and attitude than the more traditional valleys further north. Becoming trendy in Santiago wine circles, Itata is actually home to some of the oldest vineyards in the Americas, and the grapes are now turned into natural and low-intervention wines.

The Río Itata is the heart of the valley. Follow the even larger Río Biobío (Chile's widest river) and you'll end up in the largest city south of Santiago, Concepción, known for its universities, rock bands, arts scene and vibrant cafe culture.

TOP TIP

Itata Valley and Concepción are little visited by international tourists. Social media is best for contact details and intel on opening hours.

Concepción (p188)

CRISTIAN MUNOZ/SHUTTERSTOCK ©

Wine grapes

The Wild West of Chilean Wine

TASTING THE ITATA VALLEY

Ask an enologist in Santiago what region they're most excited about at the moment, and chances are they'll mention the Itata Valley. The most established of Chile's southern wine regions, it's nevertheless dominated by boutique vineyards and garage wine operations, making it very much the Wild West of wine tourism. The valley is vast in size, so it's best to concentrate your visit on the rural commune of **Guarilihue**, about 70km south of Cobquecura, which has a nascent tourism industry. **Borra Bar de Vinos** is the most alluring spot to grab lunch and find your bearings. Tucked into a charming adobe building, its young owners offer only natural or low-intervention wines, pairing them with creative seasonal plates of top quality.

Nearby, **Vinos TresC** showcases its excellent bottles of cinsault and país, while **Viña Piedras del Encanto** pours award-winning sparkling wines. **Viña Mora Reyes** highlights its wide production range, including varietals rare in Chile like chasselas and aramon. The fabulous **Viña La Fábula de Guarilihue** gives tours of its 100-year-old adobe cellar before bringing you (and some bottles) up to a sweeping viewpoint

OLD VINES, WILD WINES

With more than 500 years of history, the Itata Valley is considered one of the oldest wine-growing regions in the Americas, but because its common grape varietals were historically used for blending, it's never gotten much hype. That's changing. Vines of traditional church grapes like país (a rustic red) and Muscat of Alexandria (a slightly sweet white) can be well over 100 years old and are often made into natural wines. Enologists tend to be even more excited about the old-vine sémillon (a floral white) and cinsault (a fresh fruit-forward red), which are served at top Chilean restaurants. **Tienda Alma del Itata** in Ñipas has 160 Itata labels, making it a great stop to purchase rare bottles.

 WHERE TO STAY IN THE ITATA VALLEY

TresC
This winery has everything from hilltop domes to comfortable vine-side private rooms. $

Entre Viñedos
An agritourism operation with a spectacular pool, enthusiastic host and rooms overlooking cinsault vines. $$

Guariliwe Ecolodge & Wines
Woodsy chalet that's a great option for groups, with three rooms, a pool and hot tub. $$

Universidad de Concepción

CONCE'S ROCK HISTORY

Concepción is known as the cradle of Chilean rock. Some of the nation's biggest bands emerged from the city's vibrant live music scene, including Los Tres (one of the most influential Rock En Español bands of the 20th century) and Los Bunkers, who blend Beatles-inspired rock with the roots of Chilean folk music. Other bands originating in Conce include Emociones Clandestinas, Santos Dumont, De Saloon, Machuca and Julius Popper, while Chile's most influential musical export, Los Prisioneros (pioneers of the Nuevo Pop Chileno movement) played their first major concert here.

of the bird-filled forest that inspired its labels. Open weekends, it's the only winery in the area with English-language tours. As with all vineyards in Itata, make reservations at least 24 hours in advance.

Big-City Lights

ARTS AND CULTURE IN CONCEPCIÓN

About 125km south of Cobquecura, Concepción ('Conce') is the third-largest metropolitan area in Chile after Santiago and Greater Valparaíso. Yet this attractive university town with an energetic and youthful arts, music and culture scene receives just a fraction of the tourists who visit the nation's other hubs. Culture vultures should make the detour to see institutions like **La Casa del Arte**, located on the campus of **Universidad de Concepción** (UdeC, one of Latin America's most prestigious institutions). The star attraction is the kaleidoscopic (and fiercely political) mural **Presencia de América Latina** by Mexican artist Jorge González Camarena.

For more socially minded artwork, take a stroll around the UdeC campus and check out the vibrant public murals. Afterward, walk three blocks to **Artistas del Acero**, a cultural center with rotating art exhibitions. Check what's playing at **Teatro Biobío**, which hosts concerts, opera, theater and dance on the largest stage in Chile.

Explore Conce's vibrant live music scene at some of Chile's wildest venues, including **Casa de Salud**. This labyrinthine space blurs the lines between bar, club, concert venue, art gallery and cultural center, making it a multisensory experience for the mind, body and soul. Neighboring **La Bodeguita de Nicanor** is no less bohemian, staging everything from traditional Chilean folk music to Latin rock and roll.

GETTING AROUND

Twice daily buses connect Cobquecura with Concepción. Buses Via Itata links towns in the Itata Valley, though to visit the rural vineyards, you'll want to have your own vehicle or travel on a guided tour with an agency like Coelemu-based Itata Expediciones.

TERMAS DE CHILLÁN

Santiago
Termas de Chillán

Each winter, powder fiends flock to Termas de Chillán, Chile's prettiest ski resort, to carve turns down the longest piste in South America, which winds through dense evergreens in the shadow of the perennially puffing Volcán Chillán. After a long day on the slopes, they retreat to thermally heated pools to soothe sore muscles. Bumper-to-bumper traffic is not uncommon in high season (between June and August), though the pace is way less manic the rest of the year, when the surrounding valley, Valle Las Trancas, turns a luscious green.

From spring to fall, the rolling hills and snowcapped volcanoes lure hikers, climbers and mountain bikers. Some come simply to laze around and drink in the views. Termas de Chillán has the addictive charm of a youthful mountain town, and the area has three craft breweries. Middle Chile's best mountain lodges, hostels and cabins are here, and thankfully, the food scene is catching up.

TOP TIP

Visiting Termas de Chillán midweek can be a big money-saver on everything from lift tickets to lodging. Outside of the busy winter ski season, you'll likely have the whole valley to yourself. Be sure to stock up on supplies: a lot of establishments close down midweek during slower months.

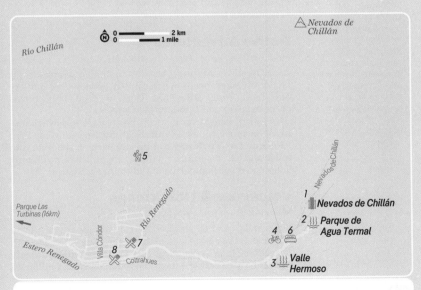

HIGHLIGHTS
1 Nevados de Chillán
2 Parque de Agua Termal
3 Valle Hermoso

ACTIVITIES, COURSES & TOURS
4 Laguna del Huemul
10 Bike Park

SLEEPING
5 Hotel Termas Chillán

EATING
8 Bistro Las Cabras
9 Las Bravas Bar & Café
see 9 Malcontenta Panadería

The Powder Capital of South America

SKIING NEVADOS DE CHILLÁN

The southern slopes of 3186m-high **Volcán Chillán** are the stunning setting of ski hub **Nevados de Chillán**. Though it draws smaller international crowds than the resorts near Santiago, in-the-know powder hounds have always had a special place in their hearts for this southerly rival. Unusual for Chile's ski resorts, many of its 34 runs track through the forest, with a good mix for beginners and more experienced skiers. Superlatives abound: Nevados de Chillán has the longest piste in South America (the 13km **Las Tres Marías**), the longest chairlift and some of the best off-piste offerings too.

The ski season can start as early as mid-June and usually lasts until mid-September. Locals swear that great snow, empty slopes and discounted ski passes make early September one of the best times to come, though seasons have been getting shorter every year. In general, the favorable climatic conditions give it some of the best powder on the continent. Hostels and discount ski rentals in town make it a more affordable option than resorts near Santiago, though if money allows, the stunning ski-in, ski-out **Hotel Termas Chillán** really is worth it. Chile's handsomest winter lodge, it has a heated indoor-outdoor pool, the nation's largest spa, haute dining options and a swirling woodsy design inspired by the surrounding forests.

Active Adventures

BIKING AND MORE IN TERMAS DE CHILLÁN

Each December to April, Nevados de Chillán swaps skis for mountain bikes, opening several lifts for downhill and enduro racers to the **Bike Park**. Open weekends only outside of the January and February high season.

For a more scenic 26km bike ride, book a day trip down the unpaved roads of picturesque **Valle de Diguillín** with Verde Tour.

Parque Las Turbinas is a private park on the road into town, and has waterfalls, zip lines, canopy walks, swimming holes and other family-friendly adventure activities

Volcanoes & Hot Springs

RELAXING IN THERMAL WATERS

What makes Termas de Chillán truly unique among global ski areas is the abundance of thermal waters where you can relax after a long day on the slopes. **Valle Hermoso** is a leafy recreation area between town and the Nevados de Chillán ski

WHERE TO EAT IN TERMAS DE CHILLÁN

Malcontenta Panadería
This hipster bakery with drool-worthy croissants and baguettes does seriously delicious pizzas too. $

Las Bravas Bar & Café
A can't-go-wrong mountain resto-bar with craft beers, burgers, pizzas, ceviches and salads. $$

Bistro Las Cabras
The valley's finest restaurant has delectable meat and pasta dishes; only open in summer and winter. $$$

resort with three open-air thermally heated pools and an on-site restaurant. Higher up the mountain is the more exposed **Parque de Agua Termal**, which has sweeping valley views and four pools. Neither are particularly fancy, and you can expect to pay a premium in winter months.

For something a bit wilder, hike out to **Valle de Aguas Calientes**, a full-day 9km journey replete with a string of thermally heated river pools. Given the volcanic nature of the area, it's best visited with a guide. **Verde Tour** (verdetour. com) is a great option for this and other active adventures in the area, such as biking, backpacking and ascending volcanoes big (**Volcán Nevado**) and small (**Volcán Renegado**) with well-trained English-speaking guides.

Hiking to Laguna del Huemul

AN EPIC ANDEAN ADVENTURE

Of all the hikes in the greater Termas de Chillán region, **Laguna del Huemul** has emerged as the most popular – and for good reason. You climb up to a dramatic overlook of an Andean lagoon, get great views of Volcan Chillán and Nevados de Chillán, and traverse dense native forests of oak, lenga and coihue. At 10km round trip, with 700m of ascent, it's enough to get your heart racing without being out of reach for most active visitors.

The trail begins near the defunct adventure park Ecoparque Shangri-La. Follow marked trails to the stone ruins of **Refugio Shangri-La**, an abandoned mountain shelter from the 1940s. The real uphill push begins from here. As you travel deep into the woods, listen for the hammering sounds of Magellanic woodpeckers. At the top, near the craggy summit of **Cerro Las Cabras** (2024m), you'll get a sweeping view of the turquoise lagoon nestled amid the surrounding peaks. Solo hikers should download the Chilean app SUDA, which offers offline trail maps from fellow users. If visiting in winter, keep in mind that the trail will likely be inaccessible, but you can still travel up to Refugio Shangri-La by snowshoe.

GETTING AROUND

Several daily buses travel to Termas de Chillán from Chillán, which is connected to Santiago by regular buses and the train. The greatest frequency is over the winter months.

The valley is exceedingly bike friendly in the summer, though many prefer to explore by rental car, typically driving in from Santiago.

Beyond Termas de Chillán

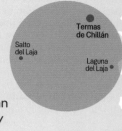

Termas
de Chillán

Salto
del Laja

Laguna
del Laja

The Andes north and south of Termas de Chillán are riddled with national parks little explored by foreign tourists.

Termas de Chillán might be the standout mountain resort of Middle Chile, but it's not the only one. Far from it; the Andes here are bisected by paved roads departing from just about every major town along Ruta 5. In general, the further south you go, the greener the mountains become and the more volcanoes there are spiking up the horizon. Antuco is the closest mountain village south of Termas de Chillán and is the gateway to Parque Nacional Laguna del Laja, a raw landscape of jagged lava fields, pounding waterfalls and crackling glaciers. The park also has one of the largest high-altitude lakes in all of the Chilean Andes.

TOP TIP

The regional capital of Chillán is an invaluable transport hub for heading south to Andean parklands or west to the coast.

Laguna del Laja

TEDDY ARAOS MOORE/SHUTTERSTOCK ©

Volcan Antuco

Volcanoes, Waterfalls & Lagoons

HIKING IN LAGUNA DEL LAJA

Laguna del Laja's **Volcan Antuco** (2979m) is perhaps the most stereotypically conical volcano in all of Chile. In winter, its perennially snowcapped summit attracts avid skiers, but the real joy of visiting comes the rest of the year when you can hike the park's myriad trails, which traverse ethereal lava fields, fast-disappearing glaciers and one of the largest alpine lakes in Chile, the namesake **Laguna del Laja**.

The two most popular trails (both 1.6km one way) set off from the Chacay lookout. **Sendero Los Coihues** traverses a forest of Chilean cedar to a fabulous volcano lookout. **Sendero Las Chilcas**, meanwhile, is the star attraction. After a 500m clifftop stretch that is wheelchair accessible, the trail dips into a lava field before making a circuit around the Río Laja to a series of powerful, splaying waterfalls. Those looking for more action should tackle **Sendero Sierra Velluda**, a 4.6km one-way hike (about five hours round trip) to the glacier at the base of Sierra Velluda (3585m). While Velluda is dormant, neighboring Antuco is very much active. The last big eruption was in 1869, but there is frequent fumarolic activity.

While close to Termas de Chillán as the condor flies, this area can take more than three hours to reach because of the horseshoe road route. Staying overnight is recommended. Options include **Antucalhue** (which has basic cabins, a pool and restaurant about five minutes outside park boundaries) and **Parque Antuco**, which lies in a dramatic valley encased in mountains inside the park with A-frame cabins and campsites.

A WORTHY ROADSIDE ATTRACTION

The Río Laja plunges nearly 50m over a steep escarpment to form the horseshoe-shaped **Salto del Laja waterfall**, which lies north of Los Ángeles off Ruta 5. Some have dubbed the sight a miniature Iguazú Falls when at full blast, though the comparison is far-fetched. Still, the falls are a great stopping point on any road trip to picnic, take a scenic boat ride, grab some souvenirs or overnight at one of the budget-friendly holiday parks, which are full of local character. For something a bit more sophisticated, try the serene **Hotel Salto del Laja**.

GETTING AROUND

Unless you're a determined public transport rider with ample time to transfer in regional capitals on Ruta 5 and wait for once-daily buses, you'll want to rent a car to explore the Andean parks north and south of Termas de Chillán. In general, roads are in great condition.

SUR CHICO

OMINOUS VOLCANOES, PRISTINE WATERWAYS AND OUTDOOR ADVENTURES

Conical volcanoes looming over picturesque turquoise lakes and rivers highlight Sur Chico's striking nature. German- and Mapuche-influenced culture and open-air escapades supplement the serene beauty.

This region is poetically labeled Sur Chico ('Little South'), but the other nicknames for this area (Zona Sur, Los Lagos, Lakes and Volcanoes) inspire equal awe. The regions of La Araucanía, Los Ríos and the Lakes District (Los Lagos) is an absolutely jarring brigade of fire-and-brimstone volcanoes whose ice-topped runoff empties into glacial lakes of impossibly hued jade and cerulean brilliance and gushing rivers carving routes through old-growth Valdivian rainforest. The entire region is an outdoor adventure Eden that dishes out thrill-seeking opportunities unrivaled on the continent, most of which present themselves in one of Sur Chico's nine national parks and reserves.

While Sur Chico's perfectly shaped volcanoes, many of which roar to life with un-settling regularity, define the landscape, it's a potpourri of seemingly opposing societies that characterize the culture. La Araucanía is the spiritual heartland of the Mapuche, Chile's largest indigenous ethnicity, and their influence is palpable in every nook and cranny of Sur Chico. Germans settled large swathes in and around Puerto Montt, Puerto Varas, Osorno and Valdivia, a result of Chile's 1845 Law of Selective Immigration that aimed to lure middle- and upper-class Europeans to settle in and develop southern Chile. The outcome is an outdoor wonderland punctuated by Mapuche spirituality and Deutschtum-accented traditions, each of which harmoniously characterizes one of the Southern Hemisphere's most stunning locales.

THE MAIN AREAS

TEMUCO
Blue-collar La Araucanía capital near extraordinary parks. p200

PUCÓN
Adventure-sports HQ under a menacing volcano. p207

VALDIVIA
Beer-loving riverside town with German soul. p214

PUERTO MONTT & LAGO LLANQUIHUE
Gorgeous lake, looming volcanoes and sublime nature. p220

SUR CHICO

LEFT: LMEDEIROS/SHUTTERSTOCK ©. RIGHT: MBPROJEKT_MACIEJ_BLEDOWSKI/GETTY IMAGES ©

Left: Parque Nacional Vicente Pérez Rosales (p226); above: Volcán Villarrica and Pucón (p207)

Find Your Way

Sur Chico takes up a nearly 100,000 sq km chunk of southern Chile, covering a stretch that begins 130km or so north of Temuco (La Araucanía) to the southern tip of Chiloé (Los Lagos).

Pucón, p207

Chile's lakeside outdoor adventure HQ, Pucón lives and plays according to the whims of the active Volcán Villarrica. Extreme sports, hot springs and entertainment abound.

Laguna Gualletué

Lago Aluminé

Lago Currhu

Lonquimay

Lago Conguillio

Pueco

Lago Caburgua

Caburgua○

Lago Pellaifa

Curacautín

Lago Collico

○Pucón

Choshue

Cherquenco   Cunco

Lago Villarrica

Lago Calafquén

Lago Panguip

San Patricio

El Pastal

Lican Ray

Rin Rini

Los Laureles

Villarrica

Vilcun○

Germania ○Choroico

Huiscapi   Panguipulli

○Mulchen

San Miguel

Arquenco

Miraflores

Radal ○Coipue

Dollinco ○

Ercilla   ○Victoria ○Perquenco

Lautaro○ ○Pillanlelbun

Malih

Collipulli

Loncoche

El Puma

Santa Elvira   El Panal

Temuco 🏛

Quepe Freire

Angol   ○Nielol

Pitrufquen

Lanco

San

Antill

Traiguen

Labranza

Reduccion

○Trintre ○Bellavista ○Galvarino

Barros ○Manquen

Jose De La Mariquina

Los○ Lumaco

Nueva Imperial

Arana

Caupolican

Tres○   Pelchua

Sauces

Capitan ○Pastene

Comuy

Aragon

Cruces   Cayumapu○

○Pillimpilli ○Puren Los

Parcelas ○Chilco

Teodoro Schmidt   Río Tolten

Valdiv

Los Notros   Contulmo

Laureles

Gualpin ○Tolten   La Barra   🏛 🍺

Lago Lleulleu

Lago del Budi

Quidico○   La Peuca

Nahuentue

Valdivia, p214

A German-influenced Pacific coast workhorse at the confluence of three rivers, the Los Ríos capital boasts a vibrant beer scene, Spanish forts and sidewalk-lounging sea lions.

Temuco, p200

A blue-collar town with a Mapuche backbone, the Araucanía capital mostly serves as the gateway for an arsenal of unmissable, eruption-shaped national parks and reserves.

TOP: WAREHOUSE OF IMAGES/SHUTTERSTOCK ©, BOTTOM: HECTOR MONTERO/SHUTTERSTOCK ©

CAR

Save a few routes to some national parks and hot springs (Conguillío, Huerquehue and Termas Geométricas, for example), Sur Chico's roads are in excellent condition and mostly paved, so renting a car is the recommended option for a fully explorative visit.

FERRY

A smattering of gorgeous lakes pepper the region, some of which require a ferry ride to cross. Examples include Lago Tagua-Tagua between Puelo and Llanada Grande, and Lago Todos Los Santos between Petrohué and Puella.

BUS

An excellent public transportation network consisting of buses, minibuses, vans and minivans operate through the region and are the most low-maintenance way to get around, but some smaller and more remote towns might require backtracking to the closest city to find the correct bus.

ARGENTINA

San Martín de Los Andes

Lago Traf ul

San Carlos de Bariloche

Lago Nahuel Huapi

Lago Mascardi

Lago Lácar

go log

Lago Moreno

Lago Puelo

rehueico

Lago Blanco

Lago Maihue

Lago Huishue

Lago Vidal Gormaz

Lago Tagua Tagua

Río Puelo

Peulla

Llifen

Lago Todos Los Santos

Lago Cayutué

Cochamó

Puelo

Futrono

Lago Ranco

Lago Puyehue

Lago Rupanco

Petrohue

Ensenada

Hornopirén

ontuela

Lago Rancho

Entre Lagos

Quillaipe

Caleta Manzano

a Pellinada hica

Río Bueno

Río Chirri

Lago Llanquihue

Seno de Reloncaví

Paillaco

Río Bueno

San Pablo

Pichil

Puerto Octay

Puerto Varas

Puerto Montt

Golfo de Ancud

Los Ulmos

La Union

Osorno

Purranque

Frutillar

Llanquihue

Los Quemas

Trumao

Río Negro

Riachuelo

Fresia

Los Muermos

Tegualda

Parga

Maullín

Carelmapu

Chiloé

rral

Hueicolla

Río Huayelhue

Bahía Mansa

Ancud

PACIFIC OCEAN

Puerto Montt & Lago Llanquihue, p220

Big-city transport and adventure tourism infrastructure work congruently as gateways to Chile's second-largest lake, the volcano-backed and incredibly picturesque Lago Llanquihue.

0

0

100 km

50 miles

Plan Your Time

Outdoor endeavors of all sorts are Sur Chico's calling, with hiking, climbing and kayaking in various national parks, reserves and other scenic settings.

Huilo-Huilo Biological Reserve (p218)

Fast and Furious

● If you only have time to do one thing in Sur Chico, check ahead on the current situation in **Pucón** (p207), and if summits are allowed, head to Parque Nacional Villarrica to climb its showpiece attraction, **Volcán Villarrica** (p211). Peering into the fiery crater of an active volcano is the thrill of a lifetime, and you will see, feel and smell incredible things that won't easily be shaken from your consciousness. After summiting, slide down on your backside and head into town, where you can swap tall tales of volcano conquering over pisco sours with fellow travelers. Don't miss a meal at **Trawen** (p209).

Seasonal Highlights

Seasonal outdoor recreations abound; winter is all about snow sports. April to June is purgatorial: sunny days have faded, but snow has yet to arrive.

JANUARY
Beginning in late January, the **Semana Musical de Frutillar** brings 10 days of world-class music to Lago Llanquihue.

FEBRUARY
Valdivians break out the beer mugs for Kunstmann's **Bierfest**, one of Chile's biggest beer festivals.

MARCH
Fall sunshine, highs around 19°C and fewer people keep **Puerto Varas** idyllic. Rivers present technical challenges for rafters and kayakers.

JÖRG SANCHO PERNAS/WIKIPEDIA/CC BY-SA 3.0 ©, JAZZ3311/SHUTTERSTOCK ©, JMAV/SHUTTERSTOCK ©

A Week to Travel Around

● If you're moving through the region and have a week to devote to Sur Chico, divide your time between the region's two magnificent adventure capitals, **Pucón** (p207) and **Puerto Varas** (p224), using them as bases for exploring their environs. From Pucón, seek out the dramatic landscapes of **Parque Nacional Villarrica** (p211), **Parque Nacional Conguillío** (p204) and **Reserva Nacional Malalcahuello-Nalcas** (p203).

● Out of Puerto Varas, spend a few days exploring the culture, cuisine and natural attractions around **Lago Llanquihue** (p220), **Reloncaví Fjord** (p228) and Chile's oldest national park, **Parque Nacional Vicente Pérez Rosales** (p226). A gorgeous, utterly menacing volcano is never out of sight.

With More Time

● Base yourself in **Pucón** (p207) and **Puerto Varas** (p224), taking in all the outdoor adventures you can muster.

● Spend a few nights at fantastic national park lodgings such as **La Baita** (p205) in Parque Nacional Conguillío, **Refugio Tinquilco** (p212) in Parque Nacional Huerquehue and **La Montaña Mágica** (p219) in Huilo-Huilo Biological Reserve.

● Bring your thirst to **Valdivia** (p214), home to one of Chile's most hop-heavy beer scenes. Pack suds to go to enjoy in more far-flung highlights such as **Caleta Cóndor** (p230), hidden away along a hard-to-reach stretch of the Osorno coast, and **La Junta** (p232), tucked 12km deep into the Río Cochamó Valley.

JULY

Ski season kicks off at Corralco Resort de Montaña, Centro de Montaña Pillán and Centro de Ski y Montaña Volcán Osorno.

SEPTEMBER

Arguably the most ideal month to visit. Rising temperatures allow for both a morning ski and an afternoon **kayak**.

NOVEMBER

Pretty perfect: Spring has sprung, and summer crowds are a month or two away. Rivers run high for optimal **rafting**.

DECEMBER

Beat the high-season crowds in **Pucón** and Puerto Varas while still enjoying dry days and warm temperatures.

TEMUCO

⚙ **Santiago**

Temuco ●

Former Temuco resident Pablo Neruda, one of most influential poets of the 20th century, once referred to the city as the Wild West. The lauded poet's take on the capital of La Araucanía is unsurprising. It's a blue-collar working town that doesn't offer much in the way of tourist pleasantries, but the surrounding nature, some of which counts as the most incredible in all of South America, would prove influential on the poet's work. His first book of poetry, 1923's *Crepuscular-io*, was largely inspired by his time in Temuco.

Today, Temuco is one of the biggest cities in southern Chile south and is fundamentally connected to the traditional land of the Mapuche, the continent's largest indigenous group. Although it's not a high-value destination in itself, most travelers spend some time here, if only to find transport to La Araucanía's arsenal of stunning national parks.

TOP TIP

Temuco's trendiest restaurants, bars and coffee houses congregate around Av Alemania west of Av Caupolicán in the surrounding vicinity of Portal Temuco, the city's nicest shopping mall. If you have only one night to spend in the city, head there for several great options.

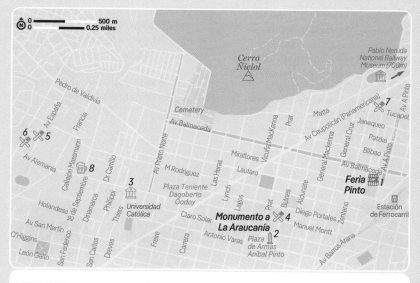

HIGHLIGHTS
1 Feria Pinto
2 Monumento a La Araucanía

SIGHTS
3 Museo Regional de La Araucanía

EATING
4 Confiteria Central
5 Gohan Sushi
6 Mercato
7 Zuny Tradiciones

DRINKING & NIGHTLIFE
8 Casa Birra

Merkén spices, Feria Pinto

Pit-Stop Temuco

LIVELY MARKETS AND MAPUCHE CULTURE

Truth be told, most visitors position Temuco in the rearview mirror as soon as possible on the way to the incredible national parks in its surroundings. Fair enough. But if you do wind up in town because of the whims of the wind (or more likely travel logistics), Temuco has culture to consume. Pablo Neruda spent much of his childhood in Temuco, having moved here in 1906 when his father came to work on the railways, commemorated at Temuco's **Pablo Neruda National Railway Museum**.

Temuco's intrinsic link to Mapuche culture is immediately evident. Spend a moment admiring the centerpiece of the leafy, palm-filled Plaza de Armas Aníbal Pinto, **Monumento a La Araucanía**, which features a Mapuche warrior and Mapuche shaman alongside a soldier, a European settler and a Spanish poet. Stroll the city's gargantuan market, **Feria Pinto**, where rows of food, produce, Mapuche spices (notably *merkén*, a smoked chili pepper), woolen goods (ponchos, blankets and pullovers) and other knickknacks fill a few city blocks. Enjoy a wonderful lunch of the simple but fabulous Chilean-Mapuche fusion of **Zuny Tradiciones**. In the afternoon, pop into **Museo Regional de La Araucanía**, housed in a handsome frontier-style building dating from 1924, for excellent regional exhibits and a Mapuche dugout canoe, as well as **Tienda Rakizuam**, a boutique for the beautiful wares from Fundación Chol-Chol, a nonprofit fair-trade organization representing 600 rural Mapuche women.

In the evening, pop into **Casa Birra**, a 35-tap hops hideaway in the Paseo Los Suizos strip mall, followed by dinner at **Gohan Sushi** (for creative, Chilean-infused sushi) or **Mercato** (an Italian-leaning spot for burgers, fresh pastas and pizzas).

I LIVE HERE: TEMUCO'S GREATEST HITS

Max Rueca (@ maxreuca) is a political activist and the *werken* (spokesperson) for Comunidad Mapuche Loncoyan in Puren. He shares his tips for Temuco.

Feria Pinto
I love this market of Mapuche handicrafts and vegetables at Balmaceda and General Pinto.

Confiteria Central
I recommend this spot for delicious coffee and pastries in the heart of downtown Temuco.

Avenida Alemania
For a night out, you can enjoy a delicious appetizer in the variety of rustic and vintage pub-restaurants in this area.

Monumento Natural Cerro Ñielol
For those who like flora and fauna, this great park is at the foot of Temuco.

GETTING AROUND

Temuco's city center is walkable, but if you're not up for legging it a kilometer or two, Uber works just fine.

Beyond Temuco

The fiercely active volcanoes around Temuco have left behind dramatically altered landscapes protected as starkly beautiful parks.

Parque Nacional Tolhuaca
Corralco Re de Montaña
Reserva Nacional Malalcahuello-Nalcas
Temuco
Parque Nacional Conguillío

Temuco is the gateway to a series of national parks and reserves within easy reach of the city, all of which feature dazzling volcanoes as protagonists. To the west and northwest of town, scenes seemingly not of this Earth emerge in Parque Nacional Conguillío and Reserva Nacional Malalcahuello-Nalcas. These side-by-side nature retreats transformed by fiery volcanic eruptions (Llaima's 2008 eruption at Conguillío and 1990's Lonquimay purge at Malalcahuello-Nalcas) serve up some of Chile's most cinematic hiking and skiing, but evocative trips by car await as well. Parque Nacional Conguillío has a drivable road straight through its heart, making for an unrivaled road trip radically unlike those that cruise along standard highways.

TOP TIP

Tickets to Parque Nacional Conguillío must be reserved in advance online (aspticket.cl). Rangers need to see the QR code for entry.

Lago Conguillío and Volcán Llaima (p204), Parque Nacional Conguillío

ROBERTO VERDE/SHUTTERSTOCK ©

Reserva Nacional Malalcahuello-Nalcas

GRA-CAIDEAS/SHUTTERSTOCK ©

Mars or Malalcahuello-Nalcas?

HIKING VOLCÁN LONQUIMAY'S SCALDED LANDSCAPES

Of the three volcanic-driven parks around Temuco, it's 303-sq-km **Reserva Nacional Malalcahuello-Nalcas**, about a two-hour drive east of the city, that will most transport you to another planet. An ashy desertscape of sand and cinders not unlike how we all imagine Mars, the reserve protects a wild singed landscape surrounding Cráter Navidad, which formed on Christmas Day 1988 when Volcán Lonquimay blew its top.

If you're short on time, you can drive to **Corralco Resort de Montaña** for a taste of these scorched-Earth badlands (snow often prevents driving deeper into the park), but even more dramatic perspectives await on a series of two- to five-hour hikes. The most easily accessible trail is **Piedra Santa** (7.5km one way, five hours), which is the beginning stretch of the longer Laguna Blanca Trail. The trail starts near the small Conaf information center near the road to the hamlet of Malalcahuello along the highway to Lonquimay. You can also trek to **Cráter Navidad** (1.5km one way, two hours), the ground-zero showpiece of this charred reserve. Find the trailhead 4.8km north of the ski resort.

THE ROAD LESS TRAVELED

As the early morning mist burns off from the surrounding hill country, flocks of parrots can sometimes be spotted on the dusty road that leads to 64-sq-km **Parque Nacional Tolhuaca**, a clear indication you're on the road less traveled. One of the park system's best-kept secrets, mainly because it's harder to get to than nearby Conguillío and Malalcahuello-Nalcas, Tolhuaca is 120km northeast of Temuco, on the north bank of the Río Malleco. The park offers hiking over elevation changes from 850m around Laguna Malleco to 1830m on the summit of Cerro Colomahuida. The 2806m Volcán Tolhuaca is beyond the park's southeastern boundaries.

 WHERE TO STAY AROUND MALALCAHUELLO

Andenrose	**Suizandina Lodge**	**Spectra Lodge**
Fully equipped lodgings built by a Bavarian carpenter along the Río Cautín; warm hospitality and great food. **$$**	German-staffed, Swiss-Chilean run ranch; roomy lodgings, horses and Swiss specialties are highlights. **$$**	Magical realism fantasy lodge dreamed up by a Kiwi-Canadian couple; incredible Lonquimay views. **$$$**

203

Llaima's Furious Heart

A 4WD vehicle is recommended for this incredible 90-minute drive through the core of Parque Nacional Conguillío, a seared, otherworldly landscape forged by the 2008 eruption of menacing Volcán Llaima (3125m). Standard cars can usually make it too, unless the road is in particularly poor condition after a hard rain. Heading south from Curacautín, an 80-minute drive from Temuco, there's one dicey uphill just after Laguna Captrén. Gun it and go!

1 Laguna Captrén

Entering from Curacautín, stop at Guardería Captrén 6km before Laguna Captrén and show your entry ticket QR code (US$13; must be purchased online in advance at aspticket.cl). The road is closed from June to September. Gaggles of submerged trees poke up through the water's surface at this small translucent lagoon, which becomes a bird sanctuary during migration season (October to March). You'll drive right past the 2008 lava flow, taking in the entire beautiful catastrophe.

The Drive: Continue south 7km. Immediately after Laguna Captrén, there's an uphill that will challenge a non-4WD car. Stay in first gear and keep your foot on the gas – we have always made it in an economy rental car!

2 Lago Conguillío

Volcano melt and numerous eruptions over the years formed this picturesque lake. Camping Los Ñirres, one of five Sendas Conguillío campgrounds, run on concession from Conaf, and has a small cafe with lake views. Fishing and kayaking are options.

ABRIENDOMUNDO/SHUTTERSTOCK ©

Lago Conguillío and Volcán Llaima, Parque Nacional Conguillío

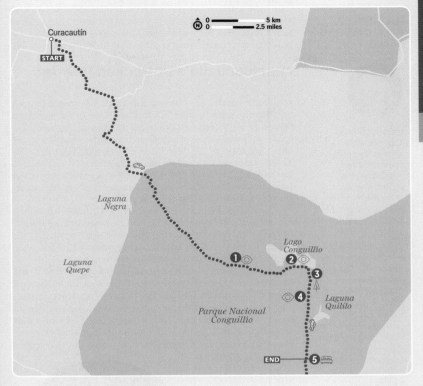

The Drive: From Lago Conguillío, the road turns into a mix of loose and compacted sand. Continue 3.5km through tangles of photogenic araucaria (monkey puzzle trees).

3 Sendero Sierra Nevada

Perfect for a pause, the Sierra Nevada Trail (7km, three hours one-way) leaves from the small parking lot at Playa Linda. Climbing steadily northeast through dense coigüe forests, the trail passes a pair of lake overlooks. From the second and more scenic overlook, you can see solid stands of araucarias beginning to supplant coigües on the ridge top.

The Drive: Head 2.5km south from Sendero Sierra Nevada.

4 Laguna Arcoíris

A small platform lookout frames this small lagoon, a translucent marriage of heavy-hued swirls of jade and turquoise that formed when lava jammed up a nearby estuary. On calm and clear days, you'll see the bottom, along with dazzling reflections of the surroundings.

The Drive: Go 6.5km south through Conguillío's blackened, jaw-dropping scenery.

5 La Baita

At the end of the trip, relax at this wonderful and stylish lodge run by ex-singer Isabel Correa. It has nine cabins and nine rooms with slow-burning furnaces, solar- and turbine-powered electricity and design-forward sinks. Even if you don't stay the night, you can refuel at the great restaurant/lounge/hangout space before continuing on.

**I LIVE HERE:
MALALCAHUELLO
BY BIKE**

Canadian **Kristin Kidd** (@k.kiddx) is the co-owner of **Spectra Lodge** in Malalcahuello and has lived in La Araucanía for seven years. She shares her favorite Malalcahuello pastime.

My favorite thing to do in Malalcahuello is riding on the **Ciclovía Malalcahuello-Manzanar** (bike lane). Whether you choose to walk, run, bike or even snowshoe in the winter, the gorgeous scenery will not disappoint. En route, you will be awed by the epic volcano views, the pristine flora and fauna, and the roaring river as you pass through antique tunnels and native forests. The best part is that the bike lane is apt for all fitness levels, so everyone can enjoy it.

In winter, the area turns into a full-blown ski resort, and snow covers the apocalyptic panorama between June and October. If you've come for the *Mad Max*-esque landscape as opposed to the powder, visit outside that time frame.

Malalcahuello's Untracked Powder

CHILE'S HOTTEST BACKCOUNTRY SKIING DESTINATION

While the novelty of skiing on an active volcano might not warrant the same wonder in Chile as it does in the Northern Hemisphere – Villarrica, Osorno and Chillán all run the risk of lava-swallowed slopes at any given moment – it's still a pretty sweet proposition. Within Reserva Nacional Malalcahuello-Nalcas, **Corralco Resort de Montaña** offers 810 vertical meters of skiing across 32 pistes, all of which are 100% above the tree line, but Malalcahuello also has some of the best backcountry skiing in southern Chile.

Experienced skiers should head up the **Cumbre** lift, which dumps you at 2400m (just 465m from Lonquimay's summit) to access the most interesting and steep ski terrain. But it's Malalcahuello's 250 sq km of backcountry skiing (off-piste access included) that have become fashionable.

If you're looking to ski tour or splitboard (a snowboard that has been split in half) and need assistance, get in touch with **Apex Backcountry Guides**, co-owned by an American former professional snowboarder and the most experienced backcountry guide in the area. The outfitter customizes your tour according to experience level and desired level of extreme. **Sled Chile** is the go-to agency for high-adrenaline backcountry snowmobile tours.

You could just ski the eight lifts, too – the US, Canadian and French Olympic ski teams have all trained here in their off-season – but that wouldn't be half as fun, would it?

VOLCANIC POWDER

Volcán Lonquimay is the best ski resort on an active volcano in Sur Chico, but it's not the only one. **Volcán Villarrica** (p211) and **Volcán Osorno** (p225) are other options. The latter has stunning views over Lago Llanquihue and Parque Nacional Vicente Pérez Rosales.

GETTING AROUND

Malalcahuello is spread out, and a car is best to get around the lodges, ski resort and national park.

PUCÓN

○ Santiago
● Pucón

Offering a world-class outdoor adventure lineup, ever-popular Pucón has drawn thrill-seekers from around the world for decades. Its setting on beautiful Lago Villarrica under the smoldering eye of the volcano of the same name seals its status as a top destination for adrenaline junkies, nature lovers and devotees of outdoor recreation of all types.

Though the city boasts the best small-town tourism infrastructure south of Costa Rica, it's struggling to keep pace. The town, home to just 28,500 people according to the 2017 census, became destination *numero uno* for folks wanting to work from home in a beautiful setting outside urban areas during the COVID-19 pandemic, resulting in some 30,000 additional residents. When coupled with alternating floods of Santiago vacationers, novice Brazilian snowboarders, adventure-seeking backpackers, new-age spiritualists and mellowed-out ex-activists turned eco-pioneers, the town can easily seem overrun, but there's no denying its allure. Life on the edge in Pucón is good.

TOP TIP

Hot springs are big business in Pucón, but not all are as natural as they claim. Some use boilers and chemicals to keep up appearances, which means you are paying a lot for what amounts to a heated swimming pool. Termas Los Pozones, Termas de Huife and Termas Geométricas are good bets.

Snowboarding, Lago Villarrica

ERIC BERGERI/GETTY IMAGES ©

I LIVE HERE: A PERFECT DAY IN PUCÓN

María Luisa Arratia is an independent mountain guide based in Pucón. Here are her top tips for spending your time in town.

The perfect day in Pucón is in the spring. Wake up early, go up to the crater of **Volcán Villarrica** and ski down to the car. And that's just in the morning! After coming down, stop to have a nice cold beer at **Restaurante El Castillo**, and then spend the afternoon on the beach or going rock climbing – everything is so close. Finish the day with friends at a barbecue or going out to **Mamas & Tapas** bar.

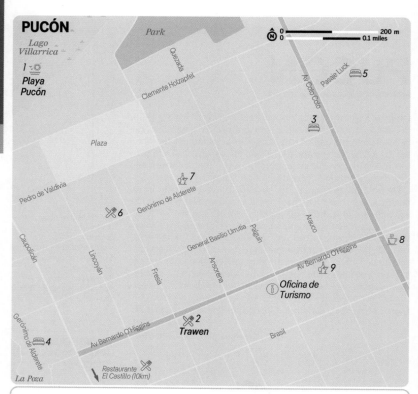

PUCÓN

1 Playa Pucón
7
6
2 Trawen

HIGHLIGHTS
1 Playa Pucón
2 Trawen

SLEEPING
3 Aldea Naukana

4 Chili Kiwi
5 French Andes II

EATING
6 La Maga

**DRINKING
& NIGHTLIFE**
7 El Camino
8 Madd Goat Coffee Roasters
9 Mama's & Tapas

Sur Chico's Outdoor Utopia

ADVENTURES IN PUCÓN

Pucón ranks up there with some of the world's great outdoor playgrounds. Take a 10-minute walk down Av Bernardo O'Higgins, Pucón's main street, and you encounter an avalanche of adventure outfitters selling every excursion imaginable. If you can hike it, jump from it, swim it, ride it or climb it, a company in Pucón is selling it. Many agencies offer the standard

WHERE TO STAY IN PUCÓN

Chili Kiwi
Pucón's most sociable hostel. Lakeside dorms, tree houses, cabins and Quonset-style huts, plus a guest-only pub. **$**

French Andes II
French-owned apart-hostel; fully equipped suites, good for longer stays. The backyard and Villarrica views delight. **$$**

Aldea Naukana
Native hardwoods and volcanic stone forms the backbone of this stylish 10-room boutique hotel. **$$$**

outings of climbing Volcán Villarrica and rafting Río Trancura. To avoid the overwhelm of options, have an idea of the adventures you want to do beforehand and peruse the *Libro de Reclamos* (tourist complaint book) at Pucón's **Oficina de Turismo** before making any final decisions.

In fact, spend a day getting acquainted with the city before committing to anything. Pucón is one of the nicest cities in Chile and offers a high standard of living. Though traditional sights and attractions are nonexistent, Pucón's charms lie in its streets, which are teeming with intrepid travelers hunched over from the weight of their trekking backpacks, swapping tall tales of high-elevation mountain escapades and plotting their next adventure. Mingle among the masses at places like **El Camino**, which draws in foreigners and locals for a bevy of creative burgers and good beers on draft (ask about Cerveza Puesco's Piedra Mala, a perfect Pucón porter often available off-menu). Don't miss the spectacular **Playa Pucón**, a black-sand beach hidden behind the Enjoy Hotels Pucón (Gran Hotel), a half moon-shaped patch of scorched tropical bliss.

After you've got your bearings, it's time to consider the highlights. **Antilco** is the go-to agency for horseback riding, mostly in the richly verdant Liucura Valley, Parque Nacional Huerquehue, Mapuche reservations, and even on to Argentina. Beginners and experts alike can opt for half- to 12-day horse treks with English-speaking guides.

If you want to get out on the water, you're spoiled for choice, though the rafting (and to a certain extent, the kayaking) in Pucón is minor league stuff. Nearby rivers (and their corresponding rapids classifications) include **Lower Trancura** (III), **Upper Trancura** (IV), **Liucura** (II–III), **Puesco Run** (V) and **Maichín** (IV–V). **Politur** and **Pucón Kayak School** are adequate for standard rafting and kayaking trips, respectively.

But honestly, you're better off saving your rafting budget for world-class Futaleufú in Patagonia and instead getting your water thrills in Pucón with hydrospeeding (whitewater swimming aided by a floating board and flippers), which packs a high-adrenaline punch for far fewer pesos compared to other places where the sport is practiced. Look at no other operator besides **Aventur** for this immersive rapids experience.

For rock climbing, contact internationally certified former Chilean climbing champion Claudio Retamal at **Summit Chile** and head to **Cerduo**, at the foot of Volcán Villarrica, where 40 climbing routes graded from 5.8 to 5.12d await. There's sport climbing as well as traditional, all surrounded by native forest, and Claudio can arrange more physically demanding routes as well.

Those activities are hardly the limit. There's also snowshoeing, skydiving, mountain paragliding, snowmobiling and exploring some of the smaller nature reserves on foot.

BEST PLACES TO EAT & DRINK IN PUCÓN

Trawen
Pucón's culinary workhorse of creativity and sustainability, with eclectic flavors enhanced by the restaurant's own certified organic gardens and fresh-baked everything. $$

La Maga
Top Sur Chico grill; a time-honored Uruguayan steakhouse excelling at *bife de chorizo* (steak) and other succulent cuts. $$$

Madd Goat Coffee Roasters
American owner Scott Roberts roasts Latin American and African beans in-house, producing southern Chile's best espresso.

Mamas & Tapas
Pucón's nightlife epicenter for years, with an all-wood interior designed by an acoustic engineer.

GETTING AROUND

Pucón proper is just a few – but growing! – lively streets easily conquered on foot.

Beyond Pucón

Fuming volcanoes, Mapuche strongholds, and a wonderland of waterfalls, alpine lakes and araucaria forests characterize Pucón's diverse surroundings.

Pucón •   Parque Nacional Huerquehue

Santuario El Cañi

Anita Epulef Cocina Mapuche

Aurora Austral Patagonia Husky

Parque Nacional Villarrica

Pleasant though it may be, Pucón mainly serves as a staging post for outdoor adventuring in its surrounds. Parque Nacional Villarrica, whose incredibly active centerpiece volcano looms over the town, is accessed in less than 15 minutes by car south of Pucón. The volcano plays host to a cornucopia of high-adrenaline happenings, including the region's signature undertaking: summiting the smoldering beast and ogling its blazing lava lakes and fountains from the crater's edge.

Beyond the show-stealing volcano, the glacial lakes and old-growth forests of Parque Nacional Huerquehue provide stunning walks in the woods along with one of Chile's most memorable *refugios* (rustic shelters), and Mapuche culture pervades everything here in the heartland of Chile's biggest indigenous group.

TOP TIP

The best time of year to ascend Volcán Villarrica is September to March, when both climatic and trail conditions are optimal.

Hikers, Volcán Villarrica crater

THOMAS HALLE/GETTY IMAGES ©

HIKE! GEE! HAW! WHOA!

German-run **Aurora Austral Patagonia Husky** is ready to take you for the ride of your life with the cutest Siberian huskies, Alaskan huskies and eurohounds (aka short sled dogs), 19km from Villarrica on the road to Lican Ray. Day trips are available in winter (and shorter 5km trips in summer), but an absolutely epic Andean crossing is a chance to bond with Latin America's fastest pups on a longer expedition. True dog lovers can stay on the grounds in four extremely nice cabins. Volunteers for stints of four to 12 weeks are also accepted.

Volcán Villarrica Five Ways

ESCAPADES ON AN ACTIVE VOLCANO

One of Chile's most active volcanoes, **Volcán Villarrica** lies just a 45-minute drive south of Pucón. This textbook-perfect stratovolcano peaking at 2847m is single-handedly responsible for putting Pucón on the global map as a center for adventure sports and is reason alone to visit this region of Chile. Its conical-shaped perfection is evidence of Mother Nature at her most flawless, but it simultaneously feeds the human need for outdoor action and escapades with a side of palpable risk.

You can tackle the volcano, the showpiece of **Parque Nacional Villarrica**, in a dizzying number of ways depending on the season, climatic conditions and, of course, whether this ominous (but gorgeous) beast is spitting lava. Topping the list is the breathtaking ascent to the volcano's crater. There aren't a lot of life experiences that can compare to summiting a roaring monster like Volcán Villarrica and peering down into the smoldering belly of the beast. It's a full-day activity, departing Pucón between 6am and 7am (depending on the season), and while no previous mountaineering experience is necessary, it's no Sunday stroll. Reaching the summit is never a guarantee, and if the weather turns, responsible agencies will always turn back, no questions asked. If summiting is allowed during your visit (it's often not because of volcanic activity), it's Pucón's signature moment. Contact **Aguaventura**, a French-owned agency with highly skilled volcano guides.

When Sernageomin (the government agency that monitors volcanic activity) shuts down ascents (or limits them to 500m from the crater, which isn't worthwhile), consider other ways of experiencing the volcano. In winter, the obvious choice is on skis or a snowboard. **Centro de Montaña Pillán**, on the northwest face of the volcano, is under concession by the same company that runs the El Colorado and Parques de Farellones ski resorts near Santiago. Safety and infrastructure improvements have been made, and at least four lifts and six slopes are available. The views from the mid-mountain lodge alone almost make the lift ticket worthwhile.

Non-skiers have a wealth of options, beginning with trekking. The **Villarrica Traverse** is the top choice. The three- or five-day outing ambles among all three of the national park's volcanoes (Villarrica, Quetrupillán and Lanín), across lenga and araucaria forest, lava fields and glacial rivers. **Ermitaño Expediciones** can handle the logistics.

It's forbidden to mountain bike on official Conaf trails, but countless volcano ride options exist. Aguaventura can

SAFETY ON VOLCÁN VILLARRICA

Summiting Volcán Villarrica is by far the top excursion in Pucón, but because of frequent volcanic activity, ascents to the crater are often suspended. A proper eruption hasn't occurred since 2015, but lava fountains inside the crater are almost always present. Check on the situation ahead of your visit with recommended agencies, as well as **Sernageomin** (sernageomin.cl), the official government agency for monitoring volcanic activity. If Villarrica is out of commission, summits are possible on nearby volcanoes Quetrupillán, Llaima and Lanín.

SKIING SUR CHICO'S ACTIVE VOLCANOES

If you're on a tour of ski resorts on active volcanoes, visit **Corralco Resort de Montaña** (p203) on Volcán Lonquimay and **Centro de Ski y Montaña Volcán Osorno** (p226) inside Parque Nacional Vicente Pérez Rosales.

 WHERE TO EAT BEYOND PUCÓN

El Sabio
Friendly Argentine couple creating wonderful uncut oblong pizzas served on small cutting boards in Villarrica. **$**

El Castillo
Homey gourmet food with an emphasis on game, including wild rabbit, venison stroganoff and wild boar. **$$**

Hotel Antumalal
Chilean-bent international cuisine making use of the hotel's organic vegetable patch. Patio views are outstanding. **$$$**

211

Parque Nacional Huerquehue

CHILE'S FIRST PRIVATE PARK

Chile has more than 2000 private parks, but it all started in 1991 when Fundación Lahuén, a small group of concerned folks, fundraised with Ancient Forests International and other organizations to purchase land near Río Liucura outside Pucón that was threatened by logging interests. From this effort, **Santuario El Cañi** was born, a drop-dead–gorgeous park that protects some 500 hectares of ancient araucaria forest, later turned over and now successfully maintained by a local guide association, Cañi Guides Group. This park is the longest-running, self-sustaining conservation project run by locals in Chile. It features a spectacular hiking trail that ascends steep terrain to Laguna Negra and onto a lookout with cinematic views of the area's volcanoes.

get you rolling and guide you. Appropriately named **El Clásico** is the most popular route, dropping 1000m along 9km of purpose-carved single track with outstanding views of Villarrica, Colico and Cabuga lakes. **Cerduo Bike Park** has five trails totaling 13km. Because of the loose and rocky terrain, downhill experience is a must – don't flip over the handlebars in the first 10 seconds like we did!

For something less active but equally thrilling, **night tours** go to Villarrica when it's particularly angry. From various vantage points on the volcano reached by car and a brief, unchallenging hike, you can ogle the volcano's fiery guts, setting the sky above the crater aglow. Weather permitting, it's a spectacular show.

Hide Away at Huerquehue

A REFUGIO TO REMEMBER

Shortly after the paved S-905 turns to dust 8km short of **Parque Nacional Huerquehue**, a 55-minute drive northeast of Pucón, it begins to snake up and over *El Alto*, local slang for the lush hilltop that leads to one of the shining stars of the south. But we're not talking about the 125 sq km park.

Non-4WD vehicles must be left behind once you reach Río Huerquehue. From here, understated signs ('*Refugio*') lead through fantastic forest, across the river and to your destination, **Refugio Tinquilco**, a luxe two-story lodge on private property at the Lago Verde trailhead 2km past the park entrance.

Designed by an architect, a writer, an engineer and an Emmy-nominated documentary filmmaker, it's the kind of place where people hide away for a week and lost souls find their way. You'll dine with your host, Patricio Lanfranco, who turns out hearty

 WHERE TO DRINK BEYOND PUCÓN

El Castillo
Haggard outdoorsy types congregate over fine beverages at this resto-bar en route to/from Volcán Villarrica.

The Travellers
LGBTIQ+-friendly traveler hub across the lake in Villarrica. Decent global grub but better drinks.

Delirium Tremens
Inviting patio and several living-room–like spaces make for cozy drinking at Villarrica's one notable brewpub.

home-style Chilean cuisine with welcome touches, such as French-press coffee and wonderful wines. He makes a great companion for sharing a bottle of Carmenere (his 2008 documentary *The Judge and the General* is a required watch on the destructive Pinochet regime). The forested 2-hectare property has it all: babbling brooks, riverside campsites, data signal-catching workstations next to massive coigüe trees and a private beach on **Lago Tinquilco**. Be sure to submit yourself to the addictive forest sauna and plunge-pool treatment. It's easy to forget you are on the doorstep of Parque Nacional Huerquehue, home to startling aquamarine lakes surrounded by verdant old-growth forests, but it might not matter. You don't have to pay the park entrance fee to come here!

Mapuche Moments

UNIQUE CUISINE AND SPIRITUAL AWAKENINGS

The land of La Araucanía is the historic and spiritual cradle of the Mapuche – the People of the Land – and their indisputable influence on modern Chilean culture spans everything from gastronomy to arts and crafts to the naming of almost every landmark of note. The Mapuche are famously insular, and being afforded the occasion to learn more about their ways and beliefs from the Mapuche themselves is an eye-opening experience.

Anita Epulef Cocina Mapuche occupies a cozy, wood-burning stove-heated cabin a 40-minute drive east of Pucón in the Mapuche stronghold of Curarrehue (home to a population that's 80% Mapuche). Anita turns seasonal ingredients into delicate Mapuche tasting menus, which are unlikely to taste similar to anything you have ever eaten before. Indigenous delicacies such as *mullokiñ* (bean puree rolled in quinoa), sautéed *piñones* (the nut of the araucaria tree – served in season only) and *brotes de colihue*, an asparagus-like plant known as Chilean bamboo, are just a few examples of the culinary adventures. **Rutas Ancestrales Araucarias** offers multiday trekking around Curarrehue as well.

Around Pucón and Villarrica, **Ruta Newen Leufu**, a Mapuche-formed cooperative, has created a four-pillar cultural immersion that includes a wellness component and trekking in **Mapuche Natural Reservation Trawünko**. For a deeper dive, **Elementos Turismo Experiencial** pioneered ethnotourism with the Mapuche. The German-run agency arranges multiday trips from the Biobío to Chiloé that include cooking lessons with Mapuche chefs, visits to *rukas* (traditional thatched Mapuche houses) and meet-and-greets with Mapuche *machi* (traditional healers).

¿QUIÉNES SON LOS MAPUCHES?

The Mapuche are Chile's largest indigenous group, making up nearly 10% of the country's population, according to the 2017 census. Well regarded as ferocious warriors, the Mapuche waged one of the fiercest and most successful defenses against the European invaders anywhere in the Americas. The Spanish were not able to settle south of the Río Biobío until the mid- to late 19th century. Today, Mapuche inhabit the land from Concepción to Chiloé (extending into Argentina as well), sharing common social, religious and economic structures, as well as various dialects of Mapudungun.

MAPUCHE MUSEUMS

If you're looking to supplement a Mapuche experience with a deeper dive into the culture, the **Museo Histórico y Antropológico** (p215) in Valdivia and **Museo de Volcanes** (p219) within the Huilo-Huilo Biological Reserve both feature excellent exhibitions.

GETTING AROUND

Most areas of interest for travelers are well served by public transport from Pucón, including Parque Nacional Huerquehue and Santuario El Cañi. For the volcano's base, a shared shuttle runs when the ski center is open. Otherwise, you need your own car or take an Uber.

VALDIVIA

The allure of Valdivia might not be as immediately evident as some of its regional sidekicks – perhaps it suffers a smidgeon for the unfortunate circumstance of being uneasy on the eyes but occupying a sweepingly beautiful location at the confluence of the Calle-Calle, Cau-Cau and Cruces rivers. Although it was founded by Spanish conquistador Pedro de Valdivia in 1552, the city began to thrive after the 19th-century wave of German immigration.

The 1960 earthquake wiped out much of the original German-style architecture, but its German effervescence carries on, along with a youthful energy and a palpable civic pride for its thriving beer scene. Besides food and drink, Valdivia's personality shines best along its pleasant waterfront, where sea lions sprawl out on the sidewalk in a food-induced comatose state brought on by gorging on scraps from the lively fish market. Find the natural attractions in and around the nearby islands of Corral, Niebla and Mancera.

✪ Santiago

Valdivia ●

TOP TIP

If you're looking to eat or drink with Valdivian trendsetters, Isla Teja, just across the bridge from the city, is home to one of the region's best collections of hip bars and restaurants along the streets of Los Robles, Oettinger, Saelzer and Los Alerces.

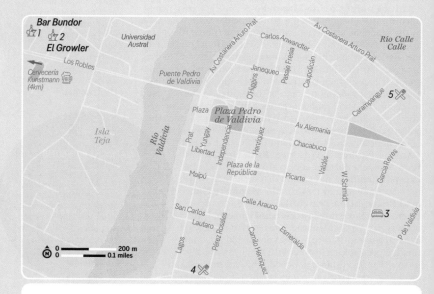

HIGHLIGHTS
1 Bar Bundor
2 El Growler

SLEEPING
3 Airesbuenos Hostel
& Permacultura

EATING
4 La Última Frontera
5 Parrilla de Thor

A VALDIVIAN RAMBLE

The action in Valdivia sits on both sides of the Río Calle-Calle, a glistening, snaking waterway that counts as the city's finest attraction. This 5.5km walking tour can be done in about an hour and takes in a perfect Valdivian trifecta of centuries-old Spanish turrets, surprisingly urban sea lions and wonderful chocolate. Start off at **1 Torreón del Barro** on Av Ramón Picarte near Valdivia's wonderful *costanera* (waterfront). It's inaccessible but was once part of a riverfront Spanish fortification built in 1774. Head north one block to the waterfront and turn west, strolling along the river towards **2 Feira Fluvial**, a lively waterfront seafood and produce market. Pay attention along the way – portly sea lions hang out right on the sidewalk. Backtrack slightly to the Puenta Pedro de Valdivia and cross onto Isla Teja, home to museums, trendy restaurants and craft beer bars. Pop into **3 RA Philippi Museo de la Exploración**, a science and nature museum focused on explorations in the region by German-Chilean paleontologist and zoologist Rodolfo Amando Philippi. Next door, the **4 Museo Histórico y Antropológico**, housed in a particularly picturesque riverfront mansion, is one of Chile's finest museums and contains household items from early German settlements on the ground floor as well as Mapuche artifacts, silver, jewelry and weaponry upstairs. Go back across the bridge, admiring the view of Valdivia as you do, and head south to **5 Torreon de los Canelos**, another Spanish turret dating from the 17th century. Head one block east on Yerbas Buenas and a few blocks north along Pérez Rosales to **6 Chocolatería Entrelagos** and indulge in a well-earned variety of sweet treats.

I LIVE HERE: VALDIVIA HIGHLIGHTS

Born and raised Valdivian, **Christián Olivares** is the founder of Cuello Negro (cuellonegro.cl), one of Chile's top craft breweries.

The best restaurants in Valdivia are on the outskirts: **De Pellin y Coigüe** for wonderful meat and sublime views of **Lago Ranco**; for finer meals, **FishCarraldo** on the shore of the **Río Valdivia**; and, in the city itself, **New Orleans**. For a drink, there is nothing like the intimacy of **Cava del Buho**. For a weekend in Valdivia, a visit to the coast is a must. The best beaches are **Playa San Ignacio**, **Playa de los Enamorados** and **Playa La Misión**. You must visit the forts in the **Bahía de Corral**. The most beautiful is on **Isla Mancera**.

Cervecería Kunstmann

Cerveza City

CHILE'S CAPITAL OF BEER

If you're looking for tastier suds than Escudo or Cristal, Chile's most popular industrial beers, you're in luck. The craft beer scene in Chile has made marked strides, and breweries around Santiago, such as Kross, Jester and Tamango, as well as Valparaíso's Granizo, produce hop-heavy IPAs and other vibrantly flavored styles on par with countries with more established craft-beer scenes. There's no denying Santiago's place as the best spot for a serious pint in Chile, but Valdivia is the heart and soul of the country's beer scene.

The city's soft water and pronounced German heritage proved a vital historical marriage. Anwandter Brewery, Valdivia's first, was founded in 1851. Destroyed in the 1960 earthquake, it rose from the rubble decades later as **Cervecería Kunstmann**, southern Chile's most widely recognized beer. Enjoy a pint of in-house–only Torobayo unfiltered on a 45-minute tour at the brewery's museum, restaurant and 32-tap bar on Isla Teja, 6km southwest of Valdivia. Hearty German fare helps fuel a fun afternoon.

In fact, beer lovers need not stray from Isla Teja at all. Just across the river from the city center, both Oregonian-owned **El Growler** (15 taps) and **Bar Bundor** (20 taps), conveniently located one easily stumbled block from each other, offer a mix of proprietary beers and Chile-wide craft. Prepare to go to war for a table on weekends. If you're around in February, Kunstmann's **Bierfest** is Chile's most rousing beer festival.

 WHERE TO STAY & EAT IN VALDIVIA

Airesbuenos Hostel & Permacultura
Valdivia's best hostel with a three-night minimum stay. **$$**

La Última Frontera
Bohemian resto-bar in a run-down but vibey restored mansion. Creative sandwiches and well-curated craft beer. **$$**

Parrilla de Thor
Waterfront Argentine steakhouse offering perfectly grilled slabs of *bife de chorizo* (steak) and accompaniments. **$$$**

Beyond Valdivia

East of Valdivia beyond the impossibly blue-hued Lago Panguipulli lies Huilo-Huilo Biological Reserve, a detour-worthy ecotourism conservation playground for nature lovers.

Termas
Geométricas

Coñaripe

Valdivia

Huilo-Huilo
Biological Reserve

Panguipulli, on the eastern flank of Valdivia Province, has some of the most breathtaking scenery in all of Sur Chico. Four ever-present volcanoes (Villarrica, Quetrupillán, Lanín and Mocho-Choshuenco) loom over the landscape, while a series of seven glacial lakes, stretching east from Lago Riñihue to Lago Pirihueico near the Argentine border, color the countryside.

Marketed as *Circuito Siete Lagos* (Seven Lakes Circuit) for tourism promotion purposes, the clever moniker is unnecessary. The intensely turquoise waters bound by verdant, forested mountains and snowcapped volcanoes need no campaigned validation. The region is home to the private Huilo-Huilo Biological Reserve, an unspoiled outdoor adventure dreamland protecting 1000 sq km of pristine temperate rainforest.

TOP TIP

Huilo-Huilo's otherworldly hotels are not for the budget-conscious. Considerable savings await for those who stay 3km away in tiny Neltume instead.

Panguipulli

GUAXINIM/SHUTTERSTOCK ©

217

GUAXINIM/SHUTTERSTOCK ©

Salto de Huilo-Huilo

LIVIN' ON THE EDGE

The Los Ríos region's northern border rubs up against La Araucanía and Parque Nacional Villarrica, home to the roaring Volcán Villarrica, one of Chile's most active volcanoes. On the southeastern shore of Lago Calafquén (which the two regions share) is the small town of **Coñaripe**, an alternative base to Pucón for exploring the park. The catch? When Villarrica blows its top, the lava usually heads straight for the town. Convivial Coñaripe boasts numerous hot springs and black-sand beaches, but because of its position in the volcano's firing line, investment has been less enthusiastic, so accommodation choices are thinner, restaurants simpler and nightlife limited.

Huilo-Huilo Wonderland

FAIRY-TALE HOTELS AND ADVENTURE TOURISM

An all-in-one high-adventure destination, **Huilo-Huilo Biological Reserve** caters to an eclectic array of enthusiasts, from nature-loving families and outdoor enthusiasts to fans of Tolkien-like high fantasy. In the shadow of Volcán Mocho-Choshuenco, between two incredibly scenic lakes (Lago Pirihueico and Lago Panguipulli) and dissected by the raging ice-blue Río Fuy, the conservation project, begun in 2000, encompasses 1000 sq km of private land that falls within a much larger Unesco Biosphere Reserve. A visit here, best enjoyed as a multiday, high-adrenaline immersion in low-impact ecotourism, leaves you dizzy on options: trekking, waterfalls, mountain biking, spas, hot springs, museums, kayaking, volcano ascents, whitewater rafting, fly fishing, climbing, horseback riding, canopy tours... There's even a microbrewery.

The endemic fauna alone is extraordinary, and you might see Darwin's frog, pudú (small deer), *monito del monte* (little mountain monkey), 111 species of birds and 35 species of ferns (second only to the Juan Fernández Islands). Fundación Huilo-Huilo, which owns and manages the reserve, has bred

 WHERE TO STAY & EAT BEYOND VALDIVIA

Treca Rupan
The Río Fuy rollicks behind this friendly Neltume lodge 3km from Huilo-Huilo. Good style-for-price ratio. **$$**

Verde Bosque
A social, traveler-friendly choice for pizza, sandwiches and Coñaripe's inaugural hometown craft beer. **$**

Cervecería Petermann
In-house microbrewery and pizzeria at Huilo-Huilo; consider it the après-ski equivalent of this outdoor wonderland. **$$**

and reintroduced the endangered huemul (South Andean deer) with startling success as well.

Start off by deciding which of Huilo-Huilo's fantasyland hotels you'd like to call home for a few nights (reserve in advance). The nine-room **La Montaña Mágica** is housed in a Frodo-approved spire with a fountain spewing from the top. Kitschy furniture and supernatural design touches abound. **Nothofagus Hotel & Spa**, the reserve's biggest hotel, has 55 rooms inside a Gaudí-inspired inverted cone suspended in the temperate rainforest treetops. **Reino Fungi Lodge** is a mushroom-mimicking, 22-room option with spa and sauna facilities included in the rates. Hardwoods feature heavily in all rooms, adding a cabin-in-the-woods vibe. Distinctly less surreal options include camping, a high-season-only hostel, well-equipped rustic tree houses, and top-end cabins with all the luxury fixings, including an open bar.

Once settled in, Huilo-Huilo's excursions desk will match your nature aspirations with the reserve's astonishing arsenal of activities, many of which require a guide. Highlights run deep, wide and tall. If time is limited, the stunning 37m **Salto de Huilo-Huilo** (no guide required) is one of the most accessible waterfalls, easily reached by car about 5km before the reserve's main entrance. Southern Chile's inaugural funicular, **Teleférico Cóndor Andino**, is also an efficient choice. The Swiss-made cableway whisks passengers away on a long 30-minute journey from the 580m base station to the 1167m summit, serving up expansive views over the entire reserve. It's also worth popping into the stone-domed **Museo de Volcanes**, the most impressive archaeological museum in Sur Chico, to eye one of the best Mapuche ornament collections in existence and a prehistoric mastodon tusk that's said to be one of only four in the world. Arrange guides at either of the two visitor centers.

The most interesting excursions require a bigger time commitment, such as the eight-hour round-trip trek to the summit of the glacier-capped Volcán Mocho-Choshuenco and the four-day **Sendero de Lagunas Andinas**. Inaugurated in 2020, it is the reserve's only long-distance trail and only the third multiday hut-to-hut hike in Chile after Torres del Paine and Parque Tantauco in Chiloé.

Huilo-Huilo Biological Reserve is a 2½-hour drive east of Valdivia that's best reached by car.

SCENIC SOAKS

For one of Chile's smaller regions, the natural beauty of the Los Ríos landscape stands out, a notion not lost on the masterminds behind **Termas Geométricas**, one of Chile's most stunning destination hot springs. Located 15km down a rough but passable road north of Coñaripe, this Asian-inspired, red-coigüe-wood-planked maze of 20 beautiful slate hot springs is straight out of the Japanese onsen playbook. There are two waterfalls and three cold plunge pools to cool off in as well. Everything is set on a verdant natural ravine over a rushing stream. In a region where hot springs are as common as the cold, none are more cinematic as this.

GETTING AROUND

If you don't have a rental car, regular buses between Puerto Fuy and Panguipulli can drop you at both Neltume and Huilo-Huilo Biological Reserve.

PUERTO MONTT & LAGO LLANQUIHUE

Santiago ✪

Puerto Montt & Lago Llanquihue

Puerto Montt – lovingly referred to as *Muerto Montt* ('Dead Montt') by comedians – is the Lakes District's commercial and transportation hub but otherwise unremarkable. There's hope for the future, however, as the city's waterfront is transformed into the CH$9 billion Parque Costanera. If you've arrived in Sur Chico to ogle its ominous volcanoes, celestial glacial lakes and mountainous national parks, or to head off to Patagonia on the Carretera Austral or the Navimag ferry, you'll cross paths with Puerto Montt.

Just 17km north as the crow flies is Chile's second-largest lake, Lago Llanquihue, and its charming gateway, Puerto Varas, a German-founded town celebrated for its glorious lakeside setting across the water from two stunning volcanoes and top-notch adventure tourism. Because of their proximity to each other, Puerto Montt and Puerto Varas are intrinsically connected, though the latter makes a more pleasant base for exploring the region.

TOP TIP

With the exception of a few good restaurants and the homespun hospitality of its *hospedajes* (guesthouses), there isn't much reason to linger in Puerto Montt. A night or two may be inevitable, but most travelers move on to Puerto Varas, a far more tourist-friendly and charming option with a beautiful lake setting.

Puerto Montt and Volcán Osorno (p225)

The Navimag Experience

SAILING ADVENTURE THROUGH PATAGONIAN FJORDS

Navimag's Patagonian fjords ferry expedition might not hog the headlines like other famed rites of passage, but this four-day journey between Puerto Montt and Puerto Natales is an unforgettable voyage through one of the world's most beautiful and remote areas.

No cruise ships ply the waters between Puerto Montt and Puerto Natales, but Navimag's *Esperanza* – a Chinese-built, Patagonian-adapted cargo ship debuted in 2021 – is a technically advanced hybrid that marries 18-wheelers and herds of cattle with tourist-friendly accommodations, bingo, yoga and reiki classes, as well as local cuisine, such as *porotos con riedas* (a spaghetti, chorizo and diced pumpkin stew), pan-fried *merluza* (hake) and *cazuelas* (meat stews). Consider it a floating hostel that sails through some of Patagonia's most stellar scenery, much of which would be otherwise inaccessible to the average traveler.

You depart from Puerto Montt on Tuesdays at 10pm (Fridays at 9pm from Puerto Natales) shortly after settling into your accommodations, which range from US$1300 per person for a private double Premium Suite to windowless shared bunkrooms from US$550. All cabins feature private bathrooms. Additional features afforded by the ship include a gym, an elevator, an infirmary, a cabin for passengers with reduced mobility, and spacious deck space where guests can bird-watch and scope the varied flora and fauna of Patagonia.

The ship plies Aisén's maze of narrow channels, navigates narrow passages like the White Channel and the Angostura Inglesa (the ship nearly kisses the shoreline on both sides) and stops at the impossibly remote Puerto Edén, a small fishing port and the last outpost of the region's indigenous Alacalufe (Kawésqar) people. The captain makes real-time decisions based on weather conditions. No specific route is guaranteed, so you might sail the open sea along the mouth of Guafo between Isla Guafo and Chonos Archipelago, the Ninualac Channel near Isla Tuap, or the lenga- and cypress-forested Pulluche Channel, for example. What is certain are waterfalls tumbling from glacial valleys to the water's edge, the sun bouncing off majestic snowcapped peaks, and the possibility of minke, Humboldt and blue whales and South American sea lions making appearances along the way.

Bonds with like-minded independent travelers quickly form after round after round of pointless card and board games, sympathizing about queasy stomachs, deck-top soccer matches, late-night dance parties, impromptu musical instrument

BEST PLACES TO STAY IN PUERTO MONTT

Sipo' Hostel
Bend-over-backwards hospitality and friendliness highlight this hostel offering both dorm and private accommodations. $

Hospedaje Vista al Mar
Puerto Montt's standout residential guesthouse features aged hardwoods and beautiful bay views. $

Casa Perla
Long-standing guesthouse full of knickknacks; legendary matriarch Perla carries on the family business around you. English and German spoken. $

Tungulú Cabañas
Stylish *cabañas* (cabins) frame panoramic sea views from their perch high on a hillside 11km southwest of the city. $$

 WHERE TO EAT IN PUERTO MONTT

Puerto Fritos
Wonderfully fresh seafood, including shellfish stew and ceviche; and has a view. $

Chile Picante
Out-of-the-box preparations of native ingredients drive unexpectedly gourmet three-course meals. $$

Cotelé
The region's most legendary steaks, meticulously cooked over an open flame in a *quincho* (barbecue hut). $$$

PUERTO MONTT & LAGO LLANQUIHUE

Puerto Fritos
(1.2km);
Puerto Varas
(see inset)
(18km)

ACTIVITIES, COURSES & TOURS	SLEEPING	EATING	DRINKING & NIGHTLIFE
1 Birds Chile	3 Casa Kalfu	9 Casavaldés	14 Caffé El Barista
2 Navimag	4 Casa Perla	10 Chile Picante	15 Taberna Nosé
	5 Compass del Sur	11 Cotelé	
	6 Hospedaje Vista al Mar	12 La Vinoteca	
	7 MaPatagonia	13 Mesa Tropera	
	8 Sipo' Hostel		

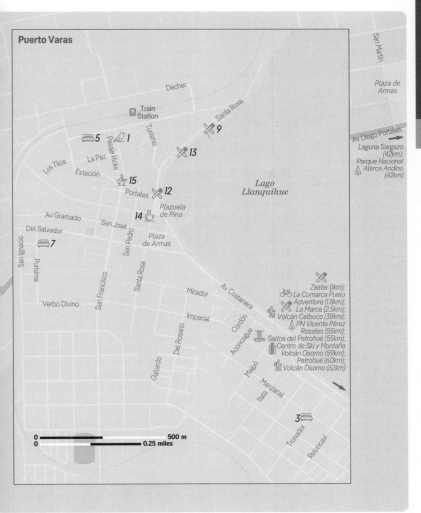

Puerto Varas

San Martín

Plaza de Armas

Decher

🚉 Train Station

Santa Rosa

🛫 9

Turismo

🛏 5 🕊 1

Pasaje Riche

🛫 13

Av Diego Portales

Laguna Sargazo (42km);
Parque Nacional
⛰ Alerce Andino (42km)

Los Tilos

La Paz

Estación

🍴 15

Portales 🍴 12

Lago Llanquihue

Plazuela de Pino

14 ☕

Av Gramado

San José

San Pedro

Del Salvador

🛏 7

Plaza de Armas

San Ignacio

Purísima

San Francisco

Santa Rosa

Verbo Divino

Mirador

Av Costanera

🍴 Zaatar (1km);
🚲 La Comarca Puelo
🍴 Adventure (1.8km);
La Marca (2.5km);
⛰ Volcán Calbuco (38km);
⛰ PN Vicente Pérez
Rosales (55km);
🏛 Saltos del Petrohué (55km);
🎿 Centro de Ski y Montaña
Volcán Osorno (59km);
Petrohué (60km);
🎿 Volcán Osorno (62km)

Imperial

Cordón

Aconcagua

Del Rosario

Maipó

Gallardo

Manzanal

Itata

3 🚗

Tronador

Reloncaví

0 ————— 500 m
0 ————— 0.25 miles

Navimag ferry through the Patagonian fjords (p221)

BELIKOVA OKSANA/SHUTTERSTOCK ©

Puerto Varas (p224)

MATYAS REHAK/SHUTTERSTOCK ©

performances and plans to meet up in Torres del Paine. Movies are available on the Navimag Travel Play platform (there is no wi-fi) and, although officially banned, contraband beers and flasks of whisky are consumed with staff often turning a blind eye. Life on deck is a shared experience that leads to lifelong friendships, with cliques forming faster than a high school orientation day.

It is this shared comradery – as much as the impossibly gorgeous landscape – that makes the Navimag experience one of the world's great journeys. Though distinctly less famous, the trip easily falls within the same vein as the Trans-Siberian Railway, hiking the Inca Trail or traversing the Amazon on a riverboat trip. In a word: Epic.

I LIVE HERE: A ROMANTIC DAY OUT

Russ Marquart is a partner at Chester Beer (@chester_beer), Lago Llanquihue's long-standing craft beer mainstay. Here's how he'd spend a day off.

A perfect outing is driving south along the **Carretera Austral** from Puerto Montt to **Parque Nacional Alerce Andino**, where you can go for a beautiful hike to **Laguna Sargazo**, a 2½-hour trek that winds through forests and along streams, a river and, of course, Laguna Sargazo. Afterward, drive back to Puerto Varas to have dinner at **La Vinoteca** on the lakefront for a great meal and glass of wine before heading back to your accommodations. Exercise, nature, great views, tasty food, fine wine – that's Puerto Varas!

Puerto Adventure

OUTDOOR ACTION AROUND PUERTO VARAS

Puerto Varas doesn't carry the same international clout as a world-class outdoor adventure hub like Pucón and it is perhaps all the better for it. The German-rooted town on Lago Llanquihue has been able to better manage its rise as a go-to destination for outdoor adventure sports and, as a result, it avoids some of the tourist-package crush that besieges Pucón while offering a similar lineup of alfresco escapades.

Much like Pucón, Puerto Varas doesn't offer much in the way of traditional attractions; rather, its defining feature is its stunning lakeside location that, on a clear day, feels like an Ansel Adams painting roared to life in vivid Technicolor. The well-organized town's hyper-maintained German architecture gives Puerto Varas a distinctive European ambiance, and shops hawk artisanal chocolate, gourmet wares and outdoor-adventure gear. Plenty of restaurants take full advantage of Lago Llanquihue's fit-for-a-postcard beauty and stunning volcano-highlighted setting.

The quickest and most obvious way to get out to the lake is on two wheels. Rent a bike from **La Comarca Puelo Adventure**, which has road and mountain bikes (book in advance for multiday rentals). Around 86km of the loop (from Puerto Varas to Las Cascadas) has been blessed with a dedicated *ciclovía* (bike lane) – Chile's longest – but you can cycle the peaceful lake's entirety (around 168km), enjoying lakeside towns and hamlets, Parque Nacional Vicente Pérez Rosales (Chile's oldest national park; p226), local breweries, German farmstead architecture as well as grazing on spit-roasted meats, *küchen* (cake) and other local specialties along the way. La Comarca Puelo Adventures offers a guided, three-day trip along this route as well.

There is great access to water sports – kayaking in particular – as well as climbing, fishing, hiking and even skiing.

 WHERE TO STAY IN PUERTO VARAS

MaPatagonia
Long-standing budget mainstay in a 1932 heritage-listed home with spacious rooms and French-Chilean hospitality. **$**

Compass del Sur
B&B occupying a rambling old German-designed home with loads of hardwood floors and high ceilings. **$$**

Casa Kalfu
A big, beautiful blue 1940s chalet with 19 renovated rooms featuring artist-designed looms as beautiful wall art. **$$**

VITALII KARAS/SHUTTERSTOCK ©

Lago Llanquihue and Volcán Osorno

BEST ADVENTURE OUTFITTERS IN PUERTO VARAS

Ko'Kayak
Recommended French-run agency for rafting trips on the Río Petrohué and sea-kayaking expeditions in the Reloncaví Fjord.

La Comarca Puelo Adventure
Friendly Ernesto Palm de Curto dreams up dramatic and tailored mountain-bike trips to less-explored areas.

Moyca Expediciones
If you're looking to scale Volcán Osorno or Volcán Calbuco, mountaineer Niccolo Caruso is the guide you'll want.

Birds Chile
Italian Raffaele Di Biase is the foremost naturalist in the area, offering fascinating bird-watching and nature-centric tours.

Nearby lakes, mountains, rivers and fjords provide a variety of activities. The two most popular trips are rafting or kayaking on the wonderfully turquoise **Río Petrohué**, whose class III/IV rapids can't compete with Patagonia's Futaleufú but are a more exciting day out than Pucón's Río Trancura. The landscape, as the river snakes from the Andes to the Pacific Ocean through Parque Nacional Vicente Pérez Rosales, is just outrageously beautiful. Contact perennial favorite **Ko'Kayak** for all things paddle-related.

For something above sea level, summiting **Volcán Osorno** (2652m) or **Volcán Calbuco** (2006m) are spectacular choices. Neither requires mountaineering experience, but Osorno is more technical than Volcán Villarrica because it features deep cracks and an ice wall. **Moyca Expediciones** is the go-to outfitter in Puerto Varas, but the companies that climb all share the same handful of guides. Independent climbers must obtain Conaf permission, but it's not recommended unless you are a highly trained technical mountaineer.

A more tranquil activity is fly fishing with John Joy at **Tres Ríos Lodge** in Ensenada or Gustavo Arenas with **Patagonia Fishing Rockers**. The Río Maullín, Río Peulo and Río Petrohué are all world-class rivers for casting a line. **Birds Chile** specializes in natural serenity as well, and its 12km interpretive geological trek between Lago Llanquihue and Lago Todos Los Santos affords the chance to make deeper connections with the landscape amid unparalleled surroundings – the reason you have come to Puerto Varas.

GET OUT

Pucón (p207), 321km north of Puerto Varas, is Chile's most popular outdoor playground, offering volcano ascents, water sports, trekking and everything in between. Between there and Puerto Varas, all your outdoor-adventure proclivities should be satisfied.

WHERE TO DRINK IN PUERTO VARAS

Mesa Tropera
Coyhaique-transplanted brewery-pizzeria overlooking the lake. Puerto Varas' best collection of craft beer on draft.

Caffé El Barista
Town social hub with commendable espresso; morphs into a bar after sunset.

Taberna Nosé
Easy-on-the-eyes bar designed by Douglas Tompkins' park architect; serves Tropera craft beer and elevated pub grub.

BEST PLACES TO EAT IN PUERTO VARAS

Zaatar
Palestinian affair doing gourmet wares of the homeland, including excellent shawarma and hummus. $$

La Vinoteca
Part wine shop, part gourmand destination; shared cast-iron-seared seafood plates and hearty, Carmenere-friendly duck, lamb and beef mains. $$$

La Marca
Hefty slabs of perfectly grilled beef maintain this steakhouse's legendary status. Finish with churros. $$$

Casavaldés
Puerto Varas' best seafood restaurant boasts lake and Volcán Calbuco views. Fresh fish pairs best with the *donostiarra* (olive oil, garlic, red chili and vinegar) preparation. $$$

Parque Nacional Vicente Pérez Rosales

Chile's Oldest National Park

GLACIAL LAKES AND DOMINEERING VOLCANOES

No matter where you are in and around Puerto Varas, the glacier-covered Volcán Osorno, the region's signature show-piece, makes its presence known. Flawlessly picturesque, its impeccable conical perfection is the stuff of storybooks and legends, a seemingly unreal illustration of nature at its finest – and most ferocious. The most obvious big day out from Puerto Varas is to head straight for this omnipresent beauty (and beast) and its phenomenal surroundings, 2530 sq km of which are protected as **Parque Nacional Vicente Pérez Rosales**, Chile's oldest national park.

On the volcano itself, you can drive to **Centro de Ski y Montaña Volcán Osorno** if for no other reason than outstanding panoramic views of Lago Llanquihue, but two lifts for skiing in winter and sightseeing and hiking in summer whisk you up as far as 1675m. If lollygagging on one of Chile's most active volcanoes isn't your thing, Petrohué's majestic lakeside setting on cerulean Lago Todos Los Santos awaits at sea level. You can kayak the stunning lake or raft its equally cinematic drainage on the Río Petrohué, two highlights of the park. Contact Ko'Kayak in Puerto Varas to organize a trip.

Don't miss **Saltos del Petrohué** while here. Located 6km southwest of Petrohué, this rushing, frothing waterfall rages through a narrow volcanic rock canyon carved by lava.

Cruce Andino offers a bus-and-boat combo transport trip between Bariloche in Argentina and Puerto Varas (and vice versa). This 12-hour journey navigates the majestic lakes and mountains of the Pérez Rosales Pass, crossing three beautiful lakes (Lago Todos Los Santos and Argentina's Lago Frias and Lago Nahuel Huapi).

GETTING AROUND

All the cities and towns around Lago Llanquihue, including Puerto Montt, are walkable, but you'll want a car to explore the lake and its environs at your own leisure.

Beyond Puerto Montt & Lago Llanquihue

THE GUIDE

SUR CHICO

Venturing beyond Lago Llanquihue means going off-grid. An isolated coastal utopia and hard-to-reach havens along the remote road toward Argentina await.

Puerto Montt and Puerto Varas sit cheek by jowl as gateways not only to the nature-rich expanse of Chilean and Argentine Patagonia to the south, but also north to Osorno's dramatic underdeveloped coast. Either direction means traversing environs flush with natural beauty and idyllic scenery that sit in isolated perfection away from the travails of mass tourism.

Remote paradises like Caleta Cóndor and La Junta deliver drastically contrasting environments with one important caveat in common. Both require a pinch more effort than average to arrive – and that is precisely the point. Along the way, rural outposts like Puelo and Llanada Grande are easier to reach but feel a world away, an ever-elusive travel ideal still attainable in southern Chile.

Caleta Cóndor

Santuario de la Naturaleza
Valle Cochamó

Puerto Montt

Termas del Sol

La Junta

TOP TIP

Access to the Río Cochamó Valley at La Junta is strictly controlled. You must register in advance at reservasvallecochamo.org.

La Junta (p232)

GERMANZELLER/SHUTTERSTOCK ©

The Road to Llanada Grande

Around 166km of road and a 45-minute glacial lake crossing separate distinctly on-the-grid PuertoVaras from wild and isolated Llanada Grande, a remote outpost of horseback-riding gaucho families and darting wild hares near the border with Argentina. Much of the journey hugs the gorgeous Reloncaví Fjord – worth the half-day trip alone – but along the way, a wealth of outdoor adventure opportunities tempt a longer linger, including sea kayaking, horseback riding and fly fishing.

1 Cochamó

The centerpiece of tiny Cochamó is the Chilote-style, alerce-shingled **Iglesia Parroquial María Inmaculada**, which hovers over the milky-blue waters of Chile's northernmost fjord (Reloncaví) like a scene plucked from a storybook. Consider sea kayaking here; Ensenada's Ko'Kayak can get you on the water. Sea lions, Chilean dolphins, kingfishers, cormorants and even penguins are served up with Volcán Yates looming in the distance. Or pack up for a few days of horse trekking with Southern Trips.

The Drive: It's 31.5km south along unpaved V-69, and the spectacular Reloncaví Fjord nearly never leaves your right side.

MAV DRONE/SHUTTERSTOCK ©

Kayaking, Lago Tagua-Tagua

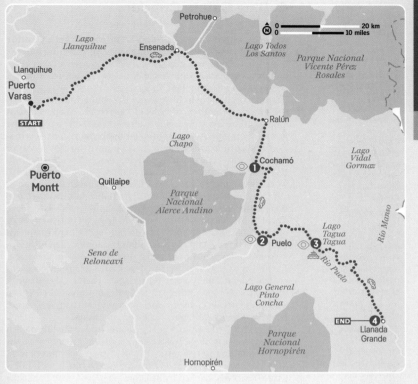

2 Puelo

The winding, jade-hued Río Puelo – particularly magnificent at sunset – cuts through the tiny hamlet of the same name, a wonderfully quaint spot to consider milling about for an evening. The spectacular destination hot springs, **Termas del Sol**, warrant lengthy soaking.

The Drive: Unpaved V-721 unravels for nearly 14km from Puelo to Puerto Canelo, where ferries cross the lake every few hours.

3 Lago Tagua-Tagua

Extraordinary Lago Tagua-Tagua is an impossibly blue jewel with tumbling waterfalls bound by mountains and virgin Valdivian forest. Fly fishing, plus trekking and bird-watching in nearby Parque Tagua Tagua) are huge draws, but the crossing itself is one for the memory books. Two isolated lodges reachable only by boat, **Lodge Tagua-Tagua** and **Mítico Puelo Lodge**, grace the lakeshore.

The Drive: The final 34km continue unpaved by mountainsides peppered with patches of dead coigüe trees before rolling into Llanada Grande.

4 Llanada Grande

This road trip is about the journey and the destination: **Campo Eggers**, an animal-packed farm in a fairy-tale Llanada Grande setting in front of the 1200m El Salto waterfall. You won't soon forget the spirited Eggers family, its arsenal of animals, and traditional lamb or wild-boar *asados* (barbecues). You are now out of bounds – the reason you have come this far.

Calling Caleta Cóndor

OFF-THE-GRID PACIFIC COAST PARADISE

BEST PLACES TO SLEEP & EAT ON THE OSORNO COAST

Hospedaje Rural Mirador
Dead simple homestay; spectacular views await a short hike above Caleta Cóndor. $

Altos de Pichi Mallay
Family-run guesthouse in Maicolpué Río Sur; a wood-fired hot tub nestled in the forest offers absolutely miraculous ocean views. $$

Hostal Caleta Cóndor
Purpose-built guesthouse sleeping 13 in rustic but comfortable rooms behind one of South America's most perfect Pacific beaches. $

La Casa de Temo
Friendly Malcalpué seafood spot with recommended shellfish *caldillos* (soups) and *chupes* (casseroles). $$

In times where almost no land is unseen, **Caleta Cóndor** stands out as one such place in the greater traveling public's blind spot. Your first glimpse of the *caleta* (cove) will completely reinvigorate your sense of discovery, but reaching its shores is no relaxing float on a lazy river.

Caleta Cóndor is hidden away in isolated tranquility in the protected indigenous zone of **Territorio Mapu Lahual** along the rugged and largely undeveloped Osorno coast. The jumping-off point to reach this impossibly gorgeous destination is **Bahía Mansa**, about a two-hour drive northwest of Puerto Montt – but you aren't driving anymore. Catch a boat from Bahía Mansa's ramshackle port, an often-rough journey that's worth every bout of queasiness that might befall you en route.

A few different boat options are available, but **Caleta Cóndor Chile** (caletacondorchile.cl) is the most reliable. Reserve a seat online ahead of time because it sets off only with 10 or more people. Boats for tourism generally operate from September to April (weekends only through December, generally daily from January to March), departing between 8am and 11am. Flexibility is key because the departures are highly weather-dependent. The journey on the open Pacific takes around two hours. Bobbing glimpses of Valdivian forested cliffs are a constant presence in your peripheral vision as the covered, Navy-certified boat navigates constant swells.

On arrival, you enter via the scenic and translucent Río Cholguaco from the Pacific Ocean and are greeted with an idyllic combination of nature (moss-strewn thatches of land that line the river like wild putting greens, flush with horses and seabirds, backed by hillsides peppered with beautiful luma and arrayán trees) and nurture (30 or so families – all running on solar power – call this piece of paradise home on a permanent basis).

As the boat makes various stops along the river to unload supplies for locals, the sense of remoteness kicks in. Month-supply sacks of potatoes, onions and dog food are dropped on the makeshift piers, liters of olive oil and canisters of natural gas follow. You might be able to post an Instagram story or two of the abandoned boats run aground along the route – these days Movistar, Claro and Wom catch a signal – but wi-fi remains elusive. It was only a decade ago that communication with the outside world from here was via VHF radio only.

The trip culminates at the river's end on a sandbar strip of out-of-place tropicalia that separates the river beach and the ocean beach. Beyond the sand, free-range horses, sheep and

WHERE TO STAY IN COCHAMÓ

Patagonia Nativa
Friendly Cristian speaks some English and runs kayak trips from this cabin-like guesthouse with fierce fjord views. $

La Frontera
Well-organized Chilean-Czech operation nearest the trailhead to La Junta; has hot showers, composting toilets and pizza. $

Las Bandurrias Eco Hostal
Swiss-run eco-guesthouse overlooking the fjord with composting, solar heating and Swiss *tresse* bread. $$

Bahía Mansa

cows graze on an equally out-of-place patch of pasture. If it's raining, it's a beautiful disaster. If the weather cooperates, it's heaven incarnate.

Once you settle in (local families have set up simple accommodations), hike 30 minutes up to the viewpoint on the hillside behind **Hostal Caleta Cóndor** for a panoramic overlook (weather permitting, of course). **Caleta Cóndor Expediciones** arranges treks, kayaking and diving, where you'll see starfish, *locos* (mollusks similar to abalone), limpets, groupers and possibly small-spotted catsharks. You're in good hands with Cristian Vargas, who was born and raised in Caleta Cóndor. Finish off with a dip in his ocean-view hot tubs.

Back in Bahía Mansa, don't miss the other Huilliche coastal communities of **San Juan de la Costa**, where a series of magnificent *caletas* – Pucatrihue, Maicolpué, Manzano, Tril-Tril – are home to windswept villages where dolphins and sea lions practically swim to shore.

BEERVANA

One of Chile's most legendary (and notoriously hard to find) home breweries is worth a detour if you are anywhere near Osorno. **Cervecería Artesanal Armin Schmid** (formerly known as 'Donde Armin?' and sometimes referred to as Cervecería Märzen) is in an unsigned private house 12km outside of Osorno on Ruta 215 toward Entre Lagos and the border with Argentina. Bavarian transplant Armin Schmid brews refreshing, unfiltered Märzen year-round, Pils in summer and Bock in winter (other styles may make occasional or seasonal appearances). Enjoy a round or three in his wonderful makeshift front-yard beer garden.

 WHERE TO EAT IN COCHAMÓ

Peumayén
You'll forgo fjord and volcano views, but house-made burgers, rustic-cut fries and craft beer ease the blow. **$$**

El Faro
Home-cooked meals on the waterfront (ceviches and fresh fish a number of ways) with Reloncaví Fjord vistas. **$$**

La Ollita
Cochamó's best-known restaurant does underwhelming seafood, but those pisco sours pair well with volcano views. **$$**

PATAGONIA'S PRESERVATION WAR WAGES ON

Southern Chile is no stranger to environmental battles. Environmentalists waged a multi-year war – and won in 2017 – over a once green-lighted hydroelectric project, HídroAysen. You can still see signs declaring the famous battle cry, '¡Patagonia Sin Represas!' (Patagonia without dams!), and the raw beauty of the region seems under constant threat. The latest flashpoint is the Río Cochamó Valley, nearly 50% of which is in the hands of a single private owner and up for sale. Organización Valle Cochamó has been campaigning to have most of the valley officially declared a nature sanctuary known as the **Santuario de la Naturaleza Valle Cochamó**, a desperately needed protective designation to help ward off development.

JUAN VILATA/ALAMY STOCK PHOTO ©

Granite mountains, Río Cochamó Valley

Livin' La Junta Vida

CLIMBING AND TREKKING EDEN

With its massive granite domes rising above the verdant canopy and colossal alerce trees dominating the rainforest, the **Río Cochamó Valley** has been billed as the Chilean Yosemite. Short of parachuting in, this haven for rock climbers and trekkers is accessible only on a five-hour, 12km hike or horseback ride. It might seem counterintuitive to hike into a place to take a hike, but trust us. Your destination? **La Junta**, a spectacular valley that almost feels under a tsunami-like threat from the looming granite domes and towering mountain surroundings.

Acclimate yourself with all things Cochamó by spending one night at **La Frontera**. It offers camping, glamping and two

 WHERE TO STAY & EAT AROUND PUELO

Isla Las Bandurrias
Isolated getaway on an island in the middle of Lago Las Rocas, 20km south of Llanada Grande. **$$**

Hostal Vuelta al Sur
Stylish five-room guesthouse in Puelo run by people from Viña del Mar. Fantastic riverside sauna. **$$**

Restaurant Tique
Rustic, family-run affair overseen by welcoming Coco; serves simple but homey Chilean dishes. **$$**

private rooms near the trailhead to La Junta, 6km down a gravel road from the main road turnoff just before crossing the Río Cochamó. Set out early in the morning (October through December and mid-March through April are best; avoid the January and February crush). As you slowly ascend alongside the river, you'll traverse quaint open meadows and deep, picturesque Valdivian rainforest before reaching La Junta.

There are four campgrounds plus the highly recommended **Refugio Cochamó**, a Chilean-Argentine-American operation with wood-fired showers, water straight from the Trinidad waterfall and homemade meals (for guests only – others must bring their own food). Stick around this gorgeous and serene spot for a while. There are six spectacular day hikes, natural swimming pools and, for climbers, more than 100 big wall-climbing routes and over 80 cragging routes.

A Soak in the Sun

HOT SPRINGS AND VOLCANO VIEWS

Owner Samuel del Sol searched far and wide across Chile for an entire year to find the natural hot water that now makes up one of southern Chile's best soaks at **Termas del Sol** in Río Puelo, a hot springs destination about a 90-minute drive south from Lago Llanquihue's southeastern corner. His perfectionism and chosen location – under the nose of the 2187m Volcán Yates – is the good fortune of all that ails you.

Dropping CH$32,000 to visit a hot spring might seem pretty splashy, but as you meander along the pinewood walkways through splendid vegetation to reach these magnificent pools of fury, the price becomes a distant memory. Some 3000 native plants, including nalca (rhubarb-like plant), *calle calle* (Chilean-iris), coigüe trees and armies of *costilla de vaca* (Chilean hard fern), envelope the 10 pools, which are framed by Piedra Laja stone from Coñaripe (it's perhaps no coincidence that del Sol's uncle, Germán del Sol, founded one of Chile's other jaw-dropping hot springs, Termas Geométricas, in Coñaripe).

The hot pools range in temperature between 36°C and 45°C, but all you need to know is that one is a cool 24°C, and bouncing between it and its 45°C neighbor is therapeutic nirvana.

Once you've had your fill, the restaurant, open to hot spring guests only, is Puelo's best outside of the luxury fishing lodges. Chase excellent pizza – try the one with *morchella* (true morels) – pulled pork and stewed beef sandwiches with craft beer from Llanada Grande. Dip. Eat. Drink. Repeat.

CAST AWAY

The Río Puelo is one of the world's last big free-flowing rivers, running unobstructed for 120km from the mountains to the ocean, making it a paradise for fly-fishing enthusiasts. The river hosts one of Chile's longest fly-fishing seasons (September to May), and an incredible variety of fish swim its waters, including rainbow, brown and brook trout, and chinook, salar and coho salmon. The outstanding assortment of fish, coupled with an abundance of luxury fishing lodges often in dramatic, far-flung spots, have sealed Puelo's fate as an idyllic destination for anglers looking to cast their lines during the Northern Hemisphere winter.

GETTING AROUND

Buses from Osorno serve the communities of San Juan de la Costa and, less frequently, buses from Puerto Montt head to Cochamó, Río Puelo and Llanada Grande, but renting a car will greatly enhance your enjoyment of both destinations.

Above: Chiloé's Pacific coast; right: Iglesia San Francisco de Castro (p247), Castro

CHILOÉ

MISTY AND MYTHOLOGICAL MARITIME ISLAND

Isla Grande de Chiloé is South America's fifth-largest island, a mysterious land of fiercely independent seafaring people, exquisite wooden churches and an outstanding cast of incredible landscapes.

There is nothing mysterious about Isla Grande de Chiloé's size – Chile's most storybook island clocks in at 8394 sq km, the country's second-largest island after Tierra del Fuego. But scrutable details trail off from there. The island's enigmatic personality reveals itself in myriad ways, from its *mestizo*-influenced Jesuit wooden churches (16 of which make up one of the world's most fascinating Unesco World Heritage Sites) to its distinctive mythology of witchcraft, ghost ships and forest gnomes.

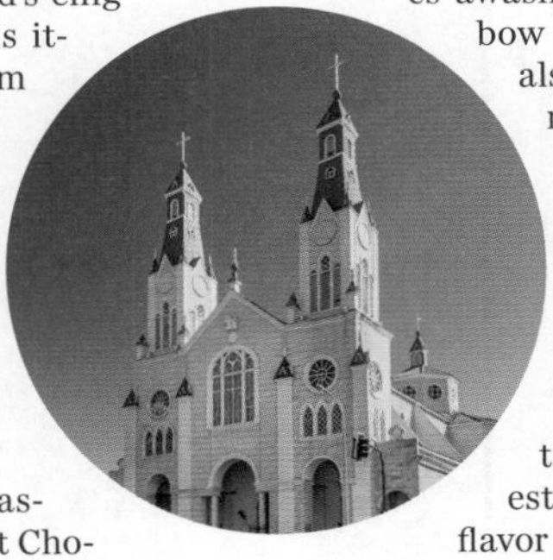

An often indomitable assortment of self-sufficient Chono, Huilliche and Cunco descendants hardened by intense wind and rain, the Chilote people dance to their own drum. Compared with Chile proper (reached by a 30-minute ferry from Pargua on the main-

land), changes in architecture, cuisine and way of life are immediately apparent. *Tejuelas* (the famous wood shingles), *palafitos* (houses mounted on stilts along the water's edge), the iconic wooden churches awash in a kaleidoscopic rainbow of unorthodox hues, and also *curanto* (the renowned meat, potato and seafood stew cooked in a hole in the ground) all stand out. All of these elements are weaved among wet, windswept and lush landscapes of undulating hills, wild and remote national parks, and dense forests, giving Chiloé a distinct flavor unique both in Chile and throughout South America. When the early morning fog shrouds misty-eyed and misunderstood Chiloé, it's clear something different this way comes.

THE MAIN AREAS

ANCUD
Low-key town with spectacular waterfronts.
p240

CASTRO
Provincial capital with atmospheric overwater architecture.
p246

Ancud, p240

Chiloé's first town of note coming from the mainland, Ancud straddles a gorgeous setting, corralling both bay and channel views. Its vicinity abounds with natural attractions.

Castro, p246

As cosmopolitan as Chiloé gets, the island capital is home to an extraordinary wooden church, remarkable *palafito* architecture and a vibrant culinary scene.

Golfo de Ancud

Tenaún

Mata

Quemchi

Lago Popetán

Achao

Chacao

Linao

Curaco

Rilan

Dalcahue

Rio Vilcun

Llau Llao

Carelmapu

Castro

Ancud

Quetalmahue

Chepu

Parque Nacional Chiloé

CAR

Driving around Chiloé opens up avenues of exploration not afforded by public transport. Renting a car is easiest in Ancud or Castro, but it's often cheaper to bring one over on the ferry from the mainland.

BUS

Major bus companies like Cruz del Sur connect Chiloé's three main towns (Ancud, Castro and Quellón) with major mainland cities. Municipal buses connect major destinations on the main island and link up with ferries to smaller islands.

Find Your Way

The Chiloè Archipelago is made up of the sizable main island, which is flanked by 40 or so secondary islands, including Quinchao, Lemuy, Tranqui and Mechuque.

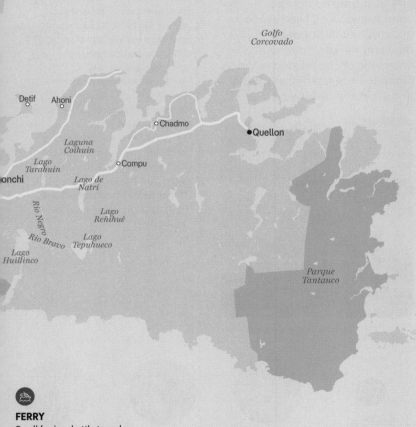

Golfo Corcovado

Detif
Ahoni
○ Chadmo
● Quellon

Laguna Coihuin

Lago Tarahuin

○ Compu

onchi

Lago de Natri

Río Negro

Lago Reñihué

Río Bravo

Lago Tepuhueco

Lago Huillinco

Parque Tantauco

FERRY
Small ferries shuttle to and from some smaller islands such as Isla Quinchao and Isla Lemuy regularly. It's also possible to move on from Chiloé to Patagonia, with infrequent departures from Quellón to Chaitén and Puerto Cisnes.

PACIFIC OCEAN

0   20 km
0   10 miles

Plan Your Time

The towns are no doubt charismatic, but Chiloé's moody and mysterious appeal is best embraced throughout its enigmatic Unesco-listed wooden churches, rugged national parks and intriguing waterways.

Iglesia Nercón, Castro (p246)

In a Rush

● **Ancud** (p240) offers a quick taste of Chilota character without having to deep dive further afield. Try a traditional *curanto al hoyo* (earthen-cooked stew; p242), enjoy craft beers with a tremendous view at **El Jardín Techado** (p241) and, between September and March, take a brief detour to the only place in the world to see Magellanic and Humboldt penguins living in harmony at **Monumento Natural Islotes de Puñihuil** (p244).

● Browsing the wooden scale models of Chiloé's 16 Unesco-listed churches on display at **Museo de las Iglesias de Chiloé** (p242) is the next best thing to seeing them in person.

Seasonal Highlights

Rain never fully fades in Chiloé, but winter is the wettest and best avoided. Overtourism in January and February can also affect your enjoyment of the bigger cities.

JANUARY
Chiloé is crowded, but numerous **festivals** around the island offer insights into the island's unique culture, food and traditions.

FEBRUARY
Chiloé's 300 native varieties of potatoes are at their ripest. Penguins boast newly hatched chicks at **Monumento Natural Islotes de Puñihuil**.

MAY
Catch fall's last days of **decent weather**, with highs around 12°C, before winter sets in, and many tourism services shut down.

A Few Days to Linger

● After time in Ancud and Monumento Natural Islotes de Puñihuil, wake up early for an epic dawn kayak in the serene sunken forest at **Chepu** (p245).

● Move on to **Castro** (p246), where highlights include a peek inside the **Iglesia San Francisco de Castro** (p247), a meal of modernized Chilota food traditions at **Rucalaf** (p248) and overnighting in a hotel along the atmospheric *palafitos*.

● Spend another day seeking out as many of the island's **Unesco-listed wooden churches** (p247) as you can. Achao, Colo and Tenaún are especially worth the effort.

10 Days to See it All

● Enjoy the natural surroundings of **Ancud** (p240), including the colony of Magellanic and Humboldt penguins at **Monumento Natural Islotes de Puñihuil** (p244).

● Set an early alarm to kayak the dramatic atmosphere at **Chepu** (p245), and then take in the beauty of the **Muelle de la Luz** (p245) art installation.

● Between meals at top-notch restaurants around **Castro** (p246), take a day trip to cinematic **Isla Mechuque** (p250).

● Move on to **Parque Nacional Chiloè** (p250), walking the wonderfully wild Sendero Chanquín-Cole Cole.

● Throughout the journey, squeeze in all of the island's **Unesco-listed wooden churches** (p247) that you can muster.

SEPTEMBER

Breeding season for Magellanic and Humboldt penguins begins at **Monumento Natural Islotes de Puñihuil**.

OCTOBER

In Achao, **Encuentro Gastronómico De Productos Del Mar** features folk music, culinary contests and innovative takes on traditional cuisine.

NOVEMBER

Rainfall in **Parque Nacional Chiloé** is relatively tolerable, and the often uncrowded park sees even fewer people than usual.

DECEMBER

The sun shines in **Ancud**, **Castro** and **Dalcahue**, and the crowded high-season onslaught hasn't materialized yet.

ANCUD

Ancud's position as Chiloé's first town of note coming from the north makes for a perfect base for exploring the spectacular natural surroundings of this lesser-visited corner of the island. It's an easy-to-digest place for a taste of Chiloé – good restaurants, trendy bars and charming lodging infrastructure abound – without committing to a deeper dive.

Historically, Ancud teemed with gracious buildings, *palafitos* (waterside stilt houses) and a railway line, all of which contributed to a distinct air of wealth about town, but the 9.5 magnitude 1960 Valdivia earthquake (and subsequent tsunami) decimated the affluence in 10 horrifying minutes. Little native architecture exists today. Ancud diverged post-rebuild into a sprawling city peppered with more hastily constructed buildings. However, the town's beautiful waterfront, which has been rebuilt in the 2020s with pedestrian boardwalks, multiple seating plazas and panoramic points both on the bay side and the channel side, should pleasantly surprise visitors.

✪ Santiago

Ancud ●

TOP TIP

The 2020s have seen Ancud become something of a surfing hot spot. A huge break off Faro Corona, 36km north of town, pulls in expert surfers, while beginners surf easier beaches like Playa Guabún, 25km to the northwest.

Ancud's waterfront

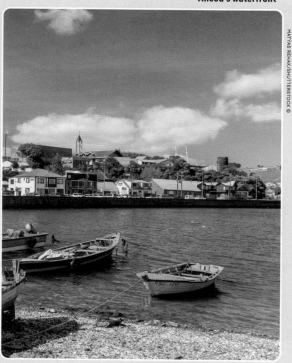

MATYAS REHAK/SHUTTERSTOCK ©

BEST PLACES TO EAT IN ANCUD

Ajo Panadería Artesanal
Two brothers devoted to producing Chiloé's best baked goods. $

Indómito
Huge, messy burgers, gourmet *pichangas* (share plates) and other stepped-up main courses highlight this always buzzing local favorite. Cash only. $$

Club Social Baquedano
This trendy resto-bar serves great ceviche, panko-crusted fish and other delights in a traditional Chilota home. $$

Wabi Sabi
Wildly popular take-out–only sushi. Order 90 minutes in advance on Instagram (@wabisabi_ sushiancud). $$

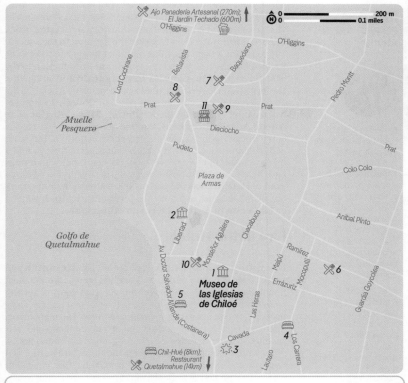

Ajo Panadería Artesanal (270m);
El Jardín Techado (600m)

O'Higgins

Muelle
Pesquero

Golfo de
Quetalmahue

Plaza de
Armas

1 Museo de
las Iglesias
de Chiloé

Chil-Hué (8km);
Restaurant
Quetalmahue (14km)

HIGHLIGHTS
1 Museo de las Iglesias
de Chiloé

SIGHTS
2 Museo Regional de
Ancud Aurelio Bórquez
Canobra

**ACTIVITIES, COURSES
& TOURS**
3 Austral Adventures

SLEEPING
4 13 Lunas Hostel
5 Hostal Mundo Nuevo

EATING
6 Café Blanco
7 Club Social
Baquedano
see 5 Indómito
8 Kuranton

9 La Corita
10 Wabi Sabi

SHOPPING
11 Mercado Municipal

Chill Out in Ancud

BREWS AND VIEWS

In Arena Gruesa, a hilltop neighborhood and waterfront, plop
down for a pint of expertly curated craft beer at **El Jardín
Techado** – revamped in 2020 and framing astonishing views
of the Chacao Channel above the secluded beach of the same

 WHERE TO STAY IN ANCUD

13 Lunas Hostel
Freshen up in hotel-standard
bathrooms and settle onto
the terrace with views at this
recommended hostel. **$**

Hostal Mundo Nuevo
Ancud's best midrange option,
this Swiss-owned lodge has
sunset-illuminated bay views
and a hostel-like vibe. **$$**

Chil-Hué
English-speaking staff, gourmet
food, eco pool, yoga: this idyllic
getaway on beachfront property
is wonderfully remote. **$$$**

name – and it's quickly evident how easy it is to fall in love with Ancud. It's about the natural surroundings, be it a brew and a view from a craft beer-focused restaurant or a sunset stroll along the revamped waterfront hugging the bay 1km to the south.

If you want a taste of Chiloé but don't have time to head as far south as Castro, Ancud is a wonderful introduction to the island. Pop into **Museo de las Iglesias de Chiloé**, occupying the former Convento Inmaculada Concepción de Ancud (1875), and peep wooden scale models of all of Chiloé's 16 Unesco-listed churches. Nearby, the worthwhile **Museo Regional de Ancud Aurelio Bórquez Canobra** houses a full-size replica of the *Ancud* – which sailed the treacherous fjords of the Strait of Magellan to claim Chile's southernmost territories – and a massive intact blue whale skeleton. Bookend your wanderings with light meals, delectable sweets and locally produced provisions at **Café Blanco** situated inside an atmospheric and rambling Chilote home, or homey and honest market-fresh seafood at **La Corita** in Ancud's **Mercado Municipal**.

Fire in the Hole!

A TRADITIONAL FEAST IN CHILOÉ

It's easy to walk into an Ancud restaurant like **Kuranton** and order *curanto* (meat, potato and seafood stew), Chiloé's most famous gastronomic endeavor, but the real coup is getting yourself invited (or paying for the privilege) to a *casa de campo* (countryside house) for a *curanto al hoyo*, the most labor-intensive, fiercely traditional version of this clambake-like stew steamed in a stone-heated dent in the ground for several hours.

Don't miss ogling the ritual. Once the stones are heated and the firewood removed, a frantic scramble begins. The shell-fish – small and large mussels, perhaps clams or simply whatever is on hand – are dumped on first, followed by alternating layers of pangue leaves (a native plant of Chile), *milcao* (Chilota potato bread) and *chapaleles* (boiled potato dumplings) and, finally, piles of chicken, smoked pork and *longaniza* sausages. It's all topped by more pangue, a damp cloth and a final vapor-sealing layer of nalca leaves (rhubarb-like plant) or tufts of peat that seals this fascinating culinary pyre.

Blink twice and it's built, done so with rousing urgency to preserve the heat of the stones. It's now an organic pressure cooker, and smoke billows skyward as it's left to simmer for an hour or two. Once plated, an intimidating mountainous feast stands before you. There's no dainty way to do it: Dig in!

If you can't weasel your way into a private family version, eateries like **Restaurant Quetalmahue**, in a small fishing village 12km from Ancud, are an option. Better yet, contact **Austral Adventures** in Ancud or **Chiloé Natural** in Castro, both of which can set you up with a more intimate affair.

GETTING AROUND

Ancud is a small town easily navigated on foot, but you'll want to rent a car to acces s the beaches and surrounding nature.

Beyond Ancud

The natural surroundings around Ancud are spectacular, harboring rare penguin enclaves, a sunken forest and breathtaking beauty at every turn.

Monumento Natural Islotes de Puñihuil

Ancud

Muelle de la Luz

Chepu

Though Ancud sits in an easy-on-the-eyes location on the Bay of Ancud and the Chacao Channel, its immediate surrounds might have leapt from a landscape painting. Vivid green pastoral hills roll under the hooves of sheep and cows and empty into an often glass-like sea in all directions.

To the west, Monumento Natural Islotes de Puñihuil protects a trio of offshore islands that serve as the world's only breeding grounds for both Magellanic and Humboldt penguins in the same place. Further southwest, rural Chepu, near the northern sector of Parque Nacional Chiloé, remains Chiloé's sanctuary of pristine beauty, highlighted by 128 bird species, a stunning coastline and gorgeous rivers congregating over a spectacular forest buried underwater.

TOP TIP

The best time to view the penguins at Monumento Natural Islotes de Puñihuil is the end of February, once the newborns have hatched.

Monumento Natural Islotes de Puñihuil (p244)

PHILIP SCALIA/ALAMY STOCK PHOTO ©

WHY I LOVE CHILÓE

Kevin Raub, writer

Even after a half-dozen trips, I feel no less intrigued by Chiloé's enigmatic culture each time I go. The extraordinary landscape – Crayola-green hills unraveling across rolling pastures peppered with alerce-shingled homes and archetypical cows and sheep – is reason enough to lure me back, but it's the unique Unesco-listed wooden churches that most warrant multiple returns. My personal favorite is San Antonio de Colo. Its radical aqua blue and salmon-trimmed interior captivates each time with the same confounding sense of awe as the first. Add to these attributes the distinctive cuisine and the whole island becomes a mystic melting pot unlike anywhere I have ever known and loved.

Humboldt penguins

In Pursuit of Penguins

PENGUIN-SPOTTING AND BIRD-WATCHING

Three islands off the coast of Puñihuil, a 26km drive southwest of Ancud, make up **Monumento Natural Islotes de Puñihuil**, a protected breeding ground for Magellanic and vulnerable Humboldt penguins, and the only place in the world where you can see both species living together in harmony.

Breeding season kicks off in September and winds down in March. Catch one of the boats leaving from the beach every 15 minutes or so between 10:15am and 5:15pm to get an upclose and personal glimpse of these remarkable birds, which waddle along the rocks among flights of cormorants (four species in total, including the chameleon-like Neotropic cormorant), flightless steamer ducks (Chile's largest duck species,

 WHERE TO SLEEP & EAT AROUND ANCUD

Agroturismo Chepu
Forgo English for the Perez-Diaz family's good-hearted nature; 10 comfortable rooms on a working farm. **$**

Alihuen
Sustainable Chepu farmstead run by a Flemish chef. The two-bedroom, recycled-corrugated-iron cabin sleeps five. **$$**

Costa Pacifico
Waves nearly sweep penguins onto the patio of this fresh seafood spot at Puñihuil Beach. **$$**

which can weigh up to a whopping 6kg/13lbs) and occasional sea lions. You might even see a blue whale or two if you're lucky.

Ecoturismo Puñihuil represents three of the seven boats licensed to provide boat excursions. If you have your own transport, you can drive right onto the magnificent rugged beach and hop on the next boat for CH$9000 per person. If you need transport, reliable agencies doing trips from Ancud include **13 Lunas Hostel** and **Casa Damasco**, but you'll pay CH$22,000 for the package. Highly recommended, US-run ecotourism agency **Austral Adventures** also includes English-language trips to see the penguins as part of their bespoke, nature-centric jaunts in the region.

KEEN ON KAYAKING?

Chepu isn't the only spot in the region for a serene kayak trip. In Cochamó, on the mainland 229km northeast of Chepu, wholly different but equally tranquil sea kayaking trips await in the **Reloncaví Fjord** (p228).

Chepu at Dawn

SUNRISE KAYAKING IN A SUNKEN FOREST

In a globally connected world, it can feel like the world has fewer opportunities to experience something new, but the rural outpost of **Chepu**, a half-hour or so drive southwest of Ancud, is one such place. Chepu's masterpiece is a breathtaking spot overlooking the confluence of three rivers and 140 sq km of sunken forest, a phenomena created by the 1960 Valdivia earthquake, which sank the ground some 2m, allowing salt water to enter the area and kill the trees. The spectacle is best seen at dawn on a surreal kayak trip that ranks as one of Chile's most serene and beautiful experiences.

As the sun breeches the horizon in front of you, you'll slowly navigate the mystical dawn landscape of the **Río Puntra** surrounded by the unusual remnants of a once-thriving forest still standing, the canopy protruding from the water like tops of flooded tombstones in a lost-in-time underwater cemetery. You'll often share the water with no one else on the 90-minute excursion, the silent lucidity broken up only by the occasional squawking of countless nesting species of birds.

Though the original visionaries behind this iconic example of low-impact ecotourism in Chepu have retired to Valdivia, their legacy is carried on by locals such as Sandra Díaz and Armando Perez at **Agroturismo Chepu**, among others. Recommended ecotourism agency **Chiloé Natural** runs overnight trips from Castro.

MISSION TO MUELLE DE LA LUZ

Muelle de la Luz is a wonderful piece of landscape art that puts a whole new meaning on taking a long walk off a short pier. Reached via a short stroll after a 30-minute boat ride (per person CH$6000; call +56 98 351 5946 or +56 93 427 1194 if no boats are present) from Muelle Anguay near Refugio Lugar de Encuentro in Chepu, the winding wooden pier (CH$2500) is dramatically perched on a cliff that drops off in startling fashion where the Chepu River meets the ocean. It's built by the same sculptor (Marcelo Orellana Rivera) as Chiloé's ruined-by-Instagram **Muelle de las Almas**, and it's at once both stunning and disconcerting.

GETTING AROUND

Renting a car is best. Public transport to Puñihuil and Chepu is sporadic and unreliable.

Ask about departures at Ancud's Terminal Inter-Rural.

CASTRO

At once both ramshackle and cosmopolitan-leaning, Chiloé's capital and biggest city is the beating heart of the archipelago. Located 85km south of Ancud on a bluff above a sheltered estuary lined with distinctive *palafito* houses (its principal attraction), Castro flirts with positioning itself as fashionable and foodie-centric before eventually revealing its true identity as a provincial town.

That's not to say it isn't likable. Castro serves up the idiosyncrasies and attractions of the archipelago within a neatly packaged urban framework and a touch of Chilota character, offering comfortable tourism infrastructure, some of the island's best restaurants and an occasional dash of big city development. With its position near the dead center of the island, it makes a perfect base for exploring attractions further afield, including Chiloé's fascinating Unesco-listed wooden churches and the island's exceptional parks and nature reserves.

✪ Santiago

Castro ●

TOP TIP

The best time of day to see Castro's *palafitos* along Pedro Montt and Puente Gamboa is sunrise and early morning when the light is just right. If you go in the afternoon, the sun will likely obscure that postcard-perfect Instagram shot.

Castro

BERND ZILLICH/SHUTTERSTOCK ©

Chiloé once boasted more than 150 stunning wooden *iglesias* (churches) and *capillas* (chapels), one of the region's main attractions. Today, some 60 or so remain, 16 of which are recognized as a collective Unesco World Heritage Site. For those who want to commit to the epic undertaking of seeing them all, contact the trilingual ecotourism agency Chiloétnico; otherwise, this half-day, 174km round-trip driving tour highlights the best and most conveniently reached choices.

Head north out of Castro to charming Dalcahue, where **1 Iglesia Nuestra Señora de Los Dolores** dominates the main square. From here, catch the 10-minute ferry (per car CH$3000) to Isla Quinchao and head southeast to Achao. As you enter town, there's a gasp-inducing view of Patagonia across the Gulf of Corcovado. On Plaza de Armas, **2 Iglesia Santa María de Loreto** stands as Chiloé's oldest church (1740). A perennial favorite, it's held together by wooden pegs rather than nails and has a mind-blowing interior. Grab the ferry back to Dalcahue and drive northeast to **3 Iglesia de Nuestra Señora del Patrocinio** in Tenaún. Its beautiful blue towers and star-adorned facade appear to reflect the cerulean blue sea across the street. **4 Iglesia San Antonio de Colo**, 13km north of Tenaún, is the smallest of the Unesco churches. Its magnificent salmon-pink and turquoise nave will recalibrate your idea of ecclesiastical interior design. Finish back in Castro, where the city's unconventionally yellow and mauve-trimmed **5 Iglesia San Francisco de Castro** beckons you into its spectacular varnished-wood interior. Try to visit on a sunny day, when the interior is illuminated by the rows of stained-glass windows.

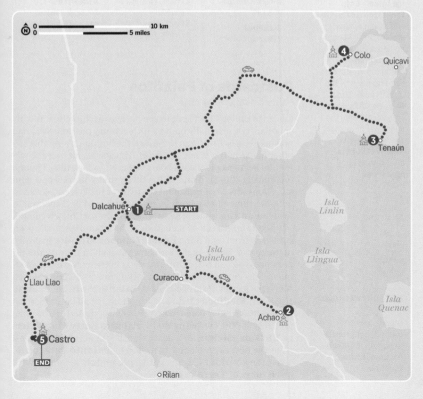

I LIVE HERE: A CHEF'S DAY OUT IN CASTRO

Lorna Muñoz Arias (@cocinerachilota) is a Chilota gastronomy researcher and the chef-owner of Restaurant Travesía.

Walk to the **Feria Yumbel** where you can stock up on fresh food and have an invigorating breakfast at **Cocinería Doña Amanda**. On the way back, look for the **Iglesia San Francisco de Castro** and its impressive architecture. At noon go to the **Humedal de Putemún** (Putemún Wetland) accompanied by the birding guide **Guía Aves de Chile**. Here you can observe the migratory birds that arrive every year. Nearby is **Rucalaf**, an exquisite local restaurant.

GETTING AROUND

Castro is foot-friendly, but prepare to huff up the steep hill from Puente Gamboa.

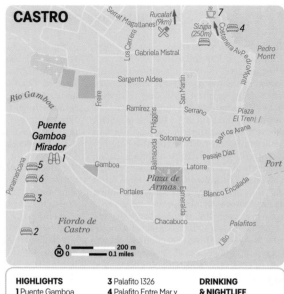

CASTRO

HIGHLIGHTS	3 Palafito 1326	DRINKING & NIGHTLIFE
1 Puente Gamboa Mirador	4 Palafito Entre Mar y Tierra B&B	7 Palafito Patagonia
	5 Palafito Hostel	see 3 Terraza 1326
SLEEPING	6 Palafito Waiwen	
2 Bledford Chiloé		

Postcards of Palafitos

CASTRO'S BOUTIQUE SIDE

Castro is Chiloé's best spot to see *palafito* architecture, a truly singular style originally built by 19th-century peasants who had nowhere else to live. From the street, the buildings resemble any other house in town, but the colorful backsides jut over the water and serve as piers with boats tethered to the stilts. Though technically illegal, demand for these shaky luma-wood constructions saw a boom around Castro over the last two decades, with boutique hotels, hostels, restaurants and bars moving in to create an atmospheric new tourism draw for Chiloé's capital.

While *palafitos* can be seen in six areas around town, the postcard view from land is the **Puente Gamboa Mirador** just west of the center. But to really immerse yourself in the *palafito* experience, you can eat, drink and sleep in them as well. Accommodations cluster along Ernesto Riquelme and Pedro Montt. Along the former, **Palafito Hostel**, **Palafito Waiwen**, **Palafito 1326** and **Bledford Chiloé** have options for all budgets, from CH$35,000 single rooms to luxuriously appointed apartments for CH$271,000. On Pedro Montt, **Palafito Entre Mar y Tierra B&B** and **Sizigia** also boast stylish stilt accommodations.

For the best espresso in town, stop by **Palafito Patagonia**. Toast the swarms of swans gathering nightly at sunset with pisco sours at **Terraza 1326**.

Beyond Castro

Parque Nacional Chiloé and Parque Tantauco safeguard pounding Pacific coastline, native evergreen forest and abundant Chilote wildlife beyond the island's capital.

Chiloé's two most protected destinations for nature lovers blanket an impossibly gorgeous chunk of South America's third-largest island south and west of Castro. Wild and windswept swaths of virgin forest shelter superlative lists of fauna. At 430-sq-km Parque Nacional Chiloé, the native evergreen forest that gives way to secluded beaches alongside the pounding Pacific makes for an inspiring day of hiking. The 1180-sq-km Parque Tantauco, a private nature reserve created and owned by former Chilean President Sebastián Piñera, canvasses the southern end of Chiloé, a three-hour drive south of the capital. It's home to one of Chile's most isolated and exclusive multiday hut-to-hut hike opportunities.

TOP TIP

Parque Nacional Chiloé is best accessed an hour's drive southwest of Castro at Cucao.

Parque Nacional Chiloé (p250)

CHILÓE IN MINIATURE

Cinematic **Isla Mechuque** (part of Islas Chauques, what some consider to be Chiloé's most beautiful island chain), offers a prettily packaged Chiloé-in-miniature experience that's perfect for a day trip. *Tejuela* (wood shingle) homes, a splendid viewpoint, a picturesque bridge, famed *curanto al hoyo* and *palafitos*: it's all here in a step-back-in-time atmosphere that is reachable on an easy boat ride from Chiloé proper. The *Niña Hermosa* leaves most frequently from Quicavi, 59km northeast of Castro, but you'll need to spend the night because of transport logistics. **Hospedaje Maria Humilde** is a good option. Most folks take a day tour instead. Castro-based **Turismo Pehuén** does it best, with private tours for up to 20 people by reservation only.

RAIMUNDO VARGAS A/SHUTTERSTOCK ©

Parque Tantauco

In Search of Unseen Sands

HIDDEN BEACH, INDIGENOUS WILDLIFE

Chiloé's 430-sq-km **Parque Nacional Chiloé** is a west coast wonderland of rugged cliffs, impeccably preserved native forest and unblemished sands that counts as the most easily accessible of the island's extraordinary protected areas. From Cucao you can waltz right into the park's **Chanquín sector** – a far simpler prospect than the park's northern sector at Chepu (which includes Isla Metalqui and its sea lion colony but is mostly inaccessible) and its middle sector at Abtao (restricted by Conaf and accessible only by an 18km hike). The park has eight official hikes of varying lengths, the most popular of which is the **Sendero Chanquín-Cole Cole**, a 25km hike along the coast, past Lago Huelde to Río Cole Cole and one of Chile's most scenic hidden beaches – the reason for this wet and wild walk in the first place.

 WHERE TO STAY BEYOND CASTRO ———————

Hospedaje Mirella
Near Tenaún's striking blue-starred church, Mirella and family dazzle overnight guests with multicourse meals. **$**

Palafito Cucao Lodge
Cucao's top digs, situated on the lake; offers fashionable private rooms and a six-bed dorm. **$**

Refugio de Navegantes
Dalcahue's most stylish option; a five-room boutique hotel above a trendy cafe full of tempting sweets. **$$$**

Visitors are at the mercy of Pacific storms, so expect rain – lots of it (300cm annually on average). Though travelers often try to manage a round-trip jaunt (returning to Cucao) in one day, most make it no further than the indigenous settlement at **Huentemó**. Instead, it's best to set out with food (Cucao is your last chance to pick up supplies) and camping equipment or arrange transport to/from Huentemó. Plan to overnight at **Cole Cole Beach**, which has indigenous-run camping and a basic *refugio* (rustic shelter). The route teems with wildlife, including the elusive pudu (the world's smallest deer, which inhabits the shadowy forests of the contorted tepú tree) and zigs and zags between extensive stands of native evergreen forest and wild beach views. File under unspoiled Pacific paradise.

A Walk in the Woods

MULTIDAY HUT-TO-HUT HIKE

Isolation, access challenges and caps on visitor numbers ensure nature lovers willing to put in the effort of taking on the six-day trek in **Parque Tantauco** are justly rewarded for their efforts. This dramatic and hard-to-reach private reserve, one of the world's 25 biodiversity hot spots identified by Conservation International, is one of the few spots in Chile where you can traverse a park on a multiday hut-to-hut hike.

An astonishing maximum of just eight trekkers per day are permitted to traverse the park's 130km of trails, which are connected by a series of six basic *refugios*. Bring all of your own supplies and provisions. A wonderful guesthouse and home-cooked meals await at the end of the line in **Inío**. Being off the grid is an entirely redefined concept as you negotiate Valdivian temperate rainforest, home to native otters, Darwin foxes and pudu. Both the world's smallest marsupial (*monito del monte* or 'little mountain monkey') and the world's largest mammal (blue whales in the surrounding seas) also call this park home. And there's little else.

The experience of hiking, camping and viewing wildlife in this magnificent park comes at a price. You need to pay for a private transfer to the trailhead at Chaiguata (CH$120,000 for up to four people), plus CH$20,000 per person per night for the *refugios* and an airlift out from Inío (per person CH$320,000). Alternatively, **Chiloé Natural**, the park's official tourism partner, can make all the arrangements for you, including a guide and a chef.

BEST REMOTE LODGES IN CHILOÉ

Isla Bruja Lodge
Cozy American-Chilean-owned hideaway on Palidad estuary 15km southwest of Queilén. $$$

Huillín Lodge
Six elevated pinewood cabins overlooking Lago Huillinco and the Quiao forests 20km east of Parque Nacional Chiloé's Chanquín sector at Cucao. $$$

OCIO Territorial Hotel
Sustainable traditionally shingled getaway framing panoramic views over Castro fjord. $$$

Tierra Chiloé
Upscale shelter dramatically perched on the edge of Chiloé's most important wetlands; an environmentally unobtrusive trifecta of incredibly beautiful native hardwoods, unfinished concrete and stunning Rilán Peninsula views. $$$

GETTING AROUND

Cucao, Parque Nacional Chiloé's main gateway near the southern Chanquín sector, is well served by Buses Unión Expresos and Buses Ojeda from Castro's Terminal de Buses Municipal. Getting to Parque Tantauco requires your own wheels or private arrangements.

NORTHERN PATAGONIA

MOUNTAINS, RIVERS, GLACIERS AND FJORDS

Northern Patagonia is a rugged, dynamic region carved by ice and water, and the whiff of adventure is perpetually on the wind.

From the formidable peaks of the Andes and the splintering glaciers of the Patagonian ice fields to the ancient alerces (Patagonian cypress) of the Valdivian forests and the rodeo-like rapids of Río Futaleufú, Northern Patagonia feels supersized and wild. These radical landscapes have long beckoned intrepid wanderers and inspired big ideas about preservation, while the unpredictable weather and occasional volcanic eruption have presented unique challenges to inhabitants.

The region's human history began with nomadic tribes that roamed the region's arid steppe and paddled its turbulent fjords, but in the early 1900s, they were violently displaced by settlers of European descent. With logging, agriculture and mining came the development of a few isolated, Wild West–style outposts, and it wasn't until 1976 that an effort commenced to connect these dots with an ambitious 1240km highway – the Carretera Austral. Today, the road remains only partially paved but it is without question one of the world's great road trips.

Aside from chatter about Carretera adventures, dinner conversation in Northern Patagonia often veers into natural resource battles: the ecological impacts of salmon farming, the ongoing effort to reject hydroelectric dams and the trade-offs of converting ranches to national parks. The region's tourism sector is still in its infancy, with all the charm and kinks you might expect. A trip here is rewarding, not only for its mind-blowing landscapes but also for the support travelers can offer to local communities.

THE MAIN AREAS

CARRETERA AUSTRAL
The ultimate road trip.
p258

FUTALEUFÚ
World-class river
adventures. **p268**

**PARQUE NACIONAL
LAGUNA SAN RAFAEL**
Glaciers, icebergs and
fjords with spectacular
waterfronts. **p272**

**PARQUE NACIONAL
PATAGONIA**
South American safari
extraordinaire. **p278**

Left: Bridge, Valle Exploradores (p273); above: Parque Nacional Laguna San Rafael (p272)

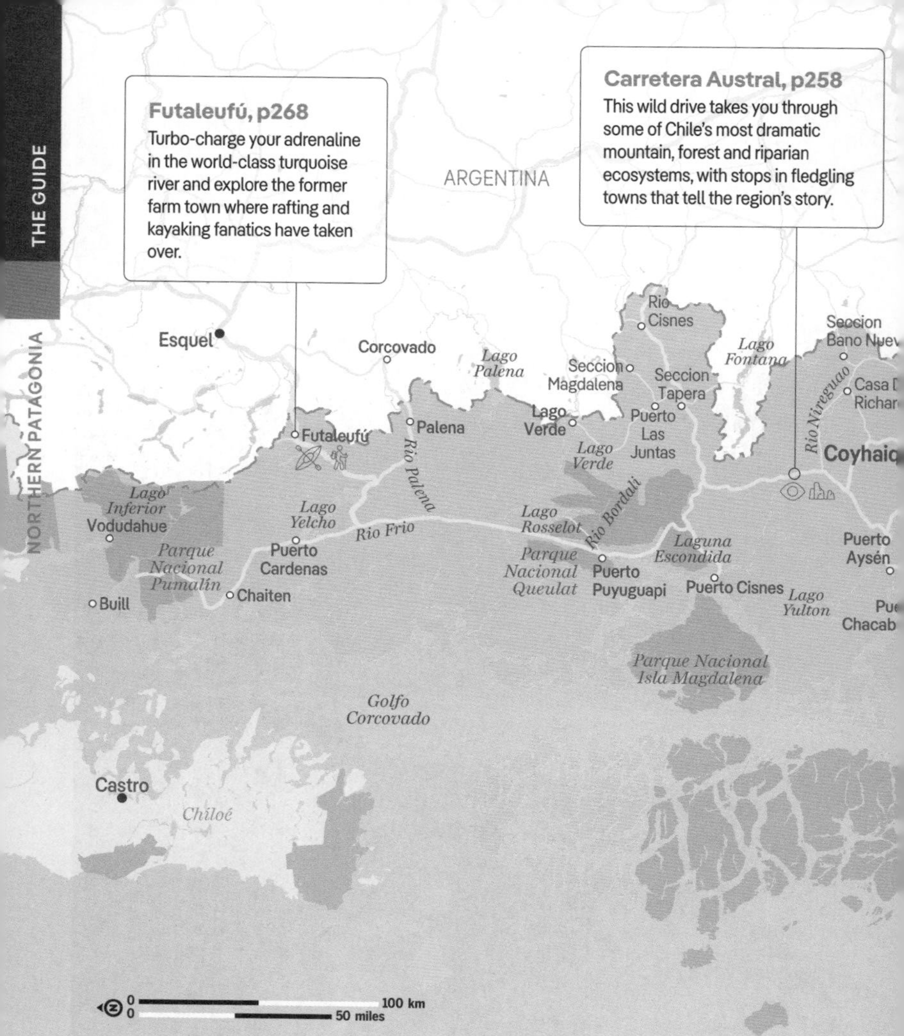

Futaleufú, p268
Turbo-charge your adrenaline in the world-class turquoise river and explore the former farm town where rafting and kayaking fanatics have taken over.

Carretera Austral, p258
This wild drive takes you through some of Chile's most dramatic mountain, forest and riparian ecosystems, with stops in fledgling towns that tell the region's story.

ARGENTINA

Esquel

Corcovado

Rio Cisnes

Lago Palena

Seccion Magdalena

Seccion Tapera

Lago Fontana

Seccion Bano Nuev

Casa D Richar

Futaleufú

Palena

Lago Verde

Puerto Las Juntas

Coyhaiq

Rio Palena

Lago Verde

Lago Inferior
Vodudahue

Lago Yelcho

Rio Frio

Lago Rosselot

Rio Bordali

Laguna Escondida

Puerto Aysén

Parque Nacional Pumalin

Puerto Cardenas

Parque Nacional Queulat

Puerto Puyuguapi

Puerto Cisnes

Lago Yulton

Buill

Chaiten

Golfo Corcovado

Parque Nacional Isla Magdalena

Pue Chacab

Castro

Chiloé

0 — 100 km
0 — 50 miles

Find Your Way

This lengthy, mountainous sliver of Chile might feel intimidating at first glance. Whether you do the whole thing or just a piece, it's the sort of place where travelers who take their time are greatly rewarded.

Parque Nacional Patagonia, p278
Once overgrazed pastureland, this park is now dominated by cruising condors, galloping guanacos, prowling pumas and furtive foxes.

CAR
Rental cars are available in Puerto Montt and Coyhaique and offer the most flexibility and independence. The road is challenging, and ferry crossings are sometimes necessary but not always reliable. Rental prices are more reasonable in Puerto Montt, but gas prices are not reasonable anywhere.

so Rio
vo

Lago Buenos Aires

Estancia Valle Huemules
Los Antiguos
ovrat
Puerto Ibanez
Puerto Avellanos
que Nacional rro Castillo
Parque Nacional Patagonia
Lago Caro
Rio Ibanez
Bahia Murta
Puerto Tranquilo
Lago Cochrane
Cochrane
Puerto Bertrand
La Colonia
Villa O'Higgins
Lago Cisnes
Laguna Larga
El Salto
Lago Berguez
Monte San Valentin
San Rafael Glacier
Parque Nacional Laguna San Rafael
Caleta Tortel
Puerto Bajo Pisagua
Parque Nacional Bernardo O'Higgins

Parque Nacional Laguna San Rafael, p272
Some of Patagonia's iciest and least inhabitable terrain is some of its most exciting and worthwhile to visit.

PACIFIC OCEAN

BUS
Some bus routes have services only a few days a week. From December to February long-distance buses often fill up. Book tickets at least three days in advance. Travelers relying on buses often end up hitchhiking (considered safe in the region but not recommended by Lonely Planet).

PLANE
When you've got long distances to travel, flying is a time-saver. LATAM, Sky Airline and Jet Smart serve the region with flights between Santiago, Puerto Montt and Coyhaique. There are also charter services, and regional flights sometimes operate between Puerto Montt, Chaitén, Coyhaique, Cochrane and Villa O'Higgins.

Plan Your Time

Northern Patagonia is a place to give yourself time to make the best of what comes. When the weather's good, seize the day. When the sky opens up, put on your raincoat and then seize the day.

Lago General Carrera (p267)

GUAXININ/SHUTTERSTOCK ©

Pressed for Time

● Head for the dreamy rafting destination of **Futaleufú** (p268) and spend a few days riding the wild, gorgeous **river** (p269) in your watercraft of choice. Once you've dried off, **hike** (271) up the scenic mountains that surround to view the river from above.

● Squeeze in a visit to the fearsome volcano and ancient alerce trees of **Parque Nacional Pumalín** (p262), one of the region's premier parks. These adventures give you a teensy taste of the **Carretera Austral** (p258), and you can even stop at a famous **hot spring** (p262) to soothe those achy muscles along the way.

Seasonal Highlights

Wildflowers explode in the spring, while summer brings the most reliable bus connections. Winter is frigid, but skiing and snowshoeing become possible.

JANUARY

Chilean **school holidays** begin, and Northern Patagonia enters peak high season, with accommodations and excursions filling up. Definitely book ahead.

FEBRUARY

Peak high season continues. **Festival Costumbrista** celebrates pioneer culture, and parties erupt across the region's small towns.

APRIL

The weather goes from **rainy** to rainier, with the western coast getting especially drenched (hence all the greenery).

MONICA QUINTA/SHUTTERSTOCK ©, RHJPHTOTOS/SHUTTERSTOCK ©, KNIK/SHUTTERSTOCK ©

A Couple of Weeks

● Fly to Coyhaique and head south on the **Carretera Austral** (p258). The first stop is **Cerro Castillo** (p266) and the jaw-dropping hike to its basalt spires and brilliant glacier-fed lagoon.

● Proceed to Puerto Río Tranquilo, where you can boat or kayak into the mind-bending **marble caves** (p267) and walk on or take a boat to glaciers in **Parque Nacional Laguna San Rafael** (p272).

● Continue down to **Cochrane** (p282) and explore the wilds of **Parque Nacional Patagonia** (p278) on foot or by boat.

● Detour off the Carretera toward **Chile Chico** (p283) if you can score a ferry ride back to Coyhaique.

With More Time

● Start in Puerto Montt and follow the **Carretera Austral** (p258) to the rainforest and volcano hikes of **Parque Nacional Pumalín** (p262).

● Detour to **Futaleufú** (p268) for an extreme **river adventure** (p269).

● Double back toward **Parque Nacional Queulat** (p263) for a fabulous glacier hike and then roll south to the **hot spring** (2620).

● Fuel up in Coyhaique and ride **horses** (p264) or visit **condors** (p265) before visiting the **marble caves** (p267) near Puerto Río Tranquilo and the calving glaciers of **Parque Nacional Laguna San Rafael** (p272).

● After spying on guanacos in **Parque Nacional Patagonia** (p278), visit the boardwalk village of **Caleta Tortel** (p276).

JUNE

Winter begins and temperatures routinely drop into the vicinity of **freezing**. Rainfall remains abundant across the region.

OCTOBER

Spring has sprung, experts start **rafting** in Futaleufú, and the river is big from all the snowmelt.

NOVEMBER

Yellow, purple, pink and white **lupines** hijack the landscape along the Carretera Austral and across parks and riverbeds.

DECEMBER

It's a fantastic month to **road trip** the Carretera Austral as temperatures have climbed and wildflowers remain, but visitor numbers aren't crazy.

CARRETERA AUSTRAL

❖ Santiago

● Carretera Austral

Carretera means highway, but that's not really the right word for this 1240km beast of a road between Puerto Montt and Villa O'Higgins. Completed in 1996 but still only partly paved, the Carretera Austral took more than 20 years and US$300 million to construct. The lion's share of the work was completed at the behest of brutal dictator Augusto Pinochet – a controversial figure around these parts – on his quest to defend Chile from Argentina and connect secluded outposts with the national identity.

Southbound visitors often bypass Northern Patagonia on a sprint to Torres del Paine, but adventurous travelers will hit pay dirt on this legendary road and its backcountry treasures. Although the northern reaches are mostly paved, ferry connections are required for roadless stretches where mountains meet the sea, and traveling over the long sections of dirt and gravel south of Villa Cerro Castillo remains an iconic challenge.

TOP TIP

Keep your itinerary flexible and be ready for anything, including storms, giant potholes, delayed ferries, flat tires or boulders blocking the road. You'll be making stops to hike, so a sturdy, comfortable pair of boots and a high-quality rain jacket are essential.

Carretera Austral, Villa Cerro Castillo

LEFT: THIAGO DICKMANN/ALAMY STOCK PHOTO © RIGHT: JHVEPHOTO/SHUTTERSTOCK ©

DRIVING TIPS

Staying safe on the Carretera Austral requires following some guidelines. Firstly, always carry a spare tire, a car jack and jumper cables. Keep your headlights on (it's the law) and avoid driving after dark. Fill up the gas tank whenever the opportunity presents itself, and carry extra water and snacks in case you get stranded. Be prepared for delays because of roadwork and livestock crossings. Book ferries in advance and realize delays are common. Stop if you see someone who needs help. Give trucks a wide berth on gravel – broken windshields are endemic to the Carretera Austral. Finally, take your time and enjoy the scenery.

Capillas de Mármol (p267),
Puerto Río Tranquilo

259

ROAD TRIP

The Carretera Austral

One serious drive, the Carretera Austral winds along some of Patagonia's most dramatic scenery, with exuberant rainforest, scrubby steppe, smoking volcanoes, snow-dusted mountains and expansive farmsteads framed in the windows. But it's water that truly defines this landscape, from the clear cascading rivers to the turquoise lakes, massive glaciers and labyrinthine fjords. This driving tour takes you through all the Carretera's major bases for exploration, refueling and cultural activities.

1 Hornopirén

Road-tripping completists begin the journey in Puerto Montt and head for this fjordside transport hub and salmon-farming settlement. Within striking distance are waterfalls and hot springs, and the alpine backcountry of Parque Nacional Hornopirén. Explore the park and grab provisions from the town's small kiosks.

The Drive: Heading south to Caleta Gonzalo requires two scenic ferry crossings (book ahead at barcazas.cl). After the ferry, it's 55km to Chaitén.

2 Chaitén

When a nearby volcano erupted on May 2, 2008, numerous homes were destroyed. Now rebuilt, the town has a museum dedicated to the eruption, which opened in 2023. Chaitén is also the main service town for Parque Nacional Pumalín, a pristine expanse of temperate rainforest, with a trail to a viewpoint of the still-smoking crater.

The Drive: Entirely paved and undeniably pleasant, the 200km trip to Puyuhuapi features fjords, lakes and river crossings out of a storybook.

3 Puyuhuapi

At the northern end of a scenic fjord, this quaint seaside village was settled in 1935 by German immigrants who farmed and made high-end carpets. Today, it's the gateway to Parque Nacional Queulat and a prestigious hot-springs resort.

The Drive: A windy, initial stretch of this 233km drive is unpaved and under construction. After the turnoff for Ventisquero Colgante (p263), the road is paved all the way to Coyhaique.

4 Coyhaique

Sprawling Coyhaique perches within an undulating range dotted with livestock and backed by rocky, snowy peaks. Travelers can get anything they need here, and it's also a launchpad for adventures like fly fishing, trekking, horseback riding and condor watching.

The Drive: A paved and scenic 100km journey south lands you at the gateway to one of the region's best hiking experiences.

Ventisquero Colgante (p263)

JENS OTTE/ALAMY STOCK PHOTO ©

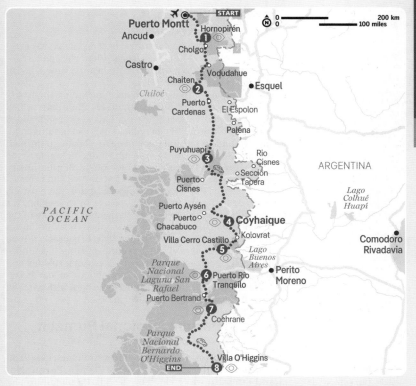

5 Villa Cerro Castillo

Under the sparkly spires of Cerro Castillo, this tiny town has a congenial, dusty-heeled feel. It's a good base to explore the eponymous national park, and the town's Festival Costumbrista offers an authentic take on Patagonian rodeo in February.

The Drive: Here's where things get bumpy. Almost none of the next 120km is paved, but the appearance of the impossibly blue Lago General Carrera makes it all worth it.

6 Puerto Río Tranquilo

This shingled-house settlement on the lake's western shores is expanding, with outdoor opportunities now including marble caves and glacier excursions to Parque Nacional Laguna San Rafael. The town also features decent (if pricey) lodgings, tasty restaurants and a small history museum that opened in 2022.

The Drive: The unpaved 115km stretch of road to Cochrane is notorious for delays. It's also strikingly beautiful, with a must-see confluence of the Ríos Baker and Neff.

7 Cochrane

An old ranching outpost, Cochrane is the southern hub of the Carretera and an up-and-coming destination thanks to nearby Parque Nacional Patagonia. The town is minutes from the park's Sector Tamango and a base for glacier treks, river excursions and fishing trips to Lago Cochrane.

The Drive: Unpaved and unruly, the 234km between Cochrane and the end of the Carretera are undoubtedly its least traveled.

8 Villa O'Higgins

This mythic village is alluring in its isolation. Settled by the English in 1914, the outpost attracted few Chileans, and the road didn't arrive until 1999. You'll explore the region on horseback or foot, and there's world-class fishing and boat access to the O'Higgins Glacier.

AGE OF ALERCE

Slow-growing conifers called alerce trees play a key role in Patagonia's temperate rainforests, but their value as a nearly indestructible hardwood meant they were logged to near extinction. Today, it's illegal to harvest live trees. You can visit them in the Lakes District and Northern Patagonian forests, and view alerce shingles on Chilote houses. Alerces rank among the oldest and largest tree species in the world, sometimes living for more than 4000 years. In fact, an alerce tree called *Gran Abuelo* in Chile's Parque Nacional Alerce Costero has been estimated at 5484 years old. Though the method for arriving at that number is controversial, *Gran Abuelo* could unseat California's 4789-year-old bristlecone pine, Methuselah, as the oldest known living tree.

Carretera Hot Stops

SOAKING IN VOLCANO-HEATED SPRINGS

When driving the Carretera Austral becomes exhausting, remember that the road slices through prime volcano territory and the resultant hot springs, with healing waters for all adventure levels and price points.

Several options lie near Hornopirén, including the toasty and accessible soaks at **Baños Termales Pichicolo**, which are just a 10km drive west. Reservations are recommended (termasdepichicolo.cl). If you're looking for something more private, **Cabañas Lahuan** can arrange a boat trip through the Comau Fjord and a hike through Valdivian jungle to the riverside **Termas Porcelana**, which offers thermal pools, massages, a mud bath, a restaurant, campsites and cabins.

Farther south, **Puyuhuapi Lodge & Spa** is the most exclusive and luxurious of the hot springs in the region. It's perched within a dripping forest on the western shore of the Seno Ventisquero and can be reached only by boat. Buildings combine the rustic look of Chilote *palafitos* (houses on stilts) with Bavarian influences, and four outdoor baths, including a fern-shaded lagoon, sit by the water – perfect for soaking and then jumping into the cool water. An elaborate indoor spa offers cold-water pools, Jacuzzis and a large pool with jets. Spa treatments and massages are also on offer.

Hiking in Parque Nacional Pumalín

TEMPERATE RAINFOREST AND TESTY VOLCANOES

A remarkable forest conservation effort stretching over 2889 sq km from near Hornopirén to south of Chaitén, **Parque Nacional Pumalín** was created by the late US philanthropist Douglas Tompkins and donated to Chile in 2017. The park encompasses vast swaths of temperate rainforest, clear rivers and smoking volcanoes, and it's a model park for the region, with well-maintained roads and trails, extensive infrastructure, and minimal impact. The isolated, northern reaches of the park are ancestral territory to the Chono people, nomads who traveled by canoe, hunting sea lions and fish, and gathering shellfish and seaweed. The only access remains by boat or kayak on the fjords, but south of Caleta Gonzalo the park bisects the Carretera Austral, and there's no entry fee.

Driving through is delightful, but get out and hike a trail or two. About 14km south of Caleta Gonzalo, **Sendero Los Alerces** takes visitors through a majestic kilometer of temperate rainforest, over a hanging bridge and into a grove of 1000-year-old alerce trees. Nearby, **Sendero Cascadas**

 WHERE TO STAY ALONG THE CARRETERA AUSTRAL

Hotel Hornopirén
This intimate hotel has Patagonian character, water views and the assuring presence of Señora Olivia. **$$**

Lodge Caleta Gonzalo
These tiny shingled cabins overlook Reñihué Fjord, with hardwood details and loft beds for kids. **$$**

Cabañas Pudu
Cozy cabins with wood stoves and comfortable beds; they are a hit with motorcyclists. **$**

© GALYNA ANDRUSHKO/SHUTTERSTOCK ©

Parque Nacional Pumalín

BEST CAMP-GROUNDS ON THE CARRETERA

Sector Amarillo
Flat, open sites and lovely views make this former farmland a top choice in Parque Nacional Pumalín. $

Camping Ventisquero
In Parque Nacional Queulat, this campground offers 10 attractive private sites with covered barbecues, picnic tables and hot showers. $

Camping Pudu
Attractive beach campground with hot showers, laundry service and a sauna in Puerto Río Tranquilo. $

Senderos Patagonia
A hub for hikers near Parque Nacional Cerro Castillo, this campground and hostel can organize hiking tours and horse-packing trips. $

Escondidas offers a glorious one-hour jaunt from a campground alongside a series of waterfalls. The most rewarding hike is the five-hour round-trip along the blast path of **Volcán Chaitén** to view its puffing crater.

Some 20km south of Chaitén, in the **El Amarillo Sector** of the park, the best hike is **Sendero Ventisquero Amarillo**, a flat, open 10km trek to the eponymous hanging glacier. It begins at the Ventisquero campground toward the base of the Michinmahuida Glacier. Alternatively, the 2.5km **Sendero Ranita de Darwin** loops through a regenerating forest with three spectacular lookouts. For more info, stop in the visitor center across from the park entrance.

Hangin' with Ventisquero Colgante

A REMARKABLY ACCESSIBLE GLACIER

For those driving the Carretera Austral, **Parque Nacional Queulat's** glacier, **Ventisquero Colgante**, is low-hanging fruit (almost literally). For a view of this striking glacier, said to be 'hanging' because of its position over a steep precipice, visitors need only register online in advance (aspticket.cl), drive off the highway about 20km south of Puyuhuapi between

Puyuhuapi Lodge & Spa
Chile's leading hot-springs resort sits in a lush forest on the shore of Seno Ventisquero. $$$

Posada Queulat
Rustic, spacious cabins with wood stoves hidden away along a fjord, offering top-notch service and activities. $$$

Huella Patagónica
Three-story corrugated-tin hostel in Coyhaique offering modern dorms with lights and outlets for each bunk. $

LEONARDO OLIVER/SHUTTERSTOCK ©

Parque Nacional Cerro Castillo (p266)

9am and 2:30pm, pay the CH$9000 park entrance, and finally traverse a 200m boardwalk (suitable for wheelchairs) to a stunning – though faraway – viewpoint.

There are two other ways to experience the glacier. The first involves a 3.2km hike across a bridge over the thundering Río Ventisquero and into a wild realm of virgin forests thick with ferns and southern beech. The hike continues along the crest of a moraine and through the 1540-sq-km park, which straddles the Carretera for 70km midway between Chaitén and Coyhaique. Rain clouds are par for the course, but when they blow over, the magical view at the end of the trail features steep-sided cliffs, cascading falls, a milky turquoise lake, and the creeping, calving Ventisquero Colgante.

The third option for viewing the glacier is from a dinghy within **Laguna de los Témpanos**. A 600m trail along the raging river leads to the dock from which lake cruises (CH$12,000, summer only) depart. There's a four-person minimum and a 10-person maximum for the 35-minute boat tour, which also includes so-close-you-get-sprayed encounters with waterfalls. However you decide to see the glacier, bring your own provisions (there's no park restaurant).

Trading the Car for a Steed

GO GAUCHO

The most rugged and remote part of continental Chile, Northern Patagonia is a place where a few hardy individuals sought out a frontier existence, and itinerant cowboys called gauchos once thrived. The *estancias* (grazing ranches) of rural Patagonia offer a rare glimpse of this fading way of life, which is best understood on horseback.

 WHERE TO STAY ALONG THE CARRETERA AUSTRAL ────────

Patagonia House
Boutique property on Coyhaique's outskirts, with understated modern style, a hot tub and gourmet dinners. **$$**

B&B Cabañas Cerro Castillo
Rooms with mountain and garden views and a tasty breakfast; on the road into the national park. **$$**

Rimaya Hostel
This cozy hostel with earth-toned decor and comfy beds offers the best value in Puerto Río Tranquilo. **$**

Up and down the Carretera, you'll find rural tourism opportunities and horseback-riding excursions, and some operators even take guests on multiday rides across the countryside. Many operators speak Spanish only, but travelers can link with rural homestays and guide services through **Casa del Turismo Rural** in Coyhaique. It's best to book a week or more in advance because intermediaries have to make radio contact with the remote hosts.

For a gander at modern *estancia* life, visit **Fundo Panguilemu**. Just outside of Coyhaique and perched beside the scenic Reserva Nacional Río Simpson, this 1000-hectare ranch uses holistic and regenerative practices to manage its cattle and sheep. On guided horseback adventures, guests can observe round-ups, visit the sheep-shearing facility and explore the vast stretches of wilderness that the owners leave untouched. Spend the night in one of the gorgeous yurts overlooking Río Simpson and indulge in the exquisite meals, which are prepared from scratch with homegrown products.

Spying on Andean Condors

AN UP-CLOSE ENCOUNTER

If you drive the Carretera Austral, you are all but guaranteed to spot an Andean condor, the largest flying bird in South America. Although these giant black, brown and white raptors are classified as vulnerable to extinction, about 6700 of them glide around, and with that 3m wingspan, they're hard to miss. A real treat is to see dozens of them – up close – as they take off in the early morning and coast on gusts of wind. Such encounters take place regularly at **Punta del Monte**, an *estancia* east of Coyhaique. The Galilea Carrillo family has been grazing cattle and sheep on the 125-sq-km ranch since 1976, and the condors were already living on the property. For years Alejandro Galilea watched them soar over, raise chicks in the rocky areas of the pampa (grasslands) and scavenge deadstock. In 2003 he started bringing visitors to see the condors too.

Over time, the experience evolved to include an overnight stay on the *estancia* (or a 5:30am pickup in Coyhaique) followed by a visit to the condor dwellings, where guests watch the majestic birds cavort and start their day. Between 20 and 50 condors are usually in view, and the photo ops are unbeatable. The experience costs CH$100,000 per person and includes a delicious breakfast, a safari in which foxes, guanacos and other wildlife can often be spotted, and a stop at an area where indigenous tribes once crafted tools. Ask Alejandro to show you the arrowheads he's collected from dry lake beds on the property.

NORTHERN PATAGONIA: THEN & NOW

For thousands of years indigenous tribes, including the Chonos and Alacalufes, lived along the channels and islands of Northern Patagonia, while Tehuelches lived on the mainland steppes. Rugged geography deterred European settlement, but late 18th- and early 19th-century expeditions did visit the area, including one that brought Charles Darwin.

In the early 1900s, the Chilean government began decimating and displacing indigenous populations and granted 10,000 sq km around Coyhaique to the Valparaíso-based Sociedad Industrial Aysén for exploitation of livestock and lumber. Colonists trickled in to claim lands for farming, and Northern Patagonia became the last area to integrate into Chile.

Today Northern Patagonia remains isolated and sparsely populated, with towns created little more than 70 years ago.

 WHERE TO EAT ALONG THE CARRETERA AUSTRAL

El Quijote
This bar-restaurant's friendly and knowledgeable owner, Javier, prepares delicious local fish with chips or salad. **$**

El Muelle
Local beer, German dishes and fish from the fjord in a shingled house with a canal view. **$$**

CB Gastronomia Patagonia
Coyhaique's top restaurant elevates regional dishes. Morels are a prominent feature, and the lamb carpaccio slays. **$$$**

DUDAREV MIKHAIL/SHUTTERSTOCK ©

Capillas de Mármol

BEST CARRETERA STOPS FOR FLOWERS

Parque Nacional Queulat
Nalca isn't technically a flower, but this giant, edible plant looks prehistoric, tastes like rhubarb and dominates the park.

Sendero Laguna Cerro Castillo
Flowers on the Chilean fire trees resemble bright red balloons, and they pop in springtime along this spectacular trail.

Puerto Río Tranquilo
Yellow lupine explodes in spring in the town and along the Carretera.

Río El Canal
About 40km south of Puerto Río Tranquilo, beds of pink and purple lupine envelop this milky river in springtime.

He's deeply knowledgeable about condors, the history of Coyhaique and the natural history of the ranch, and shares this information either in Spanish or through his English-speaking son-in-law Nicolas, who joins when necessary.

Hiking Cerro Castillo

A MAGNIFICENT ASCENT

Cerro Castillo's basalt spires are the centerpiece of **Parque Nacional Cerro Castillo**, a 1435-sq-km park located 75km south of Coyhaique. Once the stomping grounds of the nomadic Tehuelche people who hunted guanacos and ñandus with spears and arrows, this land earned national park status in 2017. Its infrastructure has yet to catch up, and the access points traverse private property, resulting in steep entrance fees. The best day hike in the park – or anywhere along the Carretera Austral, really – is **Sendero Laguna Cerro Castillo**, a 15km trek from the town of Villa Cerro Castillo. If you have a vehicle or get to the private access point (look for an open gate and a circular green 'siga' sign), you'll cut out a couple of kilometers of walking on a dirt road. At the entrance, you'll pay CH$18,000 before embarking on a 13km climb (and descent). It's pricey, but worth it.

Follow the upside-down yellow triangles up a steep path through southern beech forest (which turns brilliant red in the fall), passing several small waterfalls. After crossing some verdant meadows and hopping on logs over mud and shallow ponds, you'll cut up through an explosion of Chilean fire trees and into rocky high-alpine terrain, which offers increasingly jaw-dropping views of the valley, the town, surrounding

 WHERE TO EAT ALONG THE CARRETERA AUSTRAL

La Cocina de Sole
You can't miss these conjoined roadside buses painted in swirling pastels, serving huge steak sandwiches and juices. $

Casa Bruja
Puerto Río Tranquilo's best restaurant is set in a cozy two-story home and specializes in lamb and fish. $$

Restaurante Quiyango
A meat-lover's dream, with heaping plates of slow-cooked lamb, beef and chicken served with potatoes and salad. $$

lakes and (on a clear day) Argentina. The temperature drops, condors coast overhead, and soon you'll approach a waterfall-fed sapphire lagoon at the base of snow-patched Cerro Castillo. Sit down to eat your packed lunch while admiring this 2700m triple-tier mountaintop, which is flanked by glaciers on its southern slopes.

For a slightly longer but less challenging hike, tackle a segment of **Sendero de Chile** with the 16km trail to Campamento Neozelandés. Those with more time can take on the recommended four-day **Cerro Castillas Circuit Trek**, which leaves from Carretera Austral Km75, at the north end of the park, and winds around the peak via a high route passing glaciers, rivers and lakes to end in Villa Cerro Castillo. It's serious, remote backcountry. Before heading out, share your plans with others and check in with the ranger to avoid seasonal hazards.

Exploring the Capillas de Mármol
MARBLE CAVES

Some of Northern Patagonia's most beloved attractions are the glistening marble caves in the impossibly blue **Lago General Carrera**. Over some 6000 years, the columns and arches of these caves that formed as calcium carbonate rocks got battered by waves in the wind-whipped, glacial lake. Tours most often begin from Puerto Río Tranquilo (and less often from Puerto Sanchéz) and travel by motorboat, kayak or raft.

Going by boat is the warmest and most economical option (CH$15,000 per person), but it's a shorter excursion, and you won't get to glide beneath the tight entrances and through tunnels within the formations. For a closer encounter, opt for the kayak or raft tour (CH$37,000) with **Experiencia Chilandes**, run by Gonzalo, a knowledgeable, English-speaking Chilean. He'll drive you 8km south of Puerto Río Tranquilo to the set-off point at Bahía Manso, where he provides a kayaking skirt to keep the lower body dry, along with a life jacket, windbreaker, paddle and watercraft. Gonzalo pushes you from the pebble-covered beach into the intense blue lake, which gets its color as light refracts through the minerals within melted ice. From there, it's about 30 minutes of paddling, with breathtaking mountain scenery in every direction, to arrive at the formations, which locals have dubbed the cave, the chapel and the cathedral.

On a sunny morning, the water turns iridescent turquoise and light reflects into the caves, to surreal effect. Note that high winds can sometimes make paddling difficult and even result in canceled excursions.

WORTH A STOP: LA CONFLUENCIA

Don't miss this dramatic viewpoint along the Carretera Austral where Chile's most powerful river, Río Baker, froths into a broad, behemoth cascade before merging with the milkier, glacial-fed Río Neff in a swirling contrast of mint and electric blue. It's 80km south of Puerto Río Tranquilo and 12km south of Puerto Bertrand, and technically, it's inside Parque Nacional Patagonia (there's no entrance fee).

Park roadside in the gravel lot and follow the signs along the 800m trail. Consider packing a lunch because you'll want to spend a while at this stunning natural feature.

GETTING AROUND

Traveling the Carretera Austral, however you decide to do it, involves trade-offs. Renting a vehicle is pricey and the long stretches in poor conditions can be stressful, but for some, the independence will make it worthwhile. Taking buses are economical, but most aren't frequent, which can eat up lots of time. Some intrepid travelers do the trip by bicycle.

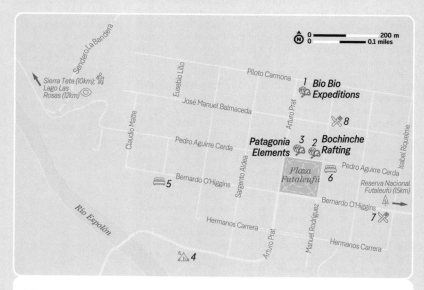

FUTALEUFÚ

Santiago

Futaleufú

Locals like to say that Futaleufú is *'un paisaje pintado por Dios'* – a landscape painted by God – and even unbelievers have a hard time disagreeing. This valley is defined by a brilliant turquoise river winding and crashing through a granite canyon, all surrounded by temperate rainforest and soaring mountain peaks. The town of Futaleufú, a lively 20-block grid of pastel houses, has become a world-famous base for river rafting and kayaking, along with expanded offerings such as fly fishing, hiking and horseback riding.

Just 10km from Argentina, Futaleufú was settled in the early 20th century by ranchers from both sides of a then-disputed border. Although livestock remains ubiquitous, the roads have vastly improved, expats have moved in and the town has boomed with river tourism. Passions for Río Futaleufú run high, and there's a strong, successful movement protecting the river from multinational energy companies that have attempted to dam it.

TOP TIP

Visit during rafting season: December to March. Experienced rafters may hit the water in October and November when the river is at its highest, but if it's too high, excursions can be canceled. When the river levels fall in late summer, boulders are exposed and whitewater increases, making the rapids more technical.

HIGHLIGHTS
1 Bio Bio Expeditions
2 Bochinche Rafting
3 Patagonia Elements

SLEEPING
4 Aldea Puerto Espolón
5 Hotel El Barranco
6 La Antigua Casona

EATING
7 La Picá de los Colonos
8 Martín Pescador

GUAXINIM/SHUTTERSTOCK ©

Kayaking the Río Futaleufú

Braving Río Futaleufú

WORLD-CLASS WHITEWATER

Río Futaleufú's adorable name means 'Big Water' in the Mapuche language, and that's actually an understatement. When professional rafters and kayakers get into this water, they ritualistically splash it on their faces and wish each other '*buenas líneas*' (good lines). On a river this wild and pushy, you really need to stay on course.

Often referred to as 'Futa' or 'Fu,' the alluring, glacier-fed river has some highly technical and demanding rapids, with some sections only appropriate for experienced rafters. Even the stretches suitable for beginners feature Class III, IV and IV+ rapids, and getting tossed by massive waves and tumbling into ice-cold, fast-moving water are distinct possibilities. Reputable operators mitigate the risks by dressing you in a wetsuit, life jacket and helmet, and placing an experienced rafting guide at the helm to teach you commands and proper paddling techniques. For extra safety, there may even be kayakers and catarafts along for the ride.

The standard beginner trip is a half-day section known as **Bridge to Bridge**, a 7km course through nearly a dozen

BEST TOUR OPERATORS

Bochinche Rafting
A small outfitter offering rafting and kayaking trips along with kayak and bike rentals and other guided activities.

Patagonia Elements
Long-standing adventure company offering rafting, kayaking, fly fishing, horseback riding, canyoning and mountain-bike rentals.

Expediciones Chile
Experienced operator with an eco-camp on Río Azul and a kayak school on the Río Espolón. Also offers mountain biking and horseback riding.

Outdoor Patagonia
Experienced local company with a riverside camp and a lively hostel, bar and restaurant in town.

 WHERE TO STAY IN FUTALEUFÚ

Aldea Puerto Espolón
Campsites and geodesic domes on a sandy riverbank flanked by mountains; has hot showers and a kitchen. **$**

La Antigua Casona
Every detail of this refurbished settler's barn expresses loving attention; rooms feature painted birds and quilted beds. **$$**

Hotel El Barranco
Elegant lodge on the edge of town with a restaurant, swimming pool and sauna. **$$$**

I LIVE HERE: WHERE TO GO ON HORSEBACK

Ervin Redlich was born on a farm in Futaleufú and owns a horseback-riding business on Lago Espolón. He recommends visiting these natural features.

Saltos del Espolón
These spectacular waterfalls are reached by boating across Lago Espolón or riding a horse along the shore and then continuing deep into the Valle de Espolón.

Lago las Rosas
This sapphire lake is unique for the island it contains, and it can be reached on a day trip or overnight excursion (recommended) on foot or horse.

Sierra Teta
This iconic mountain peak is one of the most recognized attractions in the region. It can be summited on a 13.2km out-and-back hike, and horse trails are in the process of being opened.

Río Futaleufú (p269)

challenging rapids, each with its own name and obstacles. Entrada is long and strong, Pillow involves a big rock and a massive hole to avoid being sucked into, and Mundaca smacks you in the face with its colossal waves. Rafters with more experience can continue on to run three even bigger rapids including the Terminator, one of the world's most intense to be run commercially. Before tackling these, guides stop the raft to assess the situation and decide on the safest line. During such breaks in the eddies, you may notice that the winding river, dramatic canyon and surrounding snowcapped mountains are straight out of a fairy tale. If it all sounds a little too advanced, the locally-owned company **Origines Patagonia** offers beginner 'riverbug' experiences for families.

Depending on the outfitter you choose and the services included, rafting the Futaleufú starts at CH$70,000 per person for a half day on Bridge to Bridge. A full-day trip for experienced rafters with some additional Class V sections starts at CH$90,000.

Travelers interested in whitewater kayaking will find an array of courses and runs on the Futa but also the less challenging tributaries Río Espolón and Río Azul. River kayaking is difficult for beginners, who often struggle over multiple days to master the dreaded 'roll.' Courses begin at CH$70,000 per day.

 WHERE TO EAT IN FUTALEUFÚ

Martín Pescador
Locavore eatery that takes exciting risks with local products like forest mushroom, flowers, nalca and hare. **$$$**

Restaurant Antigua Casona
Elegant Italian spot that does wonderful homemade pasta, gnocchi and lasagna with vegetarian options. **$$**

La Picá de los Colonos
There's no menu in Nelsa's home kitchen. Expect homemade pork chops and *cazuela* (stew). **$**

For travelers with a bit more wiggle room in their budget, several riverfront operations south of town provide a superior experience. The gold standard is **Bio Bio Expeditions**, a pioneering company that offers nine days of adventures from a base camp with luxury safari tents, hot tubs, a full bar, a sauna, a masseuse, delicious home-cooked meals and a rope swing over the river. Enthusiastic and knowledgeable staff members come from all over the world and are delightful to hang out with.

Hiking in Futa

KILLER RIVER VIEWS

After some close, soggy encounters with Río Futaleufú, it can be nearly as fun to dry off and gaze at the river from above. Several good hikes surround the town, the best of which involve steep climbs and high rewards.

In **Reserva Nacional Futaleufú**, a protected region south of town along the river, two recommended hikes feature panoramic views of the river. The **Condor Lookout Trail** is the more difficult option, with steep switchbacks that bring visitors up a mountain to two viewing platforms. Standing on the one at the very top, you'll be able to view the entire valley, and Andean condors may swoop right overhead. The whole thing takes around 2½ hours. The easier **Windy Rock Overlook** is only a 1½-hour commitment along a calm stretch of river, with its own lovely (if less dramatic) overlook. Hiking in the reserve is free, but you'll need to sign in at the entrance.

For a more pastoral hike, try **Piedra de Aguila** (Eagle Rock) on the north side of town. Much of the trail cuts across a private ranch (for which you'll pay CH$2000 to landowner Don Perfecto Jesus), as the distinctive rock formation comes into closer view. From the top, you can see a couple of ridiculously blue lakes and all of the northwest valley. Wear sun protection because the switchbacks are exposed for much of the way. The whole trip takes under two hours.

The path to **Lago Pinilla** (or Lago Toro, or Lago Obsession, depending on who you ask) has been generating a lot of buzz since locals started hiking it in 2019. The arduous seven-hour round-trip starts near Peuma Lodge and traverses dense groves of poplar and lengua, and then rewards with astounding views and a sparkling blue lake. Don't attempt this one in the rain because the rocky terrain becomes unsafe.

TIME TRAVELING IN PALENA

Some 90km south of Futaleufú, the quiet mountain town of **Palena** connects travelers with the pioneer lifestyle and real hospitality. The town rodeo is held on the last weekend in January, and the weeklong Semana Palena, in late February. Both feature cowboy festivities and live music.

On the plaza, the tourism office arranges horse packing, rafting and fishing trips with local guides. Allow some lead time before your trip because some rural outfitters must be reached by radio. The tourism office also connects adventurers to the wonderful Casanova family farm Rincón de la Nieve, accessed via hiking or horseback riding. Chill there or do a five-day out-and-back ride to remote Lago Palena.

GETTING AROUND

Having a rental vehicle is convenient for getting around Futaleufú; otherwise, you'll be on foot or relying on rides from tour operators. The 1½-hour drive off the Carretera Austral to the town is unpaved but relatively smooth. Buses depart from Futa somewhat regularly – but not necessarily every day – for Puerto Montt, Chaitén, Puyuhuapi, Coyhaique and Palena. International buses go to the Argentine border a couple of times a week, and public transport goes from the border to Trevelín and Esquel in Argentina. Schedules can change frequently.

PARQUE NACIONAL LAGUNA SAN RAFAEL

Santiago ✪

Parque Nacional
Laguna San Rafael ●

Established in 1959 this 17,420-sq-km park is one of Chile's largest, and its mighty but fast-melting glaciers are a major regional attraction. In demand is the frozen tongue of the park's namesake glacier, San Rafael, which descends from the Patagonian Northern Ice Field and sends house-sized chunks of broken-off glacier into the chilly lagoon. The park also boasts temperate rainforest, untamed fjords, peaty wetlands and some of Patagonia's highest mountains, all protected as a Unesco Biosphere Reserve since 1979.

Getting here used to be expensive and time consuming, but in the 2010s, a road built through Valle Exploradores allowed overland drives from Puerto Río Tranquilo, which connect with shorter boat rides into the park, and also the opportunity to don crampons and hike the Exploradores Glacier. Still, more visitors arrive by cruises and charter flights to take in the extraordinary scenery and hear the cracks and booms of calving ice.

TOP TIP

If possible, stay a few days in Puerto Río Tranquilo to give yourself a higher chance of being able to visit the park in decent weather. Conditions change quickly, so bring a good jacket, sunblock and a change of dry clothes.

Exploradores Glacier (p274)

NIXY JUNGLE/SHUTTERSTOCK ©

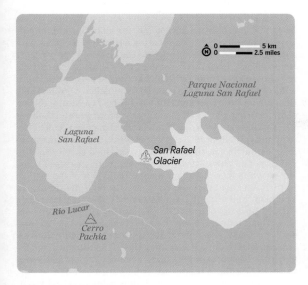

Parque Nacional
Laguna San Rafael

Laguna
San Rafael

San Rafael
Glacier

Río Lucar

Cerro
Pachía

0 — 5 km
0 — 2.5 miles

Visiting Glaciers

PUT YOURSELF ON ICE

You can visit the cerulean glaciers of Parque Nacional Laguna San Rafael by hiking, kayaking, driving, flying and boating (or a combination), and multiday adventures are ideal for enjoying this awesome and remote park. If time is short and you're looking for one top-notch glacier experience, sign up for the day trip from Puerto Río Tranquilo to the park's namesake attraction: the **San Rafael Glacier**.

The most reliable and long-standing company offering this tour, **Destino Patagonia**, picks up guests in a comfortable van for a morning drive through Valle Exploradores, where you can peer out the windows at soaring Monte San Valentín (Chilean Patagonia's highest mountain at 4058m), gushing waterfalls, distant glaciers and serene lakes. Upon arrival at Bahía Exploradores, you'll board the covered, 14-passenger boat and meet your guides, who serve sweet tea, coffee and a hearty breakfast sandwich. From there, it's a two-hour ride through the rivers and fjords that curve around the Northern Patagonian Ice Field. When the weather cooperates, the trip is relaxing, and when the water is choppy, well, that's an adventure.

PATAGONIA'S MELTING GLACIERS

In 2023 satellite images showed that Patagonian glaciers are retreating faster than anywhere else on Earth. The Northern Patagonian Ice Field – which together with the Southern Patagonian Ice Field forms one of the world's biggest ice masses – has 39 glaciers, and the San Rafael Glacier is one of the fastest-moving and most actively calving. That's great if you want to watch massive chunks of ice break off and plummet into the water, but it's depressing when you learn that 150 years ago, this glacier stretched over two-thirds of the lagoon. Although some seasonal melt is normal, this glacier flows at a speed of about 7.6km per year and is receding dramatically because of human-caused climate change.

 BEST TOUR COMPANIES FOR VISITING PARQUE NACIONAL LAGUNA SAN RAFAEL

Destino Patagonia
Full- and multiday tours to San Rafael Glacier in a covered boat, with meals and whiskey.

El Puesto Expediciones
Francisco Croxatta runs reputable ice treks on the Exploradores Glacier, including transfers and other services.

Nomade Experience
A reputable company that offers trips to Laguna San Rafael with experienced, bilingual guides.

These majestic marine mammals have elongated bodies, big heads and gray fur with light and dark spots, lending a leopard-like quality, hence the name. Weighing up to 600kg, these apex predators aren't picky. They eat fish, krill, seabirds and even other marine mammals, and spend much of their time atop icebergs resting, mating and giving birth. A monitoring program in Laguna San Rafael has identified 12 individuals with distinctive spot patterns living in the area, and when visiting the glacier by boat, you, too, have a chance at glimpsing one. Don't feed or touch them, and avoid making loud noises or throwing anything. Your boat captain should keep a distance of at least 50m from the seals.

Upon arrival at Laguna San Rafael, you'll be greeted by icebergs that look like translucent, floating mountains. Hundreds have calved off the glacier, creating a traveling ice mass with a gargantuan tongue spilling into the lagoon. If the weather is good, you'll disembark at a dock for a short hike to the ruins of old Hotel Ofqui, with a chance of seeing the smallest wildcat in the Americas, a spotted feline called a guiña. You'll then reboard the boat and climb to the bow to admire the ancient, melting glacier from a closer vantage point. It sounds like rolling thunder as ice chunks the size of semitrucks detach and drop 60m into the water. Next, typical Patagonian lunches, such as *pastel de choclo* (a smashed corn cake with red meat and chicken), are distributed with glasses of whiskey on 1000-year-old ice scooped directly out of the lagoon. In the afternoon, the boat ride back through the fjords can be choppy and difficult on the stomachs of some passengers.

If a 10-hour day sounds like a lot, opt for the glacier-lite option. About halfway down the gravel road to Bahía Exploradores, at Km52, is a sign for **Refugio de los Exploradores**. You can drive yourself here, pay the CH$8000 entrance fee and hike the short trail through the forest and to the **Exploradores Glacier Viewpoint**, from which you can see the front of the glacier. True glacier enthusiasts can take this outing a step further by continuing along the trail for another two hours with a guide through the ice moraine. Eventually, you reach a section of the glacier with white and blue ice, and your guide provides crampons to continue the trek atop the glacier and through ice tunnels. Altogether this ends up being a 10-hour day, and guests must be in good physical condition.

Those wanting an even more challenging adventure can ask **Destinos Patagonia** about two-day park trips that include trekking or kayaking and camping, three-day trips that cross the Ofqui Isthmus (where sei whales are often spotted) and six-day kayaking trips.

GETTING AROUND

A 78km road built through Valle Exploradores has created options to go part way overland. You can drive yourself or take a tour company's transport vehicle from Puerto Río Tranquilo to Bahía Exploradores, which costs a bit extra but spares you hours of driving on a rough unpaved road (4x4 recommended).

From there, it's another two hours by boat to reach the glacier. Additionally, multiday cruises sail to the park from Puerto Chacabuco and Puerto Montt. Visitors who arrive at Bahía Exploradores by cruise shift to a smaller craft to approach the glacier.

Beyond Parque Nacional Laguna San Rafael

Not your average gateway town, secluded Caleta Tortel is an old fishing and lumber village like no other.

A back way into Parque Nacional Laguna San Rafael goes through a curious old settlement called Caleta Tortel. It's defined by colorful, stilted houses cobbled around a steep escarpment and the creaky, expanding boardwalk network that connects them. This place is so distinctive that it was named a national monument. Roads are blissfully absent, and the location between two ice fields along a sea-foam–green bay and at the mouth of Río Baker is sublime.

For thousands of years, it was the territory of the nomadic, canoe-traveling Alacalufe people (Kawésqar), and colonists didn't formally settle it until 1955. The road here was built in 2003, and today locals live off cypress-wood extraction and a growing tourism industry.

Parque Nacional
Laguna San Rafael

Isla de
Los Muertos

Caleta Tortel

Ventisquero
Montt

TOP TIP

Dependence on a turbine means that the town has water shortages, and electricity is rationed during dry periods. Use water sparingly.

Caleta Tortel (p276)

ADWO/ALAMY STOCK PHOTO ©

I LIVE HERE: TORTEL'S HISTORY & CULTURE

Silvia Vega's family was one of the first to settle in Caleta Tortel. She works as a navigator for Waeskar Expeditions and a sheep-wool artisan. She recommends these adventures.

Navigating on Río Baker
The ancient settlers traveled this river on *guaitecas* cypress rafts. They also used the rafts to transport wood between faraway islands and Tortel.

Beyond the glacier
My mother's family settled near the Steffen Glacier, where several logging families still live today and transport harvested wood by raft, a risky endeavor.

Ascend Cordón las Heras
This mountain above Isla de Los Muertos has always been a point of reference for locals, and tour operators have started offering excursions to its summit.

Caleta Tortel

Touring Tortel
AN UNFORGETTABLE VILLAGE HIKE

One of the best ways to experience **Caleta Tortel** is simply to wander over its cypress footbridges. Everywhere you turn, there's something unexpected and beautiful, be it a *mirador* (viewpoint) over a hidden cove, a shop filled with artisanal crafts or a friendly village dog. If you have a solid pair of hiking shoes and a sense of adventure, **Sendero Cerro Vigía** – a 2.5km loop through the town, up over a mountain and back – is not to be missed.

The start of the trail is behind the parking lot roundabout. Head 300m north from the tourist information office and scale the narrow wooden staircase, and you'll start seeing signs for the trail. Much of it looks like a balance beam on stilts, which helps keep your feet dry (the area is swampy). Eventually, you'll reach a series of gorgeous viewpoints in all directions, with Río Baker, Cascada Pisagua, Parque Nacional Laguna San Rafael and Caleta Tortel featuring prominently.

As you continue west, the footbridges disappear, and the trail becomes less clear. For this reason, it's helpful to have a guide from the excellent tour company **Waeskar Expeditions**,

WHERE TO EAT IN TORTEL

Kuspe Patagonia
Cheerful, good-value restaurant on the edge of the village, where chef Laura expertly prepares meals. **$**

Restaurante Llao-Llao Tortel
Welcoming waterfront spot with homemade pasta, sushi, craft beer and a festive international vibe. **$$**

El Patagón Tortelino
No-nonsense eatery owned by Señoras Elvira and Fredelinda, who specialize in empanadas, fresh fish and meat dishes. **$$**

who can also share information about the region's history, carnivorous and edible plants, and hardwood trees. The guide will show you down the hill's western slope to reach the back entrance to the town. Afterward, it is 2km along the Tortel walkways back to the main docks. Along the way, you'll notice plenty of beached boats under repair, wooden statues made by village artisans and expansive, covered plazas adorned in murals. A rain jacket and a good camera are essential, and the whole experience takes around three hours.

Boat Trips Around Tortel

CRUISING IN WONDERLAND

The system of canals and fjords surrounding Caleta Tortel begs to be explored, and tour operators offer a number of excursions on the water. An hour-long boat trip takes visitors to **Isla de Los Muertos**, a lovely island in the Río Baker Delta, with a creepy history (CH$10,000 per person). At the beginning of the 20th century, a group of loggers came from Chiloé to harvest cypress from the island, and in the winter of 1906 dozens of them mysteriously died. Best guesses and a history of the place are relayed (in Spanish and English) on signs around the island, which visitors can explore on a footbridge around the perimeter that passes a cemetery.

If the weather cooperates, several more ambitious boating adventures become possible. Trips to **Ventisquero Montt** in Northern Patagonia Ice Field (CH$120,000 per person) zip passengers through archipelagos and fjords, eventually reaching an iceberg-filled canal. Some operators offer a walk through the moraine near the glacier, and all provide a homemade lunch, along with local spirits chilled with glacial ice. The tour operator **Paz Austral** offers additional two- and three-day options with add-ons including extra hikes, sunset dinners, wildlife excursions to see the endangered huemul (south Andean deer) and a trip to **Ventisquero Steffen** to the north, in Parque Nacional Laguna San Rafael.

Reputable companies with English-speaking guides offering boat trips include Paz Austral, Waeskar Expediciones and **BordeRío**, which also has kayaking options in the Río Baker Delta and around Isla de Los Muertos and Cascada Pisagua.

BEST PLACES TO STAY IN TORTEL

Hostal Natureza
A friendly two-story hotel owned by a hip Patagonian-Brazilian couple with serious boho style and a full bar. $

Residencial Estilo
Alejandra's well-kept wooden house has bright colors and tidy doubles with down duvets. $$

Entre Hielos
A cozy cypress home up a steep staircase, with modern style. Excellent breakfast and chef-prepared dinners. $$$

Camping Tortel
Platform camping with hot showers; conveniently located in the center of the village. $

GETTING AROUND

The road stops at the edge of Caleta Tortel, where those who have brought a vehicle must leave it behind. Boardwalks and staircases lead to the center and beyond to Playa Ancha, a wide beach. During high season, water taxis help people get around, but it's best to take minimal luggage (keeping in mind the numerous staircases).

All buses depart from a stop next to the tourism kiosk in the upper entrance to the village. Bus routes are run by private individuals who have to apply for the government concession, thus providers and schedules can vary from year to year.

PARQUE NACIONAL PATAGONIA

Santiago ✪

● Parque Nacional Patagonia

Gazing over the vast Parque Nacional Patagonia and its guanaco-dotted steppe, tremendous mountains, beech forests and bird-filled lagoons, it's hard to believe that much of this land was once divided by fences and intensely grazed by sheep and cattle. Today, the recovering 3045-sq-km park is one of the region's top attractions, with wildlife so abundant that some call it the 'Serengeti of the Southern Cone.'

The park is actually pretty new, created in 2018 by the Chilean government as part of an unprecedented public-private agreement with the nonprofit Tompkins Conservation, which donated 690 sq km that became Sector Valle Chacabuco. As part of the deal, Chile reclassified two nearby national reserves – now Sector Lago Jeinimeni and Sector Tamango – to enshrine this massive wildlife corridor with the highest level of protection.

Top draws include hikes long and short, safaris, cave paintings, flamingo-watching and a gorgeous visitor center.

TOP TIP

Accessibility is not this park's strong suit. The three remote entrances can't be reached via public transport, so you need wheels of some kind. If you don't have a rental car, it's recommended to arrange private transport or a guided tour well in advance.

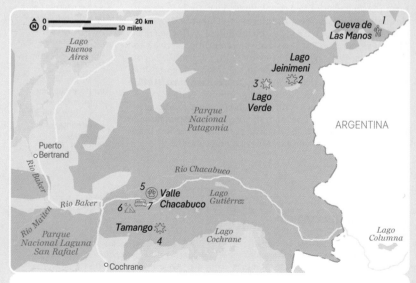

HIGHLIGHTS
1 Cueva de Las Manos
2 Lago Jeinimeni

3 Lago Verde
4 Tamango
5 Valle Chacabuco

SLEEPING
6 Camping Los West Winds
7 Lodge at Valle Chacabuco

DANITA DELIMONT/SHUTTERSTOCK ©

Guanacos, Parque Nacional Patagonia

PARQUE NACIONAL PATAGONIA'S BIG FOUR

Guanacos
Thousands of these llama cousins roam the grasslands and the highlands, and they are particularly abundant along X-83.

Huemules
The park's population of this endangered Andean deer represents 10% of the worldwide population, and studies track their movements.

Pumas
The trails around Sector Valle Chacabuco's visitor center are prime puma-spotting territory, particularly just before sunset.

Ñandus
This ostrich relative was nearly eradicated in southern Chile, but it has been successfully reintroduced and is often seen along X-83 near the border.

Exploring Parque Nacional Patagonia

DRIVES, HIKES AND A BOAT RIDE

Most travelers don't have the time to visit the whole park, so it helps to know the highlights and best hikes within each one. **Sector Valle Chacabuco** is all about wildlife, and specifically guanacos (there are thousands). The best drive is the 72km stretch from Río Baker to the Argentine border on X-83, which climbs through the valley and winds through steppe past lakes, guanacos and large rabbits. If you're lucky, you may also spot flamingos, foxes, huemules and ñandus. Drive slowly on the narrow, unpaved road.

The longer of this sector's two spectacular trails is **Lagunas Atlas Trail**. It ascends from Los West Winds camping area toward a southern ridge and heads east across open terrain and around small gemstone lakes before winding down

WHERE TO STAY IN PARQUE NACIONAL PATAGONIA

Camping Los West Winds
Valle Chacabuco's main campground with 60 sites, covered cook shelters and a bathhouse with solar showers. $

Camping at Sector Tamango
About 200m after the park entrance is a family campground with lake access, kayak rentals and bathrooms. $

Lodge at Valle Chacabuco
Stone lodges and an upscale restaurant modeled on English architecture in Argentina. Reservations required. $$$

TOMPKINS' GIFT

US entrepreneur-philanthropists Kristine and (the late) Douglas Tompkins started buying property in Chile in the 1990s, aiming to protect Patagonia's wilderness. Eventually, they accumulated 4045 sq km, and in 2018 their nonprofit Tompkins Conservation gifted the land to Chile. As part of the deal, the government incorporated another 10,115 sq km of public lands and reclassified 21,850 sq km of reserves to create five new national parks and expand three more. The protected lands are larger than Switzerland, placing Chile at the vanguard of conservation efforts worldwide. In a country with little tradition of public philanthropy, the Tompkins' sweeping purchases initially stirred up suspicion, but as time goes by, the economic value of world-class parks has become apparent.

toward the administration buildings. It has postcard-pretty views of the Chacabuco Valley, San Lorenzo, the Northern Patagonian Ice Field and the Jeinimeni Mountains. Bring plenty of water for this 23km day hike.

If you've got less time or stamina, consider the **Aviles Valley Trail**. The 16km loop through open steppe begins at the Casa Piedra camping area. You'll hike up one side of a river canyon, cross a hanging bridge, and hike down the other side, with the possibility of spotting Andean condors. Or, instead of looping around, you can continue on a stunning three- to four-day backpacking journey (about 50km) to Sector Lago Jeinimeni. This trail requires navigational skills because there are minimal markings. Arrange exit transport in advance as you'll be far from civilization with no public transport or signal.

Sector Lago Jeinimeni straddles the border with Argentina off X-753 and is worth a visit for its neon blue-green lakes and flamingo habitat. Its premier hike is an out-and-back route that takes in both the Gatorade-blue **Lago Jeinimeni** and the mint green **Lago Verde**, with options to climb to a viewpoint or camp by Lago Verde. The adjacent **Sector Cueva de las Manos**, also located along X-753, offers a spectacular 7.4km loop through an arid mountainscape. Highlights include quirky rock formations, prehistoric hand paintings and images of guanacos dating back around 10,000 years, and a 'lunar valley' with an exposed, otherworldly ridge. This remote hike is only accessible by 4x4, and the trail is sometimes hard to follow. Guide recommended.

The most accessible part of the park, **Sector Tamango**, offers a few trails in the mountains and along the impossibly blue Río Cochrane. There isn't much wildlife, and the trails aren't very dramatic, but you can explore this sector from the comfort of a boat. Just before entering the park, veer right on the dirt road and follow it down to Elvis Tomasin's residence. You can park in the grass near the riverbank and jetty, and negotiate with Elvis for a boat trip upriver (ideal for appreciating water clarity). Elvis will let you off near the source of the river for a stroll and can drop you off in the park to walk back along the 3km riverside trail.

The entrance fee is CH$9000, which covers three days in the park, although there's no fee for Sector Cueva de las Manos or for boating on the Río Cochrane. National park reservations must be made in advance online (asptticket.cl).

GETTING AROUND

A rental car is best. Tours operating out of Cochrane offer day trips and transfers in a private van to Sectors Valle Chacabuco (18km north of Cochrane) and Tamango (4km east of Cochrane). Sector Lago Jeinimeni is 54km south of Chile Chico and can be accessed via a 4x4 vehicle or on tours from Chile Chico.

Beyond Parque Nacional Patagonia

The gateway towns to Parque Nacional Patagonia – Cochrane and Chile Chico – are on the up.

Chile Chico

● Parque Nacional Patagonia

Cochrane

South of Parque Nacional Patagonia, in the old ranching outpost of Cochrane, tourism has been a catalyst for infrastructure improvements and employment opportunities. Lodgings are mostly family guesthouses and cabins, and restaurants are opening. Travelers based here can kayak, snorkel, visit Ventisquero Calluqueo and climb Monte San Lorenzo.

Nearly 200km to the northeast, sandwiched between the park and the southern shore of Lago General Carrera, the wind-whipped cherry-orchard town of Chile Chico is also booming. Locals who once earned a living raising livestock and mining are now opening accommodations, restaurants and tour businesses, and glistening hardwood facades and fresh coats of paint can be seen all over town. The latest attractions include e-biking and stand-up paddleboarding.

Chile Chico (p283)

JAN JERMAN/SHUTTERSTOCK ©

Río Cochrane

BEST PLACES TO STAY IN COCHRANE

Hotel Ultimo Paraíso
Cypress-walled gem with comfy beds and wood stoves in every room. $$

Kalfu Patagonia
Immaculate split-level apartments defined by knotty wood and winding staircases. Attached outdoor store and cafe with fabulous coffee. $$

Cabañas Sol y Luna
Well-equipped cabins slightly out of town, but worth the walk for the sauna, hot tubs and small on-site brewery. $$

Residencial y Cabañas Sur Austral
One of Cochrane's original lodgings, this dainty family guesthouse features cozy 2nd-floor bedrooms and fully equipped cabins. $$

Kickin' it in Cochrane

AQUATIC AND MOUNTAIN ADVENTURES

In addition to being the best base for accessing Parque Nacional Patagonia from the west, **Cochrane** is a pleasant place to wander with a lovely central plaza. It's also conveniently located near the azure Río Cochrane, one of the clearest rivers in the world, and it's ideal for water adventures with the company **Descubriendo**, which is co-owned by the experienced English-speaking guide Christian Restrepo. Whether you're gliding around in a kayak or plunging into the refreshingly cold river and drifting downstream, Río Cochrane is a unique and worthwhile Patagonia experience.

The meeting point is the riverside Descubriendo office, where gear gets sorted and trips begin. Kayaking trips can vary from 1½ to eight hours, with prices from CH$35,000 to CH$90,000. The shorter trips float through the national park, while the longest one brings you to Lago Cochrane and includes a tasty lunch. Descubriendo's free-diving and snorkeling tours range from three to five hours (CH$50,000 to CH$100,000). The free-diving lesson takes place right off the office dock in front of the office and then brings guests

 WHERE TO EAT IN COCHRANE

La Isla
Fish and lamb served in a lovely setting on an island outside of Cochrane; also has rental cottages. $$

La Estrella Bakery
Great option for sweet and savory baked goods including empanadas, cakes and doughnuts. $

Cervecería Tehuelche
Grab a late-night pizza and quaff some decent local beer at this small brewpub. $

down river and into Sector Tamango. All equipment is provided, including thick wetsuits.

You'll likely encounter an abundance of trout while swimming in the river, but if you're more interested in catching and eating them, reach out to Carlos from **Ultimo Paraíso**. If it's trekking at **Ventisquero Calluqueo** or mountain climbing on **Monte San Lorenzo** you're interested in, **Lord Patagonia** is your outfitter.

Chillin' in Chile Chico

KAYAKING, BIKING AND BEACHING

There's something in the air in **Chile Chico**, or maybe it's the air itself? The town's weather is different from the rest of the region: warmer, breezier and significantly less rainy. It makes for a pleasant stroll around town, along the waterfront and up to **Plaza del Viento**, a lookout structure reminiscent of the Great Wall of China at the top of a couple hundred stairs, with views of the lake, nearby islands and all of Chile Chico. Stop by the **Casa de la Cultural**, which features works by regional artists and local artifacts, including minerals and fossils. Outside is a restored boat called *El Andes*, which was brought from Europe to transport passengers and freight around the lake.

Adventure-seekers can also explore the lake with rented kayaks or on stand-up paddleboards, while land activities near town include boulder climbing, hiking, and mountain- and e-biking. **Patagonia Xpress** is a reputable outfitter that rents mountain bikes and other equipment, guides hikes and arranges transport. In addition, the municipality rents e-bikes out of the bus station, which will eventually be part of an e-bike-sharing program that helps travelers get to and from nearby Argentina. For the ambitious, a 16km ride west to the calm and warm waters of Bahía Jara offers swimming and camping, and it's a popular spot with the locals.

Nightlife is becoming a thing in Chile Chico. The town microbrewery **Puesto Pioneeros** is open late most nights, and a couple of other bars have opened around town.

WHERE TO EAT IN CHILE CHICO

Lenga Café & Bistrot
Adorable cafe serving up salads and sandwiches alongside smoothies, coffee and tea. All fresh and mostly local ingredients. $$

Restaurante Jeinimeni
Thin-crust pizzas come sizzling out of the stone oven, and seafood, sandwiches and Chilean classics are also on the menu. $$

La Cuchara e' Palo
Chile Chico's health food store and gastronomy hub invents new items regularly, making creative and delicious use of vegan and vegetarian ingredients. $$

GETTING AROUND

Buses travel daily between Coyhaique and Cochrane, and less frequent but regular service goes from Cochrane to Caleta Tortel, Villa O'Higgins and Chile Chico.

Driving the abrupt curves of Ruta CH-265 from the intersection with the Carretera Austral east to Chile Chico is one of the region's highlights. Scary and stunning, it hits blind corners and steep inclines on loose gravel high above the lake: proceed with caution. Bus routes along this road are run by private individuals who apply for the government concession, thus providers and schedules can vary from year to year.

Bus-ferry combos that take the shortcut through Lago General Carrera to Coyhaique are sometimes available. Just 9km west of Chile Chico is Argentina's Los Antiguos border. There are no buses. An e-bike sharing program to assist travelers in getting to and from the border is being developed.

Above: Colourful landscape of Tierra del Fuego; right: Guanacos

SOUTHERN PATAGONIA & TIERRA DEL FUEGO

END-OF-THE-WORLD ADVENTURES

Chile's far south combines jaw-dropping scenery and exceptional national parks with a host of outdoor activities.

Towering peaks and shimmering lakes, windswept peninsulas and seemingly endless steppe, emerald forests and vast ice fields: southern Patagonia and Tierra del Fuego boast some of the most dramatic landscapes on Earth. Sculpted by glaciers long before humans arrived on the continent, the area is sparsely populated, dotted with sheep ranches and isolated settlements.

The southern Patagonian regions of Magallanes and Última Esperanza are a haven for travelers seeking outdoor adventures, offering exceptional trekking and horse riding in particular. You'll also find intriguing cities, noisy penguin colonies and fascinating historical sites, plus breaching whales, circling condors and herds of skittish guanacos. The star attraction is the majestic Parque Nacional Torres del Paine, which attracts hundreds of thousands of visitors from across the globe every year.

South of the Strait of Magellan is Tierra del Fuego (Land of Fire), a maze of largely uninhabited islands, rocky outcrops and icy waterways that gradually crumbles away into the choppy Southern Ocean. Home to tiny Puerto Williams, the world's southernmost city, the famed Beagle Channel and lonely Cabo de Hornos (Cape Horn) – south of which lies only Antarctica – this ruggedly beautiful region retains an unparalleled frontier feel.

While you are visiting southern Chile, it is well worth popping across the border into the Argentine section of Patagonia and Tierra del Fuego, the highlights of which are covered in this chapter.

THE MAIN AREAS

PUNTA ARENAS
Engaging port city rich in history.
p290

PUERTO NATALES
Traveler hub on Last Hope Sound.
p300

PARQUE NACIONAL TORRES DEL PAINE
Sublime scenery and awesome trails.
p308

PUERTO WILLIAMS
Far-flung settlement on the Beagle Channel.
p318

Find Your Way

Southern Patagonia and Tierra del Fuego span a vast area of Chile. We've chosen the places that showcase its remarkable scenery, diverse wildlife, tumultuous history and fascinating cultures, allowing you to plot your own adventure.

Rio Gallegos

ARGENTINA

Puerto Natales, p300

A bustling traveler-focused town, Puerto Natales is the gateway to Torres del Paine, with an array of excellent places to eat, drink and stay.

Parque Nacional Torres del Paine, p308

One of South America's finest reserves, Torres del Paine's myriad trails enable visitors to soak up mesmeric views of mountains, lakes, glaciers and steppe.

El Calafate

Puerto Bories

Puerto Natales

Villa O'Higgins

Lago Argentino

Lago del Lago Toro Sofia

Lago Aniba Pinto

Laguna Larga

Parque Nacional Torres del Paine

Lago Berguez

Parque Nacional Bernardo O'Higgins

0 0
100 miles
200 M

*ATLANTIC
OCEAN*

Puerto Williams, p318
The remote settlement of Puerto Williams is a welcoming base for exploring the spectacular Dientes de Navarino range and the Beagle Channel.

Cape Horn

*Laguna
Roja*

Puerto
Williams

Ushuaia
Puerto Santa Rosa

San
Sebastian
Estancia
Rio Chico
*Lago
Lövenborg*
Caleta
Peron
Caleta
Lewaia

San
Martin
Rio
Grande

Munizaga
*Lago
Blanco*
Aserradero
La Paciencia

Tierra del Fuego
*Lago
Ofhidro*

Rio
Nuevo
*Parque Nacional
Tierra del Fuego*

Caleta
Rosario
Puerto
Yartou

San Luis

Porvenir
Mision

Punta Arenas, p290
A historic port-city on the Strait of Magellan, Punta Arenas is the biggest city in southern Patagonia and an important transport hub.

Strait of Magellan
San Juan

**Punta
Arenas**

le Puerto
Curtze

*Lago
Riesco*

*Parque
Nacional
Kawésqar*
*Lago
Titus*

*PACIFIC
OCEAN*

BUS
The main cities in southern Patagonia have good bus connections, and frequent services cross the border to the Argentine sections of Patagonia and Tierra del Fuego (the latter include a ferry crossing). By contrast, Chilean Tierra del Fuego has limited bus services.

BOAT
Ferries connect Puerto Montt with Puerto Natales, as well as Punta Arenas with Porvenir and Puerto Williams. Punta Arenas also has cruises to Ushuaia in Argentine Tierra del Fuego. Boat services between Ushuaia and Puerto Williams are suspended but expected to restart in the future.

PLANE
Many travelers fly into Punta Arenas or Puerto Natales from cities such as Santiago. Regular flights operate between Punta Arenas and Puerto Williams, which does not have road connections with the rest of Chile.

Plan Your Time

Southern Patagonia and Tierra del Fuego is a huge region overflowing with attractions, so allow plenty of time to immerse yourself in its captivating landscapes, history and cultures.

If You Only Do One Thing

● Head directly to **Parque Nacional Torres del Paine** (p308), the region's crown jewel. The most famous hikes in the park – the **W Trek** (p309) and the **Paine Circuit** (p310) – take around a week to complete, but there are shorter hikes as well as boat cruises, kayaking excursions and horse-riding trips if you are on a tight schedule. Although it is possible to visit Torres del Paine on a day trip from **Puerto Natales** (p300), it is far better to spend at least a couple of nights at one of the many hotels, lodges or campsites inside or around the park.

HUGO BRIZARD-YOUGOPHOTO/SHUTTERSTOCK ©

Hiker, Parque Nacional Torres del Paine (p308)

Seasonal Highlights

The weather in southern Patagonia is notoriously temperamental. Most travelers visit from October to March. The winter months are quieter but often more challenging.

JANUARY

It's prime time for spotting mating **sea lions** – plus all manner of whales, dolphins and seabirds – on the Beagle Channel.

MARCH

The summer winds begin to ease, **fall colors** start to appear and visitor numbers in Torres del Paine gradually drop.

JUNE

From late June until September, many places close for the winter. It's a memorable time to hike in a snowy Torres del Paine.

ANGELO DAMICO/SHUTTERSTOCK ©, GERARDO BELTRAN/SHUTTERSTOCK ©, STEVE ALLEN/SHUTTERSTOCK ©

10 Days to Travel Around

● After exploring **Parque Nacional Torres del Paine** (p308) for a few days, travel to **Puerto Natales** (p300) for a night. Stroll along the waterfront, visit the **Museo Histórico** (p301) and check out the excellent cafes and restaurants.

● Continue south to the port city of **Punta Arenas** (p290), whose historic buildings, museums and grand cemetery provide a snapshot of the wealth generated by the 20th-century sheep-ranching boom in Patagonia.

● Fit in a day trip to attractions such as **Parque del Estrecho de Magallanes** (p297), a historical site and museum, or **Monumento Natural Los Pingüinos** (p298), a significant penguin reserve.

If You Have More Time

● From **Puerto Natales** (p300), take a bus across the border into **Argentine Patagonia** (p316) and spend a few days in El Chaltén and El Calafate, the jumping-off points for a range of activities in the glorious **Parque Nacional Los Glaciares** (p308).

● From Punta Arenas, fly or catch a ferry to **Puerto Williams** (p318) in Tierra del Fuego. Hike up to the summit of **Cerro Bandera** (p321) for superb views, visit the **Museo Antropológico Martín Gusinde** (p319) and take a wildlife-watching trip along the **Beagle Channel** (p326).

● With extra days to play with, you can even hike the challenging **Dientes de Navarino Circuit** (p321).

JULY

It's the peak period for winter sports in Argentine Tierra del Fuego. Punta Arenas holds its **Winter Carnival**.

OCTOBER

Penguins return to nest at Monumento Natural Los Pingüinos and are usually around until April.

NOVEMBER

The end of spring and start of summer is a good time to **hike** ahead of the busy peak season.

DECEMBER

The start of the warmest and busiest period is ideal for hiking and ranch visits, though **national parks** are crowded.

289

PUNTA ARENAS

Santiago ✪

Punta
Arenas

Sprawling along the Strait of Magellan, Punta Arenas is the largest city in Chile's far south, a mix of the rustic and the grand. Founded in 1848, it was originally a military garrison and penal colony whose economy relied on seal skins and guanaco hides, as well as trade from ships bound for the California Gold Rush. The subsequent arrival of sheep from the Falkland Islands transformed the city – and Patagonia as a whole. It generated a booming industry, created great fortunes for a few and attracted immigrants from across Europe, but devastated the region's indigenous communities.

Today, Punta Arenas is an important transport hub and has a wide range of tourist facilities such as hotels, restaurants and travel agencies. While the outskirts are lined with huge duty-free outlets in the Zona Franca, the center is an architectural treasure trove, with elaborate wool-boom mansions and a renovated port.

TOP TIP

Punta Arenas puts on a pair of lively fiestas in the height of winter. On June 21, the city celebrates the winter solstice (the longest night of the year), while in late July, it stages the Carnival de Invierno (Winter Carnival). Expect firework displays, street parades and live music.

Chilean *baqueano* (cowboy)

MICHELE RINALDO/SHUTTERSTOCK ©

BEST BARS & COFFEE SHOPS

Wake Up
Hip baristas turn out excellent cappuccinos, cortados and espressos, as well as tasty cakes and pastries, light meals and savory snacks.

Taberna Club de la Unión
Beneath the Palacio Sara Braun, this subterranean bar-restaurant has an extensive range of piscos, gins, whiskeys and local Patagonian beers.

Café Tapiz
It's easy to while away an afternoon over a coffee or alcoholic drink at this stylish, low-lit place, especially if you snag one of the prime window tables.

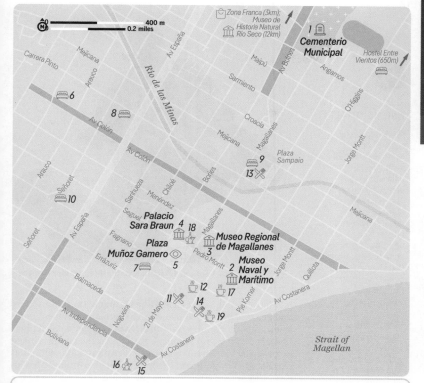

HIGHLIGHTS
1 Cementerio Municipal
2 Museo Naval y Marítimo
3 Museo Regional de Magallanes
4 Palacio Sara Braun
5 Plaza Muñoz Gamero

SLEEPING
6 Hostal Buenavista
7 Hotel Plaza
8 Ilaia
9 Innata Patagonia
10 La Yegua Loca

EATING
11 Fuente Hamburg
12 Kiosco Roca
13 La Marmita
14 La Vianda
15 Mercado Municipal

DRINKING & NIGHTLIFE
16 Bodega 87
17 Café Tapiz
18 Taberna Club de la Unión
19 Wake Up

Glimpse at a Gilded Age

THE SHEEP BARONS' LEGACY

The grand architecture of central Punta Arenas is a vivid reminder of the fortunes made by the sheep-ranching elite during their heyday in the late 19th and early 20th centuries.

 WHERE TO EAT IN PUNTA ARENAS

Kiosko Roca
Local institution specializing in bite-sized chorizo sandwiches and banana milk, a bizarre combo that somehow works. **$**

La Marmita
Cozy traveler favorite with creative meat and seafood mains, plus tasty veggie and vegan options. **$$**

La Vianda
Top-notch bakery-cafe with sumptuous breads, cakes, pastries and wholesome salads. **$**

MARINE ROYALTY

No visit to the far south of Chile is complete without sampling the delicious local *centolla* (king crab). The frigid waters here are rich in these super-sized crustaceans, which can grow to a meter or more in length, and Chile has a thriving industry dedicated to this lucrative catch, including in Puerto Williams and Puerto Toro. Restaurant menus throughout southern Patagonia and Tierra del Fuego feature *centolla* in the form of gratins, pasta dishes, risottos, crêpes, salads, soups, sandwiches and a variety of other guises. Bear in mind, though, that if you order it outside of the fishing season (roughly July to November), you might be served frozen or tinned crab, which doesn't even come close to the fresh stuff.

Ferdinand Magellan statue, Plaza Muñoz Gamero

It is most visible at **Plaza Muñoz Gamero**, the main square and heart of the city. Flanked by the cathedral, opulent mansions and other stately buildings, the plaza is the ideal place to start delving into the city's history. In the center, ringed by towering conifers, is a statue of Ferdinand Magellan that was donated by powerful sheep-ranching baron José Menéndez in 1920 to commemorate the 400th anniversary of the Portuguese navigator's voyage through the strait that now bears his name. On either side of Magellan are two rather stylized statues that represent the indigenous inhabitants of Patagonia and Tierra del Fuego. According to local legend, if you want to return to the city, you should touch or kiss the toe of the statue of the Selk'nam man.

A stone's throw from the plaza is the Palacio Braun-Menéndez, a neoclassical mansion constructed between 1903 and 1906. It now houses the **Museo Regional de Magallanes**, which offers a deeper insight into the lavish lifestyles once enjoyed by a select few in the city. The well-preserved rooms are packed with furniture imported from Paris and London, glittering chandeliers, delicate Chinese vases and stiff family portraits, while the modest servants' quarters downstairs provide a glimpse of a rather different side of life at the time. There are

WHERE TO STAY IN PUNTA ARENAS

Hostel Entre Vientos
Well-equipped hostel with dorms, private rooms, guest kitchen and lounge. A 25-minute walk from the center. **$**

La Yegua Loca
Boutique hotel on a hillside above the city with attractive rooms and a fine on-site restaurant. **$$$**

Innata Patagonia
Reliable midrange guesthouse with simple but comfortable en suites, including some good-value quads. **$$**

also displays on the history of the region, which help to illuminate its geology, Indigenous cultures, colonization and the transformative sheep-ranching boom. Ask for an English-language booklet at the desk at the entrance of the museum.

If the Museo Regional de Magallanes has piqued your interest in life in turn-of-the-20th-century Punta Arenas, head around the corner to the regal **Palacio Sara Braun**, which faces the plaza. Completed in 1905, it is now home to the upmarket Hotel José Nogueira and, in the basement, the **Taberna Club de la Unión**, an atmospheric bar-restaurant.

Naval Gazing

DIVE INTO MARITIME HISTORY

Naval buffs should stop by the **Museo Naval y Marítimo**, a couple of blocks east of the main square, which offers a snapshot of the intriguing maritime history of Patagonia and Tierra del Fuego. Its exhibits include an interesting account of the Chilean Navy's rescue of the stranded crew of polar explorer Ernest Shackleton, an array of model ships and yellowing maps, a set of fearsome torpedoes, portraits of noted naval officers and a rather hazardous-looking antique diving suit. There is also a replica ship's bridge, complete with steering wheel, portholes, charts and radio equipment, and a guide to the region's lighthouses.

Poignant City of the Dead

STORIES FROM THE CEMETERY

A 15-minute walk northeast of the main plaza, the vast **Cementerio Municipal** is one of the most captivating in South America. The 1890s cemetery spans 4 hectares, its avenues of neatly clipped Canadian cypress trees are filled with ostentatious tombs, such as the mausoleums of Sara Braun, who was part of a major sheep-ranching dynasty, and the similarly wealthy José Menéndez, and many more humble graves. Collectively, they provide a fascinating and moving insight into the history of Punta Arenas, particularly the multicultural makeup of early European settlers – Croats, Germans, British, French, Spaniards and Italians, among many others. There are also several tributes to the countless sailors who lost their lives in the often perilous seas around the coast of southern Chile.

Declared a national historic monument in 2012, the cemetery also has a statue of an unnamed Selk'nam man, the so-called *Indio Desconocido* ('Unknown Indian'), which attracts a steady stream of visitors who believe he grants wishes. The

BRUCE CHATWIN & PUNTA ARENAS

Punta Arenas played a significant role in author Bruce Chatwin's seminal travelogue *In Patagonia*. Merchant navy captain Charley Milward, a distant relative of Chatwin's, was shipwrecked on the Strait of Magellan in 1898 and subsequently settled in Punta Arenas. He later became the city's British consul, but he is best known for sending a piece of skin from a prehistoric giant sloth found in the Cueva del Milodón back to his family. The item captivated the young Chatwin, who wrote, 'I called it "the piece of brontosaurus" and set it at the center of my childhood bestiary.' It provided the inspiration for his 1977 book (whose stories are, to put it mildly, rather embellished).

Ilaia
An appealing blend of family warmth and space, contemporary style make this hotel a worthy choice. **$$**

Hotel Plaza
Converted mansion with dated but well priced rooms and an unbeatable location just off the plaza. **$**

Hostal Buenavista
Modern guesthouse with tidy doubles and triples in an elevated location overlooking the center. **$**

Punta Arenas is understandably proud of its connections to the 'heroic age' of Antarctic exploration in the late 19th and early 20th centuries, many of whose leading figures traveled through the city. This walking tour takes you to some of the key sites, starting at **1 Monumento Piloto Pardo** on the *costanera* (waterfront promenade), a short walk east of the flashy Hotel Dreams del Estrecho. Inaugurated in 2021, the monument features a statue of Chilean Naval captain Luis Pardo alongside the prow of the *Yelcho*, the vessel he used to rescue Ernest Shackleton's stranded *Endurance* crew from Elephant Island, an inhospitable mass of rock and ice just off the coast of the Antarctic peninsula, in 1916. From here, the tour follows, in part, the Circuito Turístico Antártico (Antarctic Tourist Circuit), a series of bilingual blue plaques attached to notable

historic buildings in central Punta Arenas. Walk a couple of blocks northwest to **2 Hotel de France**, which once played host to the Norwegian explorer Roald Amundsen, the first person to reach the South Pole. Two blocks further northwest, at Plaza Muñoz Gamero, you'll find the **3 old post office**, which the ill-fated Captain Robert Falcon Scott visited in 1904 to mail letters home, and **4 Residencia Blanchard**, formerly the home of a prolific French Antarctic whaler. Shackleton and his crewmen Tom Crean and Frank Worsley visited the **5 Anglican Church of St James**, a five-minute stroll northwest of the plaza. Retrace your route to the plaza before continuing on for two more blocks to the **6 Museo Naval y Marítimo**, where you can find out more about the daring exploits and feats of endurance of Pardo, Shackleton and their crews.

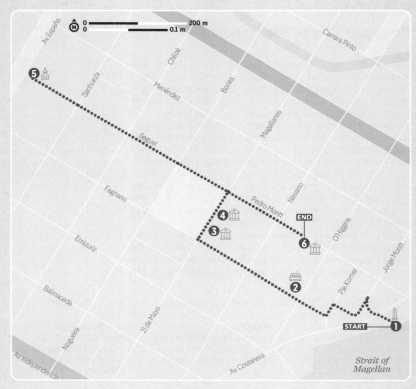

statue is surrounded by bunches of flowers, photos of loved ones and tiles with messages of thanks.

A useful map of the most notable graves in the Cementerio Municipal can be found just inside the cemetery's main entrance.

Skeletons & Sketches

MAGELLAN MARINE LIFE ENCOUNTERS

If you're interested in the creatures that inhabit the Strait of Magellan, check out the **Museo de Historia Natural Río Seco**. This privately run natural history museum – the brainchild of two brothers, one a marine biologist, the other a visual artist – has a collection of painstakingly reconstructed and imaginatively displayed skeletons, from whales and sea lions to a multitude of birds. Sets of beautiful drawings help to bring the creatures vividly to life. A good option for families in particular, the museum is in the coastal settlement of Río Seco, a 15-minute drive north of downtown Punta Arenas.

Cruise Control

SAILING SOUTH FROM PUNTA ARENAS

The opening of the Panama Canal in 1914 diminished the global importance of the port of Punta Arenas, yet more than a century on, there remains something undeniably romantic about setting sail from here. Voyaging south by **cruise ship** or **ferry** to Tierra del Fuego takes you along historic waterways, such as the Strait of Magellan and the Beagle Channel, and showcases the region's awe-inspiring scenery, much of which is otherwise inaccessible.

If money is no object, **Australis** offers luxurious four-night cruises to the city of Ushuaia in the Argentine section of Tierra del Fuego. For a cheaper, more rough-and-ready but equally memorable experience, **Transbordadora Austral Broom** has ferry services to Puerto Williams and Porvenir. More prosaically, the company also operates hourly ferries on the Primero Angostura crossing of the Strait of Magellan between Punta Delgada, 170km northeast of Punta Arenas on mainland Patagonia and Bahía Azul in Tierra del Fuego. This is the route followed by cars and buses traveling between Punta Arenas and Ushuaia.

Between November and March, Punta Arenas is also the embarkation point for a number of cruises to Antarctica.

DUTY-FREE SHOPPING

A sprawling free trade zone on the outskirts of Punta Arenas, the **Zona Franca** has a large shopping mall, hypermarkets and a variety of cavernous, warehouse-like stores, as well as a few family-friendly attractions such as an ice rink. It is worth coming here if you are in the market for outdoor gear (which is much cheaper here than in Puerto Natales), clothes, perfume, laptops, camera equipment and other electronic goods. The Zona Franca is around 4.5km north of Plaza Muñoz Gamero along Avenida España and then Avenida Bulnes. Frequent *taxi colectivos* (shared taxis) run there and back from the city center.

GETTING AROUND

Punta Arenas is relatively compact, and the center is easy to explore on foot. To reach the airport, 21km north of the city, you need to take a taxi, door-to-door shuttle service or one of the regular buses to Puerto Natales, which depart from various bus company terminals in central Punta Arenas. If you're planning to rent a car, it's cheaper to do so in Punta Arenas than Puerto Natales. Bear in mind, though, that driving a Chilean car across the border into Argentina can be costly because of international insurance requirements.

Beyond Punta Arenas

Leave the city behind and head into the wilds of southern Patagonia, whose stark, brooding scenery quickly draws you in.

Parque Nacional Pali Aike

Monumento Natural Los Pingüinos

Marine Parque Francisco Coloane

Punta Arenas

Reserva Natural Pingüino Rey

Puerto Hambre & Fuerte Bulnes

Cabo Froward

Parque Natural Karukinka

Parque Nacional Yendegaia

Cut off from the rest of the continent by frigid waters and jagged Andean ranges, the Magallanes region that surrounds Punta Arenas is desolate but beautiful. Traveling across its vast, largely treeless plains and formidable, wind-battered coastline provides you with a beguiling sense of isolation.

The area has a surprising range of things to see and do, including national parks, marine reserves, penguin colonies, hiking trails and historic monuments. A ferry ride across the Strait of Magellan takes you to Porvenir, an interesting town on Isla Grande in northern Tierra del Fuego. In the south of Isla Grande, which is divided between Chile and Argentina, is the pristine Parque Nacional Yendegaia.

TOP TIP

Strong winds and inclement weather can delay or postpone boat and kayak trips, so allow some flexibility in your schedule.

Magellanic penguin, Monumento Natural Los Pingüinos (p298)

DANI PALAZON/SHUTTERSTOCK ©

The Colonization of Patagonia

A TUMULTUOUS HISTORY

To learn more about the Spanish and Chilean attempts to colonize Patagonia, visit **Parque del Estrecho de Magallanes**, which encompasses the **Puerto Hambre** and **Fuerte Bulnes** national monuments. Puerto Hambre was one of Spain's shortest-lived outposts in South America, and Fuerte Bulnes was a fort established in 1843 after Chilean president Manuel Bulnes sent a schooner to claim the region – inhabited for thousands of years by indigenous peoples – for Chile. The fort has been impressively restored, and an informative museum with a multimedia exhibition covers the region's indigenous cultures, wildlife and geological history. Several walking trails provide a sense of the harsh terrain and climatic conditions faced by the early colonists.

Headland Hiking

REACHING CABO FROWARD

A testing but memorable two-day, 50km hike along windswept cliffs leads you to **Cabo Froward** (Cape Froward), the most southerly point on the mainland of South America. Beyond the sense of satisfaction at reaching this far-flung point, the wildlife-watching en route is top notch, particularly around the **San Isidro Lighthouse**. Expect sightings of dolphins, whales and an array of birdlife, including green-backed fire-crowns and Magellanic woodpeckers. It's possible to hike the route independently and camp overnight, but Punta Arenas tour operators such as **Turismo Comapa** offer guided treks, while **Chile Nativo** in Puerto Natales offers combined kayaking and hiking expeditions. **Kayak Agua Fresca** also runs kayaking trips off the coast.

When you reach Cabo Froward, which is inaccessible by road, you'll find a 365m hill topped with a huge metal cross. The original was erected in 1913. The current one dates from 1987 and was erected to mark Pope John Paul II's visit to Chile.

Humpbacks, Kings & Magellanics

WHALE WATCHING AND PENGUIN SPOTTING

The Strait of Magellan hums with marine life, and a range of boat and kayak tours offer excellent wildlife-watching opportunities. Spanning some 670 sq km, **Marine Parque Francisco Coloane** is home to pods of humpback whales, which feed in its waters between December and May. Minke and sei whales are also sometimes spotted alongside colonies of

COLONIAL OUTPOSTS: PUERTO HAMBRE & FUERTE BULNES

The ill-fated settlement of Puerto Hambre (Port Famine) was established by Spanish naval commander Pedro Sarmiento de Gamboa in 1584 and was also known as Ciudad Rey Don Felipe (City of King Philip). Because of a lack of food and supplies, its inhabitants starved to death or succumbed to exposure. Two and a half centuries later, the settlement of Fuerte Bulnes (Fort Bulnes) proved similarly short-lived. Faced with limited potable water and inadequate agricultural land, the Chilean colonists eventually moved north to a more promising location known to the Aónikenk as 'Lacolet' and that European sailors referred to as 'sandy point.' It became the modern city of Punta Arenas, which means sandy point in Spanish.

🐋 **MUST-SEE WILDLIFE IN SOUTHERN PATAGONIA & TIERRA DEL FUEGO**

Magellanic penguins
Found along the Patagonian coast, Magellanics are medium-sized penguins whose white chests have two black bands.

King penguins
The second-largest penguin species, kings have orange neck feathers and typically live in sub-Antarctic regions.

Humpback whales
Weighing up to 40 tons, humpbacks have small bumps in front of their dorsal fins.

A HISTORIC WATERWAY

Dividing Patagonia from Tierra del Fuego and connecting the Atlantic and Pacific oceans, the Strait of Magellan was once one of the planet's most important waterways. Navigated by indigenous Kawésqar and Yagán canoe-based societies for thousands of years, the channel is named after Fernando Magellan, who became the first European to sail its length in 1520. It later became a key commercial steamship route in the mid-19th century before declining in importance in the early 20th century thanks to the opening of the Panama Canal, which provided a handy Atlantic–Pacific shortcut. Today, the Strait of Magellan is still plied by ferries, while tour operators in Punta Arenas offer boat and kayaking excursions.

sea lions. To visit, contact **Solo Expediciones**, which offers full-day boat and kayak trips, or **Whalesound**, with three-day, science-focused boat-based expeditions.

Monumento Natural Los Pingüinos hosts tens of thousands of Magellanic penguins between November and March, as well as sea lions and birds such as black-browed albatrosses and cormorants. Five-hour boat trips from Punta Arenas – arranged through operators such as **Solo Expediciones** and **Turismo Selknam** – transport you around the islands.

On Isla Grande, **Reserva Natural Pingüino Rey** has South America's only king penguin colony. Normally found on sub-Antarctic islands, the birds unexpectedly settled here in 2010. The reserve is open from September to May. Most people visit on a day trip from Punta Arenas with a tour operator such as **Turismo Fin del Mundo**, but you can also go independently, though this requires arranging transportation to and from the reserve in the town of Porvenir.

Where the Devil Dwells

HIKING IN PALI AIKE

With a stark volcanic landscape riddled with cones, caves, craters and lava beds, it's easy to see why **Parque Nacional Pali Aike** – 'desolate place where the devil dwells' in the Aónikenk language – got its name. The 50-sq-km park is best explored on the trails that wind through mineral-rich red, yellow and gray-green rocks and a patchwork of craters, some more than four stories tall. Along the way, you pass Fell and Pali Aike caves, where excavations in the 1930s revealed evidence of human activity dating back some 11,000 years.

Most travelers visit on a full-day tour from Punta Arenas with an operator such as **Turismo Fin del Mundo**. If you have your own vehicle, you can come independently.

A Fuegian Wilderness

EXPLORING ISLA GRANDE'S RESERVES

If you're seeking a wilderness adventure, head across the Strait of Magellan to Isla Grande. The pristine **Parque Natural Karukinka** has a network of hiking routes, some suitable for mountain bikes, that take you through an expanse of coastline, steppe, forests, wetlands and mountains. Keep your eyes peeled for elephant seals, dolphins, guanacos, foxes, otters and Magellanic woodpeckers. The park has basic accommodations but nowhere to eat or buy food. Most people visit on a tour with an operator such as **Chile Nativo**,

MUST-SEE WILDLIFE IN SOUTHERN PATAGONIA & TIERRA DEL FUEGO

Guanacos
Wild relatives of the llama, guanacos are one of the largest herbivores in South America.

Andean condors
One of the world's biggest flying birds, Andean condors can have a wingspan of more than 3m.

Ñandus
Resembling ostriches and emus, ñandus are large, flightless birds found across Patagonia.

Cráter Morada del Diablo, Parque Nacional Pali Aike

GETTING TO ISLA GRANDE

The main gateway to Isla Grande is Porvenir on its northwest coast. This small, little-visited town curled around a bay has regular ferries and flights to and from Punta Arenas. A lack of public transport means it is difficult to travel around Isla Grande independently, and most people visit on an organized tour. Agencies in Punta Arenas offer day trips to Porvenir, usually including a stop at Reserva Natural Pingüino Rey. Porvenir has some simple guesthouses whose owners can arrange transport and excursions to places such as Parque Natural Karukinka. Seasonal flights operate between Pampa Guanaco, near the park, and Punta Arenas. There are no direct connections between Puerto Williams and Isla Grande.

though you can come independently if you have your own vehicle or arrange transportation in Porvenir.

In the far south of Isla Grande, **Parque Nacional Yendegaia** ('Deep Bay' in the Yagán language) receives even fewer visitors. This 1500-sq-km reserve in the Cordillera Darwin is a realm of mountains, pampas, fjords and Fuegian forest. Home to threatened species such as the southern river otter and the ruddy-headed goose, as well as a multitude of marine life, the reserve is a strategic wildlife corridor between Parque Nacional Alberto de Agostino and Parque Nacional Tierra del Fuego. The reserve has no real infrastructure, and visitor access is limited, but Chile Nativo offers off-trail hiking expeditions.

GETTING AROUND

Beyond ferries and flights to Porvenir on Isla Grande, public transport in the region around Punta Arenas is limited. Unless you rent a car or hire a taxi, you need to take an organized tour to visit the parks and reserves.

PUERTO NATALES

Once a humble port on the shores of Última Esperanza Sound, Puerto Natales is now a traveler hot spot, thanks to its role as the gateway to Parque Nacional Torres del Paine. Drawing visitors from across the globe, the town is awash with places to eat, stay and shop that are geared towards international tastes.

Despite its sky-high popularity, Puerto Natales' corrugated-tin houses, rustic bungalows, relaxed pace of life and glorious waterfront setting mean that it retains much of its rugged charm. Located some 250km northwest of Punta Arenas, it is the second-largest settlement in the region, the capital of the province of Última Esperanza (Last Hope) and the southern terminus of ferry trips through the Chilean fjords. Although the town itself is relatively short on attractions, it is an easy place to kick back, and the surrounding region has plenty of things to see and do.

Santiago

Puerto Natales

TOP TIP

Prices in Puerto Natales' shops are high, even by Patagonian standards. If you need to buy clothing, gear, food or other supplies for your Torres del Paine trek or if you plan to rent a car, it is worth doing so in Punta Arenas, which is cheaper and has a wider selection.

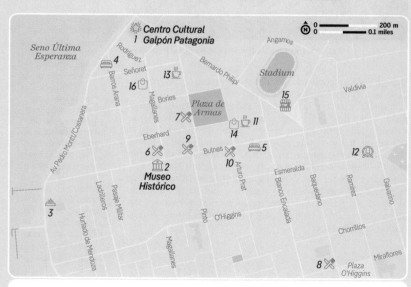

HIGHLIGHTS
1 Centro Cultural Galpón Patagonia
2 Museo Histórico

ACTIVITIES, OURSES & TOURS
3 Navimag

SLEEPING
4 Kau Patagonia
see 12 Vinnhaus
5 Wild

EATING
6 Afrigonia
7 Aluen

8 Cafe Kaiken
9 El Bote
10 Vinnhaus

DRINKING & NIGHTLIFE
11 Holaste!
12 Last Hope Distillery

13 Ludopía

SHOPPING
14 Espacio Ñandu
15 Pueblo Artesanal Etherh Aike
16 Wine & Market Patagonia

A Costanera Saunter

MONUMENTS, ARTWORK AND VISTAS

As well as offering sweeping views across the waters of Seno Última Esperanza to the snow-covered mountains beyond, a stroll along the **Costanera** – the pedestrianized waterfront of Puerto Natales, running alongside Av Pedro Montt – takes you past a series of interesting monuments, sculptures and pieces of contemporary art.

A short walk north of the ferry dock is a tribute to Hermann Eberhard Schmith, one of the first European settlers in the Seno Última Esperanza region. He famously discovered the remains of a mylodon (a prehistoric giant sloth that has become a symbol of the town) in a nearby cave in the 1890s; the site is now open to the public (p307). If you continue walking north, you'll soon come to a small skateboard park, beside which rises an eye-catching pair of flying figures known as the *Amores de Viento en Natales* (*Lovers of Wind in Natales*).

Head further north to see another impressive artwork, a giant hand seemingly reaching out from the sidewalk as if ready to snatch up unsuspecting passersby. The final monument, just to the north in the middle of a roundabout on the edge of Puerto Natales, is a large mylodon statue. Display panels provide some background on this fascinating creature, whose image adorns many of the street signs in the center of the town.

Perspectives on Patagonia

HISTORY LESSONS AND CULTURAL CONTEXT

For an illuminating insight into the turbulent history of southern Patagonia, head to the small but information-packed **Museo Histórico**, which has exhibits on the prehistoric flora and fauna; the Aónikenk, Kawésqar, Selk'nam, Yagán and Haush cultures; and the seismic impact of the sheep-ranching industry in the late 19th and early 20th centuries.

Commendably, the museum does not shy away from issues such as the devastating impact of colonialism on the indigenous peoples of Patagonia, who had lived in the region for at least 10,000 years before the arrival of European explorers and Chilean settlers. In a section titled 'Genocide and Indigenous exile in Patagonia,' displays in English and Spanish outline how these communities were 'persecuted... deported... exhibited as animals... shown as the last step of human evolution in Europe and the United States... [and] massacred by gangs of mercenaries, losing their freedom and their lands.'

Other sections of the museum provide interesting context on other notable, but often overlooked, events in the history of

BEST PLACES TO SHOP IN PUERTO NATALES

Pueblo Artesanal Etherh Aike
Indoor market in the city center with a selection of small, locally run stores selling crafts, artworks, clothes and souvenirs.

Wine & Market Patagonia
Smart deli with an extensive range of gourmet products, including local cheeses, charcuterie, chocolates, wines, and craft beers and spirits. Regular tasting sessions are available too.

Espacio Ñandu
A useful one-stop shop diagonally opposite the main square selling outdoor gear and accessories, books on Patagonia, local food products and a selection of souvenirs.

 WHERE TO STAY IN PUERTO NATALES

Wild
Hostel with private rooms (some with shared bathrooms) and cabins, a restaurant-bar and tour agency. **$**

Vinnhaus
Elegant guesthouse with a swish vintage feel to its rooms and suites. Great breakfasts. **$$$**

Kau Patagonia
Modern, wood-paneled hotel with comfy en suites, unrivaled fjord views and popular on-site coffee shop. **$$**

Navimag ferry

I LIVE HERE: LURE OF PUERTO NATALES

Kiera Shiels and **Matt Oberg**, owners of the Last Hope Distillery, share what they love about Puerto Natales.

Puerto Natales is a stunning location full of adventurers, but it also feels like a charming and sleepy little town. It's an amazing base for one of the world's most incredible hikes. We love this part of the world for what it looks and feels like, but also for the people it attracts. It takes a certain kind of person to spend their limited vacation hiking in the wild and unpredictable Patagonian weather, and we love meeting these people in our bar. We also love the community formed by the Chileans who come here to live and work.

southern Patagonia. They include displays on the large-scale migration of people from the Chiloé archipelago to work in the burgeoning sheep-ranching industry in and around Puerto Natales in the early years of the 20th century. Another display details the anarchist-led rebellion against exploitative conditions by workers in the meatpacking plants and ranches of the Última Esperanza region in 1919.

Follow up your visit to the Museo Histórico with a trip to the **Centro Cultural Galpón Patagonia**, a cultural center, workspace and gallery in a converted warehouse on the waterfront of Puerto Natales. It hosts regular exhibitions of works by artists from the town and beyond, as well as screenings of films and documentaries and occasional food markets featuring items from local producers.

G&T Time

CRAFT GIN DISTILLERY TOUR

Puerto Natales is not the most obvious location for a craft gin producer, and that makes the **Last Hope Distillery** all the more welcome. Founded by Australian couple Matt and Keira, who fell in love with this part of Patagonia after hiking

 WHERE TO EAT IN PUERTO NATALES

Afrigonia
A sophisticated African-Chilean restaurant providing a welcome injection of spice, creativity and culinary flair. **$$**

El Bote
Rustic restaurant with hearty Patagonia fare, such as lamb chops, guanaco stew and king crab gratin. **$$**

Café Kaiken
An intimate restaurant with a relaxed vibe and delicious dishes including sun-dried tomato and spinach ravioli. **$$**

the W Trek in Parque Nacional Torres del Paine in 2015, it offers excellent free tours that draw a steady stream of visitors (Wednesday to Sunday, 5.30pm in English, 6.30pm in Spanish). On the tours, you learn about the gin-making process, taste the various botanicals that give the spirit its distinct flavor, find out how Last Hope's gin has been given a uniquely Patagonian twist and of course sample the finished product.

Afterward, grab a seat in the attached bar for a perfectly mixed cocktail featuring the house dry gin or a deep-purple version flavored with sweet-sour calafate berries. Whiskey production is in the pipeline, but in the meantime, the bar has an extensive range of whiskeys produced by other distilleries. The inventive snacks and sharing platters are to die for. Highlights include a reuben sandwich made with guanaco pastrami, hummus with hazelnut dukkah (a tasty Middle Eastern spice blend) and, for those with a sweet tooth, a sticky date pudding with a bourbon butterscotch sauce.

Fjords, Forests & Ferries

SETTING SAIL FROM PUERTO NATALES

A spectacular cruise through the forest-fringed fjords strung between northern and southern Patagonia, the **Navimag ferry** voyage from Puerto Natales to the city of Puerto Montt (or vice versa) is, for many travelers, one of the highlights of their trip to Chile. On a four-day, three-night journey, the ship travels through the glorious Parque Nacional Bernardo O'Higgins, immersing you in a remote, largely inaccessible realm studded with giant glaciers. It is also excellent for wildlife-watching. Whales, penguins, dolphins and albatrosses are among the species you are likely to spot en route.

The **Transbordadora Austral Broom** ferry offers a more basic but similarly scenic service between Puerto Natales and the far-flung fishing village of Puerto Yungay, with a stop at the isolated settlement of Puerto Edén, which is home to an indigenous Kawésqar community, inside the national park. The voyage takes approximately 41 hours. As with the Navimag ferry, this memorable journey is more environmentally friendly than flying between northern and southern Patagonia.

Tickets for both routes should be booked well in advance. Schedules and journey times vary depending on weather conditions and tides, so allow some leeway in your itinerary in case of delay.

BEST CAFES & BARS IN PUERTO NATALES

Aluen
Top-notch *heladería* (ice cream shop) serving toothsome treats. Flavors range from dulce de leche to rice pudding. $

Vinnhaus
Classy restaurant-bar with well-mixed cocktails, good selection of wines and tempting snacks. $$

Last Hope
Unmissable Aussie-run bar and gin distillery with the finest cocktail list in Puerto Natales.

Holaste!
Tiny coffee shop offering superb espressos, cappuccinos and cortados. Busy but worth the wait.

Ludopía
Cafe-shop with a compendious selection of board games to play (and buy).

GETTING AROUND

Puerto Natales is a small city, and most travelers explore on it foot. Many hostels and some travel agencies rent bikes, which can be handy if you're planning on visiting outlying areas. Renting a car is more expensive here than in Punta Arenas. Buses to and from Punta Arenas, Parque Nacional Torres del Paine and El Calafate use the Rodoviario (bus terminal), which is around 1.5km southeast of the city center. Puerto Natales' small airport, which has flights to Santiago, is 8km north of the city. Taxis are available at the bus station, the airport and around the main square. Alternatively, ask your accommodation to book one for you.

Beyond Puerto Natales

Estancia
Laguna Sofía
Cueva del
Milodón
Parque Bahía
Esperanza
Puerto
Bories
Estancia
La Peninsula
Puerto Natales

Although it may have a forbidding name, Última Esperanza (Last Hope) province has stunning landscapes and intriguing historical sites to explore.

Última Esperanza is renowned for Parque Nacional Torres del Paine, but many of its other attractions fly under the radar, despite being easily accessible on day trips from Puerto Natales. They include Puerto Bories, a former industrial complex that once drove the economy across Patagonia, and privately run nature reserve Parque Bahía Esperanza, which offers hiking and wildlife-watching opportunities.

There's also the curious historical and archaeological site of Cueva del Milodón, plus a pair of sheep ranches – Estancia La Peninsula and Estancia Laguna Sofía – that offer superb horse riding. The landscapes of the Última Esperanza region are also a major draw in their own right: ice-blue fjords, rugged steppe and soaring peaks swirling with clouds.

TOP TIP

For a greener way to get around the area, Patagonia Zero Emission in Puerto Natales rents e-bikes.

Cueva del Milodón (p307)

ADRIAN WOJCIK/ALAMY STOCK PHOTO ©

Industrial scale, Singular hotel's museum

A Slice of Industrial History

DRIVING PATAGONIA'S ECONOMY

As unlikely as it may seem today, the Última Esperanza region was once a thriving hub of industrial activity. Some 6km north along the coast from Puerto Natales is the former company town of **Puerto Bories**, which grew up around a vast meat- and wool-processing plant owned by the Sociedad Explotadora de Tierra del Fuego commercial empire. For anyone interested in learning more about the history of Patagonia, a visit here is a must.

Opened in the 1910s, the plant received sheep from the Chilean and Argentine sides of Patagonia, slaughtering the animals, processing the carcasses and freezing the meat, which was exported to Europe and beyond, generating sky-high profits. At its height, it got through a staggering 150,000 to 250,000 animals every year. The complex operated until the mid-1980s before closing. Thanks to its cultural, industrial and architectural significance, it was declared a national monument in 1996.

The *frigorífico* (cold storage plant) has since been thoughtfully converted into the luxury **Singular** hotel, which retains much of the heritage. An informative **museum** inside the hotel whisks you through the history of Puerto Bories – and by

PATAGONIAN LAMB AT ITS BEST

Spit-roasted lamb, butterflied open and slow-cooked to perfection over a wood fire, *cordero al palo* is a classic Patagonian meal. The leisurely cooking process results in a succulent and smoky dish that features prominently on restaurant menus in Puerto Natales and throughout southern Patagonia. But without a doubt the best places to sample authentic *cordero al palo* are on the sheep ranches themselves. Try **Estancia La Peninsula** or **Estancia Laguna Sofía**, which both offer rib-sticking lamb barbecues served with all the trimmings, including salads, potatoes, home-baked bread, the ubiquitous *pebre* salsa (diced onions and tomatoes, chili, parsley, cilantro and vinegar), and, of course, excellent Chilean wine.

WHERE TO STAY AROUND PUERTO NATALES

Singular Patagonia
Accessed via a funicular railway, this characterful waterfront five-star draws heavily on its industrial heritage. **$$$**

Puerto Bories House
A trio of charming homes in Puerto Bories that resemble English country houses. Good for groups. **$$$**

Simple Patagonia
Distinctive lodge in Puerto Bories with modern, pared-back design and epic views of the sound. **$$$**

TRACING THE ROUTE OF PARKS

Stretching 2800km from Puerto Montt to Cape Horn, the **Ruta de los Parques** (Route of Parks; rutadelosparques. org) is a network of 17 national parks in Patagonia and Tierra del Fuego (that includes Torres del Paine) offering sensational scenery, trekking and wildlife-watching. It was launched in 2018 after pioneering environmental organization Tompkins Conservation donated 4045 sq km of land to create five new national parks and expand three others. The government contributed an additional 10,115 sq km of land and reclassified a further 21,850 sq km of nature reserves as national parks. As well as protecting ecosystems, the project aims to boost the economic development of local communities, connect isolated regions and promote sustainable tourism.

Estancia La Peninsula

extension, much of 20th-century Patagonia – showcasing an array of vintage machinery, much of which originated in the UK and looks as if it could jolt back into operation at a moment's notice. It is open to guests and nonguests, and guided tours are available.

Afterward, pop into the Singular's **restaurant-bar** for a drink overlooking Seno Última Esperanza.

Estancia Experiences

LIFE ON THE RANCH

A quintessential Patagonian sheep ranch, **Estancia La Peninsula** is a wonderful spot for multiday horseback adventures. Run by a family that has been ranching in the region for some six generations, the *estancia* also offers day trips featuring shorter horse rides or hikes, a hearty meal of *cordero al palo* (spit-roasted lamb), sheep-shearing and sheepdog demonstrations, and the chance to immerse yourself in the activities of a working ranch. If you get a taste for the lifestyle, there is also a volunteer programme and a more in-depth trainee scheme. Estancia La Peninsula is on Península Antonio Varas, across the water from Puerto Natales and accessed via a dock at Puerto Bories.

The equally beautiful **Estancia Laguna Sofía**, 30km north of Puerto Natales next to Lago Sofía, has similar activities. As well as one-hour, half-day and full-day horseback rides with *baqueano* (cowboy) guides, there are guided hikes to waterfalls, archaeologically significant caves and the summit of Cerro Mocho, plus sheepdog and herding-dog demonstrations, and delicious lamb barbecues. You can kayak and camp here too.

 WHERE TO STAY AROUND PUERTO NATALES

Estancia Laguna Sofía camping
Well-equipped campsite in a tranquil ranch location; good if you have your own vehicle. **$**

Remota Patagonia Lodge
Secluded hotel just outside Puerto Natales with contemporary decor, spa and lots of excursions. **$$$**

Casa Bahía Esperanza
This bright and breezy ranch house can be booked by families and groups. **$$$**

Trail Mix

PRIVATE NATURE RESERVE

Although only a 15-minute boat ride from Puerto Bories, **Parque Bahía Esperanza** provides a taste of the Patagonian wilderness. A ranch turned nature reserve, it allows you to hike, ride a horse or e-mountain bike through ancient woodlands echoing with birdsong along the shore of jewel-like lagoons and across undulating hills whose summits offer panoramic views. Visitors can also follow the Monument Trail to the park's most eye-catching structure, the elevated bow of a 40m wooden ship.

The trails, which are 1km to 5.2km in length, are well marked and can be tackled independently, though guides are available. The ticket price includes boat transfers from a dock at Puerto Bories.

A Subterranean Sloth

CAVES, VIEWPOINTS AND PREHISTORIC REMAINS

In 1895, a German named Hermann Eberhard Schmith discovered the partial remains of a mylodon (an enormous ground sloth) in a large cave in the side of Cerro Benítez, 24km northwest of Puerto Natales. This long extinct, slow-moving herbivore, nearly 4m tall, quickly attracted international media attention. A scrap of its skin eventually found its way to Bruce Chatwin, inspiring him to write his travel classic *In Patagonia* (the author originally thought the fragment was from a brontosaurus).

The **Cueva del Milodón** has since been named a natural monument. A kitsch scale replica of the mylodon stands outside the main cave where the remains were discovered, while paths take you into the inky cavernous depths. Two smaller caves are also open to the public, Cueva Chica and Cueva del Medio. In the latter, archaeologists discovered evidence of human activity dating back 11,000 years.

Another path leads to a strange rock formation known as Silla del Diablo (Devil's Seat), while a series of lookouts offers expansive views and, with a bit of luck, condor sightings. A visitor center has displays on Patagonia's prehistoric fauna and geological history.

Travel agencies in Puerto Natales run half-day tours to Cueva del Milodón. Alternatively, hire a taxi and ask the driver to wait while you look around. Buses to Torres del Paine pass the turning to the site, but it's an 8km walk from here to the main cave.

BEST PLACES TO EAT & DRINK AROUND PUERTO NATALES

Singular Patagonia
A sophisticated hotel restaurant and bar with a romantic atmosphere, an expert take on local ingredients and a strong wine list. Well worth a splurge. $$$

La Caldera
Cozy, wood-paneled cafe with good coffee, teas and cakes, plus wonderful Seno Última Esperanza views. It's 2km north of central Puerto Natales. $

Estancia Laguna Sofía
Settle down for a lavish *cordero al palo* (lamb barbecue) at this beautiful sheep ranch. Book in advance; minimum six people. $$$

GETTING AROUND

The region surrounding Puerto Natales has little in the way of public transport, so unless you rent a car, hire a taxi or – for shorter journeys – ride a bike or e-bike, you'll be largely reliant on organized tours. Alternatively, many of the *estancias* (ranches) can arrange transfers to and from Puerto Natales.

PARQUE NACIONAL TORRES DEL PAINE

Santiago ✪

**Parque Nacional
Torres del Paine**

One of South America's finest – and most popular – national parks, Parque Nacional Torres del Paine is a trekking haven. Spanning 1810 sq km, it is dominated by the eponymous Towers of Paine, a set of 2800m granite pillars that soar near vertically into the sky. They are part of a dazzling range of landscapes, from emerald forests and open steppe to azure lakes and shimmering glaciers. The park is home to a similarly wide range of wildlife, including ostrich-like rheas (known locally as *ñandus*), circling condors, guanacos, endangered huemul deer and growing numbers of pumas. Extensive accommodation options allow you to hike the famous W Trek or Paine Circuit trails in comfort, though unpredictable weather means that the park never feels fully tamed. You won't have the place to yourself though: Torres del Paine is a travel hot spot, which is proving challenging for its infrastructure and the environment.

TOP TIP

The weather in Parque Nacional Torres del Paine is notoriously prone to change, so pack for all four seasons, no matter what time of year you visit. The wind can be incredibly strong in the summer – as much as 120km/h.

Hiking towards Los Cuernos, Parque Nacional Torres del Paine

BLEUNG/SHUTTERSTOCK ©

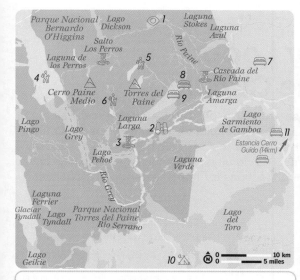

SIGHTS	ACTIVITIES, COURSES & TOURS	SLEEPING
1 Lago Paine		**7** Awasi
2 Mirador Nordenskjöld	**4** Glacier Grey	**8** EcoCamp Patagonia
	5 Mirador Las Torres	**9** Hotel Las Torres
3 Salto Grande	**6** Valle Francés	**10** Patagonia Camp
		11 Tierra Patagonia

World-Renowned Trail

ON THE W TREK

The most popular hike in Torres del Paine, the **W Trek** showcases the park's incredible scenery to the fullest. Taking its name from the shape it traces on the map, the route offers superior views of the black sedimentary peaks known as Los Cuernos (The Horns) when hiked from west to east (though you can also hike from east to west).

Open year-round, the W Trek is around 71km and generally takes four to five days, plus a day or two to get to and from the park. If you're short on time, you can hike individual sections of the route – the Mirador Las Torres leg is a popular choice. Don't expect much in the way of peace or solitude, though. The trails get extremely busy, especially in summer.

When hiking from west to east, the first leg is from Guardería Paine Grande to Refugio Lago Grey (13km, four hours one

PLANNING A VISIT TO TORRES DEL PAINE

Many visitors come on an organized day trip, tour or trek, and to visit Parque Nacional Torres del Paine independently requires some advance planning. The park is open all the year, but from May to September you must have a licensed guide because the trails are more perilous in the winter. Park entrance tickets must be booked online (aspticket. cl) at least 24 hours before you arrive. You also need to bring your passport and tourist card with you. Accommodations should be booked well in advance. The park has no ATMs, so bring sufficient cash with you from Puerto Natales. Most hotels and *refugios* accept credit and debit cards.

WHERE TO STAY IN & AROUND PARQUE NACIONAL TORRES DEL PAINE

Tierra Patagonia
Gorgeous hotel blending into the landscape, with views across Lago Sarmiento to the Paine massif. **$$$**

EcoCamp Patagonia
Carbon-neutral lodge with a mix of basic and deluxe domes, sociable restaurant-bar, yoga sessions and massages. **$$**

Estancia Cerro Guido
Working ranch with rooms in a renovated 1920s farmhouse at the foot of its namesake peak. **$$$**

A Longer Loop: the Paine Circuit

If you want to immerse yourself in the scenery of Torres del Paine, set off on the epic 112km Paine Circuit trek. Also known as the O Trek, it includes the W Trek as well as the backside between Refugio Grey and Refugio Las Torres. The circuit typically takes seven to nine days, plus a day or two for connections to/ from the park, and it's quieter than the W Trek.

1 Laguna Amarga

You have to hike the Paine Circuit counter-clockwise, starting from the shores of Laguna Amarga (or Refugio Las Torres) in the east of the park and finishing at Valle Francés and Los Cuernos. The circuit is closed to trekkers during the winter season, unless you go with a certified tour operator with permission from Conaf. From the outset, there are classic Torres del Paine views from Laguna Amarga ('Bitter Lake,' a reference to its salinity).

The Hike: The opening leg of the circuit is relatively easy with largely open terrain. The hike to Campamento Serón is 15km and takes four to five hours.

2 Campamento Serón

Expect strong winds and vague trail markings as the spectacular route from this

MOCHILAOSABATICO/SHUTTERSTOCK ©

Lago Dickson

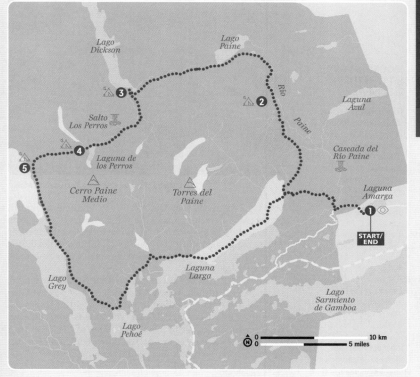

rustic campsite curls around the shores of the shimmering Lago Paine. Stick to the trail furthest away from the lake to avoid getting lost.

The Hike: The second stage of the hike takes you to Campamento Lago Dickson. It is 18.5km and takes six to seven hours.

3 Campamento Lago Dickson

In a peaceful spot beside Lago Dickson in the north of the park, this campsite is the jumping-off point for the walk southwest to Campamento Los Perros, which takes in the Perros lagoon and glacier.

The Hike: This leg is a fairly simple but windy section of the route. It covers 9km and takes around five hours.

4 Campamento Los Perros

The high point – in all senses of the word – of the stretch beyond Campamento Los Perros is the 1241m Paso John Gardner. Of-

ten covered with knee-deep mud or sometimes snow, it is the most extreme part of the whole Paine Circuit, but provides you with stellar vistas. After crossing the pass, don't be confused by what appears to be a campsite immediately afterward. Keep going until you see a shack.

The Hike: This stage of the Paine Circuit is physically challenging, especially in the winter, but rewarding. It is 8.6km to Compomento Paso, which takes roughly four hours.

5 Campamento Paso

The last leg of the hike offers stunning glacier views. From Campamento Paso, you head steeply downhill – trekking poles are a great help here – and cross a series of three hanging bridges over narrow gullies.

The Hike: The final stage of the Paine Circuit takes you to Refugio Lago Grey. It is a 10km hike that takes around two hours.

RENATO GRANIERI/ALAMY STOCK PHOTO ©

Puma, Parque Nacional Torres del Paine

way). It's a relatively easy trail with some challenging uphill sections and a glacier lookout. You then return to Guardería Paine Grande before hiking to the beautiful Valle Francés (9.5km, five hours). With Los Cuernos looming overhead, this section skirts Lago Skottsberg, ascends to the valley and crosses a suspension bridge.

The next stage, to Los Cuernos/Lago Pehoé (10km, five hours), is a wonderful stretch. Hugged by glaciers, it winds between Cerro Paine Grande (3050m) in the west and the Torres del Paine and Los Cuernos to the east. You then head to Refugio Las Torres (9.5km, four to five hours). Keep to the lower trail because hikers often get lost on the upper trail, which is unmarked on maps. Expect fierce summer winds.

The final leg, to Mirador Las Torres (10.5km, four hours), is a moderate hike up the Río Ascencio to a treeless tarn below the eastern face of the Torres del Paine before a final stretch across a scree field of giant boulders. Enjoy glorious close-up views of the towers but expect deep snow in the winter. You then retrace your route to Refugio Las Torres. This section is heavily touristed, and a new trail is being built to ease the pressure.

Trails for Tight Schedules

TORRES DEL PAINE DAY HIKES

In addition to the epic trails, Torres del Paine has plenty of shorter hikes that can be completed in a day or less. The highlights of the W Trek – **Mirador Las Torres**, **Valle Francés** and **Glacier Grey** – can each be hiked to and from in a single day. The trail to Mirador Las Torres starts at Refugio Las

 WHERE TO STAY IN & AROUND PARQUE NACIONAL TORRES DEL PAINE

Patagonia Camp
Yurts in a tranquil forest overlooking Lago Toro. Green credentials include a water treatment plant. **$$$**

Awasi
Stylish five-star in a remote location. Secluded villas are dotted around the main lodge. **$$$**

Hotel Las Torres
A large, well-equipped and handily located hotel with comfy en suites and a spa. **$$$**

Torres, while routes to Valle Francés and Glacier Grey start at Guardería Paine Grande.

From Guardería Pudeto, easy walks that take roughly one hour head to **Salto Grande**, an impressive waterfall, and **Mirador Nordenskjöld**, a viewpoint offering panoramas of the mountains and its namesake lake. A longer, more challenging option is the four-hour hike from Laguna Azul to **Lago Paine**, which provides a taste of the park's gorgeous scenery.

Various day hikes set off from Guardería Lago Grey, including to **Playa Grey**, which crosses a hanging bridge and offers lake and glacier views; **Cascada Pingo**, a riverside walk leading to a dramatic waterfall (accessible only with an accredited guide); and **Mirador Ferrier**, which leads to a viewpoint with superb vistas.

Tour operators **Antares**, **Chile Nativo** and **Erratic Rock** offer a good range of guided hikes.

For something a little different, **Bigfoot Patagonia** runs ice-hiking trips across the top of Glacier Grey. They last approximately five hours and involve gear such as crampons and ice axes.

Paddles to Pumas

KAYAKING, HORSE RIDING AND WILDLIFE-WATCHING

You don't have to hike to explore Torres del Paine. Tour operators in Puerto Natales and hotels in and around the park offer myriad minibus trips that take in a series of viewpoints. Although they provide only a snapshot of the park, they are a good option for visitors with mobility issues.

Bigfoot Patagonia runs a variety of kayaking excursions, including on iceberg-dotted Lago Grey and along the Pingo and Serrano rivers, while **Navegación Glacier Grey** has three-hour catamaran cruises between October and April that allow you to view the glacier up close. You can go horse riding with operators such as **Baqueano Zamora**, **Las Torres** and **Chile Nativo**, and mountain-biking trips are possible on certain trails. Several operators offer trips that focus on bird-watching, wildlife, photography and even fossil hunting in the Zapata Valley.

Puma tracking tours have become increasingly popular too. Seeing these big cats in the wild is an incredible privilege, and numbers in the park have grown. However, some tours get too close to and spend too long with the animals, so choose a responsible operator, such as Chile Nativo. Just outside the park, **Estancia Cerro Guido** offers conservation-focused 'safaris.'

THE DANGERS OF OVERTOURISM

The hundreds of thousands of annual visitors to Torres del Paine take a heavy toll on the environment and infrastructure. Trail deterioration, erosion and increasing waste are major issues. To help conserve the park, follow the regulations, avoid bottled water and pack out garbage. Don't make campfires – they're illegal – and be careful with cigarettes, lighters and stoves. Avoid the peak summer period, opt for quieter trails and park sections (or explore the surrounding area), and stay at sustainably run camps. Choose responsible local operators (such as the ones we recommend). You can also donate to the **Torres del Paine Legacy Fund** (tdplegacyfund.org), which works on conservation and community projects.

GETTING AROUND

If you haven't booked an organized tour or trek, public buses run to several destinations inside Parque Nacional Torres del Paine from Puerto Natales, which lies 112km to the south. A variety of shuttle bus and catamaran/ferry services can get you around the park. Luxury hotels, lodges and eco-camps in and around Torres del Paine provide transfers to and from the park as part of their all-inclusive packages.

Beyond Parque Nacional Torres del Paine

Don't limit yourself to the national park – the surrounding region offers similarly impressive scenery and far fewer fellow travelers.

The majority of visitors understandably focus their attention on Parque Nacional Torres del Paine, but visiting attractions in the surrounding area allows you to escape the crowds and reduce the growing pressure on the park. Neighboring *estancias* (ranches) offer a host of outdoor and wildlife-focused activities, while further afield lies Parque Nacional Bernardo O'Higgins, a huge but little-touristed reserve studded with looming glaciers. Many travelers combine their visit to this part of Chile with a trip across the border into neighboring Argentina, whose section of Patagonia provides a similar mix of jaw-dropping scenery – huge ice fields in particular – as well as exceptional hikes, extensive tourist facilities and useful transport connections.

Parque Nacional Bernardo O'Higgins

MAKINAJP/SHUTTERSTOCK ©

TOP TIP

Parque Nacional Los Glaciares gets uncomfortably crowded in the summer. Visiting during the quieter shoulder or winter seasons can be far more enjoyable.

BEST PLACES TO DRINK IN EL CALAFATE & EL CHALTÉN

La Vinería
This El Chaltén bar-restaurant has a superior wine and beer list, plus tapas and steaks for sustenance.

La Zorra
Lively El Calafate taproom serving excellent craft beer, including draft IPAs, stouts, golden ales, and fruit and honey beers.

Kau Kaleshen
An enjoyable El Calafate spot for a leisurely *merienda* (afternoon tea and cakes).

El Chaltén

Parque Nacional Los Glaciares   El Calafate

Parque Nacional Bernardo O'Higgins

Parque Nacional Torres del Paine

Tracking Patagonia's 'Ghost Cats'

PUMA CONSERVATION PROJECT

Ever since sheep were first brought to Patagonia in the late 19th century, there has been conflict between ranchers and the native wildlife, above all pumas. Although the practice is illegal, puma hunting remains common in the region, but a ranch on the edge of Parque Nacional Torres del Paine is aiming to show that another way is possible.

Estancia Cerro Guido (estanciacerroguido.com) runs a pioneering conservation program that involves using trained trackers to study the pumas, while humane strategies – including camera traps, light devices and 'sheep protection dogs' that live with the flocks – deter the endangered big cats from preying on the sheep. Its objective is to show that it is possible to have 'respectful livestock farming that coexists with the native species.' As part of a wide range of hiking, horse riding, jeep and culture-focused excursions, it offers enlightening 'conservation safaris' that allow travelers to accompany the ranch's professional puma trackers as they monitor these illusive 'ghost cats' in areas such as the spectacular Condoreras ridge, which, as the name suggests, is also a good place for spotting condors.

Land of Glaciers

SAIL THROUGH PARQUE NACIONAL BERNARDO O'HIGGINS

Northwest of Torres del Paine, **Parque Nacional Bernardo O'Higgins** encompasses a sizable chunk of the Southern Patagonian Ice Field. It is home to some 49 giant glaciers, including Pío XI, the largest in the Southern Hemisphere outside Antarctica. Over the last half a century, it has grown by more than 9.5km.

The only way to explore the park is by boat or kayak, traveling along channels and fjords strewn with icebergs. At almost 35,260 sq km – roughly the size of Taiwan – it is the biggest national park in Chile but receives few visitors thanks to its inaccessibility. Beyond glaciers, wildlife such as sea lions, fur seals, gray foxes, otters and – if you are lucky – huemules can be seen here.

You can't visit the park independently, but Puerto Natales-based tour operator **Turismo 21 de Mayo** runs day cruises to it that also take in the Balmaceda Glacier in Torres del Paine. Alternatively, you can visit the O'Higgins and Chico glaciers on a boat or kayak tour from Villa O'Higgins in northern Patagonia. Ferries traveling between Puerto Natales and Puerto Montt/Puerto Yungay pass through the park too.

CALAFATE BERRIES

The yellow-flowering *calafate* (Berberis microphylla) bush is a common sight across Patagonia. According to local legend, if you eat its berries, you are guaranteed to return to the region in the future, a story that has its origins in Aónikenk mythology. Also known as the box-leaved or Magellan barberry, *calafate* berries are small, dark blue-purple in color and have a distinctive sweet-sour taste. They are commonly used to make jams, ice cream, sweets and even beer, as well as to add a Patagonian twist to a pisco sour. *Calafate* products are widely available in shops and on menus in Puerto Natales, Punta Arenas, El Calafate and El Chaltén.

 WHERE TO STAY IN ARGENTINE PATAGONIA

América del Sur
Well-established backpacker favorite in El Calafate with neat and tidy dorms and private rooms. **$**

Estancia Cristina
Inside the national park and only accessible by boat, this lodge has sparkling modern cabins. **$$$**

Nothofagus B&B
Friendly and economically priced guesthouse in El Chaltén with a charming personal touch. **$$**

Going to Argentine Patagonia

CROSSING THE FRONTIER

Just across the border in Argentine Patagonia, the unmissable Parque Nacional Los Glaciares offers trekking trails that rival those in Torres del Paine, as well as the chance to observe up-close some sublime glaciers.

Visiting the region from Última Esperanza could hardly be easier. Regular buses connect Puerto Natales with the touristy town of **El Calafate**, the gateway to the southern section of the park. Named after a Patagonian berry, it has countless places to sleep, eat, drink, and arrange tours and activities, as well as a well-connected bus station and airport. The town itself is relatively short on attractions, though visitors should check out the impressive **Glaciarium**, a modern museum dedicated to the world of ice.

Buses run from El Calafate to **El Chaltén**, which manages to retain a frontier feel despite its popularity with trekkers and climbers and a prime location inside the northern section of Parque Nacional Los Glaciares. The village was founded in 1985 in a rush to beat Chile to the claim on the land. During the spring and summer, it is a hive of activity, drawing ever-increasing numbers of travelers eager to hike the surrounding trails. By contrast, in winter (May to September), many of El Chaltén's tourist-oriented business shut down for the season, and transport connections are significantly reduced.

Ice Field Encounters

EXPLORING THE PERITO MORENO GLACIER

Nothing prepares you for your first glimpse of the awe-inspiring **Glaciar Perito Moreno**. At 250 sq km, this immense tongue of blue-white ice is bigger than Buenos Aires and gradually creeps forward into Lago Argentino, the largest body of water in the country. Periodically, large chunks of the glacier calve off and plunge into the lake below to form icebergs. While most of the world's glaciers are receding, Perito Moreno is currently considered to be stable.

It is the centerpiece of the southern section of the majestic **Parque Nacional Los Glaciares**, a 7300-sq-km Unesco World Heritage Site that encompasses one of the world's largest and most accessible ice fields. The glacier can be viewed from a network of wooden boardwalks or on a boat trip across the iceberg-studded lake. The most exhilarating way to experience it is to strap on a pair of crampons and ice-hike across its groaning surface on an organized tour run by El Calafate-based **Hielo & Aventura**. The trip is perfect for wannabe

---

I LIVE HERE: PUMAS OF PATAGONIA

Ricardo Muza explains a day in his life as a puma tracker for Estancia Cerro Guido's conservation program.

Pumas are perfectly evolved for this landscape – they blend right into it. For sheep farmers, pumas are a threat, but for the ecosystems, they are a positive influence on wildlife diversity. They also mean opportunities for tourism. A typical day starts before dawn. I visit the base of the Condoreras ridge and then the top. If we find a puma, we stay, observe and take notes, especially if we find an active kill site. It is a long day, especially in the summer, but it's a beautiful, quiet, peaceful place to work. It's just you and nature.

 WHERE TO EAT IN EL CALAFATE & EL CHALTÉN

Pura Vida
Vegetarians are well catered for at this homely restaurant on El Calafate's main street. **$$**

Domo Blanco
El Chaltén ice cream parlor that also has a selection of savory snacks and lunches. **$**

Don Pichon
For expertly cooked beef and Patagonian lamb, try this classic Argentine *parrilla* (steakhouse) in El Calafate. **$$$**

OLEG SENKOV/SHUTTERSTOCK ©

Glaciar Perito Moreno

BEST TOUR OPERATORS IN PARQUE NACIONAL LOS GLACIARS

Hielo y Aventura
Ice-hikes across the Glaciar Perito Moreno, catamaran cruises, and boat and walking tours.

Glaciar Sur
Offers a day trip featuring a visit to Estancia Nibepo Aike and glacier-viewing from a less-touristed area of the park.

Fitz Roy Expediciones
Treks in the park's northern section, climbing expeditions and half-day kayaking excursions.

Walk Patagonia
Guided hikes in and around the park's northern section.

Chaltén Mountain Guides
Extensive trekking, mountaineering and skiing expeditions, plus climbing courses.

polar explorers, and you spend up to three hours on the glacier, visiting its caves, fissures and sapphire pools of meltwater.

If the ice-hike whets your appetite, head over to El Chaltén, the gateway to the park's northern section, which is dominated by the shark-toothed Fitz Roy range. Mesmerizing mountain scenery and a network of world-class trails have made this area the trekking capital of Argentina, while Cerro Torre and Cerro Fitz Roy attract mountaineers from around the world eager to test their mettle on their notorious ascents.

GETTING AROUND

Buses travel regularly between Puerto Natales and El Calafate; El Calafate and El Chaltén; and El Calafate and the southern section of Parque Nacional Los Glaciares. Services are much reduced in the winter. Driving a Chilean rental car across the border is an expensive endeavor because of international insurance. If you need a car in Argentina, rent one in El Calafate.

It's possible to get between El Chaltén and the Chilean settlement of Villa O'Higgins on an adventurous, if convoluted, one- to three-day journey. Possible only between November and April, it involves trekking or horse riding, boat or ferry crossings, and a bus. El Chaltén's Rancho Grande hostel can help with information and logistics.

PUERTO WILLIAMS

Looking out onto the Beagle Channel and backed by the Dientes de Navarino range, Puerto Williams is the most southerly city on Earth. Antarctica lies less than 1000km to the south, while Santiago is more than 2400km north. Located on Isla Navarino in Tierra del Fuego and home to around 2000 people, Puerto Williams was upgraded to city status by the Chilean authorities in 2019, but it looks and feels like a small town. It was founded in 1953 as a naval base in an area inhabited by the indigenous Yagán for thousands of years.

Today, Puerto Williams is developing fast. New infrastructure, notably a large modern dock, is being built, and growing numbers of Antarctic cruise ships call in. For travelers, it offers stunning scenery, a superb hiking base and, above all, the unrivaled sensation of being at *el fin del mundo* – the end of the world.

Santiago

Puerto Williams

TOP TIP

Puerto Williams has no road connections with the rest of Chile. You have to fly or take the ferry from Punta Arenas. Inclement weather can cause delays, so allow some leeway in your itinerary. At the time of writing, boat services between Puerto Williams and Ushuaia, Argentina, were suspended but should restart soon.

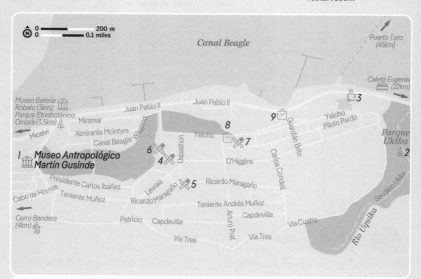

HIGHLIGHTS
1 Museo Antropológico
Martín Gusinde

SIGHTS
2 Parque Ukika

EATING
3 Campero
4 Restaurante Dientes
De Navarino

5 Resto del Sur
6 Resto Express
7 Worus

SHOPPING
8 Comercial Antarctica
9 Jardín Fuegia

PEP ROIG/ALAMY STOCK PHOTO ©

Puerto Williams

Indigenous Insights & Antarctic Exploration

ANTHROPOLOGY MUSEUM AND SHACKLETON EXHIBIT

The modern and well-designed **Museo Antropológico Martín Gusinde** on the western side of Puerto Williams explores the natural and human history of Tierra del Fuego. Artifacts such as harpoons, canoes and a replica shelter provide an insight into the remarkable culture of the Yagán, whose nomadic, canoe-based societies flourished in the southern reaches of Tierra del Fuego for thousands of years despite an incredibly challenging environment.

The museum also covers the impact of the arrival of Europeans on the region. Just across from the main entrance is Casa Stirling, a prefab building that was brought to Tierra del Fuego from the UK in 1869. It was used by British Anglican missionaries, who were soon followed by waves of sheep ranchers and gold miners, a process that devastated the Yagán

YAGÁN COMMUNITY OF VILLA UKIKA

On the eastern outskirts of Puerto Williams, a 1km walk from the center, **Villa Ukika** is a small Yagán community. Founded in the 1960s, it is home to a traditional-style timber building known as the Kipa Akar ('House of the Women' in the Yagán language) in which handicrafts are sometimes for sale. The hamlet sits alongside **Parque Ukika**, a park with a forest trail that runs along the bank of the Río Ukika, with various spots for picnics. Keep an eye out for the bulbous clumps of the *Cyttaria hariotii* on the trees. These orange, golf-ball-shaped mushrooms, commonly known as *pan de indio* ('Indian bread'), were traditionally eaten by indigenous peoples across Patagonia and Tierra del Fuego.

 WHERE TO STAY IN PUERTO WILLIAMS

Hotel Fio Fio
Excellent midranger with knowledgeable staff, top breakfasts and cozy rooms with thick Berber carpets. **$$**

Hostal Pusaki
Long-running guesthouse with simple, good-value rooms (some of which are en suite) and home-cooked meals. **$**

Lakutaia Lodge
Smart, modern lodge 2km outside of town, with attractive rooms, a restaurant, tours and activities. **$$$**

SAFELY TREKKING THE DIENTES DE NAVARINO CIRCUIT

Apart from the initial Cerro Bandera leg, Dientes de Navarino Circuit trail markings are minimal, and conditions can be treacherous. It is advisable to go with a guide (check their level of experience, first-aid certification and language skills before setting off). Use a GPS device in conjunction with maps, take a VHF radio and register with the police in advance. Make a plan B in the case of bad weather because you might need to postpone, take extra time or alter your route. The trek is best attempted in the summer season (January to March). Winter treks are suitable for experienced mountaineers only. The tourist office (visitacabodehornos.cl) can provide more information and recommend guides.

View of the *dientes* along the Dientes de Navarino Circuit

and other indigenous communities such as the Selk'nam, who inhabited the northern parts of Tierra del Fuego. Many died of diseases such as measles and smallpox that were brought over by the settlers. Others were displaced from their ancestral lands or killed by bounty hunters working for ranchers.

The museum also has a collection of evocative black and white photos of Tierra del Fuego and displays on the flora and fauna found in the region.

After your visit, head back into the center of Puerto Williams to learn about one of the most famous events from the 'heroic age' of Antarctic exploration in the late 19th and early 20th centuries. Outside the naval quarters, you will find a replica of the prow of the **Yelcho**, the ship that was used

 WHERE TO STAY IN PUERTO WILLIAMS

Errante Ecolodge
Sleek, sustainability focused option in a tranquil location near the end of the Dientes de Navarino trek. **$$**

Refugio El Padrino
Sociable hostel on the waterfront with clean and compact dorms, plus a nearby camping area. **$**

Hostal Akainij
A handful of spick and span en-suite rooms in a welcoming family home. **$$**

to rescue polar explorer Ernest Shackleton's stranded *Endurance* crew from Elephant Island in 1916, as well as display boards that provide some background on the story. The original prow, incidentally, is now on display on the waterfront in Punta Arenas.

Summiting Cerro Bandera & Beyond

END-OF-THE-WORLD HIKES

For sensational views of the Beagle Channel and the Dientes de Navarino, follow a well-marked forest trail up to the stony, windswept summit of **Cerro Bandera** (610m). A fluttering Chilean flag appears to mark the top, but if you continue to ascend for a further 45 minutes to one hour following a series of cairns, you are rewarded with even more sublime vistas of the Dientes as well as the channel.

The 12km hike can be done independently without a guide. It takes approximately four to five hours round-trip and starts at the Plaza de la Virgen altar, a 1km walk west of Puerto Williams along Vía Uno. From here, a track leads to a dam with a visitor information center before heading uphill to the summit, which can be very cold, windy and often wet. Make sure that you wear appropriate gear and take drinking water and snacks.

The hike up Cerro Bandera is the first stage of the **Dientes de Navarino Circuit**, a testing 53km trail that winds through the spectacular Fuegian wilderness. Taking four to five days in total, the route features a series of glorious lakes and truly awesome views of the appropriately fang-like peaks of the *dientes* (teeth). The number of people hiking the circuit has increased in recent years, but it is not suitable for casual walkers. You need far greater navigational skills and backcountry experience than for treks in Parque Nacional Torres del Paine, for example. Out here, you are basically on your own.

The rewarding 41km trek to the remote and little-visited **Lago Windhond** is a good alternative to the more popular Dientes de Navarino Circuit, particularly if conditions are too windy to attempt the latter. Lasting three to four days and following a relatively sheltered route, the trek takes you through a wild landscape of forests, peat bogs and mountains. The icy, crystal-clear lake is also popular with anglers, who come to fish for brown and rainbow trout. For information, guided tours and fishing trips, get in touch with **Turismo Shila** (turismoshila.cl).

WHERE TO EAT IN PUERTO WILLIAMS

Resto Express
Nautical decor and a wide-ranging menu of fried fish, schnitzels, pastas, burritos and stir fries. $$

Campero
Delightful bakery-cafe serving focaccia, mini pizzas, cinnamon rolls, doughnuts and coffee. $

Restaurante Dientes De Navarino
Colombian-run restaurant with tasty dishes, including *bandeja paisa* (a combo of beans, rice, plantain, eggs and meat). $$

Resto del Sur
This friendly restaurant is a good spot for beer and pizza. $$

Worus
Burgers, sandwiches (including king crab) and sharing platters, plus karaoke nights. $$

 BEST TOUR OPERATORS IN PUERTO WILLIAMS

Turismo Shila
Guided treks, fishing trips, and gear and bike rental.

Explora Isla Navarino
Trekking, mountain biking, kayaking, stand-up paddleboarding and more.

Serendipia
Sailing trips to Puerto Toro, Cabo de Hornos and Parque Nacional Alberto de Agostini.

'Miniature Forests' & Military Sites

NATURE TRAILS AND HISTORIC RELICS

Parque Etnobotánico Omora is a nature reserve, scientific research center and conservation project that seeks to educate people about the flora and fauna of Tierra del Fuego. It is open for nature tours led by specialist guides, which are available via advance reservations only (omora.org).

Taking its name from the Yagán word for hummingbird, Omora has a network of walking trails (which each take 1½ to three hours to complete) through pristine forests and boglands. Plants and trees are labeled with their Spanish, Yagán and Latin names. The park is known in particular for its incredible array of moss, lichen and fungi species. These tiny organisms blanket the tree trunks and branches, forming 'miniature forests' that are best observed with the aid of a magnifying glass. The park is around 3km west of Puerto Williams along the Y-905 road.

Meanwhile, close to the turnoff for Parque Etnobotánico Omora is the **Museo Batería Róbalo**, a small open-air museum with military vehicles, weapons and equipment from the 1978–83 border dispute between Chile and Argentina over the islands of Picton, Lennox and Nueva. Just beyond the site, a turning to the north leads to **Península Zañartu**, where you will find a lake and sweeping views.

Road's End & Beyond

VISITING CALETA EUGENIA AND PUERTO TORO

If Puerto Williams isn't far south enough for you, you can visit two even further-flung settlements. Some 25km east of the city along the coastal Y-905 road, which is dotted with Yagán archaeological sites, **Caleta Eugenia** is the most southerly point you can drive to on Earth. On the edge of a bay facing the Beagle Channel and sometimes frequented by boats catching *centolla* (king crab), the *estancia* (ranch) is owned by the Chilean Navy and maintained by a father and son. A couple of weekly minibuses run between Puerto Williams and Caleta Eugenia if you fancy taking a quick look. Ask at the tourist office for details on the schedule. Tour operators such as Explora Isla Navarino also offer half-day tours.

Puerto Toro, the most southerly village on Earth, is even more isolated. Founded in 1892, it is located on the eastern shore of Isla Navarino and reachable only by boat. Puerto Toro is permanently home to around a dozen people, plus a few naval personnel, but the population jumps during the

Puerto Toro

 BEST TOUR OPERATORS IN PUERTO WILLIAMS

Parque Etnobotánico Omora
Guided walks around the nature park.

Denis Chevallay
Multilingual guide offering day hikes, bird-watching and city tours. Contact by email (denischevallay@gmail.com).

Tourist office
Staff can put you in touch with local guides, including ones focusing on Yagán culture.

GEERT SMEY/SHUTTERSTOCK ©

Fishing nets, Isla Navarino

WHY I LOVE PUERTO WILLIAMS

Shafik Meghji, writer

Like most visitors, I was initially drawn to Puerto Williams by its isolated location at the southern tip of the Americas and stunning setting on the Beagle Channel in the shadow of the Dientes de Navarino range. But I quickly came to appreciate the incredible warmth of the local community, as well as the city's role as a gateway to some of the world's most dramatic landscapes. From the summit of nearby Cerro Bandera, the vast, seemingly untouched wilderness of Tierra del Fuego stretches away into the distance. It feels as if you have it all to yourself.

centolla-catching season. There are no road connections to the rest of Isla Navarino – though plans to build one have been mooted in the past – but a free ferry runs between Puerto Williams and Puerto Toro on the last Sunday of every month (three hours each way, with an hour in Puerto Toro; reserve your place in advance at the tourist office). **Serendipia** also has a sailing trip that calls in at the village.

Puerto Toro has no tourist facilities, and other than a short walk around the village, there is not much to do. The key reason to visit is simply to get a taste of what life is like at the very end of the world.

GETTING AROUND

Puerto Williams is small enough to explore on foot. Rental bikes – available from Turismo Shila and other places – are useful for reaching some of the outlying attractions such as Parque Etnobotánico Omora, Museo Batería Róbalo and Península Zañartu. Weekly minibuses travel to Caleta Eugenia, and a monthly ferry goes to Puerto Toro. Check the schedules for both at the tourist office. The airport, which has regular flights to and from Punta Arenas, is around 3km northwest of Puerto Williams by road. Accommodation rates generally include free airport pick-up and drop-off. Ferries to and from Punta Arenas use the main dock, and an upgraded version is being built.

Beyond Puerto Williams

Parque Nacional
Alberto de
Agostini
Tren del Fin
del Mundo Ushuaia
Parque Nacional
Tierra del Fuego
Puerto
Williams

Cabo de
Hornos

If you want to get away from it all, there are few better places than Tierra del Fuego (Land of Fire).

Exploring the southern part of Tierra del Fuego takes time, flexibility with regards to itineraries and – especially for the most isolated areas – a fair amount of expense, but the rewards are immense. Once the realm of indigenous people such as the Yagán and Selk'nam, whose fires inspired its evocative modern name, this tangle of largely uninhabited islands is an expanse of ragged mountain ranges and wind-whipped forests, serpentine coastlines and crystalline lakes, as well as a scattering of isolated settlements and hardscrabble ranches.

Few travelers make it out to Cabo de Hornos or Parque Nacional Alberto de Agostini in Chilean Tierra del Fuego, but the Argentine section of the archipelago is surprisingly touristy.

TOP TIP

While some notable Tierra del Fuego attractions can be visited from Puerto Williams, others require traveling via Punta Arenas.

Pia Glacier, Parque Nacional Alberto de Agostini

LEONARD ZHUKOVSKY/SHUTTERSTOCK ©

ALEXANDRE G. ROSA/SHUTTERSTOCK ©

Cabo de Hornos

Rounding the Horn

REACHING CABO DE HORNOS

The farthest-flung headland on Isla Hornos and reaching out into the notoriously rough Drake Passage, **Cabo de Hornos** (Cape Horn) is a place that evokes tales of seafaring adventure and disaster – more than 700 shipwrecks have been recorded in the area. The meeting point for the Pacific and Atlantic oceans, it is covered in peat bogs and sub-Antarctic forests and is rich in marine birds, including albatrosses, southern giant petrels and Magellanic penguins. **Explore Isla Navarino** and **Serendipia** can organize sailing trips, and many Antarctic and Beagle Channel cruises pass by. Sightseeing flights are another option to visit this isolated outpost.

Pristine Glaciers, Forests & Fjords

VISITING PARQUE NACIONAL ALBERTO DE AGOSTINI

In the western reaches of Chilean Tierra del Fuego, **Parque Nacional Alberto de Agostini** is a virtually untouched landscape. Home to the striking 34km-long Cordillera Darwin, a succession of thickly forested hillsides and plunging fjords, and a constellation of giant glaciers, as well as numerous wildlife species, including elephant seals, it is the third-largest national park in the country, spanning more than 14,600 sq km.

LEAVE IT TO BEAVERS

As you explore Tierra del Fuego's forests, you will find yourself periodically coming across patches of devastation: tangles of broken branches and denuded trunks. It looks as if these areas have been struck by a hurricane, but it is actually the work of *castores* (beavers). In an attempt to develop a fur trade in the 1940s, the Argentine authorities recklessly introduced 20 Canadian beavers to the archipelago. The industry didn't take off and the beavers, free of natural predators, reproduced and spread rapidly. In the process, they have damaged a quarter of Tierra del Fuego's forests. Eradication efforts have proved ineffectual, and there are now thought to be around 200,000 of the animals.

WHERE TO STAY IN & AROUND USHUAIA

Estancia Harberton
This historic Anglo-Argentine ranch has great food and atmospheric accommodations in a variety of cottages. **$$**

Antarctica Hostel
Backpacker favorite in the heart of Ushuaia with a welcoming vibe and clean rooms and dorms. **$**

Tierra de Leyendas
Charming boutique hotel southwest of central Ushuaia, with top views and a superb restaurant. **$$**

Train to Ushuaia

WHERE TO EAT & DRINK IN USHUAIA

Kalma Resto
Sophisticated restaurant with a seasonally changing menu that takes a creative approach. $$$

Ramos Generales
Atmospheric bakery-restaurant-bar with house-baked goodies, tasty sandwiches and classic Argentine meals. $

Freddo
An outpost of the famous Argentine ice cream chain; try the dulce de leche flavors. $

Kaupé
Long-established restaurant renowned for fish and seafood dishes such as *centolla* (king crab) crêpes. $$

María Lola Restó
A winning combination of superb views and top-notch fish, seafood, meat and pasta options. $$

Getting to Alberto de Agostini is something of a challenge. There is no access by road or trails, but luxury **Australis** cruises between Punta Arenas and Ushuaia provide short excursions into the park. **Serendipia** runs sailing trips along the park's coastline from Puerto Williams. **Transbordadora Austral Broom** ferries traveling between Punta Arenas and Puerto Williams also provide glimpses of it.

Exploring Argentine Tierra del Fuego
BUSY PORTS, NATIONAL PARKS AND HISTORIC ESTANCIAS

The **Argentine section of Tierra del Fuego** attracts considerably more travelers than its Chilean counterpart. The hub of the region is **Ushuaia**, a touristy city that sits below the snowy Martial range on the north shore of the Beagle Channel. Thanks largely to the busy port – the embarkation point for the majority of Antarctic cruises from South America – the city has countless hotels, hostels, restaurants, shops and tour operators, plus some excellent museums that introduce you to the region's turbulent history.

Housed inside a former prison, the **Museo Marítimo** and **Museo del Presidio** vividly explore the region's maritime history and the city's origins as a penal colony, respectively. Wandering through the old cells, which have display panels telling the stories of noted inmates, is a haunting experience. **Museo del Fin del Mundo** has a mix of natural history exhibits, photos of the early days of the city and displays on the region's indigenous people, who paid a heavy price for the colonization of Tierra del Fuego.

Ushuaia is a good base for exploring the rest of Argentine Tierra del Fuego. Several tour operators offer **boat trips** along

 WHERE TO STAY IN & AROUND USHUAIA

La Posta
Good-value, well-equipped apartments with kitchenettes are on offer at this reliable Ushuaia option. $$

Arakur
High above Ushuaia, this five-star delivers the goods; highlights include the heated indoor-outdoor infinity pool. $$$

Posada Fin del Mundo
Characterful Ushuaia B&B with distinctive rooms (the best are upstairs) and a cozy lounge. $$

the Beagle Channel, visiting lighthouses, sea lion colonies and small islands with ancient Yagán middens (heaps of discarded mollusk shells). In the winter, you can ski and snowboard at resorts such as **Cerro Castor**, easily accessible from Ushuaia.

Around 85km east of the city, **Estancia Harberton** is the oldest ranch in Tierra del Fuego, founded in 1886 by missionary Thomas Bridges (who produced the first Yagán-English dictionary) and his family. It offers guided history-focused tours, a marine-life museum and a great restaurant, as well as trips to an island colony of Magellanic and gentoo penguins.

Hiking, Bird-Watching & Train Rides

EXPLORING PARQUE NACIONAL TIERRA DEL FUEGO

A realm of sub-Antarctic forests, lakes, bogs and bays, **Parque Nacional Tierra del Fuego** is a wonderful place for hiking and bird-watching. The park has 40km of well-marked trails, with plenty of short options that can be completed in less than an hour. Longer trails include the testing hike up to the 970m summit of Cerro Guanaco, which offers excellent views; the more relaxed Costera trail, which hugs the coastline; and the Pampa Alta route, which heads through patches of forest to the Río Pipo. Keep your eyes peeled for birds such as condors, orange-billed steamer ducks, oystercatchers, kelp geese and Magellanic woodpeckers. Most people visit for the day, but if you want to stay overnight, there are several campsites.

Minibuses run regularly to the park from the center of Ushuaia, or you can catch a ride on the **Tren del Fin del Mundo** (End of the World Train), the world's southernmost railway. It was built in the first decade of the 20th century by inmates of Ushuaia's prison – whose fearsome reputation earned it the nickname the 'Siberia of the south' – to transport timber. Today, it is a touristy but fun experience.

Next Stop: Antarctica

CRUISES TO THE WHITE CONTINENT

If Tierra del Fuego isn't far enough south for you, **Antarctica** is only 1000km away across the Drake Passage. Most cruises depart from Ushuaia, though some companies use Punta Arenas or Puerto Williams instead. Regular voyages travel between November and March and generally last one to three weeks. Longer itineraries often visit the Falkland Islands and South Georgia too. Cruises are expensive, but last-minute deals are sometimes available, especially in Ushuaia toward the end of the season.

GETTING TO ARGENTINE TIERRA DEL FUEGO

From Punta Arenas, buses go regularly to Ushuaia via the Punta Delgada ferry crossing and the city of Río Grande. There are also buses from Río Gallegos and El Calafate in Argentine Patagonia and regular flights from Buenos Aires.

If you've rented a car in Argentine Patagonia, you will have to drive through Chile to reach Argentine Tierra del Fuego, which requires special documents and extra international insurance coverage. Most car rental companies can arrange this for you.

Boat services between Ushuaia and Puerto Williams were suspended at the time of research, but are due to restart in the future. Multiday cruises also run from Punta Arenas to Ushuaia.

GETTING AROUND

Traveling across southern Tierra del Fuego can be challenging, time-consuming and costly. Visiting Cabo de Hornos requires a boat trip or sightseeing flight, while Parque Nacional Alberto de Agostini is accessible only by cruise or ferry. There are no direct connections between Puerto Williams and the Argentine section of Tierra del Fuego, so traveling between the two is relatively convoluted.

RAPA NUI

POLYNESIA'S LEGENDARY OPEN-AIR MUSEUM

The unsolved mysteries of the *moai* lure travelers to Rapa Nui, but it's the endless ocean, stellar seafood and strong Polynesian culture that make the trip unforgettable.

Nothing can fully prepare you for your first encounter with the enigmatic *moai*. These improbably placed megalithic statues – representations of Polynesian ancestors – line the entire coastline of Rapa Nui (Easter Island), looking inward over its 8500 modern-day inhabitants. What inspired their creation? How did they get to their distant *ahu* (ceremonial platforms)? Why were they all toppled to the ground by the 19th century? We may never know the answers to Rapa Nui's biggest mysteries, but that's what makes it such an alluring destination for thinkers and dreamers.

The astounding isolation is another draw. Rapa Nui is one of the most remote inhab-ited places on Earth. Its nearest neighbor, the Pitcairn Islands, is 2080km to the west. You have to travel 3700km east to hit mainland Chile, the closest point on a continent. The horizon is so empty that you can see the curvature of Earth. Meanwhile, the Pacific Ocean is so alive that chefs plate fresh-caught tuna and mahi-mahi so exquisite it's often served raw.

Be warned: Rapa Nui is not the Polynesia of popular imagination. The island has only one major beach (Anakena), and palm trees are few. At times, the landscape looks more like Ireland than Tahiti. Yet the barren slopes of its dormant volcanoes are a hiker's nirvana, and the town of Hanga Roa is getting greener every year.

THE MAIN AREAS

HANGA ROA
The heart of the island.
p334

PARQUE NACIONAL RAPA NUI
Beaches, volcanoes and *moai*.
p341

Left and above: Ahu Tongariki *moai* **(p342)**

Cabo
Norte

△ Maunga
Terevaka

Motu
Hepo

Cer
P

Hanga Roa, p334

The only town on the island is where you'll find nearly all of Rapa Nui's hotels, restaurants, shops and cultural institutions.

Museo
Rapa Nui

Ahu Tahai

Caleta
Hanga Roa

Ahu
Tautira

Hanga
Roa

Maunga
Orito

Rano Kau

Motu
Kao Kao
Motu Iti

Motu
Nui

CAR

A car is the easiest and most comfortable way to get around Rapa Nui, especially if you stay at a hotel in Hanga Roa but want to spend plenty of time at the beach in Anakena. Find rental agencies along Atamu Tekena street.

Find Your Way

Rapa Nui is an incredibly small island, just 25km from end to end, in the middle of the world's largest ocean. Nearly all of its infrastructure lies in its one town, Hanga Roa.

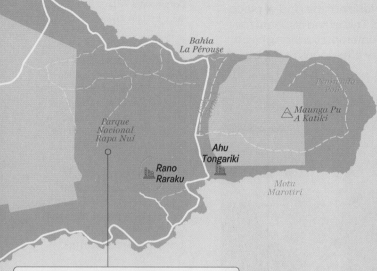

Bahía La Pérouse

Península Poike

△ *Maunga Pu A Katiki*

Parque Nacional Rapa Nui

Ahu Tongariki

Rano Raraku

Motu Marotiri

P A C I F I C O C E A N

Parque Nacional Rapa Nui, p341

This national park covers much of the island and contains its archaeological treasures, including a quarry home to hundreds of monolithic human figures.

BICYCLE

Active travelers enjoy cycling around Rapa Nui because the weather is usually pleasant and the interior hills aren't too steep. The road along the south coast, while in poorer condition, is flatter and more scenic than the central thoroughfare.

TOUR

Because of rules implemented in 2022 that require a certified guide at most archaeological sites beyond Hanga Roa, many visitors travel around the island on a private or group tour. Higher-end hotels sometimes include guides and transfers as part of their packages.

Plan Your Time

Rapa Nui is not the kind of place to rush. This island is meant for slow contemplation, long hikes and lazy afternoons at the beach.

THOMAS LUSTH/SHUTTERSTOCK ©

View from the rim of Rano Kau (p339)

Three Days to Travel Around

● Three days is the absolute minimum to see Rapa Nui's highlights. Start at **Orongo Ceremonial Village** (p339) to delve into the mysterious birdman cult.

● On day two, travel back to the time of *moai* building, visiting the quarry of **Rano Raraku** (p342) and the magnificent **Ahu Tongariki** (p342), with its 15 monolithic stone statues. Finish with a dip at the beach in **Anakena** (p342).

● Dedicate your final day to exploring **Hanga Roa** (p334), getting context for everything you've seen at **Museo Rapa Nui** (p336). Cap off your trip with a dance show at **Kari Kari** (p334).

Seasonal Highlights

Summer (January to March) is high season on subtropical Rapa Nui, making the shoulder seasons of April to June and October to December the most appealing times to visit.

JANUARY

High season kicks into full gear with warm waters for **snorkeling and swimming** at Anakena.

FEBRUARY

Visitors plan entire trips around the two-week-long **Tapati Rapa Nui** festival, the island's biggest event with music and cultural competitions.

APRIL

Local artists and craftspeople display their wares at the annual **Arts and Culture Week** in Hanga Roa.

JHVEPHOTO/SHUTTERSTOCK ©, JHVEPHOTO/SHUTTERSTOCK © , ALEXANDRALAW1977/SHUTTERSTOCK ©

Rapa Nui in Five Days

● Add on a snorkeling trip, either in the open ocean at **Motu Nui** (p339) or off the beach at **Ovahe** (p343). Afterward, tackle the moderate hike up **Terevaka** (p342), the island's highest point, to survey the land and the empty horizon beyond. Hikes typically begin and end at **Ahu Akivi** (p340), an atypical inland platform whose seven *moai* look toward the sea.

● Travel to the source of the red topknots adorning many *moai* on a visit to the quarry at **Puna Pau** (p340).

● Spend your final evening watching the sunset behind **Ahu Tahai** (p336) in Hanga Roa, which is surrounded by stellar seafood restaurants.

If You Have More Time

● Extend your trip on the island's best hikes, such as the remote **North Coast** (p339), which is full of archaeological sites most visitors never see.

● The little-visited peninsula of **Poike** (p342) has several oddly placed *moai,* as well as the island's best photo op looking south over Ahu Tongariki from above.

● Tour the 'B-side' archaeological sites along the south coast, including **Ahu Hanga Te'e** (p340), which has an interpretation center. These off-the-beaten-path platforms with toppled *moai* give you an idea of how the island looked before the statues were restored to their platforms beginning in the 1950s.

JUNE
Runners from around the globe converge for the most remote marathon in the world: **Maraton Rapa Nui**.

JULY
Islanders gather en masse at Anakena to commemorate the arrival of the first settler **Hotu Matu'a**.

SEPTEMBER
Mild temperatures for hiking combined with Polynesian-infused **Fiestas Patrias** (national holidays) celebrations make this an alluring off-season month.

NOVEMBER
Local schools celebrate **Mahana O Te Re'o** (Day of Our Language) with recitals, art shows and documentaries.

HANGA ROA

● Hanga Roa

✪ Santiago

Hanga Roa is Rapa Nui's de facto capital – and only real town – but it's as laid-back as a place can be. Tourism is the main industry, and yet it never feels overly touristy in the way many Polynesian hubs do. The main drag, Atamu Tekena, has a small collection of shops, hotels and cafes interspersed between flowering hibiscus and bougainvillea. Along the coast, kids play in protected swimming coves, surfers ride gentle waves and athletes battle it out on the soccer field under the watchful eyes of distant *moai*.

Meanwhile, scuba divers set off in small boats from the harbor, passing a row of seafood restaurants on their way to distant dive sites. When the sun finally plunges into the Pacific, the grass skirts come out, and performers take to stages across Hanga Roa to share Polynesian legends through song and dance.

TOP TIP

Rapa Nui is the most expensive destination in Chile. Flight tickets often allow you to bring two large suitcases, meaning you can pack a few bottles of Chilean wine, pisco and some groceries from the mainland to cut down on expensive on-island purchases.

Boat, Hanga Roa

TERO HAKALA/SHUTTERSTOCK ©

BEST LIVE MUSIC & DANCING

Kari Kari
Rapa Nui's longest-operating song and dance troupe, Kari Kari is so highly regarded that it's toured the world. The elaborately costumed and talented group revives traditional war dances, ancestral songs and island legends.

Te Ra'ai
Beyond the music and dancing, Te Ra'ai offers a traditional (if highly theatrical) umu ceremony, where fish and meats are cooked in the ground with hot stones.

Iti Lafken
For something less touristy, commune with island residents at this live music venue where local artists regularly perform.

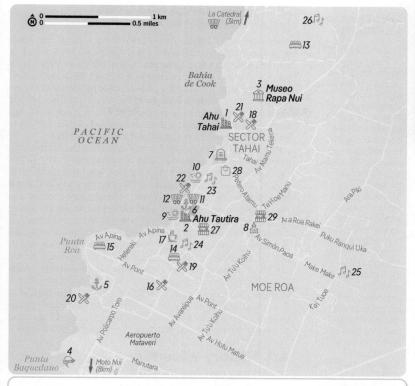

La Catedral (3km)

Bahía de Cook

Museo Rapa Nui **3**

21 **1** **18**

Ahu Tahai

PACIFIC OCEAN

SECTOR TAHAI

7

10 **28**

22 **23**

12 **11**

9 **6** Ahu Tautira

2 **27**

29

8

17 **24**

15 **14**

5 **19**

20 **16**

25

MOE ROA

Punta Roa

Av Apina Av Apina

Hetereki

Av Pont

Petero Atamu

Av Atamu Tekena

Tahai

Te Hoe Manu

N a Roa Rakei

Av Simón Paoa

Av Tuu Koihu

Av Pont

Av Avareipua

Av Tuu Koihu

Av Hotu Matua

Av Policarpo Toro

Aeropuerto Mataveri

Manutara

Punta Baquedano

4

Moto Nui (8km)

Ara Piki

Puku Ranqui Uka

Make Make

Kai Tuoe

26

13

HIGHLIGHTS
1 Ahu Tahai
2 Ahu Tautira
3 Museo Rapa Nui

SIGHTS
4 Ana Kai Tangata
5 Caleta Hanga Piko
6 Caleta Hanga Roa
7 Catholic Cemetery
8 Iglesia de Santa Cruz
9 Playa Pea
10 Playa Poko Poko

ACTIVITIES, COURSES & TOURS
11 Mike Rapu Diving Center
12 Orca Diving Center

SLEEPING
13 Altiplanico Rapa Nui
14 Hare Nua Hotel Boutique
15 Nayara Hangaroa

EATING
16 Aloha Food Trucks
17 Polynesian Coffee & Tea
18 Puka Puka
19 Taina Beer Garden
20 Tataku Vave
21 Te Moai Sunset
22 Te Moana

ENTERTAINMENT
23 Iti Lafken
24 Kari Kari
25 Te Ra'ai
26 Toki

SHOPPING
27 Feria Artesanal
28 Mana Gallery
29 Mercado Artesanal

 WHERE TO STAY IN HANGA ROA

Hare Nua Hotel Boutique
Downtown's smartest property with a lush interior patio and Instagram-worthy aesthetic. **$$$**

Altiplanico Rapa Nui
This midranger offers striking ovular bungalows (with outdoor showers!) strewn along a verdant Pacific-facing hill. **$$**

Nayara Hangaroa
This playful all-inclusive seafront resort with an Orongo theme is Hanga Roa's most luxurious. **$$$**

A MORE SUSTAINABLE FUTURE

Rapa Nui shut itself off from the world for 2½ years during the coronavirus pandemic. No commercial flights from mainland Chile also meant few imported supplies. Instead, islanders returned to ancestral principles like *umanga*, growing their own food and sharing it freely with neighbors. Residents created a whopping 1300 family gardens in a push for greater food sovereignty, making it possible to now eat 100% locally sourced meals. Meanwhile, out-of-work guides planted trees and cleaned 10 tons of trash from both the seabed and coastline. When Rapa Nui reopened in August 2022, it was lusher and more sustainable than ever.

Moai kavakava

NURPHOTO SRL/ALAMY STOCK PHOTO ©

Along the Hanga Roa Coast

SWIMMING AND STROLLING PAST *MOAI*

The coastline of Hanga Roa is perfect for a stroll, but don't forget your bathing suit. Take a taxi to the southern outskirts and begin at **Ana Kai Tangata**, a seafront cavern with rock paintings depicting curvy anthropomorphic birdman motifs. Heading north, you'll find a path leading to a natural swimming pool and **Caleta Hanga Piko**, a small fishing harbor used for outrigger canoe racing. For lunch, grab a bite up above at **Tataku Vave**, a dreamy seafood restaurant overlooking the ocean that's remained a hidden secret.

Playa Pea, the town's de facto beach, is on the far side of a small but scenic peninsula. Take a cooling dip in the swimming cove protected by a rock barrier from the small crescent of introduced sand. Just a stone's throw away is **Caleta Hanga Roa**, the town's main port, where many dive companies have their storefronts. Visitors often encounter their first *moai* here at **Ahu Tautira**, which lies in front of the harbor.

Continue north along the coast past a lovely children's playground to another swimming cove, **Playa Poko Poko**, which is also a popular picnic location that's dotted with public art. Nearby is the island's main **Catholic Cemetery**, which is notable for its religious syncretism. Some tombstones, for example, have *moai* statues holding crosses. **Ahu Tahai** is the climax and most striking feature along this coast. Try to time your arrival with sunset when low rays of gold turn the five *moai* on the central platform into glowing silhouettes.

Art, History & Identity

DISCOVERING POLYNESIAN CULTURE

Museo Rapa Nui is a necessary stop to get a sense of Rapa Nui culture and history. Nowhere else on the island can you learn about the mysterious rongorongo tablets, only 23 of which exist (all in foreign museums and private collections; Rapa Nui is, incomprehensibly, left with replicas). These tablets display an intricate system of glyphs that, to this day, no one has been able to decipher. The museum also showcases skeletal *moai* kavakava carvings, basalt tools, funerary cists, petroglyphs and even a repatriated *moai*.

For modern art and artifacts, head to **Mana Gallery**, where you'll find unique pieces from the island's top painters and craftspeople. The two traditional craft markets, **Feria Artesanal** and **Mercado Artesanal**, are more of a mixed bag with genuine carvings and jewelry alongside trinkets made in China. The latter lies across the street from **Iglesia de la Santa Cruz**, a Catholic church well worth a peek for

 WHERE TO FIND CHEAP EATS IN HANGA ROA

Aloha Food Trucks
Shaded food truck patio with sushi, burgers and creative empanadas, including one filled with ceviche. **$**

Taina Beer Garden
Sometimes you just need the comforts of pizza and craft beer; this place makes both. **$**

Polynesian Coffee & Tea
Seafront lattes and omelets at breakfast segue to acai bowls and bountiful sandwiches for lunch. **$**

its spectacular wood carvings, which integrate Christian doctrine with Rapa Nui traditions. Visit on Sunday mornings to hear psalms and songs in the Rapa Nui language. Occasionally, you can catch more Rapa Nui melodies at concerts put on by **Toki**, the island's music school. It lies north of town in a striking Earthship-style structure shaped like a flower and built from upcycled trash.

THE CULT OF THE BIRDMAN

Visit **Orongo Ceremonial Village** (p339) to learn more about the competition that took place at Motu Nui. It was central to the birdman cult, which was the island religion between the *moai* era and Christian era.

Diving & Snorkeling

EXPLORE THE CRYSTALLINE WATERS

Rapa Nui may be best known for what lies above the ocean, but increasingly, scuba diving has become one of its biggest secondary draws. Boats leave from either Caleta Hanga Roa or Caleta Hanga Piko and depart for dive sites like **La Catedral**, an underwater cavern, and **La Pyramide**, a seamount covered in corals. You can also dive down to the **Underwater Moai**, but know that it isn't authentic – it was built for Kevin Costner's 1994 movie *Rapa-Nui* (which sparked the first big boom in tourism here).

While these gin-clear waters, which boast visibility up to 60m, have plenty of pristine coral formations, tropical fish are less prevalent. That said, the sea does contain 142 marine species found nowhere else, including the rare Easter Island butterflyfish, which has a flat body, upturned snout and uninterrupted dorsal fin.

Snorkeling trips invariably depart from Hanga Roa to **Motu Nui**, an islet made famous by the birdman competition at Orongo Ceremonial Village up above. With a bit of luck, you may encounter green or hawksbill sea turtles. If not, you might see them by the boats in the harbor. Snorkeling and diving are possible year-round as water temperatures vary from 20°C in winter to 26°C in summer. Recommended outfits include **Mike Rapu** and **Orca Diving Center**, which have decades of experience safely guiding travelers to the island's top sites.

BEST SEAFOOD RESTAURANTS

Puka Puka
Calm vibes and a small menu. Come for the shrimp *pil pil* (in a white wine and garlic sauce) or the fresh mahi-mahi ceviche. $$

Te Moai Sunset
The Tiradito de Ika – sashimi-style fish in a mango and *aji* pepper coulis – is as wowing as the views over Ahu Tahai. $$

Te Moana
Oozing tiki vibes, this oceanfront staple crafts seafood dishes as flavorful as they are bountiful. The playful Ceviche Te Moana arrives inside a conch shell. $$$

GETTING AROUND

Hanga Roa is a small town, so unless your lodging is in the outskirts, it's unlikely you'll need a car. Taxis are expensive but handy for small trips (to the airport, for example). Many hotels offer bikes, and the weather is generally pleasant for walking, though there are hills. Tickets for activities like evening dance shows often include transport.

● Ahu Maitake Te Moa

● Ahu Akivi

Ana Kakenga
●

Hanga Roa ●   ● Puna Pau

Orongo Ceremonial
● Village

Beyond Hanga Roa

Some of the island's wildest coastlines, most
intriguing historical sites and best preserved
ruins lie just beyond the town limits.

A quick stroll or drive beyond town makes it abundantly
clear that Hanga Roa wasn't always the only hub of activity. To the southwest, the vast ceremonial village of Orongo
is precariously set along the crater rim of Rano Kau, one of
the three principal volcanoes whose ancient eruptions formed
this triangular island. The two are Poike and Terevaka. The
latter looms on the northeastern horizon, cradling most of
the island's agricultural fields along its verdant slopes. Several archaeological sites are within easy reach of Hanga Roa,
but oddly, they get far less foot traffic than the more famous
places in the heart of Parque Nacional Rapa Nui further east.

TOP TIP

Internet and cell service are
poor at the best of times
in downtown Hanga Roa.
Once you leave, expect to
be incommunicado.

Moto Nui islet

CHILE DESCONOCIDO/ALAMY STOCK PHOTO ©

History at Rano Kau & Orongo Ceremonial Village

THE CULT OF THE BIRDMAN

When the era of *moai*-building (1250–1500 CE) came to a close, island resources were depleted, and Rapa Nui devolved into civil war. That's when the *Tangata manu* (birdman) cult arose as a religion that might unite islanders once again. At its heart was a competition that took place each year at the **Orongo Ceremonial Village** atop the **Rano Kau** volcano. Competitors would race down to the coast, swim to the **Motu Nui islet**, retrieve an egg of the migratory sooty tern and try to be the first to return so that their clan could rule Rapa Nui for the coming year.

As you climb up to the crater's rim today, you'll find 54 circular homes with walls made of stone slabs and arched roofs covered in earth. Of the more than 300 petroglyphs recorded on the island, most are here. Down below, the Rano Kau crater resembles a giant witch's cauldron and is a wild greenhouse of endemic biodiversity. The only *moai* found at Orongo, Hoa Hakananai'a, was taken away in 1868 and is still in the British Museum in London (one of roughly a dozen Rapa Nui hopes to repatriate).

Orongo is either a short scenic drive or steep climb from Hanga Roa. Don't miss the little-visited **Ahu Vinapu** on the volcano's backside. It's home to not only a rare female *moai* made of red scoria but also extraordinary Inca-like stonemasonry on the platform, which some archaeologists believe shows contact with ancient Peru.

Hiking the North Coast

WALK ON THE WILD SIDE

The North Coast is Rapa Nui's wildest and least visited corner, stretching for nearly 16km from the outskirts of Hanga Roa to the sandy shores of Anakena. To hike it, follow the road north from Ahu Tahai until it peters out into a path near **Ana Kakenga**, which has two large sea-facing caves. The route north from here is riddled with even more caves, which were used as hideouts during the island's civil war period and European slave raids. Many incorporate stones borrowed from the visible ruins of boat houses (ancient homes that looked like upturned ships).

None of the archaeological sites along the North Coast have been restored because there's no road access. Interestingly, you'll find recycled *moai*, which, for unknown reasons, weren't propped up on platforms, incorporated into the backsides of

I LIVE HERE: RAPA NUI TRAVEL TIPS

Sebastián Paoa, CEO and founder of Kava Kava Tours, shares his advice for visiting Rapa Nui.

Advance tickets
Get tickets for Parque Nacional Rapa Nui in advance (rapanui nationalpark.com), allowing you to avoid delays and make the most of your visit.

Guides
It's mandatory to have an accredited guide to visit the park. They are experts in history, culture and geography.

Rapa Nui nectar
Purchase Rapa Nui honey, which is considered one of the purest and highest quality in the world, produced by bees that pollinate the endemic flowers of the island.

Plastic-free
Bring an aluminum bottle to contribute to the care of the island, save money and support local companies, which offer filtered water charging points.

 WHERE TO SLEEP IN A CABIN

Cabañas Christophe
These four hardwood bungalows at Rano Kau's base are the best deal on the island. **$$**

Hare Swiss
Sunset views over the Pacific are the highlight of these well-managed cabins north of Hanga Roa. **$$**

Pikera Uri
Horse-lovers use these spacious and beautifully decorated cabins to explore the island on the saddle. **$$$**

LESSER-VISITED RUINS

Puna Pau
The rust-colored *pukao* (topknots) were quarried from this site rich in red scoria. Sixty of these stylized 'man buns' were transported to spots around the island.

Ahu Akivi
This *ahu* is located inland from the coast, and its seven *moai* face outward to the Pacific – both unusual features. It was the first scientific restoration on the island in 1960.

Ahu Hanga Te'e
Most visitors stop to look at the interpretive village without realizing an *ahu* with eight toppled *moai* lies just beyond.

Moai

ahus at locations like **Ahu Maitake Te Moa**. You'll also find newer *poe-poe* (ramp-shaped) platforms like **Ahu Atanga**, which were built after European contact in the 18th century to resemble the bow of a ship. After rounding the northern-most point on the island, you'll reach the small fishing cove **Hanga Oteo** before skirting below tall cliffs over to **Anakena** (beware of the guard dogs on the final stretch, where there are some squatter homes).

The North Coast has so many hidden sites that it's best to travel with a guide, or perhaps even on horseback with tour company **Cabalgatas Pantu**. Either way, you'll want to arrange a transfer from Anakena back to Hanga Roa through a taxi tour company in town, allowing yourself plenty of time to cool off at the beach.

GETTING AROUND

Many archaeological sites are within easy walking distance of Hanga Roa. Taxis circle around town, and shops on Atamu Tekena rent bicycles, motorbikes, buggies and SUVs. Beware of cows, horses and stray dogs on the roads.

PARQUE NACIONAL RAPA NUI

Parque Nacional Rapa Nui has nearly all of the archaeological sites that give this small outcrop such an outsized reputation. A Unesco World Heritage Site, it covers much of the island beyond Hanga Roa, including the Rano Raraku *moai* quarry, the Ahu Tongariki ceremonial platform and Anakena beach. Many visitors breeze through the park in about three days, but it has enough hidden ruins and scenic hiking trails to hold your attention for at least a week.

In 2017, Chile handed control of the park over to the Ma'u Henua Indigenous Community, a Rapa Nui–led organization. To see the park's vast archaeological sites, you need to purchase a pass at the Ma'u Henua office by the Feria Artesanal in Hanga Roa. Tickets cost foreigners US$80 and last 10 days, though certain sites, such as Orongo and Rano Raraku, can be visited only once.

TOP TIP

A certified guide is required to visit most archaeological sites beyond Hanga Roa (with the exception of Anakena). The Ma'u Henua office has a list of guides. If you arrive at a site without a guide, the ranger might be able to accompany you for around CH$5000 per person.

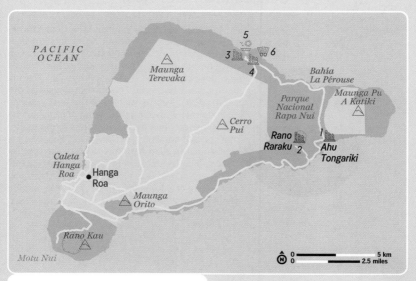

Parque Nacional Rapa Nui

Santiago

PACIFIC OCEAN

Maunga Terevaka

Bahía La Pérouse

Maunga Pu A Katiki

Parque Nacional Rapa Nui

Cerro Pui

Rano Raraku **2**

1 Ahu Tongariki

Caleta Hanga Roa

Hanga Roa

Maunga Orito

Rano Kau

Motu Nui

0 — 5 km
0 — 2.5 miles

HIGHLIGHTS
1 Ahu Tongariki
2 Rano Raraku

SIGHTS
3 Ahu Ature Huki
4 Ahu Nau Nau
5 Anakena
6 Ovahe

BEST VOLCANO HIKES

Maunga Terevaka
This 9.5km round-trip hike from Ahu Akivi takes you to the top of the island's highest peak, where ancient Rapa Nui would teach their youth how to navigate by the stars. Nowhere else can you truly appreciate the emptiness of the horizon.

Poike
It's 12km to circumnavigate the Poike peninsula or 8km to cross it, hiking from Ahu Mahatua up to the crater at Maunga Pu A Katiki before descending into the eroded cliffs above Ahu Tongariki, the island's most spectacular viewpoint.

The Mighty Moai

WHERE HISTORY WAS MADE

Of the 887 known *moai*, 396 lie in **Rano Raraku**. The ancient Rapa Nui carved nearly all of these statues out of this quarry's volcanic tuff, and you can walk back in time and view a number of them in various stages of progress. Most lie on the outside of the volcanic crater, but about 20 *moai* stand on the inside and were burned in a 2022 fire. Look out for **El Gigante**, which, if it had been completed, would have weighed up to 182 tons. The kneeling *moai* called **Tukuturi** has confounded archaeologists for decades.

Remarkably, less than 20% of the *moai* carved here made it to their final *ahu*. Ninety-two fell in transit. You can trace the fate of nine of them on a trail leading out toward the coast.

Many of the *moai* at Rano Raraku are more recent and stylized than elsewhere, with elongated faces, square heads, prominent jaw lines and large noses. Nearby **Ahu Tongariki**, the largest *ahu* ever built, has 15 older *moai* with more distinct Polynesian features. Devastated in a 1960 tsunami and restored with funding from Japan in the 1990s, it is one of the island's most dramatic sites, particularly when viewed at sunrise. At the entrance to Tongariki is the so-called **Traveling Moai**, who flew to Japan and back in the 1980s. The site also features petroglyphs and the remains of ancient boat houses.

Sun, Sand & More Moai

A POLYNESIAN PARADISE

If you've come to Rapa Nui for sun, sand and sea, then **Anakena** is the tropical paradise you've been waiting for. Nowhere does the island look more stereotypically Polynesian than here, with dozens of perky palms swaying in the wind and a perfect crescent of bone-white sand leading to the gem-colored sea. This protected cove is both the safest place to swim and the best place to day drink, with a handful of happening bars on the grassy slope up above. What really makes it special, however, are the *moai*. The lonesome statue atop **Ahu Ature Huki** was the first re-erected on its platform in 1956 during the expedition of Norwegian explorer Thor Heyerdahl, who had the help of a dozen islanders. The seven *moai* of nearby **Ahu Nau Nau** are among the best preserved and are some of the only ones with restored topknots on their heads.

Ahu Nau Nau *moai*

FCG/SHUTTERSTOCK ©

WHERE TO CAMP ON RAPA NUI

Camping Mihinoa
Hot showers, tent rental, wi-fi and kitchen are great, but the seafront location sells it. **$**

Tipanie Moana
Campgrounds don't get any cleaner than this. Non-campers are welcome in the great-value rooms. **$**

Camping Anakena
This basic campground is further from Hanga Roa, but it's just steps from the beach. **$**

FCG/SHUTTERSTOCK ©

Traditional boat, Anakena

Mark Johanson, writer.

This island is scarred onto my body thanks to a motorbike accident in 2017. That daily reminder – my permanent souvenir – kept Rapa Nui on my mind in the years that followed as I dreamt of an eventual return. Of course, the *moai* inevitably lured me back. They have an energy that's hard to explain until you experience it in the flesh. Maybe it's their aura of mystery? Most tropical islands are meant for tuning out, but Rapa Nui demands that you tune in. It asks big questions. It offers prescient warnings. It makes your mind spin. I've never been anywhere else quite like it.

Anakena is often the site of celebrations as it's considered the birthplace of Rapa Nui history. According to oral tradition, it's where the powerful Polynesian chief Hotu Matu'a arrived with the island's first settlers, an event that's reenacted each July. Anakena gets packed on weekends, making neighboring **Ovahe** more ideal for those who want to escape the crowds. This smaller beach, split by a rocky outcrop, is also *the* place to go for snorkeling as corals are more abundant here than elsewhere.

GETTING AROUND

It used to be simple to explore Parque Nacional Rapa Nui on your own by renting a car or bicycle in Hanga Roa. You can still do that, but rules implemented in 2022 mandate guides for most archaeological sites, so the majority of visitors tour the island in vehicles provided by a Hanga Roa–based agency.

TOOLKIT

The chapters in this section cover the most important topics you'll need to know about in Chile & Rapa Nui. They're full of nuts-and-bolts information and valuable insights to help you understand and navigate Chile & Rapa Nui and get the most out of your trip.

Arriving
p346

Getting Around
p347

Money
p348

Accommodations
p349

Family Travel
p350

Health & Safe Travel
p351

Food, Drink & Nightlife
p352

Responsible Travel
p354

LGBTiQ+ Travel
p356

Accessible Travel
p357

How to Visit Robinson Crusoe Island
p358

Nuts & Bolts
p361

Language
p362

Estación Central, Santiago (p44)

✈ Arriving

Aeropuerto Internacional Arturo Merino Benítez, 15km northwest of downtown Santiago, is Chile's principal international gateway. Calama's El Loa Airport and Puerto Montt's El Tepual International Airport are also popular entry points into Chile's north and south, respectively.

Visas

Citizens of the US, Canada, Australia, New Zealand, Japan, South Africa and the EU do not need a visa to visit Chile for stays of up to 90 days.

SIM Cards

SIM cards are not available at Santiago's airport. Skip the touts in the streets and metro stations and go to the actual shop of mobile providers, such as Movistar, Entel, Claro or Wom.

ATMs

The arrivals hall at Santiago's airport has two ATMs, and you pay a hefty CH$7000 transaction fee for the privilege. They are located on the left end as you enter the hall from customs.

Wi-Fi

Complimentary wi-fi is available as soon as you step into the terminal. Connect to 'Airport WiFi – Free' and enter your email, year of birth, nationality and gender.

Public Transport from Airport to City Centre (CH$)

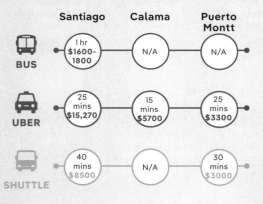

	Santiago	Calama	Puerto Montt
BUS	1 hr $1600–1800	N/A	N/A
UBER	25 mins $15,270	15 mins $5700	25 mins $3300
SHUTTLE	40 mins $8500	N/A	30 mins $3000

CUSTOMS

Customs inspections are fairly routine but more heavy-handed than many destinations. Don't forget about any unpackaged or fresh food in your baggage because big fines are imposed for fruit, dairy, spices, nuts, seeds, meat and organic products. SAG (*Servicio Agrícola-Ganadero;* Agriculture and Livestock Service) checks bags (often using dogs) and levies fines to prevent the spread of diseases and pests that might threaten Chile's fruit exports. You must fill out an online affidavit within 48 hours of arrival at sagingresoachile.cl. Duty-free allowances include 400 cigarettes, 500g of tobacco, 50 cigars and 2.5L of alcoholic drinks.

Getting Around

Chile has excellent roadways and an expansive long-distance bus network, though getting around is trickier in Chilean Patagonia.

TRAVEL COSTS

Rental **From CH$36,800/day**

Petrol **Approx CH$1396/liter**

Bus from Santiago to Pucón
From CH$31,400

Flight from Santiago to Calama
From CH$23,990

Plane

Chile's biggest domestic airline is LATAM. Sky Airlines and JetSmart also serve major Chilean cities, while Punta Arenas–based DAP operates passenger and charter flights connecting Santiago with Chilean Patagonia. Air taxis link up isolated regions.

Bus

A huge bus network canvasses the country. Service is efficient, affordable and spans all comfort levels, from *clásico* (barely reclining seats, no bathrooms) to luxury sleeper coaches known as *salóncama*. Turbus and Pullman Bus are Chile's two biggest bus companies.

FERRYING THE CHILEAN SOUTH

Navimag's ferry service running between Puerto Montt and Puerto Natales is one of the continent's great travel experiences, and the intricately spun web of essential passenger-ferry services traversing southern Chile's jigsaw-puzzle coast is essential to travel in the region. Popular routes include Castro to Laguna San Rafael, La Arena to Puelche, Puerto Montt to Laguna San Rafael and Chacabuco, Pargua to Chiloé, Chiloé and Puerto Montt to Chaitén, Puerto Ibáñez to Chile Chico, and Punta Arenas to Tierra del Fuego.

TIP

Carrying extra fuel is wise along the Carretera Austral and in remote areas. Ask the rental agency for a *bidón* (fuel container).

DRIVING ESSENTIALS

Drive on the right.

60

Speed limit is 60km/h in urban areas, 100km/h on secondary roads and 120km/h on highways.

.03

Blood alcohol limit is 0.03g/L

Boat

Chile's preposterously long coastline is strung with a necklace of ports and harbors, but opportunities for travelers to get around by boat are concentrated south of Puerto Montt. Chilean Patagonia and Tierra del Fuego are accessed by ferries traveling the intricate maze of islands and fjords.

Road Conditions

Chile's longest roadway, Ruta 5 *(Carretera Panamericana)*, is a top-quality highway running from the Peruvian border to Chiloé, with periodic toll booths known as *peajes* (check toll rates at concesiones.mop.gob.cl). Off the highway, the further south you go, the more likely you are to encounter unpaved roads.

Car Rental

To rent a vehicle in Chile, you must have a valid driver's license, be at least 21 to 25 years of age (varies by company) and possess a major credit card (Mastercard or Visa; or be prepared to pay a large cash deposit). Drivers from some countries require an International Driving Permit.

$ Money

CURRENCY: **CHILEAN PESO (CH$)**

ATMs

Chile's many ATMs ('*un Redbanc*' in local vernacular) are the easiest and most convenient way to access funds, but fees can be high (up to CH$8000). ATMs are widely available everywhere except along the Carretera Austral. Credit cards are accepted at most places, but some restaurants accept cash or bank transfers only.

Tipping

Restaurant and bar servers usually ask if you'd like to include the 10% service fee ('*servicio*') before running your plastic in the card machine. If paying with cash, 10% is customary. Taxis do not expect tips, though locals generally round up the fare. Tour guides appreciate a 10% tip.

Contactless Payments

Contactless payment has been slow to roll out. Apple Pay has been pushed back again and again. Google Wallet is supported but remains uncommon.

Taxes and Refunds

A 19% value-added tax (*impuesto de valor agregado;* IVA) is levied on all goods and services.

HOW MUCH FOR...

subway fare
CH$720

museum entry
CH$8000

movie ticket
CH$4000

Parque Nacional Torres del Paine entry
US$18

HOW TO... Buy a Domestic Flight

Want to save some pesos? Don't buy your domestic flights from abroad bundled with your international flight without first checking the price in Chilean pesos direct from Sky Airlines, LATAM or JetSmart. Often, separating out this leg of your journey and paying in pesos – depending on the exchange rate – can net you a better deal than an international online travel agency.

LOCAL TIP

Use your foreign debit card to avoid tiered processing fees on foreign Mastercard and Visa credit purchases. Fees range from CH$347 (for purchases between US$1 and US$20) to CH$2677 (for purchases over US$80).

CHILE AIN'T CHEAP

Chile is the most developed country in South America and, as such, also clocks in as the continent's most expensive country to visit. If you've hopped over from Peru or Bolivia, you're in for a shock. Prices aren't quite what you'd see in Europe or North America, but they seem pricey by South American standards (depending on what's going on with the exchange rate in Brazil, one of South America's other notoriously expensive countries).

Accommodations

Guesthouses

Hospedajes (guesthouses) form the cozy backbone of Chile's lodging options, especially in smaller towns and rural locations. These homey accommodations, which often offer both private and shared bathroom options, are simple, family-run affairs. Expect foam-mattress beds, hard pillows, clean sheets and warm blankets. Breakfast is usually Nescafé with *hallullas* (Chile's ubiquitous round flatbread), butter and marmalade (and scrambled eggs if you're lucky).

Lodges

When Explora opened its luxury lodge in Torres del Paine National Park in 1993, it set the standard for stunning remote lodges amid spectacular South American scenery, and an entire industry of well-appointed accommodations coupled with incredible outdoor adventures kicked off. Find design-forward adventure lodges in Patagonia, Atacama, Rapa Nui, Chiloé and elsewhere.

Homestays

For a true taste of local character and culture, bed down at a *casa de familia* (homestay). Particularly in Chiloé and throughout the south, where tourism is less formal, it's common for families and rural farms to open up their homes. Guests do not always have kitchen privileges, but usually can pay fair prices for abundant meals or laundry service. Tourist offices maintain lists of such accommodations. Achitur (Asociación Gremial de Turismo Rural; achitur.cl) provides Chile-wide listings.

HOW MUCH FOR A NIGHT IN...

a hostel dorm
CH$12,600

a *hospedajes*
CH$23,000

a top-end hotel
CH$210,000

Camping

Chile has a developed camping culture, though it's more of a sleepless, boozy sing-along atmosphere than a back-to-nature escape. Most organized campgrounds are family-oriented with large sites, full bathrooms, laundry, firepits, a restaurant or snack bar, and a grill for the essential *asado* (barbecue). Remote areas have free camping, often without potable water or sanitary facilities.

Hostels

Chile is home to a large network of excellent hostels. Dorm-style accommodations usually set aside a few more expensive doubles for couples who want a social atmosphere but greater creature comforts. Backpackers Chile (backpackerschile.com) is a good resource for hosteling nationwide.

TAX-FREE ACCOMMODATIONS

Foreigners visiting Chile are exempt from the 19% IVA (*impuesto de valor agregado;* value-added tax) charge levied by hotels in the country when paying in US dollars or with a foreign-issued credit card. You'll need to prove your tourist status by showing the paper *Tarjeta Unica* *Migratoria* (tourist card) given to you by the Investigations Police of Chile (PDI) at immigration, along with your passport. The catch is that it works only at lodgings registered with Chile's Internal Tax Service, which many smaller *casas de familia* (homestays) and *hospedajes* (guesthouses) are not.

Family Travel

Chile is one of the best destinations for family travel in South America, and it offers an incredible array of kid-friendly natural attractions, active adventures, and family-oriented resorts and lodgings. The culture of the country welcomes and treasures little ones, and empathy for parents is widespread. Even strangers offer help, and hotels and services tend to accommodate children.

Best Regions for Kids

Santiago Chile's capital has plenty of options for visiting families, including museums, parks and winter resorts with easy terrain, fun events and kids' classes.

Sur Chico Volcano thrills, horseback riding, lake beaches and plenty of watersports are highlights in high-adventure Sur Chico towns like Pucón and Puerto Varas.

Norte Chico Penguin enclaves and seaside resorts provide beach fun and wildlife viewing, while epic stargazing awaits in the Elqui Valley.

Dining Out

It's uncommon for Chilean restaurants to offer kids' menus or special meals for children, but the average eatery has plenty of kid-suitable options to choose from. Because portions are substantial, kids can often split a single dish. High chairs are sometimes available. Latin dining habits mean dinner might be later than you're used to at home, with most restaurants open for dinner no earlier than 7pm.

Discounts

Children under two travel free on a parent's lap on LATAM and Sky Airlines (the latter offers a fare discount up to 12 years of age). Major bus companies offer free child fares, with the maximum age varying by operator.

Facilities

Diaper-changing stations are common in airports and shopping mall bathrooms, but you won't often find them in restaurants. Odds improve slightly in other public restrooms, but bring a changing mat. Most midrange and top-end hotels provide cots and cribs on request.

KID-FRIENDLY PICKS

Parque Metropolitano (p59) Santiago's largest green space has great playgrounds and kid-friendly attractions.

Huilo-Huilo Biological Reserve (p218) Spectacular ecotourism conservation project and family-friendly nature reserve.

Artequin (p168) Viña del Mar's children's museum features play areas and a collection of reproduced masterpieces.

Centro Cultural La Moneda (p52) Santiago cultural center with a playful and imaginative art gallery for children.

Cueva del Milodón (p307) Pose with a kitsch replica prehistoric ground sloth outside Puerto Natales.

BREASTFEEDING IN CHILE

While Chile is generally considered a conservative country, it's far less prudish about breastfeeding than many countries that might like to consider themselves enlightened. Huge strides in women's rights have been made in the country, and breastfeeding in public without hesitation or shame sits firmly on the list of liberties. At feeding times, women should operate within their personal comfort zones, but in bigger cities, you don't have to duck into a bathroom to feed your child. However, in more traditional areas, you might still get the stink eye from those around you if you don't cover up.

LEFT: RASTKO BELIC/EYEEM/GETTY IMAGES ©; RIGHT: YAMAOYAJI/SHUTTERSTOCK ©

Health & Safe Travel

DOGS & BUGS

Stray dogs are an issue in Chile. An estimated 2.5 million wayward canines roam the streets, often saddled with scabies, which is contagious. Resist the urge to interact with dogs with obvious skin problems. In the Chilean South, the pesty *tábano*, a large biting horsefly that is more an annoyance than a health risk, wreaks havoc on outdoor enthusiasts in summer.

Earthquakes & Volcanoes

One-third of the world's earthquakes greater than 8.5 magnitude have occurred in Chile, mainly because of the Nazca Plate, an eastward shifting tectonic plate rubbing elbows with the South American plate off the Chilean coast. Many structures do not meet seismic safety standards, and adobe buildings are especially vulnerable. Chile is also home to 19 active volcanoes, the fifth most in the world.

Crime & Protests

Compared with other South American countries and much of North America, Chile is remarkably safe. However, since the *Estadillo Social* – the country's wave of social unrest in 2019 and 2020 sparked by fare increases on Santiago's public transportation – petty crime (pickpocketing, purse-snatching) is on the rise in dense urban areas. Protests can erupt on short notice and turn violent.

TAP WATER

Chilean tap water is generally safe to drink, but delicate stomachs beware: High mineral content can cause stomach upsets.

Rural Healthcare

Modern healthcare facilities, such as Santiago's Clinica Las Condes and Clinica Alemana, are available in large cities, but medical care on Rapa Nui (Easter Island) and the towns of Northern Patagonia is extremely limited. Rural *postas* (clinics) are rarely well stocked with medicine and are usually attended by paramedics only. Bring a first-aid kit and familiar medicines when traveling in these areas.

Solo & Female Travel

Chile is one of South America's safest countries. Solo travel, including female travel, is easy, but petty theft isn't uncommon. Be aware of your surroundings.

SWIM SAFELY

Apto para bañar	No apto para bañar	Peligroso
Safe to swim	Unsafe to swim	Danger – do not enter the water

CHILEAN RECLUSE SPIDER

While not aggressive, the brutal bite of the venomous Chilean recluse spider (*araña de rincón)* can cause lesions, renal failure and even death. It's found throughout the country (and most of the continent) and is identified by its brown color, violin-like markings and unusual six eyes (most spiders have eight). If bitten, put ice on the bite and seek medical attention immediately.

Food, Drink & Nightlife

Where to Eat

Cafes Social dining with less formality and a bar or coffee shop vibe.

Cocinas costumbristas Popular on waterfronts, these stall-style kitchens usually offer home-style soups and seafood.

Fuentes de soda Casual snack bar or diner-style eatery.

Marisquerías Restaurants specializing in seafood.

Restaurants Range from fast-food to *cocina de autor* (gourmet nouvelle and fusion cuisine).

When to Eat

Desayuno (breakfast; 8am to 10am) is simple: white rolls, butter and jam, tea or instant coffee.

Almuerzo (lunch; noon to 3pm) is the main meal. Hearty soups and casseroles are common. Fixed-price *menú del día* (menu of the day) usually includes juice, salad and a main course.

Once (teatime; 5pm to 9pm) is mainly in the German-influenced south, with cakes, fresh bread, cheese and deli meats. Can replace dinner.

Cena (dinner; 8pm to 10pm) can be similar to lunch but often lighter.

MENU DECODER

Asado Barbecue.

Caldillo de mariscos Shellfish stew.

Cazuela Meat stew.

Centolla King crab.

Chacarero Steak sandwich with green beans and spicy peppers.

Chorrillana Fries topped with meat, fried egg and caramelized onions.

Churrasco Grilled steak sandwich.

Completo Italiano Hot dog with avocado, chopped tomato and mayonnaise.

Congrio A type of cusk-eel (fish) similar to kingclip.

Curanto Clambake-like stew from Chiloé.

Empanada Sweet or savory turnover.

Humita Corn tamale.

Küchen Sweet, German-style cakes.

Loco Mollusk similar to abalone.

Lomito Braised pork sandwich.

Machas a la parmesana Razor clams baked with parmesan cheese.

Manjar Dulce de leche.

Merkén Mapuche spice-smoked chile.

Merluza Hake.

Mote con huesillo Peach juice with barley and cinnamon.

Pastel de choclo Meat and maize casserole.

Pastel de jaiba Crab casserole.

Pebre Spicy salsa.

HOW TO... Drink Pisco

Most visitors will encounter pisco, Chile's national spirit, in the country's refreshing cocktail, the pisco sour, a sort of margarita–whisky hybrid made with cane sugar, egg whites, lemon and a dash of Angostura bitters. (We'll leave the war with Peru over pisco's origins for another day.)

This regional brandy commonly made from quebranta or muscat grapes can be appreciated in a number ways. Pisco comes in four variations: *corriente* (traditional, young, clear), *especial* (aged slightly, light birch color), *reservado* (aged, medium amber color) and *gran pisco* (well-aged, dark amber color). The simplest *pisco tragos* (cocktails) are usually made with *corriente* for obvious reasons. *Piscola* is pisco mixed with cola, and *chilcano* pairs pisco with fresh lemon juice and ginger ale. As quality improves, pisco can be appreciated on its own, much like a fine wine or any other refined spirit, from a tulip-shaped pisco snifter.

HOW MUCH FOR...

Espresso
CH$2200

Pisco sour
CH$4900

Pint of craft beer
CH$4500–
6000

Glass of
Carmenere
CH$4900

Sánguche de
lomito completo
CH$8500

Pastel de choclo
CH$9200

Caldillo de
congrio
CH$10,200

Tasting menu
at a fine-dining
restaurant
CH$126,000

HOW TO... Enjoy Curanto Al Hoyo

One of Chile's most famous culinary adventures awaits on the island of Chiloé, renowned for a local delicacy known as *curanto*. No words can quite prepare you for the first moment a piping hot bowl of *curanto* lands on the table in front of you, but 'what did I get myself into?' comes to mind. Rest assured, however, your slack jaw will come in handy when it's time to shove all that food in.

At its most traditional, *curanto* is made by heating up stones in a hole in the ground until they crackle and then directly piling on shellfish, pork and chicken, followed by nalca (a rhubarb-like plant) or pangue (a native plant of Chile) leaves and damp cloths before the whole shebang is covered in dirt and grass and left to simmer for nearly two hours. Locals still prepare it this traditional way, called *curanto al hoyo,* as do a few traditional restaurants around the island. Think of *curanto al hoyo* as similar to a New England clambake, a cherished event – part feast, part social gathering – with plenty of drinking and revelry while the food slowly cooks.

Once the food arrives – an intimidating mountain of steaming-hot shellfish (mussels, clams), meat (chicken, sausages), potatoes, *milcao* (Chilota potato bread), *chapaleles* (boiled potato dumplings) and assorted vegetables – there's no dainty way to do it. Go big or go home!

Curanto's Origins

Chiloé's most traditional dish is of unknown origins, but historically its preparation harkens back to the earth ovens of Polynesian culinary ancestry. The word itself evolved from the Mapuche word *kurantu* ('stony' or 'ground full of rocks').

CARMENERE'S IMPROBABLE CONQUEST

Despite being considered part of the New World of wine, Chileans began their winemaking crusade in the 16th century, when Spaniards transported common grape vines *(Vitis vinifera)* to South America. A few centuries later, the French planted cabernet sauvignon, merlot and, most interestingly, Carmenere, all of which were kept mostly for Chileans to enjoy until the mid-1990s.

Military dictatorships, high taxes and stifling bureaucracy made tapping Chile for wine exports more trouble than it was worth – until the world rediscovered Carmenere, anyway. This cousin of cabernet originally hails from the Médoc region of Bordeaux and is widely considered one of that famous wine region's original six varietals. But when the black plague of the wine world, phylloxera, nearly wiped out the European wine industry in 1867, the sought-after varietal was thought to have been rendered extinct.

Meanwhile, in Chile, the grape was inadvertently preserved and flourishing right under the noses of oenophiles until 1994, when 50% of what was thought to be Chilean merlot was found to be Carmenere. And just like that, Chile's signature varietal was set, given the seal of approval by the Chilean Department of Agriculture in 1998. Chile's explosive climb onto the world's most selective wine lists – and subsequently its entire wine tourism industry – began their improbable journey. Today, Chilean Carmenere's coveted characteristics (medium tannins, medium body, notes of red and black fruits on the palate, and a peppery aroma) have catapulted it into a world-class wine that's reason alone for wine lovers to travel to Chile.

Responsible Travel

Climate Change & Travel

It's impossible to ignore the impact we have when traveling, and the importance of making changes where we can. Lonely Planet urges all travelers to engage with their travel carbon footprint. There are many carbon calculators online that allow travelers to estimate the carbon emissions generated by their journey; try resurgence.org/resources/carbon-calculator.html. Many airlines and booking sites offer travelers the option of offsetting the impact of greenhouse gas emissions by contributing to climate-friendly initiatives around the world. We continue to offset the carbon footprint of all Lonely Planet staff travel, while recognizing this is a mitigation more than a solution.

Support Local

- Stay in family-run *hospedajes* (guesthouses) and homestays.
- Shop Mapuche weaving and textiles from fair-trade organizations like Fundación Chol-Chol.
- Drink wines from sustainable wineries like Emiliana, Lapostolle and Cono Sur.
- Hike locally run nature reserves like Santuario El Cañi.

Rural Tourism

Find rural homestays and guides through Casa del Turismo Rural in Coyhaique, which can connect you with rural tourism opportunities and horse-riding excursions along the Carretera Austral, including multiday jaunts in the countryside and through the pampas.

Give Back

AMA Torres del Paine (@amatorresdelpaine) Works with a limited number of volunteers in Parque Nacional Torres del Paine.

Experiment Chile (experiment.cl) Organizes social-enterprise volunteer programs.

Un Techo Para Chile (cl.techo.org) Coordinates home construction for low-income families throughout Chile.

Ecotourism Hot Spots

Eat, sleep and play in Sur Chico's Huilo-Huilo Biological Reserve, a private conservation project falling within a much larger Unesco Biosphere Reserve. Roaring rivers, towering waterfalls, extraordinary endemic fauna and low-impact ecotourism are highlights.

Support community conservation efforts in the threatened Río Cochamó Valley, where concerned residents are banding together – armed with ecotourism as their weapon – to ward off development by obtaining official nature sanctuary status for the area.

Embark on a bird-watching nature trek with enthusiastic Italian naturalist Raffaele Di Biase at Puerto Varas–based Birds Chile, the country's only tour operator with a Level 3 Sustainable Stamp according to Sernatur, Chile's national tourism board.

Indigenous Ruins

Visit Aldea de Tulor near San Pedro de Atacama, a fascinating archaeological site of ruined circular dwellings owned and run by the indigenous Likan Antay people. The area was settled 2500 years ago and abandoned in 300 CE.

Sustainable Trekking

Hike the 2800km Route of the Parks, a trail protecting some 113,300 sq km of Chilean Patagonia and traversing 17 national parks. The route is an economic driver for more than 60 surrounding communities.

Puma Preservation

Accompany professional puma trackers on a 'conservation safari' at Estancia Cerro Guido, part of a pioneering puma conservation project in a region near Parque Nacional Torres del Paine where sheep farming and wildlife often conflict.

Sleep under the Elqui Valley stars in Bedouin tents from Morocco at solar-powered Campo de Cielo.

Avoid farmed salmon in Chile unless it's certified by the Aquaculture Stewardship Council (ASC).

Metro

Since 2017, the forward-thinking Metro de Santiago (Santiago Metro), Latin America's second-largest metro system after Mexico City, has sourced at least 60% of its operational electricity needs from renewable solar and wind-generated energy.

Patagonia Parks

Hike vast swathes of temperate rainforest, smoking volcanoes and breezy fjords in Parque Nacional Pumalín and pasture-converted steppe, forests, mountains, lakes and lagoons at Parque Nacional Patagonia, both forged from preservation efforts.

Trash to Musical Treasure

Enjoy a concert at NGO Toki Rapa Nui, the first fully sustainable music school in Latin America and Oceania. Visits to the school, made entirely from upcycled trash, support classes for local children, who study instruments and traditional disciplines.

RESOURCES

tompkins conservation.org Nonprofit focused on rewilding and park creation.

fondonaturaleza. org Nonprofit managing resources for large-scale nature conservation in Chile.

chile.wcs.org International organization working tirelessly to conserve Patagonian wildlife.

LGBTIQ+ Travelers

A landmark law recognizing gay marriage came into effect in 2022 in Chile (same-sex civil unions had been legal since 2015), a major step forward for one of South America's most conservative and overwhelmingly Catholic countries. Chileans are generally tolerant, especially in bigger cities. In smaller and more rural towns, public displays of affection still come with a 'proceed with caution' caveat.

Gay Chile

Santiago has a good gay scene, and nightlife centers on Barrio Bellavista, especially along the bar-lined street of Bombero Núñez. Station RestoBar, Bar 105 Fetish, Blondie and Club Soda are staples in the gay scene. Lesbians head to Chueca Bar or parties organized by Realidad Paralela. Hotspot Club is the gay equivalent of Chueca Bar. Many of the hipper urban bars and clubs also have an active gay scene. Beyond the capital, Valparaíso and Viña del Mar are home to Chile's most robust gay scenes.

TORTA GOLOSA

The lesbian-feminist reggaeton act Torta Golosa has become the soundtrack for Valparaíso's history of intolerance toward lesbians, specifically masculine-appearing lesbians, who are derogatorily referred to as *camionas* (similar to 'butch' in English). Several high-profile murders have taken place and remain unsolved. Travel cautiously.

FESTIVALS

Every November in celebration of Día Nacional de la Diversidad, the Santiago Parade, Open Mind Fest marries a diversity march with one of Chile's biggest electronic music festivals. The event takes place at Plaza Baquedano (Plaza Italia), across the Mapocho River from Barrio Bellavista.

Left, Right, Left

Right-wing former Chilean president Sebastián Piñera signed Chile's *Ley de Matrimonio Igualitario* (Equal Marriage Law) into law in late 2021, a bill that was originally sent to the congress during the second term of his left-wing predecessor, Michelle Bachelet. But the political ping-pong didn't start there. Bachelet saw through Chile's same-sex civil unions bill in 2015, a law originally introduced during Piñera's first term in 2014.

RESOURCES

Movil H (Movement for the Integration and Liberation of Homosexuals; movilh.cl) advocates for gayrights in Chile. Regional chapters include Aysén, Bío-Bío, Maule, Los Lagos and Valparaíso.

Out Adventures (outadventures.com) and **Pride Tours Chile** (pridetours.net) run gay-friendly trips to Chile.

International Gay and Lesbian Travel Association (IGLTA; iglta.org) is a solid source for LGBTIQ-friendly businesses in Chile.

Pride Parade

Santiago's annual gay pride parade, Marcha del Orgullo Gay, is Chile's largest pride event, organized by the Movil H and Fundación Iguales on the last Saturday in June. The 2022 event drew 80,000 attendees.

Accessible Travel

Chile remains a robust but improving challenge for travelers with disabilities. Ramp access is common in shopping malls, public buildings, museums and many higher-end hotels (legislation now requires new public buildings to be accessible), but advance planning through a relevant organization is best for ensuring a wonderful experience.

Getting Around Santiago

Santiago's metro has elevators, and Transantiago has access ramps and spaces for wheelchairs on newer buses. Some street lights have noise-indicated crossings for the blind. Unfriendly sidewalks remain problematic.

Airport

Santiago's Aeropuerto Internacional Arturo Merino Benítez offers complimentary wheelchair and assistance services for passengers with reduced mobility. Reserve 48 hours in advance at nuevopudahuel.cl. Travelers with invisible disabilities can request a special lanyard for personalized airport attention.

Accommodations

Historically, ramps and adapted rooms were no guarantee even in top-end hotels, but a 2019 law decreed universal accessibility in all hotels and lodgings in Chile within three years. Expect changes.

National Parks & Reserves

According to Chile's official tourism website (chile.travel), at least 40 of the country's national parks, reserves and natural monuments are accessible. Adaptations include access ramps, braille signage and more.

Valparaíso

Because of its steep slopes, Valparaíso might seem an intimidating choice for those with limited mobility, but a huge universal access project is underway, including Metro Valparaíso's adapted ticket offices, tactile paving, accessible benches and additional elevators.

WHEEL THE WORLD

Using a special all-terrain ride, Chilean Alvaro Silberstein was the first wheelchair user to explore Torres del Paine National Park in 2016, leading to the creation of Wheel the World (wheeltheworld.com), a US-based, Chilean-founded accessible travel agency.

RESOURCES

Sernatur (sernatur.cl/accesibilidad-turistica) Government accessibility travel initiative.

Fundación Eres (fundacioneres.cl) Nonprofit organization for inclusionary rights, especially in culture, tourism and recreation.

Corporación Ciudad Accesible (ciudadaccesible.cl) Provides advice for those with disabilities about travel in Chile.

SATH (Society for Accessible Travel & Hospitality; sath.org) Resource for travelers with disabilities.

Jass Puerto Varas (jasspuertovaras.com) Offers accessibility-friendly sea kayaking and trekking excursions.

Senior Travel

Seniors, known as *tercera edad* (literally 'third age'; 60 and up) in Chile, often receive discounts at museums and attractions and on the metro. Those 55 and up receive preferential healthcare in Chile.

JEREMY RICHARDS/SHUTTERSTOCK ©

San Juan Bautista, Robinson Crusoe Island

HOW TO...

Visit Robinson Crusoe Island

'If the island wants you to stay, you stay' is a popular adage among the people living on Robinson Crusoe. Getting to the island, located nearly 700km off Chile's Pacific coast, is an adventure that requires patience and luck – and might just be one of the most memorable journeys you ever embark on. By Shivya Nath

Robinson Crusoe might seem small at only 48 sq km, but it packs in an incredible diversity of natural experiences. We've picked the most unique, sprinkled with the distinct island culture and practical planning, for your own castaway adventure.

HOW TO GET AROUND

More than 90% of the island is a protected national park, so all amenities are concentrated in the remaining 9%. All facilities are within walking distance in San Juan Bautista. There are no taxis on the island, but accommodation hosts and locals with cars happily offer rides.

How to Get to Robinson Crusoe Island

Travelers have two options to get to Robinson Crusoe Island.

Lassa, Aerocardal and Ata run flights between Santiago and the island at an average cost of US$745 for a round trip. Lassa is the most frequent service, with a capacity of six people. Ata has lower frequency with a slightly bigger plane to seat eight people, and Aerocardal is more expensive but the preferred choice of many islanders. Flights can be reserved by email or phone, but they are confirmed based on weather conditions only a day (and sometimes a few hours) before departure. Most airlines accept 15kg of luggage per passenger. Small soft-top bags are recommended because bags are loaded directly behind the seats. The boat transfer from the landing strip at Robinson Crusoe to the

village of San Juan Bautista is included in the airline ticket. Carry a rain jacket and be prepared for a choppy boat ride.

Taking the boat is also an option. Transmarko runs a weekly boat service from Valparaíso to the island at US$310 for a round trip, including all meals on board. The journey takes three days and two nights, and accommodations are dorm-style, with four people to a room. The water can be extremely choppy, so if you're prone to sea sickness, it's better to fly. Wind conditions need to be stable for the boat to dock at the island, so be prepared for delays. For bookings, check with accommodations providers on the island.

Whether you take the air or sea route, keep a few days of buffer for your return journey. Wind and water conditions need to align for your departure from the island too.

Where to Eat

Matemala Charming mountain-top restaurant with stellar views over the Pacific. Indulge in local ingredients and try the house-brewed beer. Book in advance by phone (+569 9324 2280). $$

Bahia A family-run eatery offering fresh catch and comfort foods. Friday nights are the perfect time to join islanders for a game of pool. $$

Tamara (home chef) Chef Tamara and her son used to run the island's first vegan restaurant and now offer delicious deliveries from their home kitchen. $

Plan Your Time

The essence of Robinson Crusoe is in slowing down. Hike to Villagra to witness the island's diverse landscapes and snorkel or dive with the Juan Fernandez fur seals.

A running joke on Robinson Crusoe is that if you don't like the weather, come back in five minutes. It's not rare to experience all four seasons, scattered with rain and rainbows, on the same day. Summer (November to February) is the best time to visit for moderate weather and wind. May to August experience heavy rainfall and colder days.

Hike to Plazoleta El Yunque

The short self-guided hike from the village of San Juan Bautista to Plazoleta El Yunque – which lies at the base of the highest peak on the island – goes through the incredible slow-growth forest that evolved over centuries of isolation. As you follow the boardwalk, look out for the otherworldly umbrella-like pangue plant, ancient canelo trees and the flutter of the red Juan Fernandez firecrown (pictured), a hummingbird endemic to the island.

Before you set out for the hike, register at the Conaf office in the center of San Juan Bautista and pay the nominal entrance fee of CH$8000.

KNOW BEFORE YOU GO

Money Carry enough cash for your time at Robinson Crusoe Island, as well as some buffer in case of departure delays, perhaps about US$50 per day, not including accommodation and food expenses. There are no ATMs or official money exchanges on the island. Credit cards are rarely accepted.

Packing Prepare for all weather, even for a short trip in the middle of summer. Pack a rain jacket and sturdy walking shoes.

Internet Decent wi-fi is available in most accommodations. Connectivity can be slow or unsteady on windy days.

Special diets A health food store on the island stocks vegan and gluten-free options. Most restaurants and accommodations cater to special diets with advance notice.

SLOW TRAVEL EXPERIENCES

Kayak On a calm day, rent a free kayak from Conaf and paddle into the Pacific to spot Juan Fernandez fur seals.

Buy Order a customized souvenir made from rare coral negro (pictured) from local craftswoman Brenda Coral. Black corals are allowed to be pulled out of the water only when they naturally come apart or accidentally get stuck in fishing nets.

Eat Organize a farm-to-table meal on one of the island's only organic farms with a local fishing family. Book through Turisma Aventura (+569 9235 9324).

Snorkel or Scuba Dive with the Juan Fernandez Fur Seals

Head into the turquoise Pacific with local dive shop Marenostrum to spend an afternoon snorkeling or diving with the island's endemic seals (pictured). These spirited creatures, especially the young ones, might come close to check you out, but as with any wildlife experience, keep a safe and responsible distance. Rent a wetsuit from the dive shop to brace yourself for the chilly waters.

Hike from the Airport to Villagra & Camp Overnight

The diversity of scenery between the airport (which is really just a landing strip) and Villagra is breathtaking. Hike in coastal, desert, mountain and forest landscapes before arriving at the dramatic campsite at Villagra, surrounded by hills jutting out of the Pacific. Trek back to San Juan Bautista past the stunning viewpoints at Punta De Isla and Mirador Selkirk, a loop that allows you to get to know and experience much of the island. The hike is demanding in parts and requires a moderate level of fitness. A licensed guide is necessary, so organize it through the Conaf office in San Juan Bautista.

Where to Stay

Isla Pacifico Ecolodge Modern, family-run lodge with spacious rooms or cozy self-contained *cabañas* (cabins). Enjoy lavish breakfasts and sunrise views out to the Pacific. $$$

Casa Isla A creative residency in a quieter part of town, home to a Chilean art collector. Also hosts artists based on art exchange. $$

Cabanas Baron de Rodt Three rustic *cabañas* run by the island's oldest family. Delve into the fascinating history of the island over their famous kingfish sandwich. $

➕ Nuts & Bolts

OPENING HOURS

Banks 9am–2pm weekdays, sometimes 10am–1pm Saturday

Government offices & businesses 9am–6pm weekdays

Museums Often close Monday

Post offices 9am–6pm Monday to Friday, to noon Saturday

Restaurants Noon–11pm, many close 4–7pm

Shops 10am–8pm, some close 1–3pm

Internet Access

Internet connectivity in most of Chile is excellent. Hotels, hostels and coffee shops typically offer wi-fi. However, don't expect a connection in much of Patagonia. Look for free public wi-fi on the plaza in some communities.

GOOD TO KNOW

Time Zone
GMT-4 (GMT-3 mid-December to late March)

Country Code
56

Emergency number
131

Population
19.6 million

PUBLIC HOLIDAYS

Año Nuevo (New Year) January 1

Semana Santa (Easter Week) March or April

Día del Trabajo (Labor Day) May 1

Glorias Navales Commemorating the naval Battle of Iquique; May 21

Corpus Christi May/June; dates vary

Asunción de la Virgen (Assumption) August 15

Día de Unidad Nacional (Day of National Unity) First Monday of September

Día de la Independencia Nacional (National Independence Day) September 18

Día del Ejército (Armed Forces Day) September 19

Día de la Raza (Columbus Day) October 12

Todo los Santos (All Saints' Day) November 1

Inmaculada Concepción (Immaculate Conception) December 8

Navidad (Christmas Day) December 25

Smoking

Smoking is banned indoors in public places, including restaurants, bars and public transport.

Toilets

Public toilets are poorly maintained. Carry toilet paper, which is not flushed but put in the trash.

Electricity 220/50Hz

Type C
220V/50Hz

Type L
220V/50Hz

📖 Language

With an entire continent of gregarious Spanish-speaking locals to chat with, you don't want to be limited to 'gringo lingo' – and you'll find that revving up your *eres* 'e·res' (r's) and grunting out your *jotas* 'kho·tas' (j's) is fun.

Basics

Hello. Hola. *o·la*
Goodbye. Adiós. *a·dyos*
Yes. Sí. *see*
No. No. *no*
Please. Por favor. *por fa·vor*
Thank you. Gracias. *gra·syas*
Excuse me. Perdón. *per·don*
Sorry. Lo siento. *lo syen·to*
What's your name? ¿Cómo se llama Usted? *ko·mo se ya·ma oo·ste* (pol)
¿Cómo te llamas? *ko·mo te ya·mas* (inf)
My name is ... Me llamo ... *me ya·mo ...*
Do you speak English? ¿Habla inglés? *a·bla een·gles* (pol)
¿Hablas inglés? *a·blas een·gles* (inf)

Directions

Where's ...?
¿Dónde está ...? *don·de es·ta ...*
What's the address?
¿Cuál es la dirección? *kwal es la dee·rek·syon*
Could you please write it down?
¿Puede escribirlo, por favor? *pwe·de es·kree·beer·lo por fa·vor*
Can you show me (on the map)?
¿Me lo puede indicar (en el mapa)? *me lo pwe·de een·dee·kar (en el ma·pa)*

Signs

Abierto Open
Cerrado Closed
Entrada Entrance
Hombres/Varones Men
Mujeres/Damas Women
Prohibido Prohibited
Salida Exit
Servicios/Baños Toilets

Time

What time is it? ¿Qué hora es? *ke o·ra es*
It's (10) o'clock. Son (las diez). *son (las dyes)*
Half past (one). Es (la una) y media. *es (la oo·na) ee me·dya*
morning mañana *ma·nya·na*
afternoon tarde *tar·de*
evening noche *no·che*
yesterday ayer *a·yer*
today hoy *oy*
tomorrow mañana *ma·nya·na*

Emergencies

Help! ¡Socorro! *so·ko·ro*
Go away! ¡Vete! *ve·te*
I'm ill. Estoy enfermo/a. *es·toy en·fer·mo/a* (m/f)
Call ...! ¡Llame a ...! *ya·me a ...*
　　a doctor un médico *oon me·dee·ko*
　　the police la policía *la po·lee·see·a*

Eating & Drinking

What would you recommend?
¿Qué recomienda? *ke re·ko·myen·da*
Cheers! ¡Salud! *sa·loo*
That was delicious.
¡Estaba buenísimo! *es·ta·ba bwe·nee·see·mo*

NUMBERS

1
uno *oo·no*

2
dos *dos*

3
tres *tres*

4
cuatro *kwa·tro*

5
cinco *seen·ko*

6
seis *seys*

7
siete *sye·te*

8
ocho *o·cho*

9
nueve *nwe·ve*

10
diez *dyes*

DONATIONS TO ENGLISH

Numerous – you may recognise armada, aficionado, embargo, fiesta, machismo, patio, plaza ...

Rapa Nui Language

Although the people of Rapa Nui speak Spanish, among themselves many of them use the island's indigenous language (also called Rapa Nui). Due to the island's isolation, the Rapa Nui language developed relatively untouched but retains similarities to other Polynesian languages, such as Hawaiian, Tahitian and Maori. These days the language increasingly bears the influence of English and Spanish. The hieroglyph-like Rongorongo script, developed by the islanders after the Spanish first arrived in 1770 and in use until the 1860s, is believed to have been the earliest written form of Rapa Nui. The written Rapa Nui used today was developed in the 19th century by missionaries, who transliterated the sounds of the language into the Roman alphabet. Sadly, while most understand Rapa Nui, few of the younger islanders speak it fluently, though work is being done to keep this endangered language, and the culture it carries, alive.

Hello. 'Iorana.
Goodbye. 'Iorana.
Thank you. Maururu.

DISTINCTIVE SOUNDS

The strong and rolled r, and kh (pronounced as in the Scottish loch).

To Lisp or Not to Lisp

If you're familiar with the sound of European Spanish, you'll notice that Latin Americans don't 'lisp' – ie the European Spanish th is pronounced as s in Chile and elsewhere in Latin America.

Grammar

Spanish has a formal and informal word for 'you' (Usted and tú respectively). The verbs have a different ending for each person, like the English 'I do' vs 'he/she does'.

SPANISH AROUND THE WORLD

Over the last 500 years, Spanish in Latin America has evolved differently to the Spanish spoken in Europe. Influenced by indigenous languages, Latin American Spanish varies slightly from country to country, especially when it comes to vocabulary.

300 million speak Latin American Spanish as their first language

100 million speak Latin American Spanish as their second language

Mexico
Cuba
Guatemala
Costa Rica
Colombia
Ecuador
Peru
Bolivia
Paraguay
Chile
Argentina

STORYBOOK

Our writers delve deep into different aspects of Chile & Rapa Nui life

A History of Chile & Rapa Nui in 15 Places

These places offer an insight into how Chile became the country it is today.

Isabel Albiston

p366

Meet the Chileans

Living in a time of transition, Chileans might come off as quite reserved, but they will win you over with their friendliness.

Soledad Balduzzi

p370

'Chile Woke Up'

Though now years in the past, Chile's 2019 social unrest has shaped the modern nation.

Mark Johanson

p372

The Planet on an Island

Robinson Crusoe is a microcosm of our whole planet – and a peek into its future.

Shivya Nath

p375

Guanacos, Parque Nacional Torres del Paine (p308)

A HISTORY OF CHILE & RAPA NUI IN
15 PLACES

An improbably long and narrow sliver of land, Chile's geography has shaped its past. Its relatively isolated location, sandwiched between the Andes Mountains and the Pacific Ocean, has meant its cultures and traditions have remained distinct from its neighbors. These places offer an insight into how Chile became the country it is today. By Isabel Albiston

HOME TO THE oldest inhabited site discovered in the Americas, Chile is a country where people have thrived in challenging environments for thousands of years. Extreme climates in the north and south and the ever-present threat of earthquakes pay testament to the hardy spirit of those who live here.

But Chile has long simmered with the tensions of socio-economic inequalities, with a small landowning elite and a long history of mineral exploitation. Since the Spanish colonists arrived in 1535, the oppression of indigenous groups has created wounds and led to their marginalization. Indigenous Mapuche in La Araucanía fought to retain their autonomy for hundreds of years. In 2018, the police shooting of Mapuche farmer Camilo Catrillanca prompted a wave of clashes between Mapuche activists and the Chilean state.

In 2019, thousands of protesters took to the streets to demand that inequalities be addressed with a new constitution. Their demands were met with the proposal of a new constitution, which included a recognition of the rights and autonomy of Chile's indigenous people; however, the constitution was rejected in a national referendum in 2022. It was a moment of sadness and celebration that shone a light on societal divisions.

1. Villa Ukika
TIERRA DEL FUEGO'S FIRST INHABITANTS

Though the indigenous Yagán community at Villa Ukika was founded in the 1960s, the people here could be the descendants of some of Patagonia's earliest inhabitants. The early Yagán people were nomadic, canoe-based societies that survived the challenging climate of Tierra del Fuego for thousands of years. Remains found at the Tres Arroyos rock shelter showed evidence of human occupation from 12,000 BCE. The cave is just one of several sites to have been excavated at Cerro de los Onas on Tierra del Fuego. Further north, evidence uncovered at Monte Verde near Puerto Montt suggests human activity as early as 16,500 BCE.

For more on Villa Ukika, see p319

2. Museo de Sitio Colón 10
CHINCHORRO MUMMIES OF THE AZAPA VALLEY

In 2004, when architects began excavating the foundations of a 19th-century house in Arica to prepare the ground for a hotel, they uncovered a burial site from the

Chinchorro culture. The Chinchorros were nomadic coastal dwellers who lived in the area between 8000 and 2000 BCE. The burial ground at Sitio Colón 10 is believed to date from between 4200 and 3800 BCE, when burial procedures involved covering the bodies with plant fibers and feathers. Nearby, several older burial sites have been found where the bodies were mummified; these are the oldest known intentionally preserved mummies in the world.

For more on Museo de Sitio Colón 10, see p117

3. Parque Nacional Rapa Nui
MYSTERIOUS MEGALITHIC HUMAN FIGURES

Researchers in Rapa Nui have long puzzled over the story behind the *moai,* large representations of the islanders' Polynesian ancestors. What inspired their creation and how they were transported to their *ahu* (platforms) remains a mystery, and there is no consensus on when they were made. Most of the figures were produced in the Rano Raraku quarry. The 396 statues there were carved out of volcanic turf and are positioned in or around a volcanic crater. At the nearby Ahu Tongariki ceremonial platform are several older *moai.* Both these

Moai, Ahu Tongariki (p342)

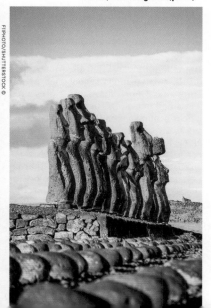

FIIPHOTO/SHUTTERSTOCK ©

archaeological sites lie within the Parque Nacional Rapa Nui.

For more on Parque Nacional Rapa Nui, see p341

4. Pukará de Quitor
DEFENDING AGAINST SPANISH COLONIZERS

Hundreds of years before the town of San Pedro de Atacama was founded, a nearby hillside was the site of a 12th-century fortress that housed and protected the indigenous Lickan Antay people, who grew potatoes, maize and quinoa on terraces nearby. In 1536, the area was under Inca control when news reached Pukará de Quitor of the Spanish invasion. The fortress was well prepared when Pedro de Valdivia's men arrived several years later, but the Lickan Antay were eventually overcome by the Spanish, who killed the fortress' defenders. The ruins of Pukará de Quitor can be seen from a walking trail.

For more on Pukará de Quitor, see p98

5. Monumento a la Araucanía
CENTER OF MAPUCHE CULTURE

La Araucanía is the heart of indigenous Mapuche culture. At Plaza Aníbal Pinto in Temuco, Monumento a la Araucanía features a Mapuche shaman and *toqui* (Mapuche military leader) who fought against Spanish invaders. Starting in 1536, the Arauco War was a long-running series of conflicts in which the Mapuche resisted the Spanish for 300 years. From 1861 to 1883, the 'pacification' of La Araucanía involved Chilean troops finally taking control of the region. Tensions between the Mapuche people and the Chilean state have started to increase once again, sparked by conflicts over ancestral land rights and police violence.

For more on Monumento a la Araucanía, see page 201

6. Plaza de Armas
COLONIAL SQUARE AT SANTIAGO'S CENTER

Santiago's main square has been the city's centerpiece since its founding in 1541 on the orders of Pedro de Valdivia, who appears astride his horse in statue form. During colonial times, Plaza de Armas was the site of the city's gallows. Chile's independence from Spain in 1818 is commemorated with a statue of South

American liberator Simón Bolívar, who led an army south from Venezuela to Peru. It was another liberator, the Argentinian José de San Martín, who crossed the Andes from Mendoza to liberate Santiago in 1818 before sailing north to Lima to drive Spain out of Peru.

For more on Plaza de Armas, see p54

7. Itata Valley Vineyards
CHILE'S OLDEST WINES

The earliest vineyards in Chile are believed to have been planted by European missionaries in the 16th century. Jesuit priests cultivated país grapes in the Itata Valley, which is considered one of the oldest wine-growing regions in the Americas. Indeed, some of the vines in the valley were planted hundreds of years ago. For many years, país was considered an inferior grape, so these vineyards produced país grapes to be used in blends. País has now come back into fashion, with sommeliers comparing it to Beaujolais. Drinking a glass is like imbibing Chilean history.

For more on the vineyards of the Itata Valley, see p187

8. Corbeta Esmeralda
WAR OF THE PACIFIC BATTLESHIP

In Iquique, the replica of the sunken *Esmeralda* tells the story of the War of the Pacific (1879–83), in which Chile defeated a Peruvian-Bolivian alliance and increased its territory in the north. Before then, Iquique and the province of Tarapacá were part of Peru. During the war, Chile quickly occupied Antofagasta (then part of the Bolivian coastal region) and then faced naval battles against Peru. The victory at Iquique in 1879 enabled Chile to invade Peru and occupy Lima. Peru signed a peace treaty in 1883 that ceded Tarapacá to Chile, and in 1929, Peru formally recognized Arica as Chilean territory.

For more on the Corbeta Esmeralda, see page 111

9. Ruinas de Huanchaca
REMAINS OF A BOLIVIAN MINING COMPANY

Antofagasta was once a Bolivian town, and its strategic importance grew with the nitrate boom that began in 1866 and the discovery of silver in Caracoles in 1870. The battle for control over the region's mineral resources was one of the causes of the War of the Pacific (1879–83), during which Bolivia lost the territory to Chile. Today, the Huanchaca ruins are all that remains of the Bolivian Huanchaca Company site. Built in the late 19th century, it was used as a refinery for raw materials. The site is now a museum, and the port of Antofagasta remains a major import-export point for Bolivia.

For more on the Ruinas de Huanchaca, see p105

10. Humberstone & Santa Laura
GHOSTS OF CHILE'S NITRATE MINING BOOM

Empty streets and abandoned buildings are all that remain of the once thriving nitrate mining communities of Humberstone and Santa Laura, in the desert near Iquique. Today, the eerie ghost towns are preserved as museums where you can see how mining families lived in the pampas towns that supported the mines during the nitrate boom of the late 19th and early 20th centuries. With the development of synthetic nitrates, demand declined and the site closed in 1960. Explore theaters, houses, schools, stores and industrial hangers with mining machinery, all in varying states of decay.

For more on Humberstone and Santa Laura, see p114

11. Museo Casa-Escuela Gabriela Mistral
A LAND OF POETS

In the Elqui Valley village of Montegrande, the small primary school once attended by poet Gabriela Mistral is preserved as a small museum. The poet is buried in a nearby mausoleum that reflects her status as the first Latin American to win the Nobel Prize in Literature, in 1945. Together the two sights tell the story of Mistral's rise from humble beginnings to international acclaim and of her enduring love for the Elqui Valley. The celebration of Mistral also reflects how Chile sees itself as a nation of poets. Chilean bards include Pablo Neruda, Vicente Huidobro and Nicanor Parra to name just a few.

For more on Museo Casa-Escuela Gabriela Mistral, see p141

Carretera Austral (p258)

12. Palacio de La Moneda

SCENE OF THE 1973 COUP

The late 18th-century Palacio de La Moneda was first used for minting currency but later became the president's office. It is most closely associated with the events of the coup of September 11, 1973, in which military general Augusto Pinochet's rebel forces bombarded the building with air-force missile attacks, surrounded it with tanks and seized control of the government. Inside, President Salvador Allende, who had become Chile's first socialist president in 1970, refused to leave. When troops entered the palace, they found Allende dead, apparently by suicide. Today, a statue of Allende stands in the square in front of the palace.

For more on Palacio de La Moneda, see p54

13. Carretera Austral

HISTORIC HIGHWAY THROUGH PATAGONIA

The construction of a highway linking the rural outposts of southern Patagonia was initiated by Pinochet in 1976, in part to strengthen Chile's standing in the region in the face of increasing tensions with Argentina. Before the construction of the Carretera Austral, road traffic had to pass through Argentina to reach Chile's southernmost territory. In 1978, the two countries almost went to war over three small islands in the Beagle Channel, but the Pope stepped in to mediate and the conflict was settled in 1979. In the end, the Carretera Austral took more than 20 years and US$300 million to construct.

For more on the road, see p258

14. Museo de la Memoria y los Derechos Humanos

REMEMBERING CHILE'S DISAPPEARED

The military dictatorship headed by General Pinochet began with the coup of 1973 and continued until the democratic elections of 1989. During that time, large-scale human rights violations were perpetrated by the regime against its own citizens. More than 40,000 people were subjected to imprisonment and torture, of which 3000 were executed. Meanwhile, hundreds of thousands of Chileans were forced into exile. In Santiago, the Museum of Memory and Human Rights is a sobering but vital space that serves as a record of what happened, an arena in which to learn about it and as a moving memorial to those who died.

For more on Museo de la Memoria y los Derechos Humanos, see p65

15. Mina San José

DRAMATIC RESCUE OF 33 TRAPPED MINERS

In a barren patch of the Atacama Desert near Copiapó, the San José copper mine was the scene of the dramatic rescue of 33 trapped miners who, on August 5, 2010, had become stranded 700m underground after a cave-in. After a two-month rescue effort that cost an estimated US$20 million and was covered tirelessly by international media, as many as one billion viewers tuned in to watch live coverage of the miners being raised to safety in a specially designed capsule on October 13. The mine is no longer in operation but is open as a visitor attraction.

For more on Mina San José, see p147

MEET THE CHILEANS

Living in a time of great political and social transition, Chileans might come off as quite reserved at first encounter, but they will win you over with their friendliness. SOLEDAD BALDUZZI introduces her people.

CHILE'S UNIQUE GEOGRAPHY has shaped our character. Our country – this long and narrow strip of land –can sometimes feel like an island. We have the Atacama Desert to the north, Antarctica to the south, the Andes to the east and the Pacific Ocean to the west. Perhaps being in this 'enclave' has made us more reserved and less extroverted than other Latin American folks, but we're just as friendly.

Chile has a population of 19.5 million. Waves of immigration have brought different cultures here since Spanish colonization, as well as after Chile gained independence and declared itself a republic in 1818. During the 19th and 20th centuries, Europeans arrived, and you can still find big communities continued by their descendants. This century has seen the arrival of immigrants from South America and the Caribbean. About 12% of Chileans identify as belonging to an indigenous group.

Once considered among the most conservative countries in Latin America, Chile has taken steps toward becoming a more liberal and modern society, codifying same-sex marriage and abortion laws. Around 45% of Chileans today identify Catholics, a figure that has decreased over the years, but Catholicism still remains as the predominant religion. Chile's population is also aging rapidly; 16.5% of Chileans are over 60. Meanwhile, the birth rate has fallen. On average, 1.44 children are born per woman, one of the lowest rates in the region.

If you speak some Spanish and don't understand a word we're saying, rest assured it's not your problem – it's ours. Enunciation is not our strength, and we're usually not even understood by other Spanish speakers. To make it worse, we use so much slang that you'll probably think we're speaking in code. Some of the words we use on a daily basis come from the language of indigenous people. For example, *yaya* means a boo-boo or cut in Aymara, *pichintún* is something tiny in Mapuche, and the lovely *nanay* is an expression for comforting someone or calming pain in Quechua.

One of our best features is solidarity. People might think differently in many aspects – polls in 2022 showed an increase of sociopolitical polarization in Chile – but whenever a tragedy or natural disaster strikes, we come together to lift one another up. Chile is one of the most seismically active countries in the world, and I believe this fact has made us more unified, resilient and even defiant. How else can you explain that the same country that experienced the strongest earthquake ever registered also has the tallest building in South America?

WHERE DO MOST CHILEANS LIVE?

The Santiago Metropolitan Region constitutes only 2% of the country's area but has about 40% of its population. The other most populated regions are Biobío and Valparaíso. Almost 90% of Chileans reside in urban areas, while the remaining 10% live in the countryside.

Clockwise from top left: Mapuche woman; a Chilean mother and son; parade in Santiago; a shop owner in Santiago

A MIXTURE OF CULTURES

I'm a journalist living in Santiago. I moved here when I was 18 years old to study journalism, and I fell in love with the capital's cultural and bohemian lifestyle.

My family is from the Maule Region, a three-hour drive to the south. Many Chilean families are tight-knit, a loving yet sometimes worrying part of our culture, and I visit my family perhaps too often and let myself be spoiled with my favorite childhood food.

My mom is Ecuadorian, my dad is Chilean, and my paternal grandmother is Italian, so I experienced a mixture of cultures growing up. I learned at an early age to appreciate the customs and rituals of each, most of which were usually associated with some type of meal. The Chilean *once*, for example, is an evening snack or light dinner consisting of tea and bread with something delicious, such as *palta* (avocado), a tradition I still cherish and follow devotedly.

'CHILE WOKE UP'

Though now years in the past, Chile's 2019 social unrest has shaped the modern nation. By Mark Johanson

IT WAS OCTOBER 18, 2019, when a relatively low-key student protest against increased fares on the Santiago metro exploded into a full-blown social uprising against inequality that would galvanize the nation for years to come. Thousands of protesters clashed with police at locations across the Chilean capital, though the epicenter was Plaza Italia, where rioters blocked Santiago's main thoroughfare with fiery barricades. Police raced after them with tanks, turning the air over the city sour with tear gas. Meanwhile, public transportation ground to a halt just in time for the afternoon rush hour. As 2.5 million stranded workers walked across town to their homes, many stopped at key Santiago plazas to join peaceful protests in

support of the fare-dodging students, banging pots and pans into the darkening night.

By the time midnight approached, rioters had torched 20 of the empty metro stations. Another 57 were seriously damaged. The headquarters of Chile's largest electricity company was on fire too. Dozens of stores across Santiago were in the process of being looted. The center-right president, Sebastián Piñera, watched all of this happen from a pizza restaurant in the ritzy neighborhood of Vitacura. It wasn't until after midnight that he finally went back to the presidential palace, La Moneda, and appeared on television with an announcement: Soldiers would now patrol the streets of the capital.

Protesters, Santiago

Chileans hadn't seen something like this since the end of the dictatorship of Augusto Pinochet in 1990, and it set the stage for a prolonged conflict. Santiago went into a weeks-long state of emergency with nightly curfews and heavy-handed armed officials calling the shots. It was clear to many that Chile – seen for decades as a beacon of stability in a rocky region – was headed toward an uncertain future.

The End of the Chilean Dream

A week later, 1.2 million Chileans marched on Plaza Italia in a peaceful protest. The metro fare hike was the spark that lit the fire. Now protestors had a growing list of demands for a more just society. *Chile despertó* ('Chile woke up') became the chant of the crowd: no longer would they accept poor education, low wages, expensive health care, meager pensions and entrenched inequality. Chile, they said, had to change.

From afar, the nation had often been heralded as Latin America's greatest success story, with migrants pouring in from across the region in search of the 'Chilean dream.' It was the story many Chileans on the political right told themselves too: that they'd somehow cracked the code to live better lives than their neighbors. The nation's free-market model – instilled during the dictatorship and inspired by American economist Milton Friedman (advisor to both US President Ronald Reagan and UK Prime Minister Margaret Thatcher) – was credited with driving down poverty from more than 50% to under 5% over three decades, turning Chile into the richest nation per capita in the region. But those numbers only told part of the story.

At the time of the social uprising (known as the *Estallido Social*), half of Chile's wealth was held by the top 1% of society. Meanwhile, half of all workers were earning US$550 or less each month, making the successive rises in the prices of basics like water (a private entity in Chile), electricity and public transportation enough to push many over the edge – to make them 'wake up' to the perceived inequities.

The Crisis Simmers

Protests raged on in Santiago – and other cities from Arica to Punta Arenas – until the start of the pandemic in March 2020. By then, some 36 people had been killed, and thousands more were injured and arrested. The United Nations High Commissioner for Human Rights – Chile's leftist ex-president Michelle Bachelet – had kept a close eye on the situation. Concerned, she sent a team to investigate abuses on the part of the government, whose security forces had been accused of aiming rubber bullets not at the legs, as UN guidelines implore, but rather into the eyes of protesters, blinding them. What Bachelet's team uncovered was 350 cases of eye trauma, 113 cases of torture and ill treatment, and 24 cases of sexual violence.

Most Chileans were outraged, but they finally had cause for hope (and a potential end to the billowing crisis). Protesters channeled their energy into the push for a new constitution, which might act as a kind of panacea for the wide swath of demands. The government begrudgingly agreed to put the idea to a ballot. A date was set: On April 26, 2020, all Chileans would vote in a national plebiscite for or against drafting a new constitution. Of course, by April, the country was in lockdown because of the COVID-19 pandemic. The *Estallido Social* simmered in the background until October 25, when Chileans finally got the chance to make their voices heard.

A New Constitution?

The results were resounding: 78% of Chileans voted for a Constitutional Convention to draft a new constitution. A Pinochet-appointed commission wrote and approved the old charter in a controversial referendum during his authoritarian rule. Now, representatives voted on by the people would write the new version. For many Chileans, it felt like they were finally stomping out the last ashes of the dictatorship era.

Voters delivered plenty of surprises a few months later when they overwhelmingly chose left-leaning independents– rather than candidates linked to major political parties – to fill many of the seats on the Constitutional Convention. The political right didn't even secure one-third of the seats needed to block legislation. Drafting began, in earnest, in July 2021, and hopes were high among the newly empowered left that this body could come up with a charter to lead Chile into a new era. It was, after all, to be the first constitution in the world drafted with gender parity and one of the few to set aside seats for representatives of indigenous groups. It was even led by Elisa Loncón, a Mapuche linguist and indigenous rights activist.

Meanwhile, a 35-year-old leftist named Gabriel Boric – who rose to fame in the student protests of 2011 demanding a new framework for public education – captured the zeitgeist of the moment to become Chile's youngest-ever president. He was heavily involved in pushing constitutional reform through Chile's lower house of Congress in 2019, and the national plebiscite in September 2022 was to be his first major test as president. But by the time that date came around, the political tides were shifting once again.

An Uncertain Future

Though more than three-quarters of all Chileans had voted for a new constitution in 2020, just 38% voted to ratify the draft charter that was ultimately put up for a vote in 2022. Chile's new constitution was dead on arrival.

The criticisms were many. With 388 articles, the verbose charter would have been one of the longest in the world. Many argued that, despite its length, the text seemed vague on important details. Perhaps more than anything else, it was simply too progressive for a conservative Catholic nation that had only just legalized gay marriage earlier that year (and didn't allow divorce until 2004).

The constitution would have enshrined gender parity in politics, vastly expanded LGBTIQ+ rights, made the government responsible for mitigating climate change and recognized Chile as a plurinational state, giving indigenous groups more autonomy. The changes it proposed were so sweeping

THOUSANDS OF PROTESTERS CLASHED WITH POLICE AT LOCATIONS ACROSS THE CHILEAN CAPITAL, THOUGH THE EPICENTER WAS PLAZA ITALIA, SANTIAGO'S MAIN THOROUGHFARE.

and so progressive that the majority of the nation just couldn't get on board.

If anything, the social uprising and subsequent referendums showed the strength of Chile's democracy in the face of myriad challenges. Yet the one thing that was meant to bring about change to Chilean society – to make it more fair, equal and representative of all – failed spectacularly. With no resolution in sight, Chile went back to the drawing board in 2023 in an attempt to elect a new body that might draft a different kind of constitution that the majority of the nation could support.

Lingering Effects

The *Estallido Social* is now years in the past, but it remains a constant topic among Chileans. It was, for many, the defining moment of a generation, with the largest marches this nation has ever seen. In Santiago, the streets are no longer paralyzed by protests, but evidence of the social uprising is everywhere. The historic buildings of Centro are the most obvious examples. They were canvases for discontent and remain covered in graffiti. Many popular restaurants and bars in this district and in neighboring Bellavista decamped for richer parts of town, leaving the city's historic heart less dynamic than it once was.

Much of Santiago Centro is now populated by newly arrived immigrants from Venezuela, Peru and Colombia, as natural-born Chileans move east toward the Andes. The unrest also led to increased crime in the capital, though it's still considered among the safest big cities in Latin America. Plaza Italia, where it all began, now goes by a new name: Plaza de la Dignidad. It's a reference to the lingering demands of protesters, who are still pleading, years later, for more dignity.

IGNACIO BUSTAMANTE/SHUTTERSTOCK ©

THE PLANET ON AN ISLAND

Robinson Crusoe is not only a stunningly remote destination, but it's also a microcosm of our whole planet – and a peek into its future.
By Shivya Nath

ON A BALMY coastal morning nearly 700km off Chile's Pacific coast, I set out on a hike on Robinson Crusoe Island, originally called Mas a Tierra ('Closer to Earth'). Despite the island's compact nature – a mere 48 sq km – the landscape transforms every few hundred meters from ocean to hills to forest to desert.

At the start of the trail, the Pacific Ocean is bathed in brilliant shades of blue. Gradually, dramatic hills shaped by centuries of wind and water comes into view, jutting out of the ocean. Among patches of slow-growth forest filled with centuries-old towering endemic luma and canelo trees, I linger in the shade with national park

rangers. The trail winds past an eroded valley and leads us into a dramatic red-soil desert scattered with small craters and odd volcanic formations that nearly trick us into believing that we have somehow left Earth altogether.

The island's original claim to fame may be that it inspired Daniel Defoe's novel *Robinson Crusoe,* which it was renamed after in 1966, but perhaps what deserves more attention is that it's home to greater biodiversity than even the Galapagos, according to a 2021 report by Island Conservation.

About 10km later, with tired feet but surging hearts, we finally arrive at our destination – not a place, but a tree.

Robinson Crusoe Island

A Tree the World Might Never Know

Perched precariously in a dry ravine, I see the island's – and the planet's – last remaining *Dendroseris neriifolia*. At the age of 140, it has short and slender bark, long droopy leaves and pretty white snowflake-shaped flowers. Like many species that have evolved over millions of years of isolation on Robinson Crusoe, it is found nowhere else on the planet. Crowded out by invasive species that were mostly introduced by human settlers nearly 600 years ago and unable to keep up with increasingly erratic weather patterns caused by climate change, this tree before me is the last remaining member of its entire species.

Over the past decade of being a travel writer, I've been fortunate enough to experience the wild beauty of our planet in many forms, and I've felt driven to advocate for its protection. I've often read that we're living through a sixth mass extinction, but to stand before the last of one such species puts everything I had imagined about our future into perspective. Robinson Crusoe is not just a little-visited wild Pacific island but also a microcosm of our planet and a window into how delicately our future hangs in the balance.

A Journey Not for the Faint-Hearted

I had never dared to put the Juan Fernandez Archipelago – which Robinson Crusoe is part of – on my 'someday' list. Getting there is no easy feat. Plenty of intrepid travelers have tried but failed. You need the perfect combination of money, time, luck, patience and hyperlocal weather conditions.

When I was selected as one of only five people from around the world to participate in the first phase of the Work For Humankind project on Robinson Crusoe in 2022, it felt like the island was calling me. The goal was to test Lenovo technology (internet access was almost nonexistent on the island until 2022), prove that remote work was possible from such a distant corner of the world and volunteer alongside the island community to pilot sustainable development solutions to local challenges.

In early 2022, at the tail end of the travel restrictions that accompanied the COVID-19 pandemic, the prevailing regulations demanded that we quarantine for six nights on mainland Chile before setting out for the island. But the right weather conditions eluded us for days, and when the stars finally aligned, I understood what the fuss was about.

From a rustic navy airstrip in Santiago, we boarded the tiniest twin-prop plane I've ever flown. Its capacity was four passengers and two pilots. Our luggage was piled up at the back, and the unwieldy seatbelt was optional. For nearly two hours, we flew low over the Pacific until we finally caught the first glimpse of our secluded destination, the surreal sight of rugged hills shrouded in mist jutting out of the blue water.

On a short, thin strip sandwiched between desolate hills and the vast ocean, we made a perilous landing, not an experience for the faint-hearted. I'd later learn that regulations for flying to the island were not always so strict. In 2011, a famous Chilean actor and 20 other passengers lost their lives in a plane crash on the same journey. The resulting public outrage led to stringent rules around the optimal wind speed before twin-prop planes are allowed to take off in either direction.

As we waited for a boat to ferry us from the landing strip to San Juan Bautista, the only inhabited village on Robinson Crusoe Island that's home to about 1000 people, we were surprised to spot wild Juan Fernandez fur seals hanging around the water. Endemic to the island, these seals evolved differently from other seal species and have tiny ears and the ability to stand on their front flippers. American ships hunted these playful creatures for their waterproof fur, and legend has it that Napoleon Bonaparte's army wore winter coats made from it. The population of four million seals was driven to extinction in the 1800s. In 1965, a resident from Alexander Selkirk Island (part of the same archipelago) unexpectedly found a handful of seal pups in a cave, and the community made it their mission to protect them from hunting. The Chilean authorities eventually banned hunting them, and populations have since rebounded to several thousand. A few days later, in the chilly Pacific waters, I'd spendsome precious moments snorkeling among the seals.

Learning About Species Extinction

During my month on the island, I witnessed the jaw-dropping biodiversity of Robinson

Crusoe and the effect of human presence. On hikes across the island, 91% of which is a protected national park, it seems like an idyllic green haven. When the first European settlers arrived on this uninhabited island some 600 years ago, they carried with them many invasive species. Wild plants like mora (blackberry) were used for fencing, and rats arrived on boats. Rabbits and gautis (wild cats) were introduced to deal with the rats, while domesticated animals like cats, dogs, goats, horses and cows were brought for entertainment and agriculture. Cypress, eucalyptus and pine trees were planted for familiarity.

These non-native species grow faster, consume more water, adapt better to climate change and have been crowding out the slow-reproducing, slow-growing, endemic flora, which evolved for centuries without any foreign threats. Rats and rabbits gobble up the endemic seeds, and horses, cows and goats munch on the seedlings, making it nearly impossible for the native species to propagate. Across the island, it is rare to spot native trees in their adolescence.

A 30-minute hike from San Juan Bautista, Plazoleta El Yunque is an example of what's possible with thoughtful human intervention. Hundreds of hectares of invasive species have been painstakingly removed from this area to allow the endemic trees to reclaim their territory. I spent many quiet afternoons on the wooded trail, spotting pretty crimson *picaflores* (hummingbirds) flit around the umbrella-like pangue and the delicately branching ferns to the magnificent roots of canelo trees and the swishing canopies of the lumas. Called the Juan Fernandez firecrown, these hummingbirds are found only on Robinson Crusoe, but they are threatened by cats and birds that eat their eggs, the non-endemic hummingbirds that destroy their nests, and the effects of climate change, which has been leading to late nesting and broken nests because of stronger winds. Oikonos, a nonprofit organization, has set up local operations on the island to study their habitat, and estimates that fewer than 500 of Juan Fernandez firecrowns survive on the island today.

DARIO CASTRO/SHUTTERSTOCK ©

Almost every conversation I had with islanders was laced with concern over the future of the island and the colossal loss should some of this endemic biodiversity disappear in the near future. Conservationists estimate that 60% of the native forest will be lost by 2070 – or sooner – because of the dual impact of invasive species and climate change.

600 YEARS OF HUMAN INHABITATION HAS BROUGHT SPECIES THAT EVOLVED OVER MILLIONS OF YEARS TO THE BRINK OF EXTINCTION.

Rethinking Travel

Ever since I returned home to the other side of the world, I haven't stopped wondering what it meant for me to travel to a land as remote as Robinson Crusoe. Sure, there's the thrill of going somewhere that few have been. But what good is the journey if it doesn't contribute in some way toward conserving the island's extraordinary biodiversity? If it doesn't stop us from viewing the world as one large Instagram backdrop and rethink travel as a powerful way to learn about climate change, species extinction and human impact on the environment?

Robinson Crusoe – where 600 years of human inhabitation has brought species that evolved over millions of years to the brink of extinction – is not just another destination. It's a journey to learn about an incredible planet in peril.

For more information on visiting Robinson Crusoe Island, see p358.

INDEX

Map Pages **000**

Ahu Tongariki (p342), the largest *ahu* ever built, has 15 older *moai* with more distinct Polynesian features.

[In Parque Nacional Lauca] Several viewpoints take in the perfect, snowcapped cone of Volcán Parinacota (p123). Walk along the trail at the shores of the glistening Lago Chungará where picnic tables make an idyllic spot for lunch.

THIS BOOK

Design Development
Marc Backwell

Content Development
Mark Jones, Sandie Kestell, Anne Mason, Joana Taborda

Cartography Development
Katerina Pavkova

Production Development
Sandie Kestell, Fergal Condon

Series Development Leadership
Darren O'Connell, Piers Pickard, Chris Zeiher

Destination Editor
Sarah Stocking

Production Editor
Kathryn Rowan

Book Designer
Dermot Hegarty

Cartographer
Hunor Csutoros

Assisting Editors
Carly Hall, Soo Hamilton, Lauren Keith, Jenna Myers

Cover Researcher
Mazzy Prinsep

Thanks Katie Connolly, Karen Henderson

MIX
Paper from responsible sources
FSC™ C021741
www.fsc.org

Paper in this book is certified against the Forest Stewardship Council™ standards. FSC™ promotes environmentally responsible, socially beneficial and economically viable management of the world's forests.

Published by Lonely Planet Global Limited
CRN 554153
12th edition – Sep 2023
ISBN 978 1 78701 676 7
© Lonely Planet 2023 Photographs © as indicated 2023
10 9 8 7 6 5 4 3 2 1
Printed in China